REBELS™

THESE FREE AND INDEPENDENT STATES

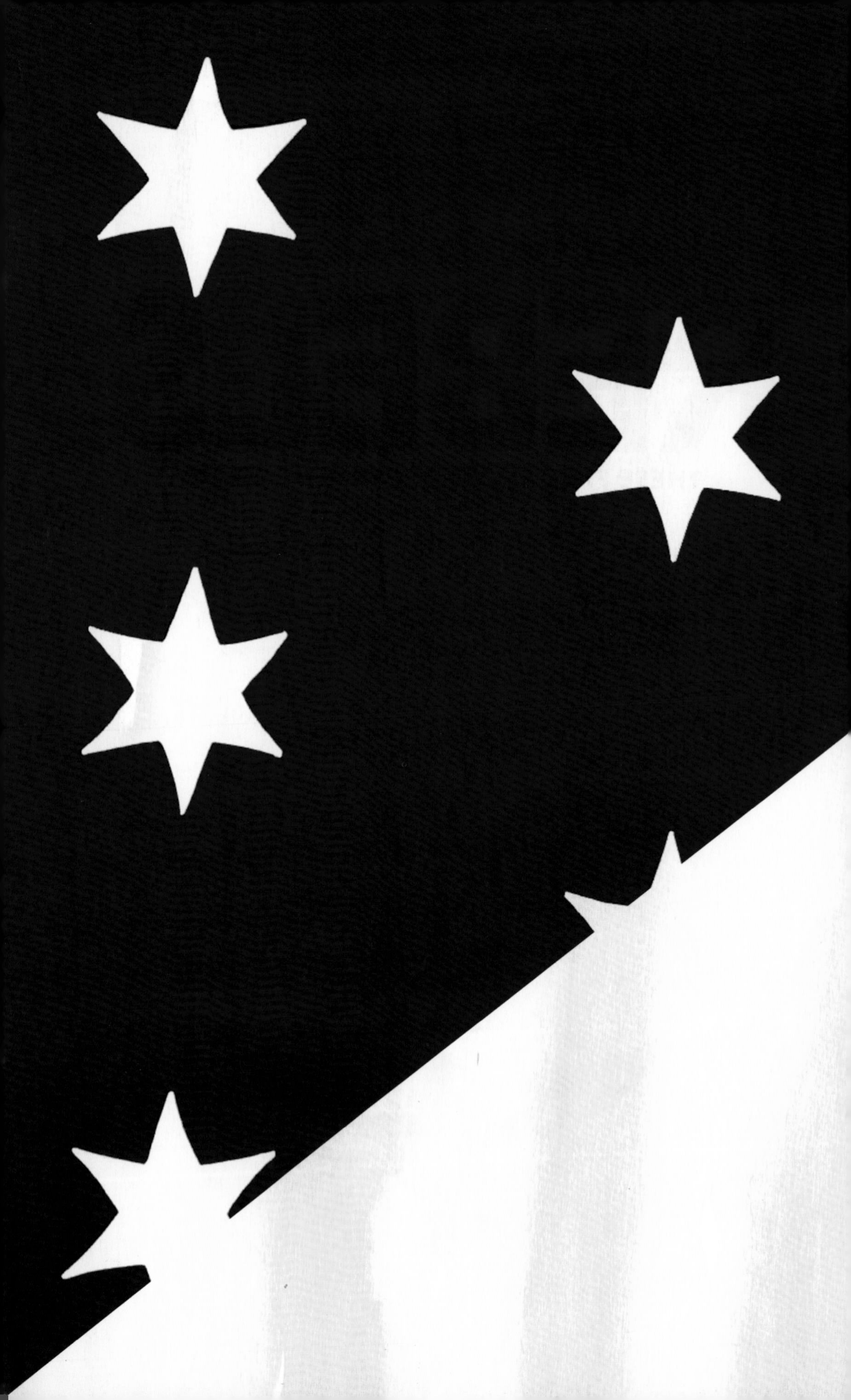

REBELS™

THESE FREE AND INDEPENDENT STATES

STORY
BRIAN WOOD

ART
ANDREA MUTTI (CHAPTERS 1–6)
LUCA CASALANGUIDA (CHAPTER 7)
JOAN URGELL (CHAPTER 8)

COLORS
LAUREN AFFE

LETTERING
JARED K. FLETCHER

COVER ART
MATT TAYLOR

PRESIDENT & PUBLISHER
MIKE RICHARDSON

EDITOR
SPENCER CUSHING

ASSISTANT EDITOR
KEVIN BURKHALTER

COLLECTION DESIGNER
BRENNAN THOME

DIGITAL ART TECHNICIAN
ALLYSON HALLER

PUBLISHED BY DARK HORSE BOOKS
A DIVISION OF DARK HORSE COMICS, INC.
10956 SE MAIN STREET
MILWAUKIE, OR 97222

DARKHORSE.COM

FIRST EDITION: MARCH 2018
ISBN 978-1-50670-203-2

1 3 5 7 9 10 8 6 4 2

PRINTED IN CHINA

TO FIND A COMICS SHOP IN YOUR AREA,
VISIT COMICSHOPLOCATOR.COM

INTERNATIONAL LICENSING: (503) 905-2377

REBELS VOLUME 2: THESE FREE AND INDEPENDENT STATES
REBELS™ © 2017, 2018 BRIAN WOOD AND ANDREA MUTTI. DARK HORSE BOOKS® AND
THE DARK HORSE LOGO ARE REGISTERED TRADEMARKS OF DARK HORSE COMICS, INC. ALL
RIGHTS RESERVED. NO PORTION OF THIS PUBLICATION MAY BE REPRODUCED OR TRANS-
MITTED, IN ANY FORM OR BY ANY MEANS, WITHOUT THE EXPRESS WRITTEN PERMISSION
OF DARK HORSE COMICS, INC. NAMES, CHARACTERS, PLACES, AND INCIDENTS FEATURED
IN THIS PUBLICATION EITHER ARE THE PRODUCT OF THE AUTHOR'S IMAGINATION OR ARE
USED FICTITIOUSLY. ANY RESEMBLANCE TO ACTUAL PERSONS (LIVING OR DEAD), EVENTS,
INSTITUTIONS, OR LOCALES, WITHOUT SATIRIC INTENT, IS COINCIDENTAL.

THIS VOLUME COLLECTS THE COMIC BOOK SERIES REBELS: THESE FREE AND INDEPENDENT
STATES #1–#8 FROM DARK HORSE COMICS.

NAMES: WOOD, BRIAN, 1972- AUTHOR, CREATOR. | MUTTI, ANDREA, 1973- ARTIST. |
  CASALANGUIDA, LUCA, ARTIST. | URGELL, JOAN, ARTIST. | AFFE, LAUREN,
  COLOURIST. | FLETCHER, JARED K., LETTERER. | WOODSON, MATTHEW, ARTIST.
TITLE: THESE FREE AND INDEPENDENT STATES / STORY, BRIAN WOOD ; ART, ANDREA
  MUTTI, LUCA CASALANGUIDA, JOAN URGELL ; COLORS, LAUREN AFFE ; LETTERING,
  JARED K. FLETCHER ; COVER ART, MATTHEW WOODSON.
DESCRIPTION: FIRST EDITION. | MILWAUKIE, OR : DARK HORSE BOOKS, MARCH 2018. |
  SERIES: REBELS ; VOLUME 2 "THIS VOLUME COLLECTS THE COMIC BOOK SERIES
  REBELS: THESE FREE AND INDEPENDENT STATES #1-8 FROM DARK HORSE COMICS."
IDENTIFIERS: LCCN 2017044018 | ISBN 9781506702032 (PAPERBACK)
SUBJECTS: LCSH: UNITED STATES--HISTORY--REVOLUTION, 1775-1783--COMIC BOOKS,
  STRIPS, ETC. | COMIC BOOKS, STRIPS, ETC. | BISAC: COMICS & GRAPHIC NOVELS
  / GENERAL.
CLASSIFICATION: LCC PN6728.R42 W66 2018 | DDC 741.5/973--DC23
LC RECORD AVAILABLE AT HTTPS://LCCN.LOC.GOV/2017044018

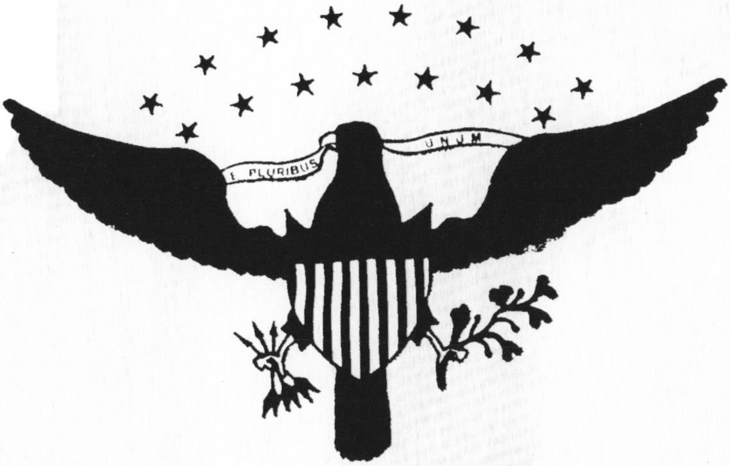
E PLURIBUS
UNUM

The first volume of *Rebels* was an attempt to connect the events of the American Revolution with where I grew up in rural Vermont. It was my way to create a sense of belonging to the heroes I grew up reading about, their stories, and the landmarks I'd pass on my way to school. Raising two children a stone's throw from where the Battle of Brooklyn was fought was yet another way to connect with its history, for me and for them.

So, what to do for a sequel story? If the Revolution is considered the birth of the United States, it seems fitting to also look at its troubled adolescence, when the idealism of its creation collided with the realities of governing and learning how to get along with the world. Answer: The War of 1812.

One of the things driving me to co-create and write *Rebels* was the dismay I felt seeing this history misused and twisted to support partisan politics. There's a saying I've heard that American is a perfect idea imperfectly executed, and I feel the truth in that. I think, on paper, the concept of America is open, inclusive, secular, and welcoming, and that patriotism isn't a dirty word. I also recognize all the times we've failed to live up to the ideal. I reject the use of history and those ideals as tools to divide.

Even though we're past the era of the Tea Party and in a lull between elections, I can't fail to see parallels. In 1812, America was struggling with its trading partners, struggling with piracy on the high seas, isolationists within its government, and a worsening of relations with its neighbors. It was growing pains, straight up, and it took a war, a messy war with lots of buildup and lots of fallout, for America to come to grips with itself and mature a little.

John Abbott, the protagonist of our first story in this volume, is himself a sort of symbol for American stubbornness, of idealism set in stone, unyielding and unapologetic. If you're inclined to assume that means things work out for him in the end, don't. Instead, consider other founding men and women of America who held similar traits.

Like in the first volume, we round out this one with short stories that paint a fuller picture of the times, ones that go beyond the story of the Abbotts and the major wars. We turn our view back decades to a young, entitled George Washington and the power that the Virginia colony held during the French and Indian War. Washington, a beloved figure, as flawed and complex as anyone, is the perfect-imperfect personified. The Battle of Brooklyn is viewed through the eyes of two orphans trying to hold on to their farm in Brooklyn Heights. And the Green Mountain Boys come full circle as they prove the value of the American militia.

TABLE OF CONTENTS

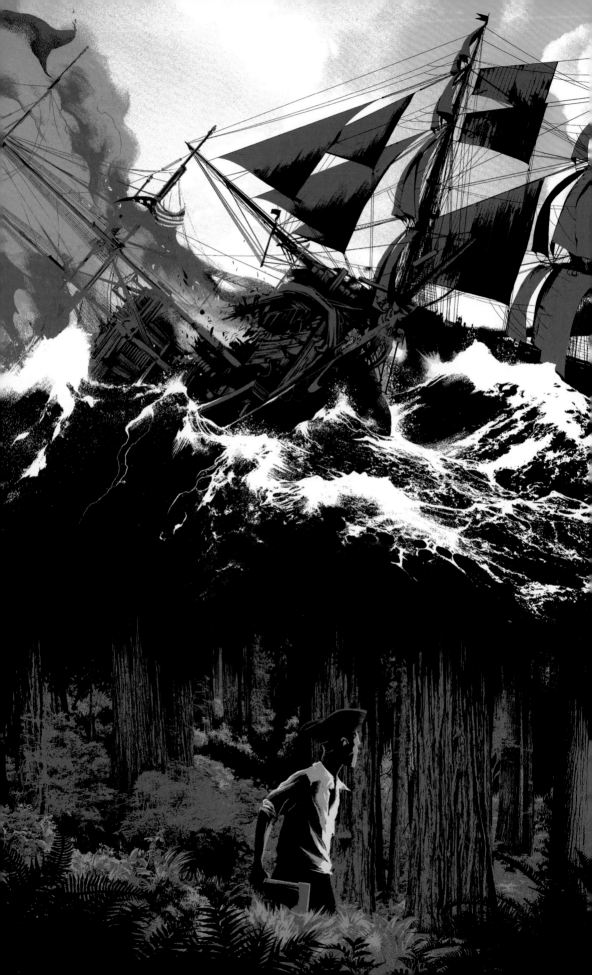

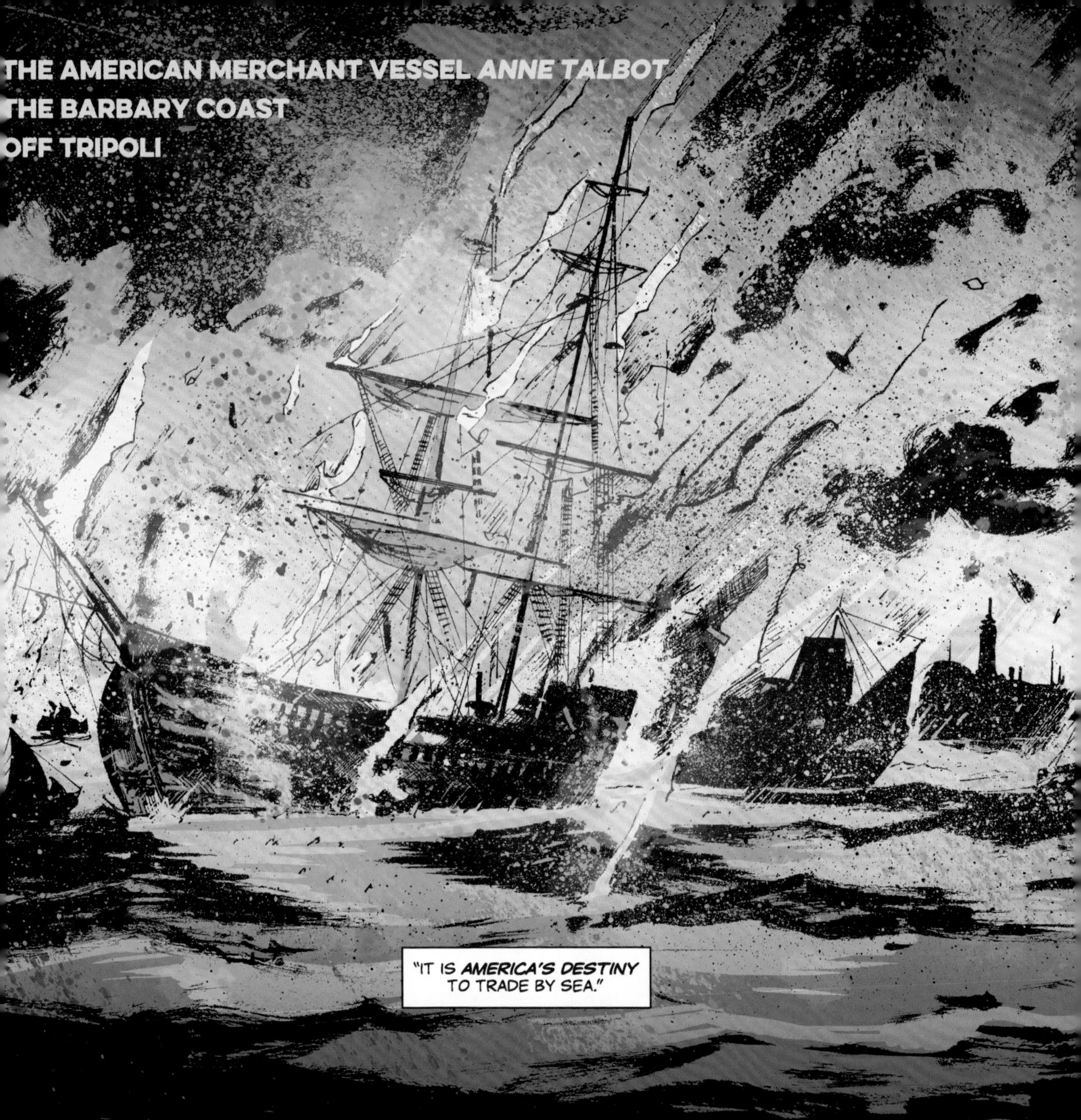
THE AMERICAN MERCHANT VESSEL *ANNE TALBOT*
THE BARBARY COAST
OFF TRIPOLI
"IT IS *AMERICA'S DESTINY* TO TRADE BY SEA."

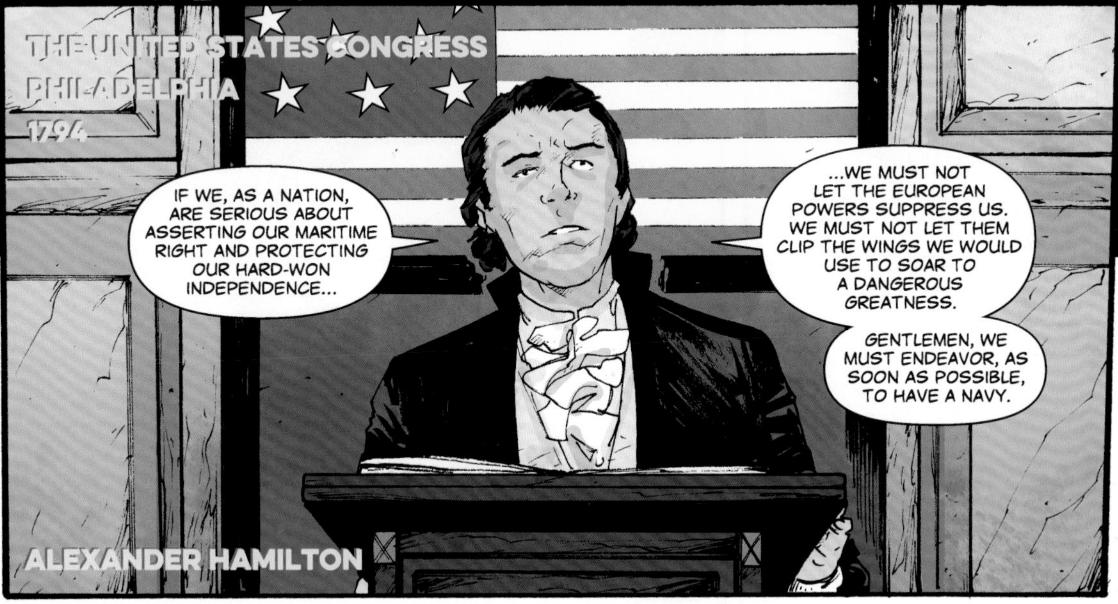
THE UNITED STATES CONGRESS
PHILADELPHIA
1794
IF WE, AS A NATION, ARE SERIOUS ABOUT ASSERTING OUR MARITIME RIGHT AND PROTECTING OUR HARD-WON INDEPENDENCE...
...WE MUST NOT LET THE EUROPEAN POWERS SUPPRESS US. WE MUST NOT LET THEM CLIP THE WINGS WE WOULD USE TO SOAR TO A DANGEROUS GREATNESS.
GENTLEMEN, WE MUST ENDEAVOR, AS SOON AS POSSIBLE, TO HAVE A NAVY.
ALEXANDER HAMILTON

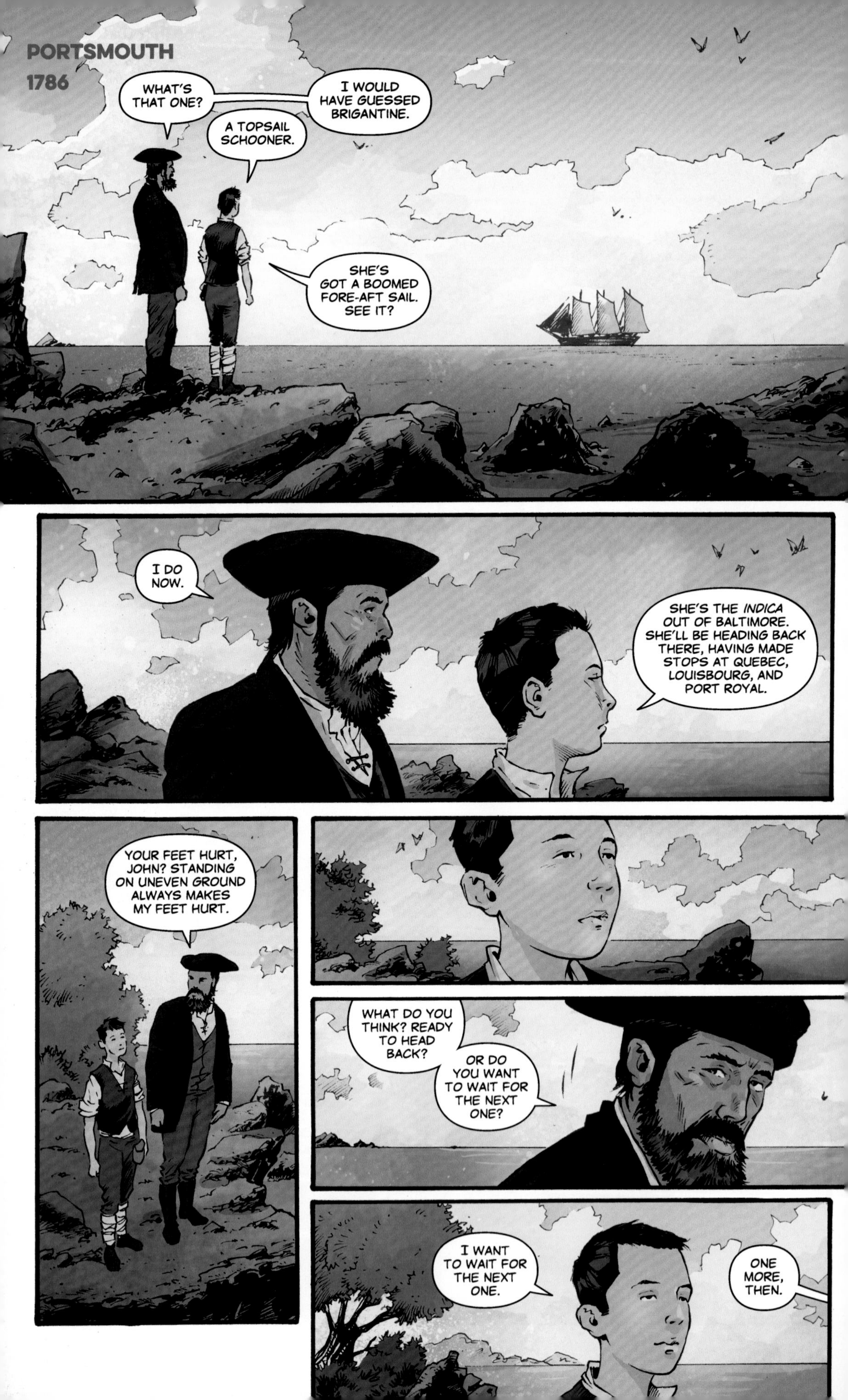
PORTSMOUTH
1786
WHAT'S THAT ONE?
A TOPSAIL SCHOONER.
I WOULD HAVE GUESSED BRIGANTINE.
SHE'S GOT A BOOMED FORE-AFT SAIL. SEE IT?
I DO NOW.
SHE'S THE *INDICA* OUT OF BALTIMORE. SHE'LL BE HEADING BACK THERE, HAVING MADE STOPS AT QUEBEC, LOUISBOURG, AND PORT ROYAL.
YOUR FEET HURT, JOHN? STANDING ON UNEVEN GROUND ALWAYS MAKES MY FEET HURT.
WHAT DO YOU THINK? READY TO HEAD BACK?
OR DO YOU WANT TO WAIT FOR THE NEXT ONE?
I WANT TO WAIT FOR THE NEXT ONE.
ONE MORE, THEN.

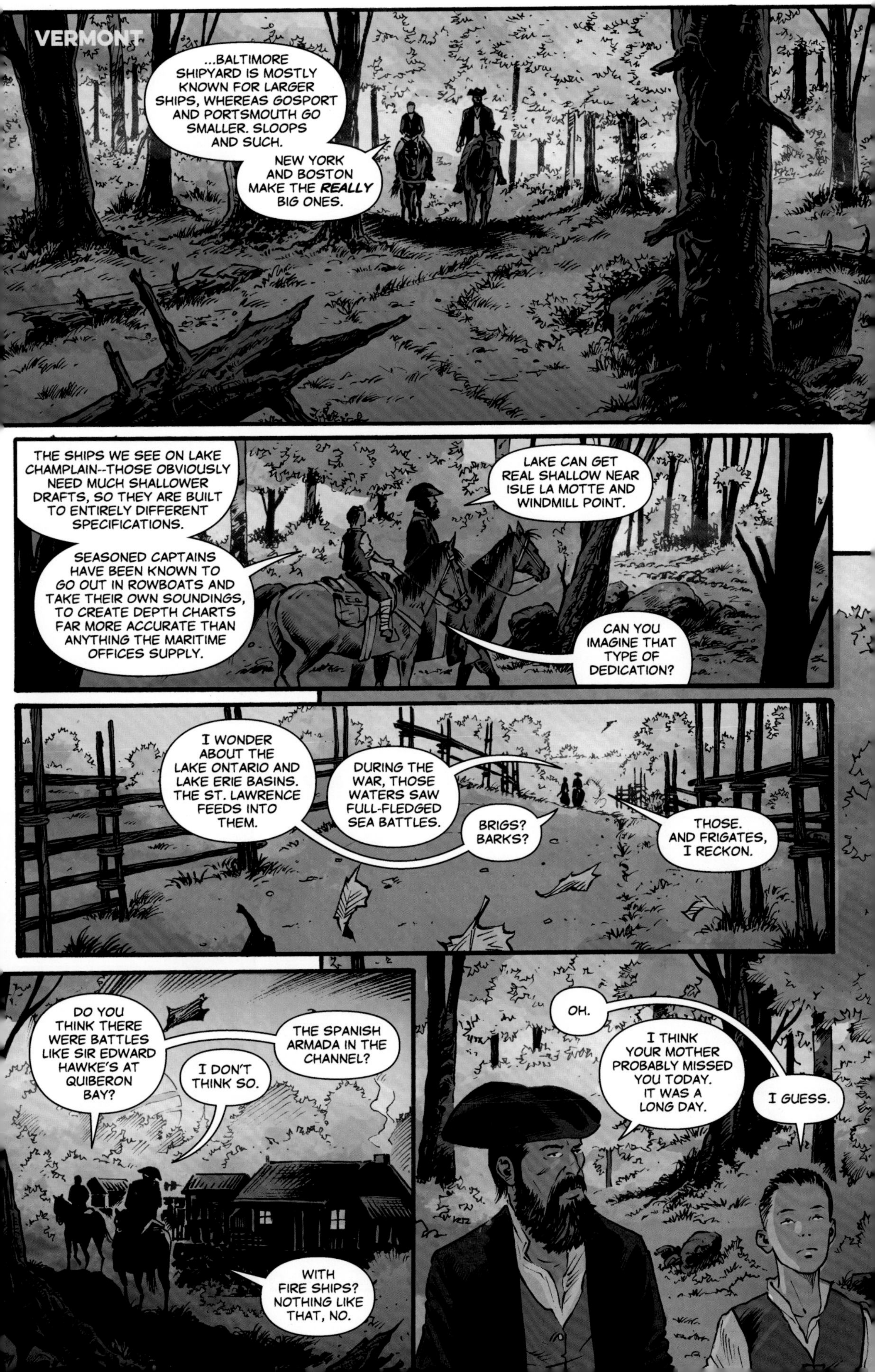
VERMONT
...BALTIMORE SHIPYARD IS MOSTLY KNOWN FOR LARGER SHIPS, WHEREAS GOSPORT AND PORTSMOUTH GO SMALLER. SLOOPS AND SUCH.
NEW YORK AND BOSTON MAKE THE *REALLY* BIG ONES.
THE SHIPS WE SEE ON LAKE CHAMPLAIN--THOSE OBVIOUSLY NEED MUCH SHALLOWER DRAFTS, SO THEY ARE BUILT TO ENTIRELY DIFFERENT SPECIFICATIONS.
LAKE CAN GET REAL SHALLOW NEAR ISLE LA MOTTE AND WINDMILL POINT.
SEASONED CAPTAINS HAVE BEEN KNOWN TO GO OUT IN ROWBOATS AND TAKE THEIR OWN SOUNDINGS, TO CREATE DEPTH CHARTS FAR MORE ACCURATE THAN ANYTHING THE MARITIME OFFICES SUPPLY.
CAN YOU IMAGINE THAT TYPE OF DEDICATION?
I WONDER ABOUT THE LAKE ONTARIO AND LAKE ERIE BASINS. THE ST. LAWRENCE FEEDS INTO THEM.
DURING THE WAR, THOSE WATERS SAW FULL-FLEDGED SEA BATTLES.
BRIGS? BARKS?
THOSE. AND FRIGATES, I RECKON.
DO YOU THINK THERE WERE BATTLES LIKE SIR EDWARD HAWKE'S AT QUIBERON BAY?
THE SPANISH ARMADA IN THE CHANNEL?
I DON'T THINK SO.
WITH FIRE SHIPS? NOTHING LIKE THAT, NO.
OH.
I THINK YOUR MOTHER PROBABLY MISSED YOU TODAY. IT WAS A LONG DAY.
I GUESS.

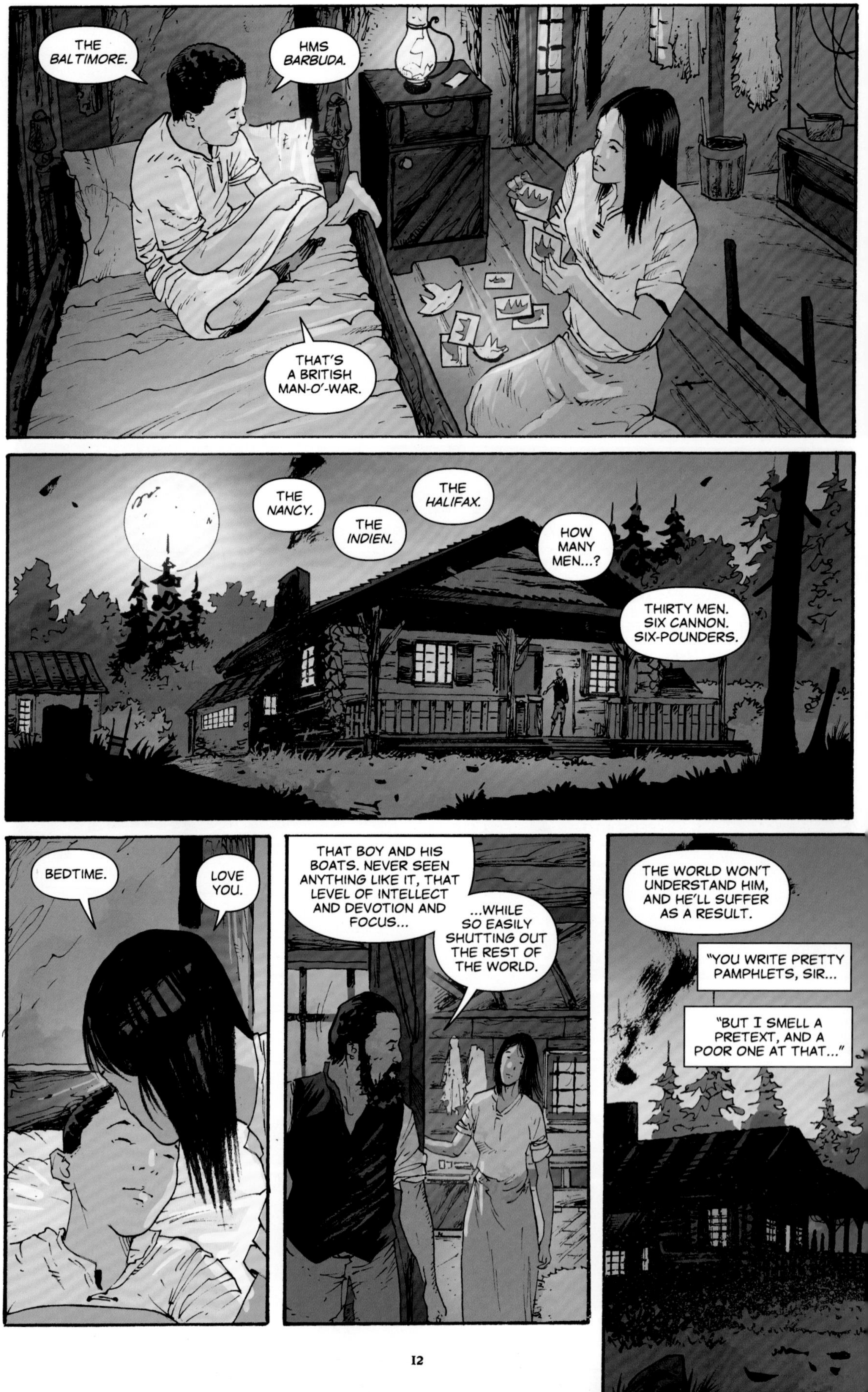
THE BALTIMORE.
HMS BARBUDA.
THAT'S A BRITISH MAN-O'-WAR.
THE NANCY.
THE INDIEN.
THE HALIFAX.
HOW MANY MEN...?
THIRTY MEN. SIX CANNON. SIX-POUNDERS.
BEDTIME.
LOVE YOU.
THAT BOY AND HIS BOATS. NEVER SEEN ANYTHING LIKE IT, THAT LEVEL OF INTELLECT AND DEVOTION AND FOCUS...
...WHILE SO EASILY SHUTTING OUT THE REST OF THE WORLD.
THE WORLD WON'T UNDERSTAND HIM, AND HE'LL SUFFER AS A RESULT.
"YOU WRITE PRETTY PAMPHLETS, SIR...
"BUT I SMELL A PRETEXT, AND A POOR ONE AT THAT..."

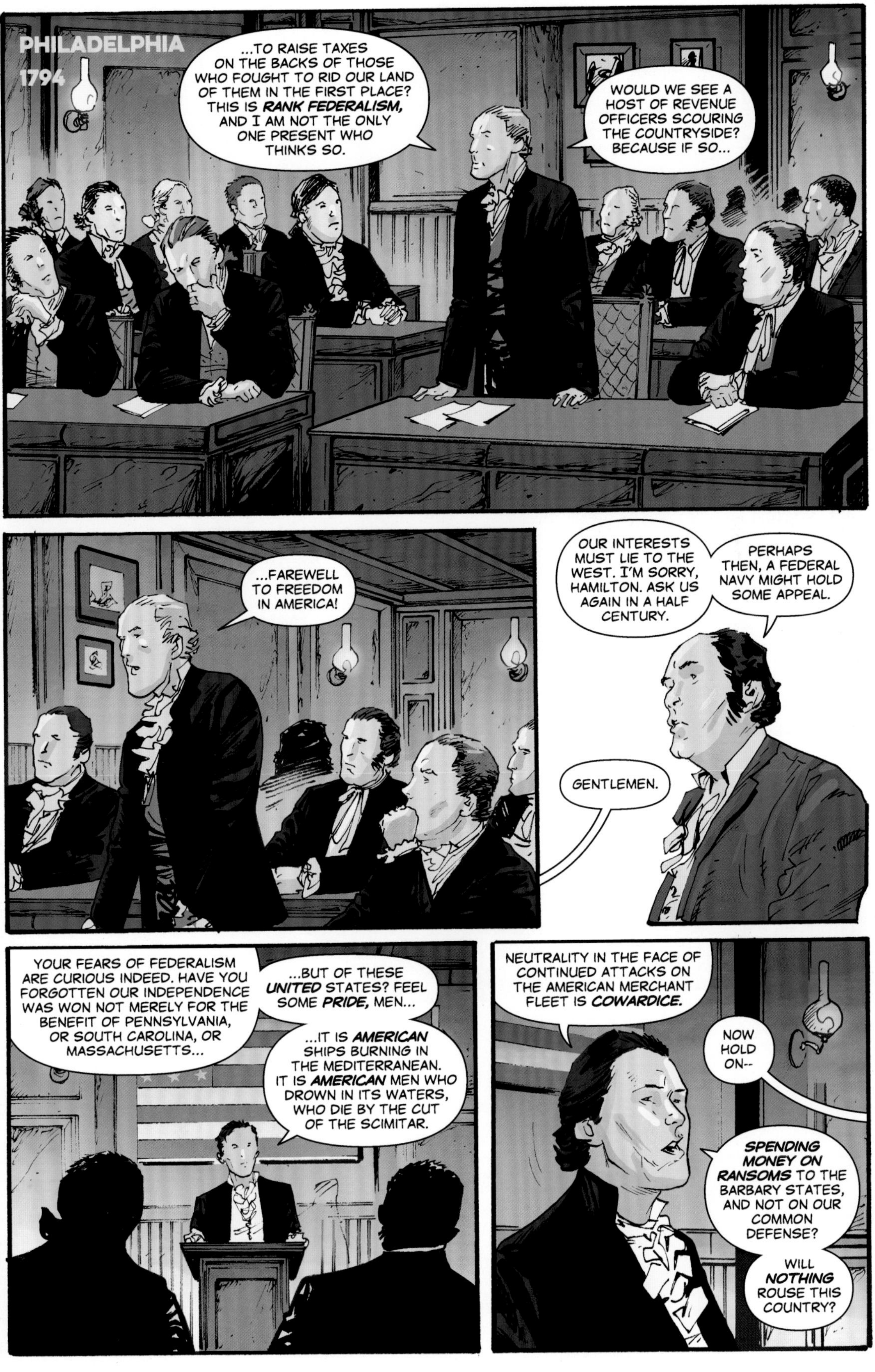
PHILADELPHIA 1794
...TO RAISE TAXES ON THE BACKS OF THOSE WHO FOUGHT TO RID OUR LAND OF THEM IN THE FIRST PLACE? THIS IS RANK FEDERALISM, AND I AM NOT THE ONLY ONE PRESENT WHO THINKS SO.
WOULD WE SEE A HOST OF REVENUE OFFICERS SCOURING THE COUNTRYSIDE? BECAUSE IF SO...
...FAREWELL TO FREEDOM IN AMERICA!
OUR INTERESTS MUST LIE TO THE WEST. I'M SORRY, HAMILTON. ASK US AGAIN IN A HALF CENTURY.
PERHAPS THEN, A FEDERAL NAVY MIGHT HOLD SOME APPEAL.
GENTLEMEN.
YOUR FEARS OF FEDERALISM ARE CURIOUS INDEED. HAVE YOU FORGOTTEN OUR INDEPENDENCE WAS WON NOT MERELY FOR THE BENEFIT OF PENNSYLVANIA, OR SOUTH CAROLINA, OR MASSACHUSETTS...
...BUT OF THESE UNITED STATES? FEEL SOME PRIDE, MEN...
...IT IS AMERICAN SHIPS BURNING IN THE MEDITERRANEAN. IT IS AMERICAN MEN WHO DROWN IN ITS WATERS, WHO DIE BY THE CUT OF THE SCIMITAR.
NEUTRALITY IN THE FACE OF CONTINUED ATTACKS ON THE AMERICAN MERCHANT FLEET IS COWARDICE.
NOW HOLD ON--
SPENDING MONEY ON RANSOMS TO THE BARBARY STATES, AND NOT ON OUR COMMON DEFENSE?
WILL NOTHING ROUSE THIS COUNTRY?

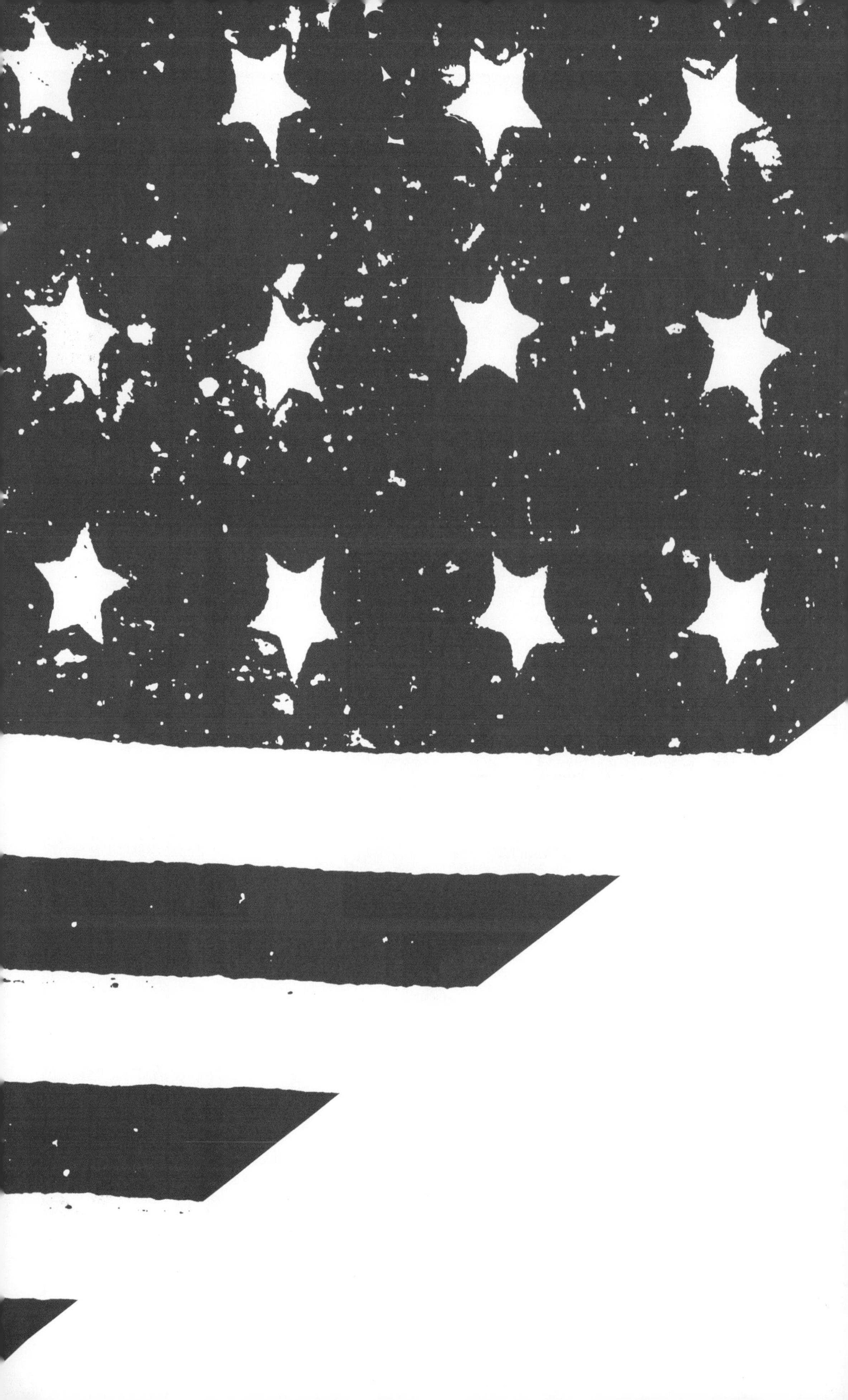

REBELS

"THESE FREE AND INDEPENDENT STATES" PART 1 OF 5

*IN WHICH A DIVIDED AMERICA ONCE AGAIN MARCHES TOWARD WAR,
AND YOUNG JOHN ABBOTT DISPLAYS A REMARKABLE APTITUDE.*

BRIAN WOOD · ANDREA MUTTI · LAUREN AFFE · MATT TAYLOR

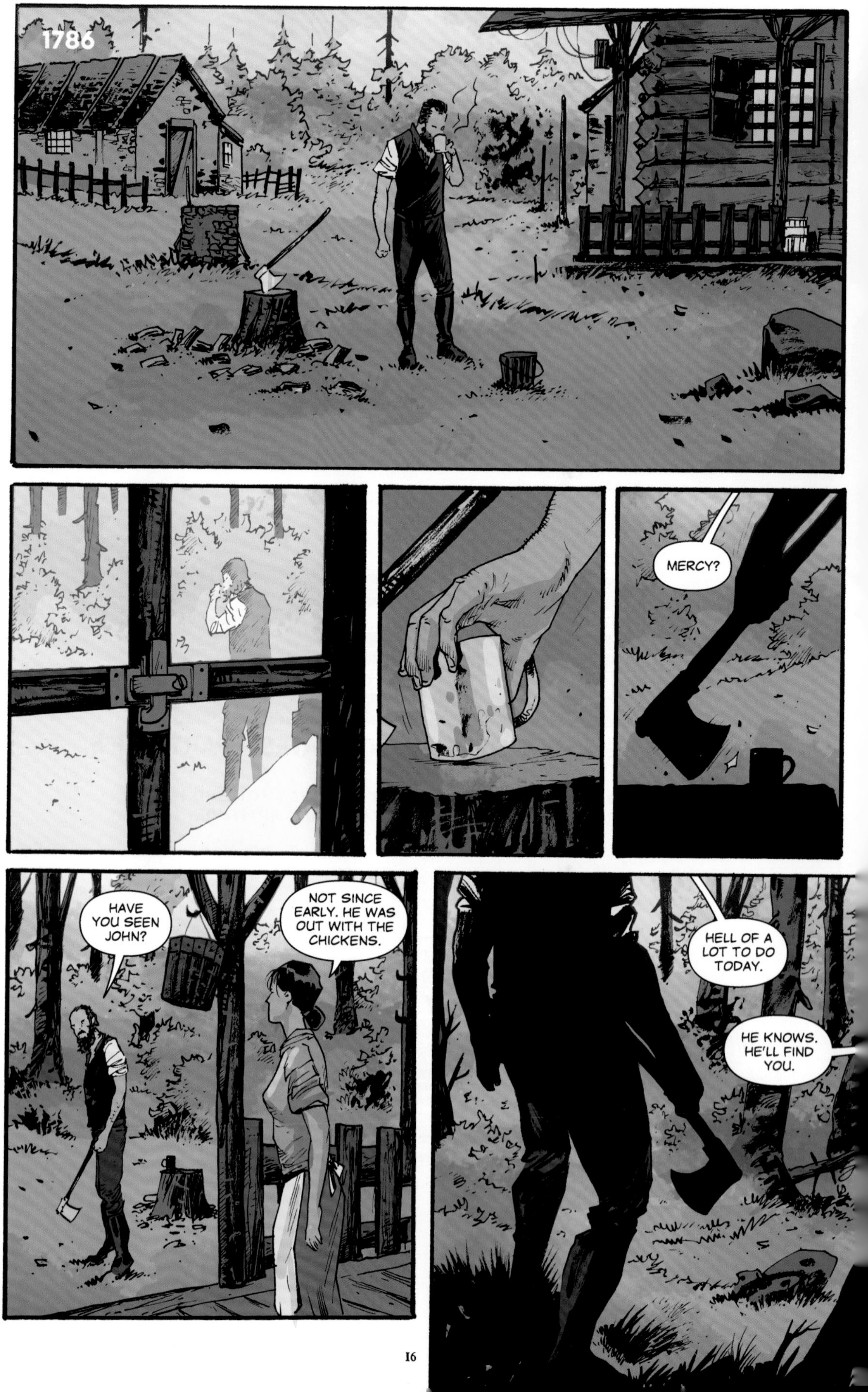
1786
MERCY?
HAVE YOU SEEN JOHN?
NOT SINCE EARLY. HE WAS OUT WITH THE CHICKENS.
HELL OF A LOT TO DO TODAY.
HE KNOWS. HE'LL FIND YOU.

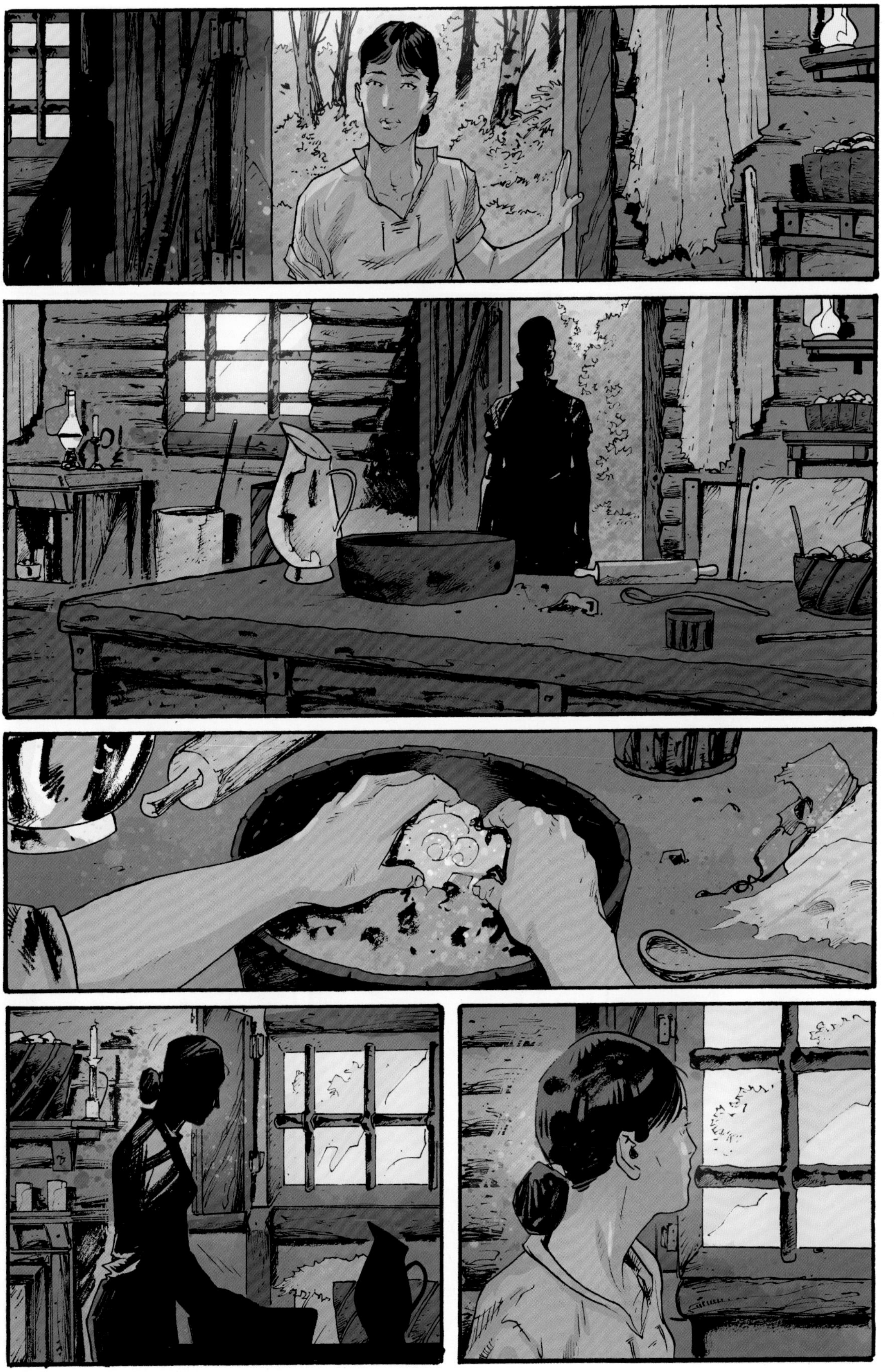

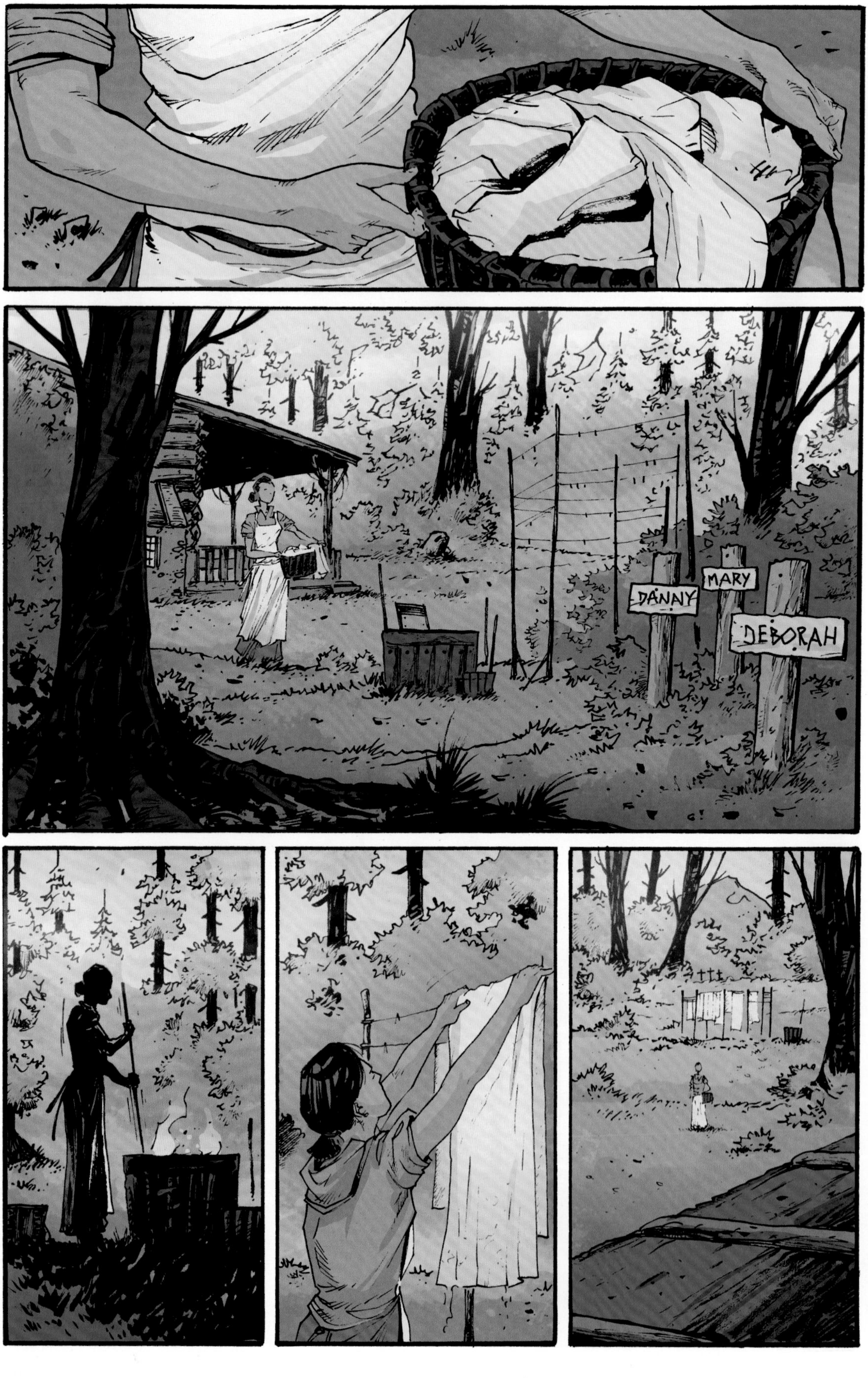
DANNY
MARY
DEBORAH

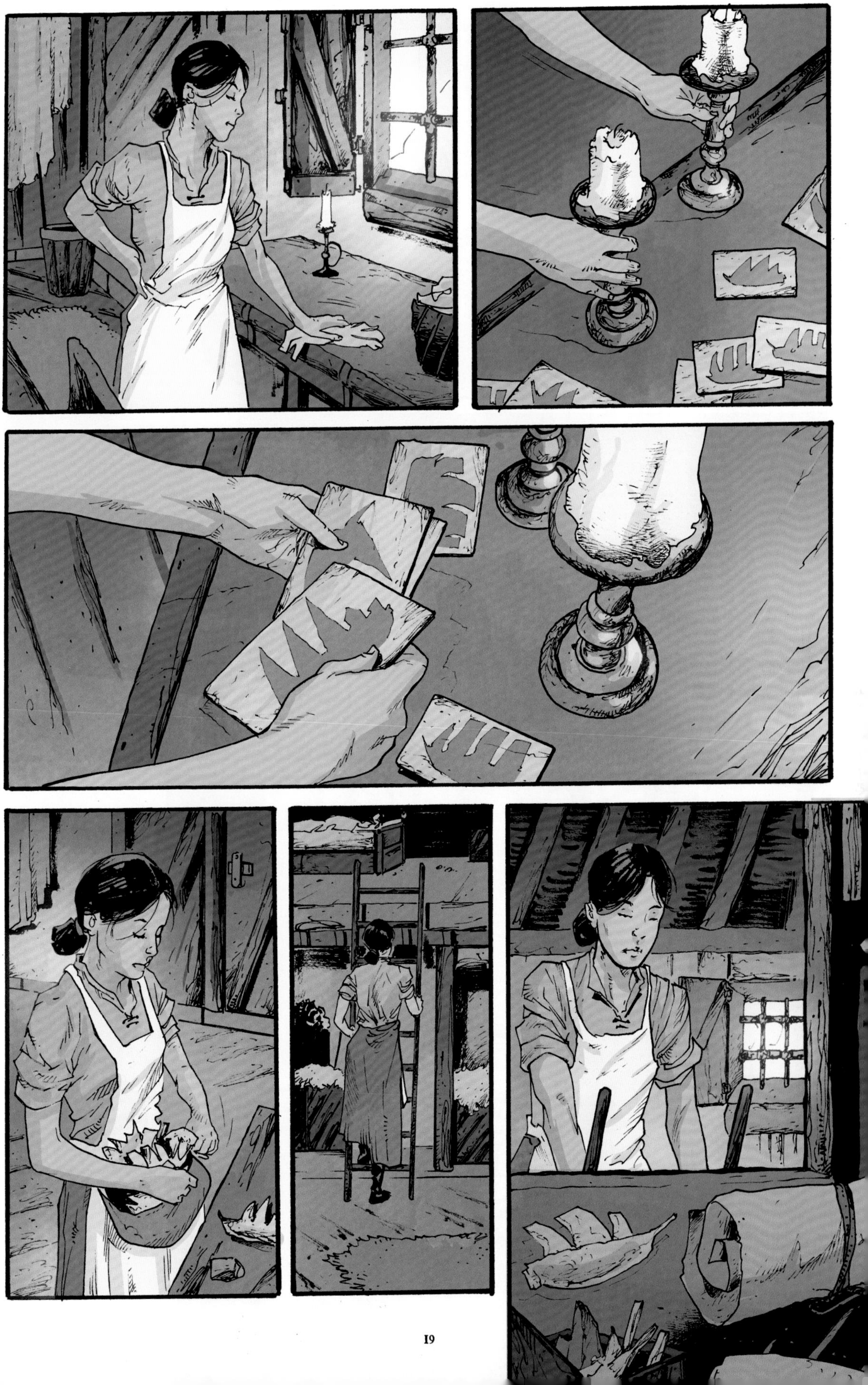

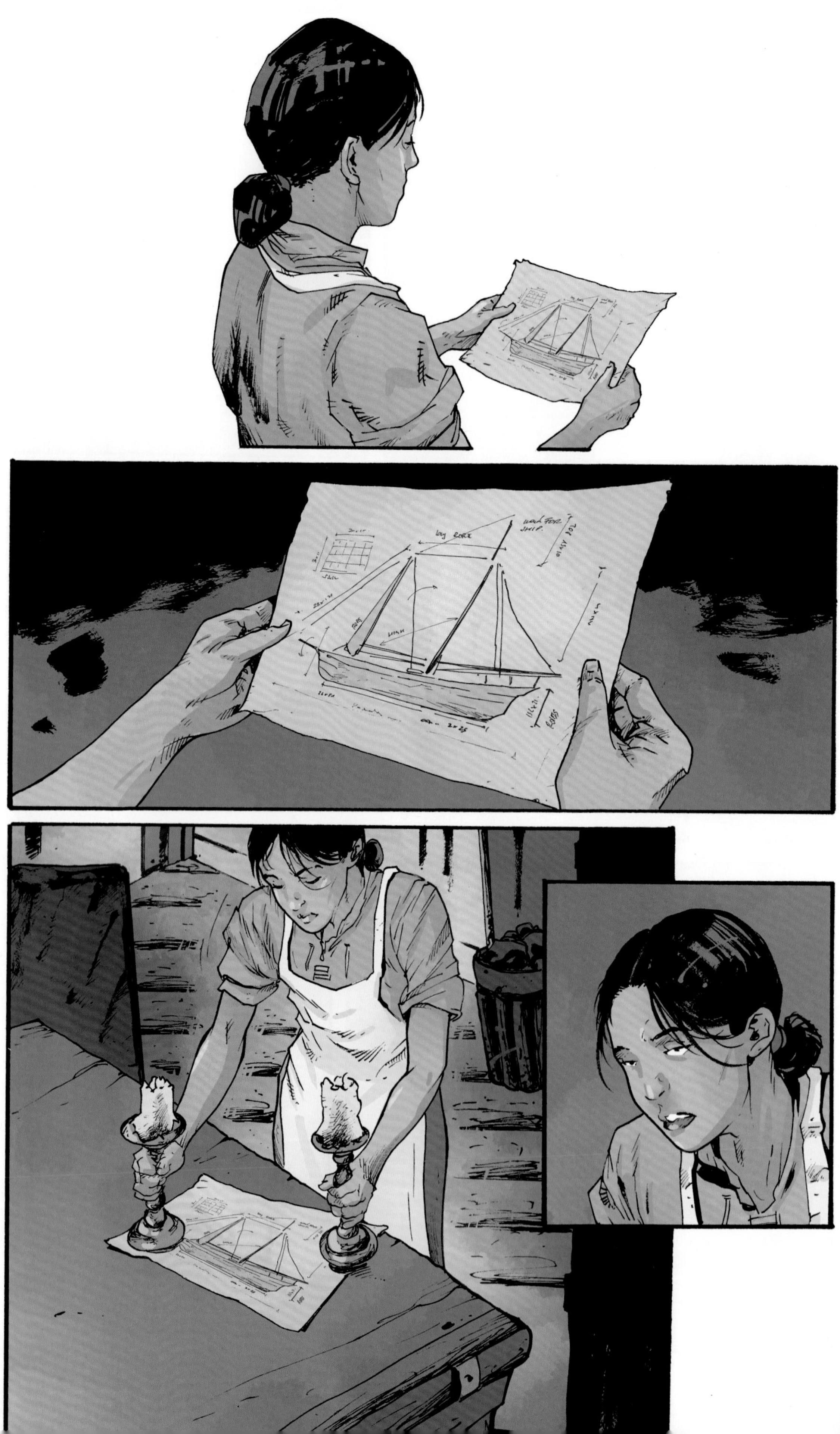

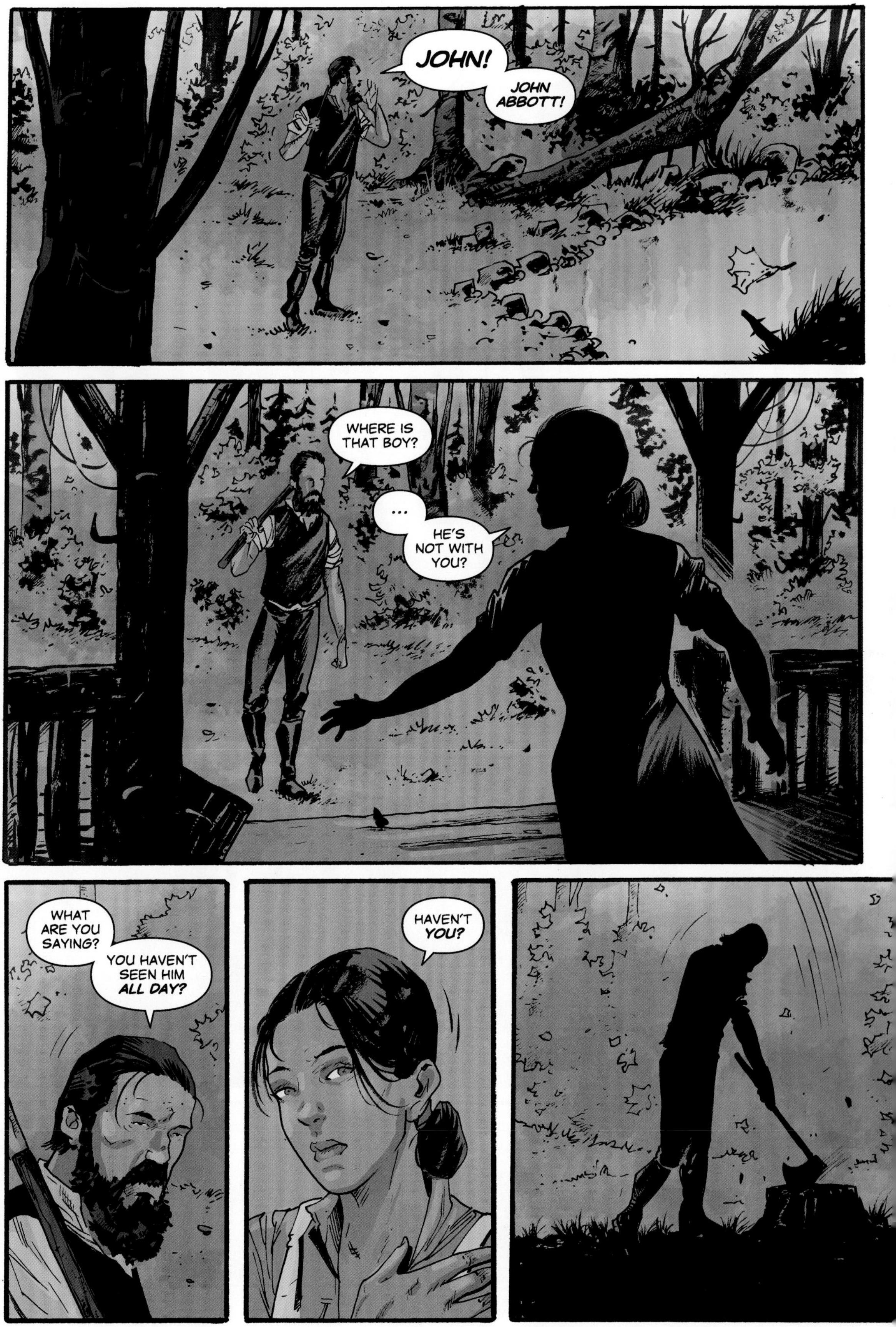
JOHN!
JOHN ABBOTT!
WHERE IS THAT BOY?
...
HE'S NOT WITH YOU?
WHAT ARE YOU SAYING?
YOU HAVEN'T SEEN HIM ALL DAY?
HAVEN'T YOU?

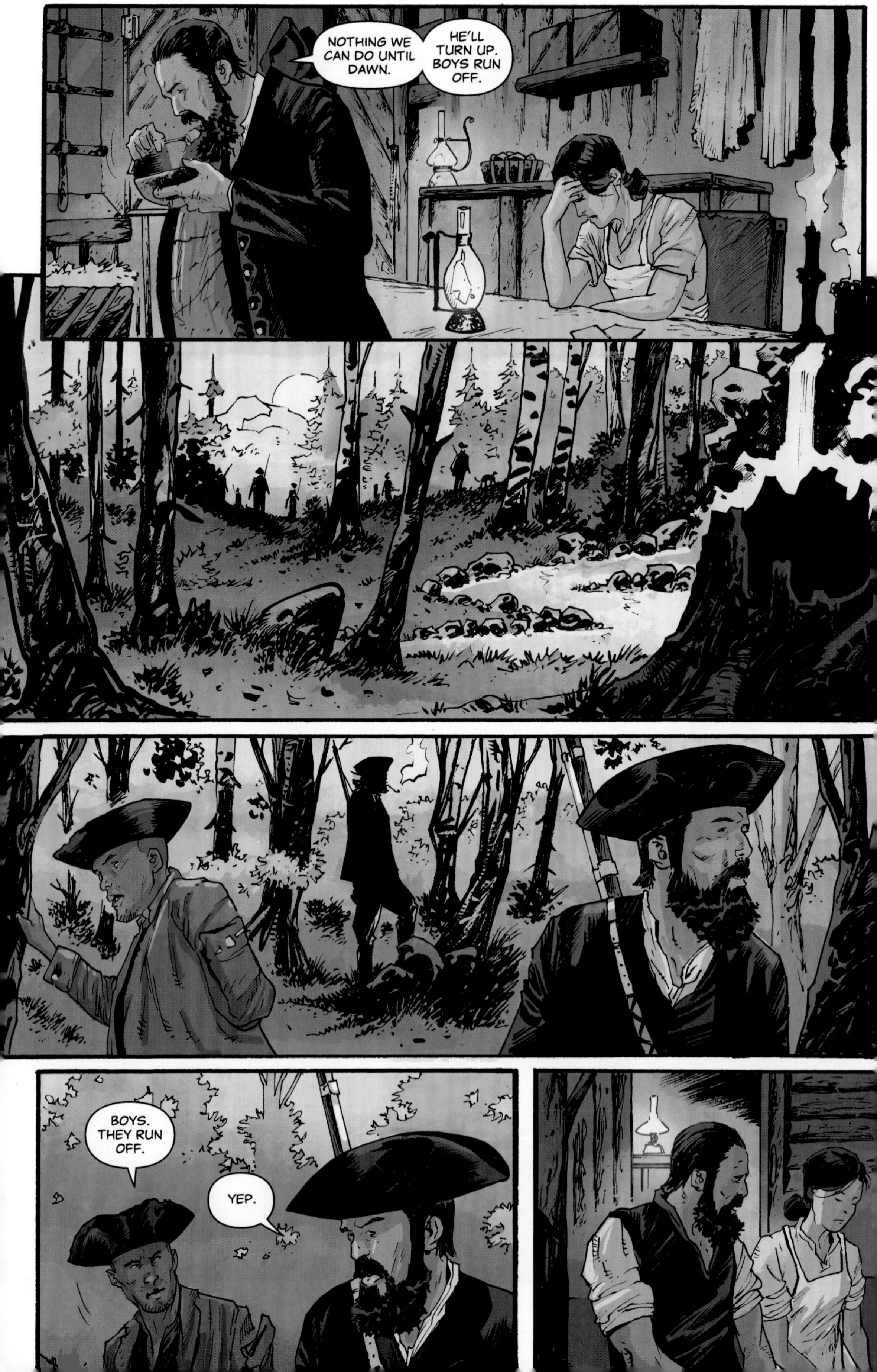
NOTHING WE CAN DO UNTIL DAWN.
HE'LL TURN UP. BOYS RUN OFF.
BOYS. THEY RUN OFF.
YEP.

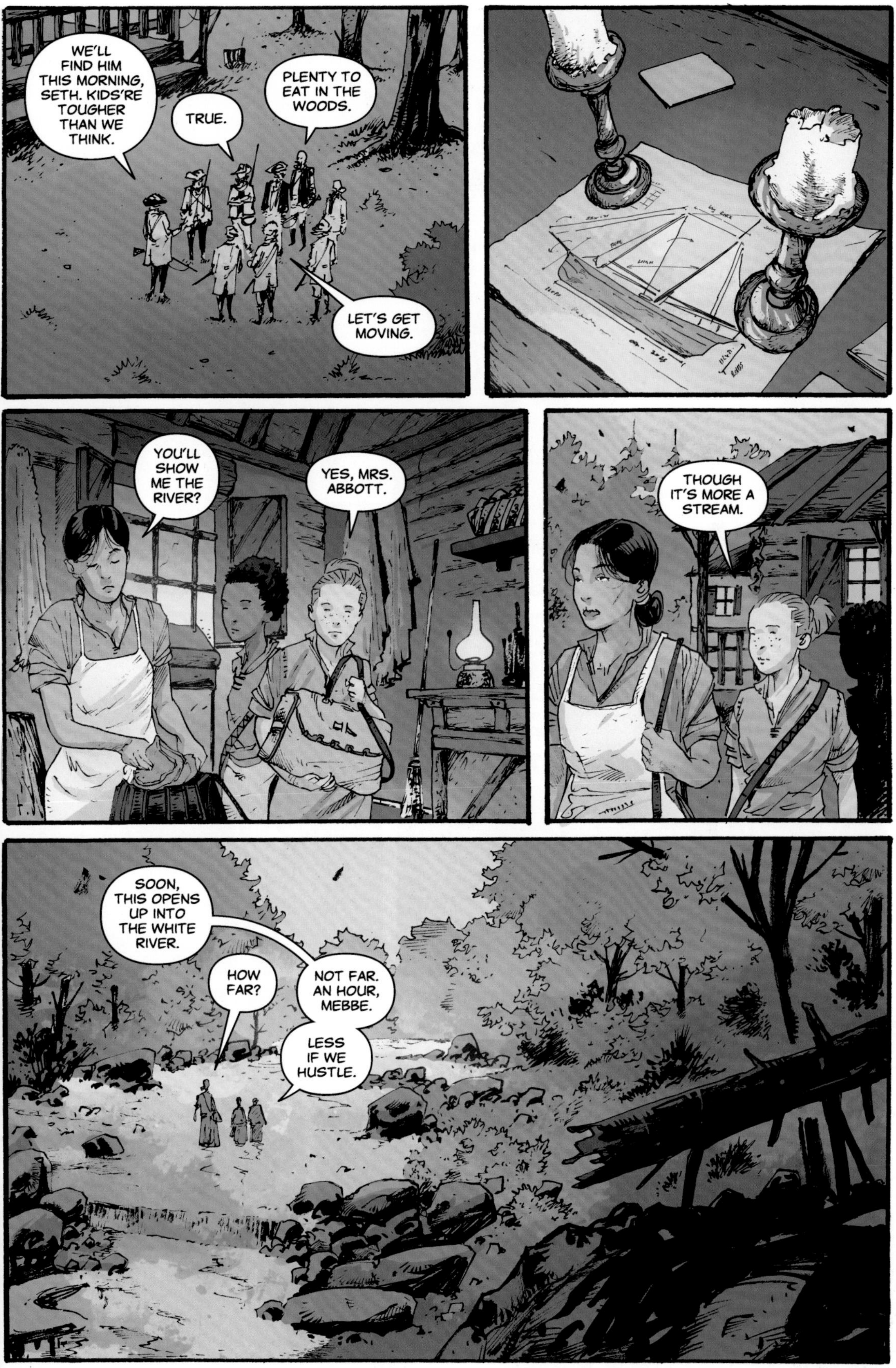
WE'LL FIND HIM THIS MORNING, SETH. KIDS'RE TOUGHER THAN WE THINK.
TRUE.
PLENTY TO EAT IN THE WOODS.
LET'S GET MOVING.
YOU'LL SHOW ME THE RIVER?
YES, MRS. ABBOTT.
THOUGH IT'S MORE A STREAM.
SOON, THIS OPENS UP INTO THE WHITE RIVER.
HOW FAR?
NOT FAR. AN HOUR, MEBBE.
LESS IF WE HUSTLE.

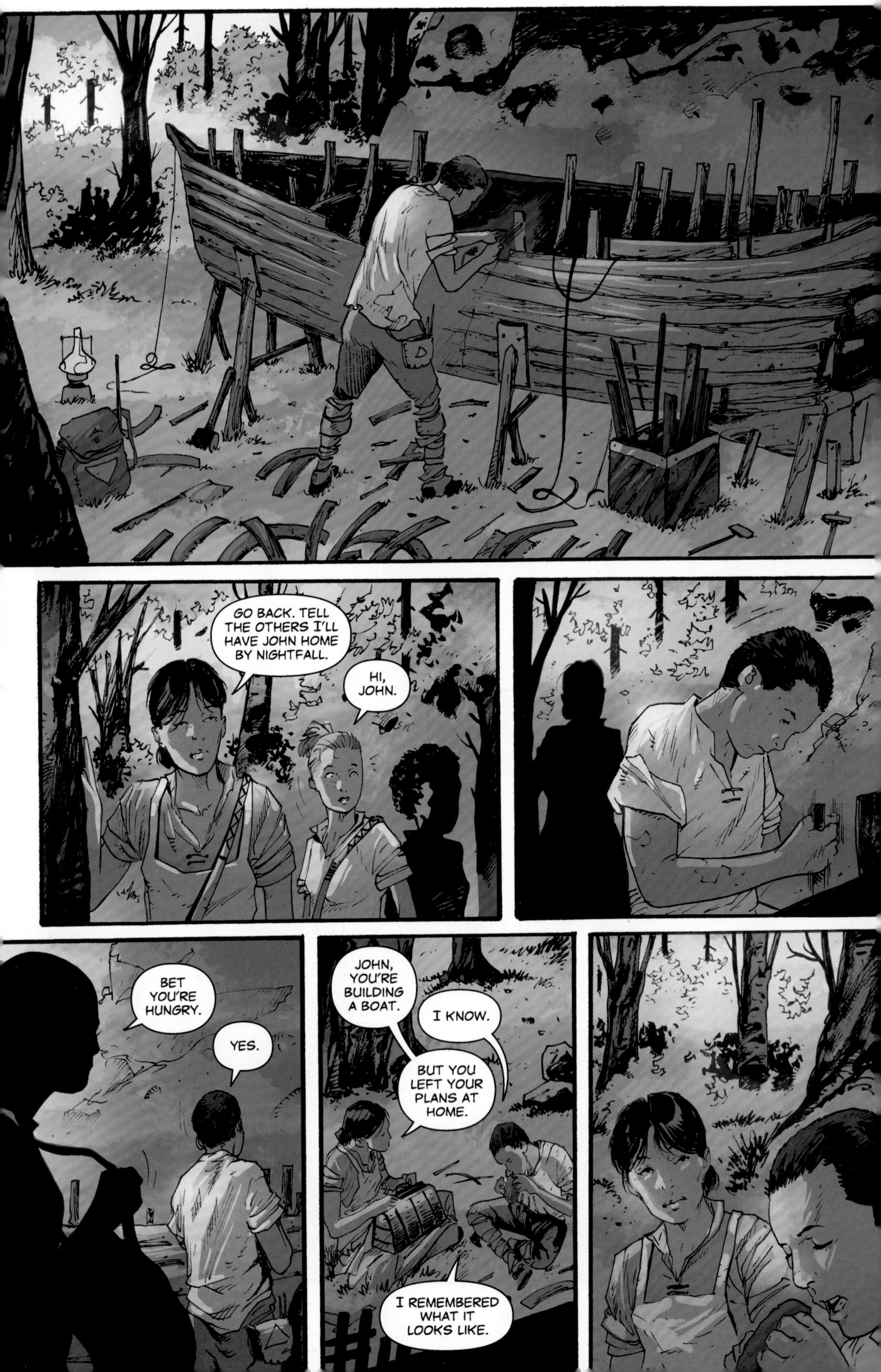
GO BACK. TELL THE OTHERS I'LL HAVE JOHN HOME BY NIGHTFALL.
HI, JOHN.
BET YOU'RE HUNGRY.
YES.
JOHN, YOU'RE BUILDING A BOAT.
I KNOW.
BUT YOU LEFT YOUR PLANS AT HOME.
I REMEMBERED WHAT IT LOOKS LIKE.

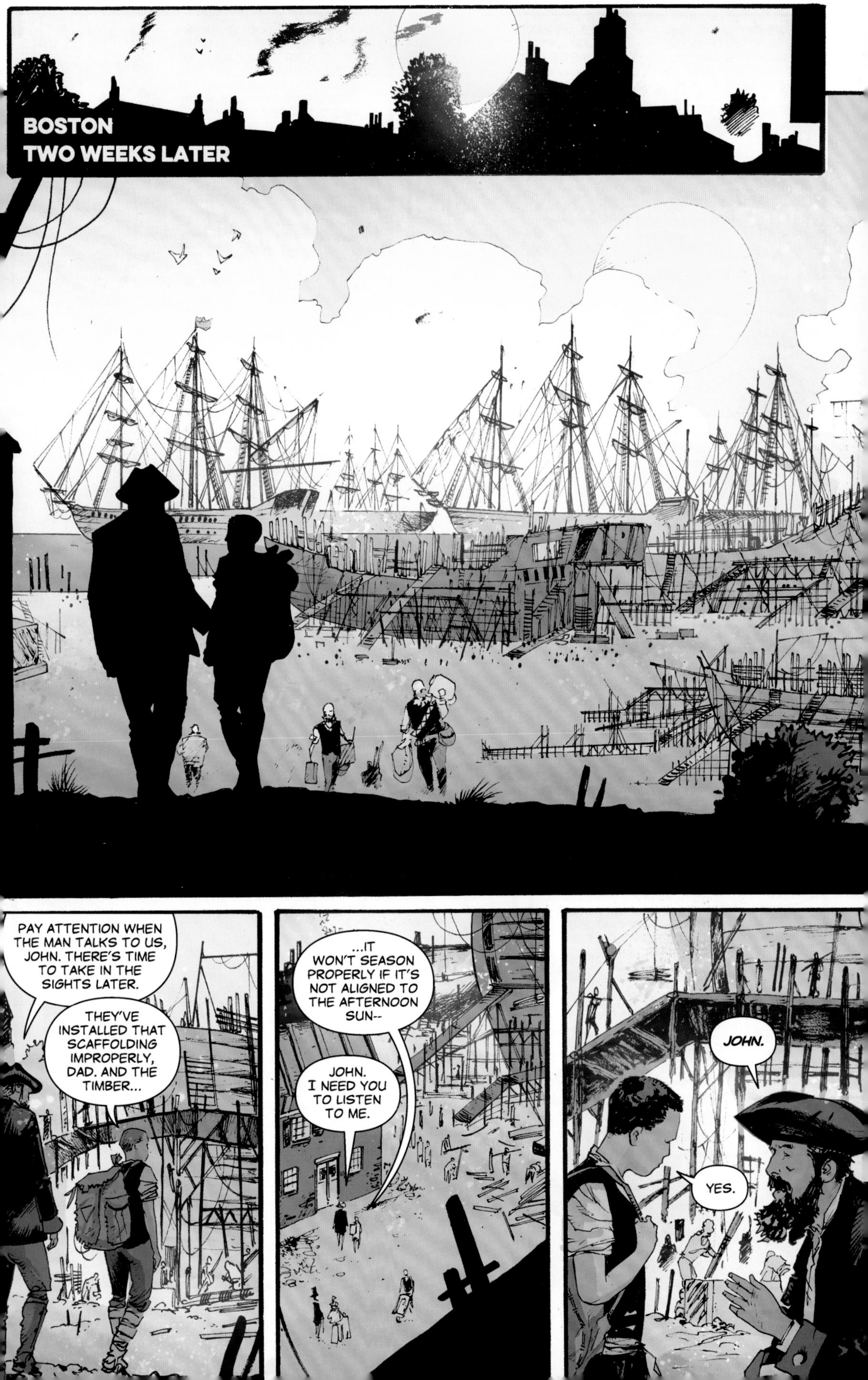
BOSTON
TWO WEEKS LATER
PAY ATTENTION WHEN THE MAN TALKS TO US, JOHN. THERE'S TIME TO TAKE IN THE SIGHTS LATER.
THEY'VE INSTALLED THAT SCAFFOLDING IMPROPERLY, DAD. AND THE TIMBER...
...IT WON'T SEASON PROPERLY IF IT'S NOT ALIGNED TO THE AFTERNOON SUN--
JOHN. I NEED YOU TO LISTEN TO ME.
JOHN.
YES.

WE'RE GOING TO SEE THE SUPERINTENDENT. HIS NAME IS SAMUEL NICHOLSON. YOU'LL BE WORKING FOR HIM.

YOU'RE A SMART BOY, JOHN. CHRIST, YOU'RE THE SMARTEST PERSON I KNOW OUT OF *ANYONE.*

BUT YOU HAVE TO HOLD YOUR TONGUE.

THESE PEOPLE ARE QUAKERS. THEY'RE GOOD PEOPLE. MORAL PEOPLE, KIND TO A FAULT, AND THEY'LL HOUSE YOU AND FEED YOU AND YOU'LL HELP BUILD THE BEST SHIPS THIS COUNTRY HAS TO OFFER. YOU WANT THAT, RIGHT?

YES.

BUT EVEN A QUAKER ISN'T READY FOR A TEN-YEAR-OLD BOY THAT'S AS SMART AS YOU ARE. YOU'RE HERE AS AN *APPRENTICE,* UNDERSTAND?

STAY QUIET UNLESS ASKED A QUESTION. LEARN EVERYTHING YOU DON'T KNOW.

I HAVE LOTS OF TIME.

YES.

I DON'T HAVE TO RUSH IT.

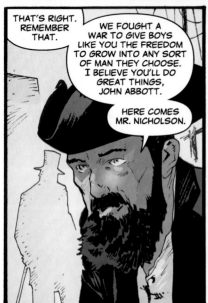

THAT'S RIGHT. REMEMBER THAT.

WE FOUGHT A WAR TO GIVE BOYS LIKE YOU THE FREEDOM TO GROW INTO ANY SORT OF MAN THEY CHOOSE. I BELIEVE YOU'LL DO GREAT THINGS, JOHN ABBOTT.

HERE COMES MR. NICHOLSON.

SETH ABBOTT?

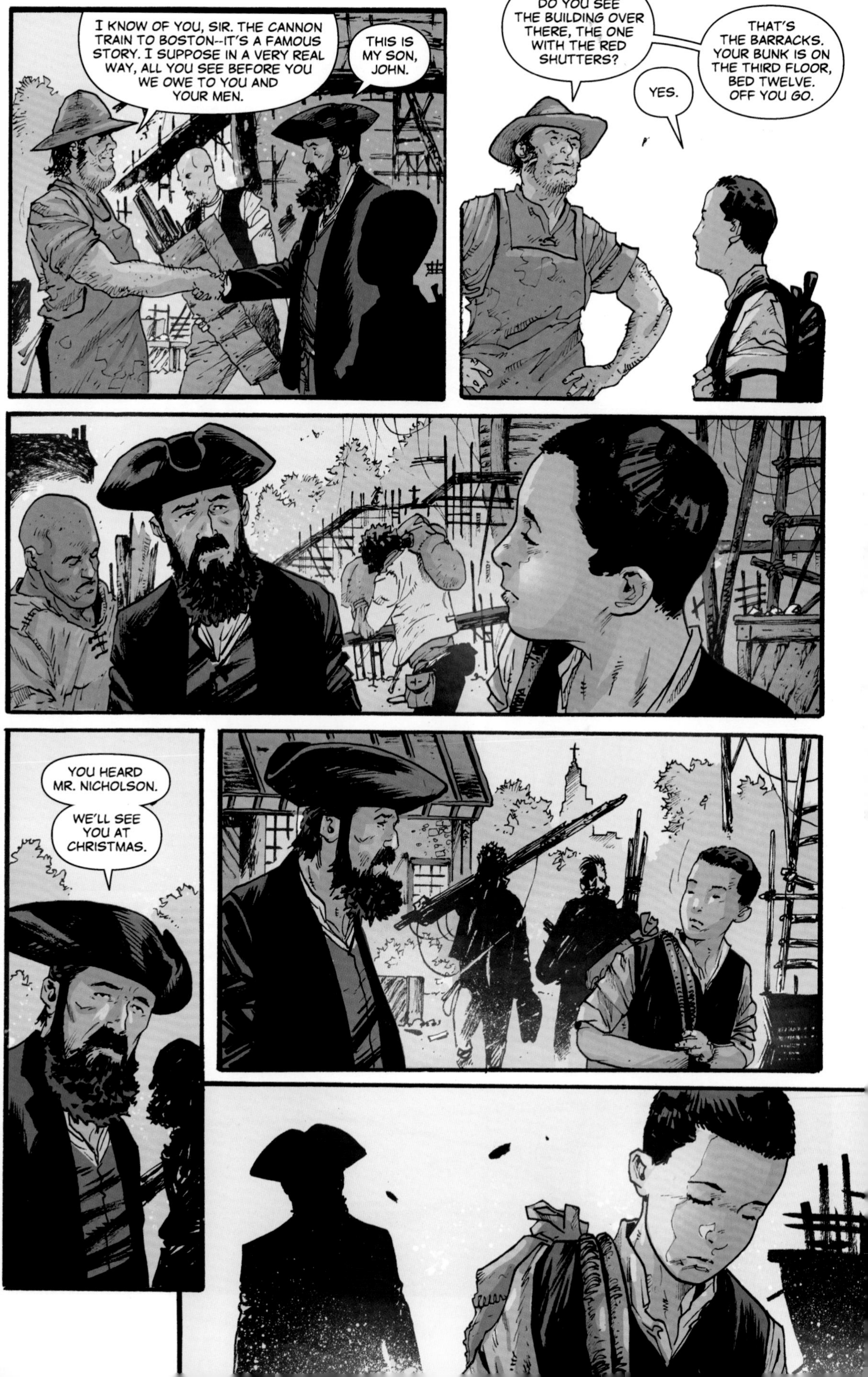
I KNOW OF YOU, SIR. THE CANNON TRAIN TO BOSTON--IT'S A FAMOUS STORY. I SUPPOSE IN A VERY REAL WAY, ALL YOU SEE BEFORE YOU WE OWE TO YOU AND YOUR MEN.
THIS IS MY SON, JOHN.
JOHN. DO YOU SEE THE BUILDING OVER THERE, THE ONE WITH THE RED SHUTTERS?
YES.
THAT'S THE BARRACKS. YOUR BUNK IS ON THE THIRD FLOOR, BED TWELVE. OFF YOU GO.
YOU HEARD MR. NICHOLSON.
WE'LL SEE YOU AT CHRISTMAS.

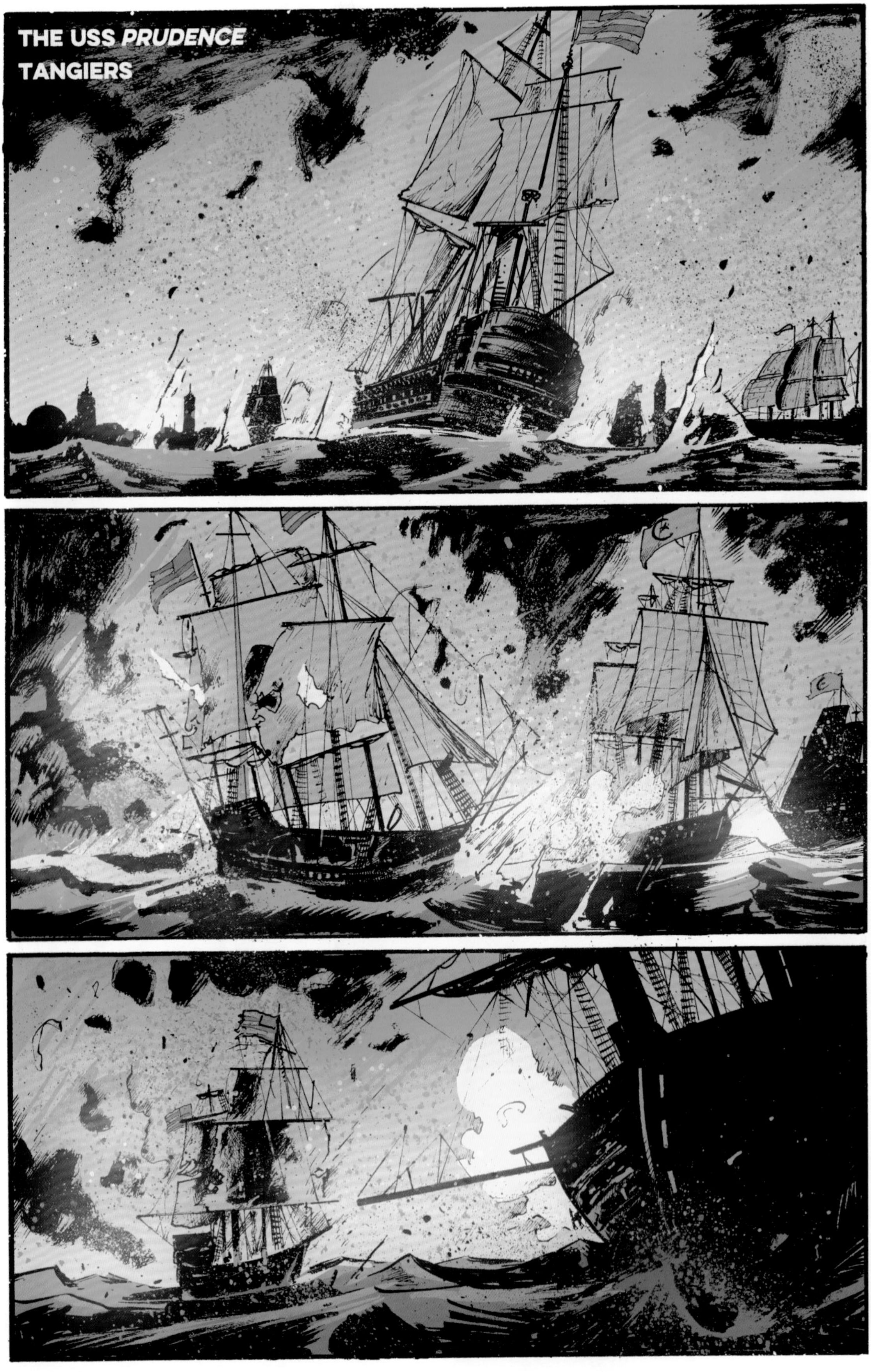
THE USS *PRUDENCE*
TANGIERS

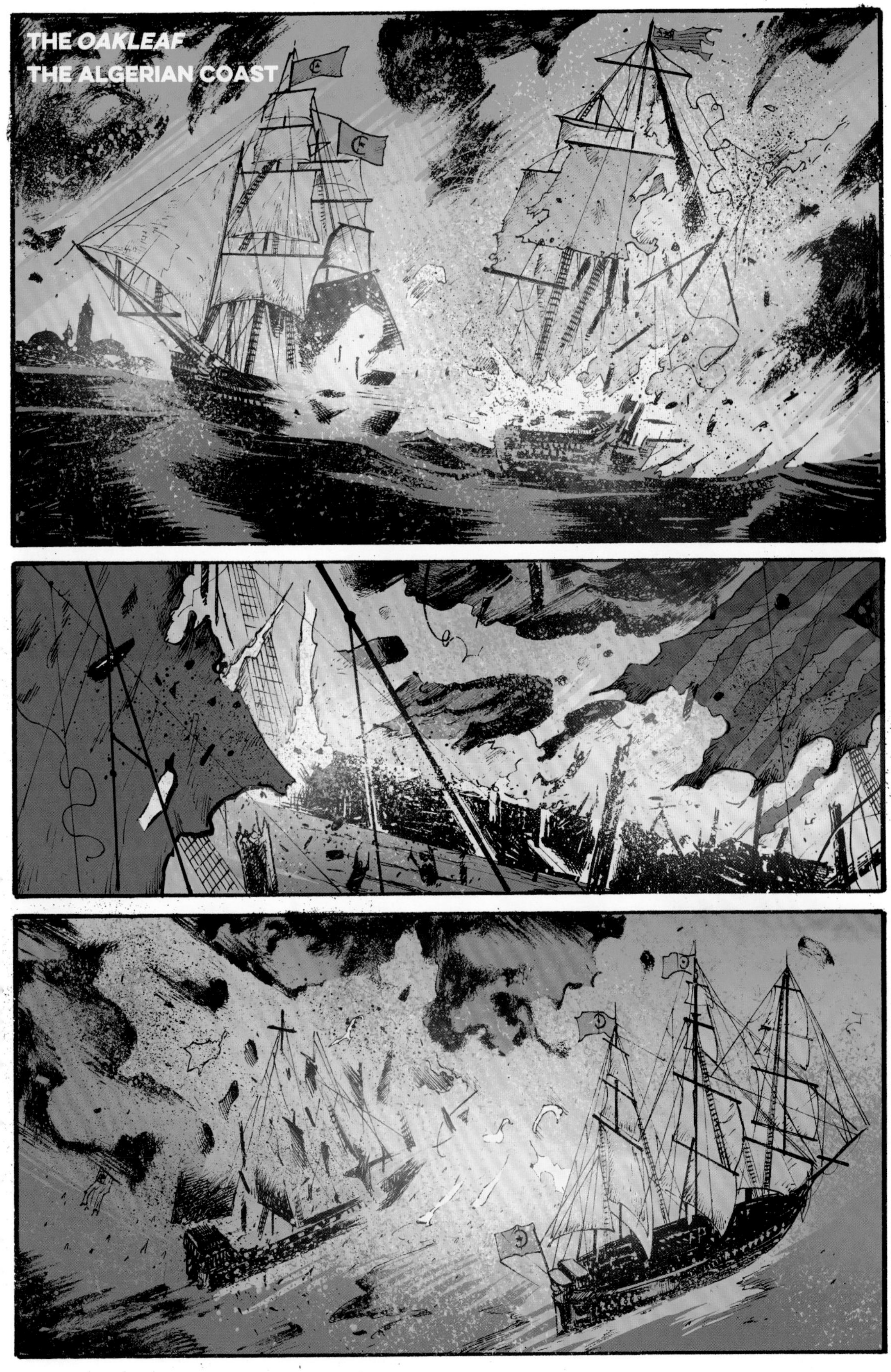
THE *OAKLEAF*
THE ALGERIAN COAST

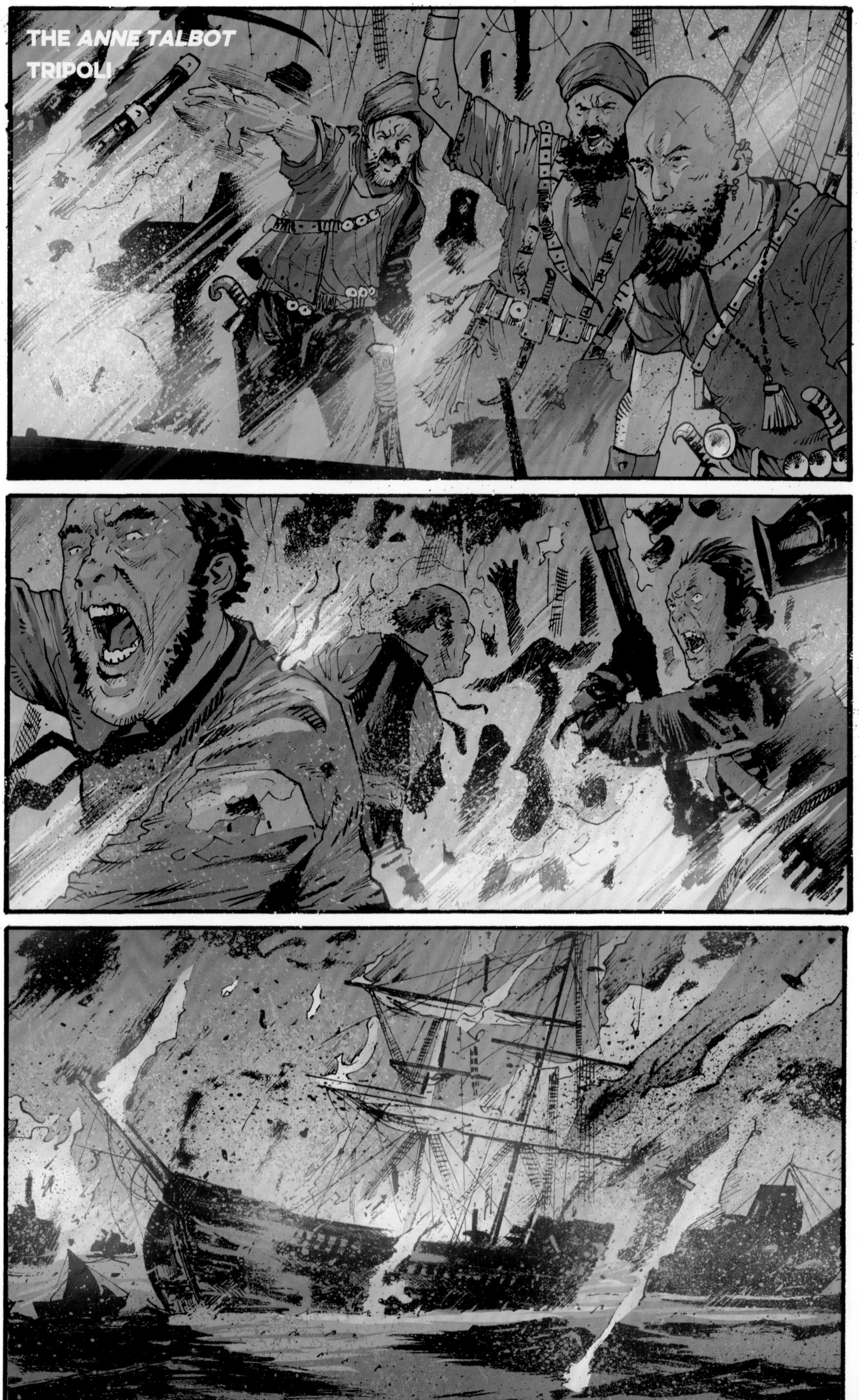
THE *ANNE TALBOT*
TRIPOLI

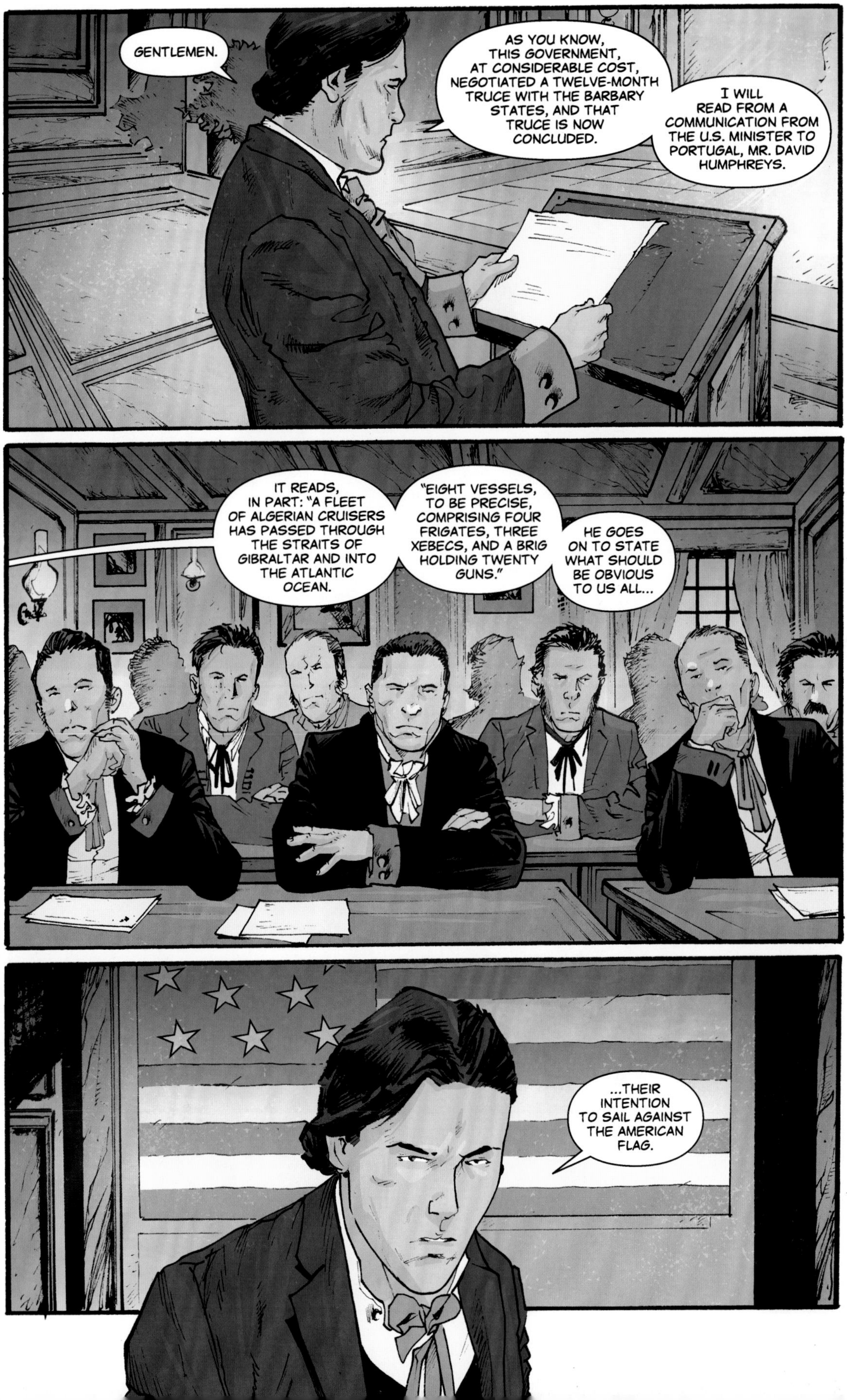
GENTLEMEN.
AS YOU KNOW, THIS GOVERNMENT, AT CONSIDERABLE COST, NEGOTIATED A TWELVE-MONTH TRUCE WITH THE BARBARY STATES, AND THAT TRUCE IS NOW CONCLUDED.
I WILL READ FROM A COMMUNICATION FROM THE U.S. MINISTER TO PORTUGAL, MR. DAVID HUMPHREYS.
IT READS, IN PART: "A FLEET OF ALGERIAN CRUISERS HAS PASSED THROUGH THE STRAITS OF GIBRALTAR AND INTO THE ATLANTIC OCEAN.
"EIGHT VESSELS, TO BE PRECISE, COMPRISING FOUR FRIGATES, THREE XEBECS, AND A BRIG HOLDING TWENTY GUNS."
HE GOES ON TO STATE WHAT SHOULD BE OBVIOUS TO US ALL...
...THEIR INTENTION TO SAIL AGAINST THE AMERICAN FLAG.

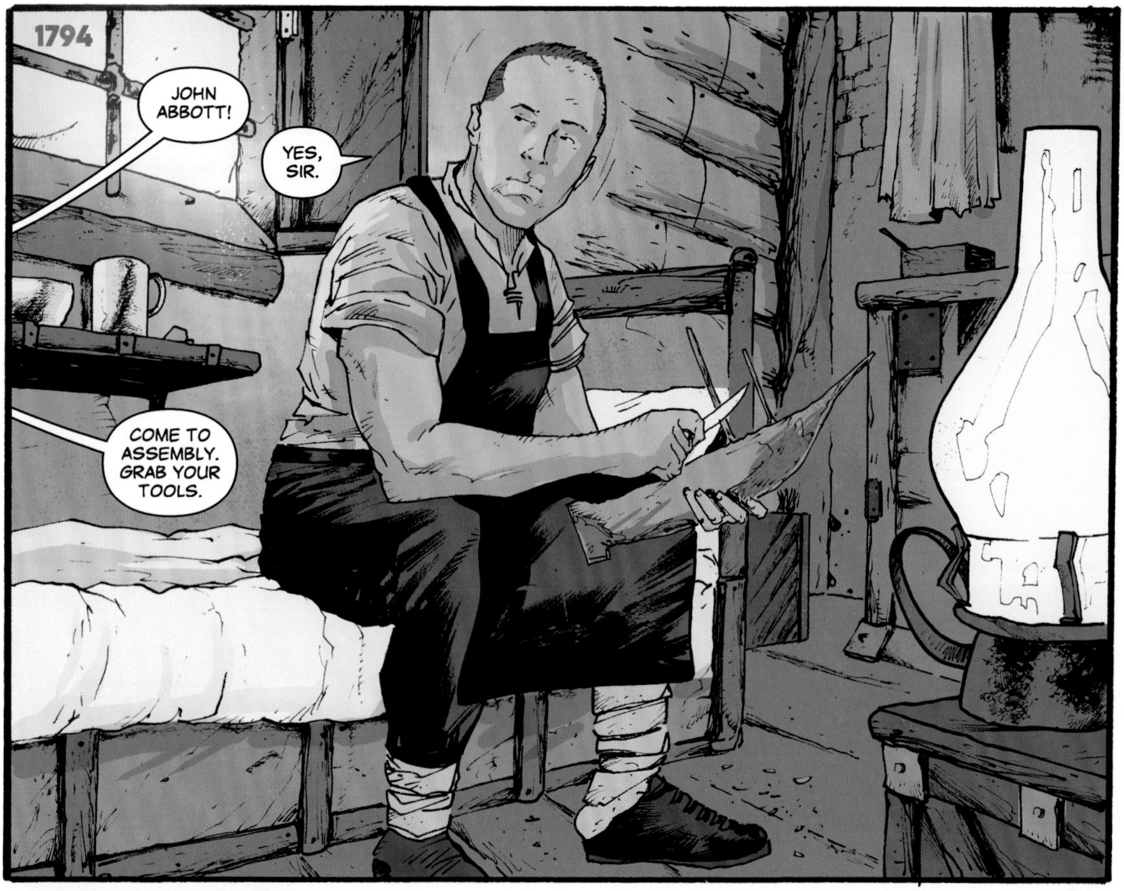
1794
JOHN ABBOTT!
YES, SIR.
COME TO ASSEMBLY. GRAB YOUR TOOLS.

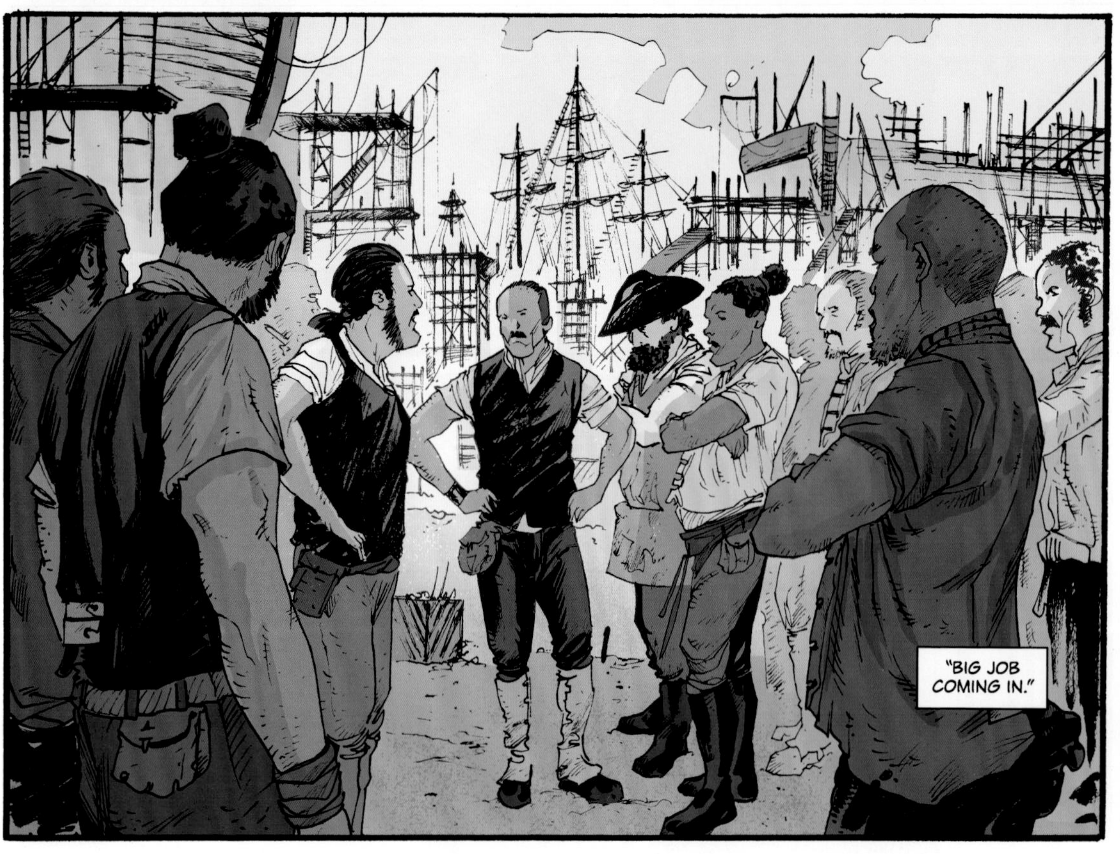
"BIG JOB COMING IN."

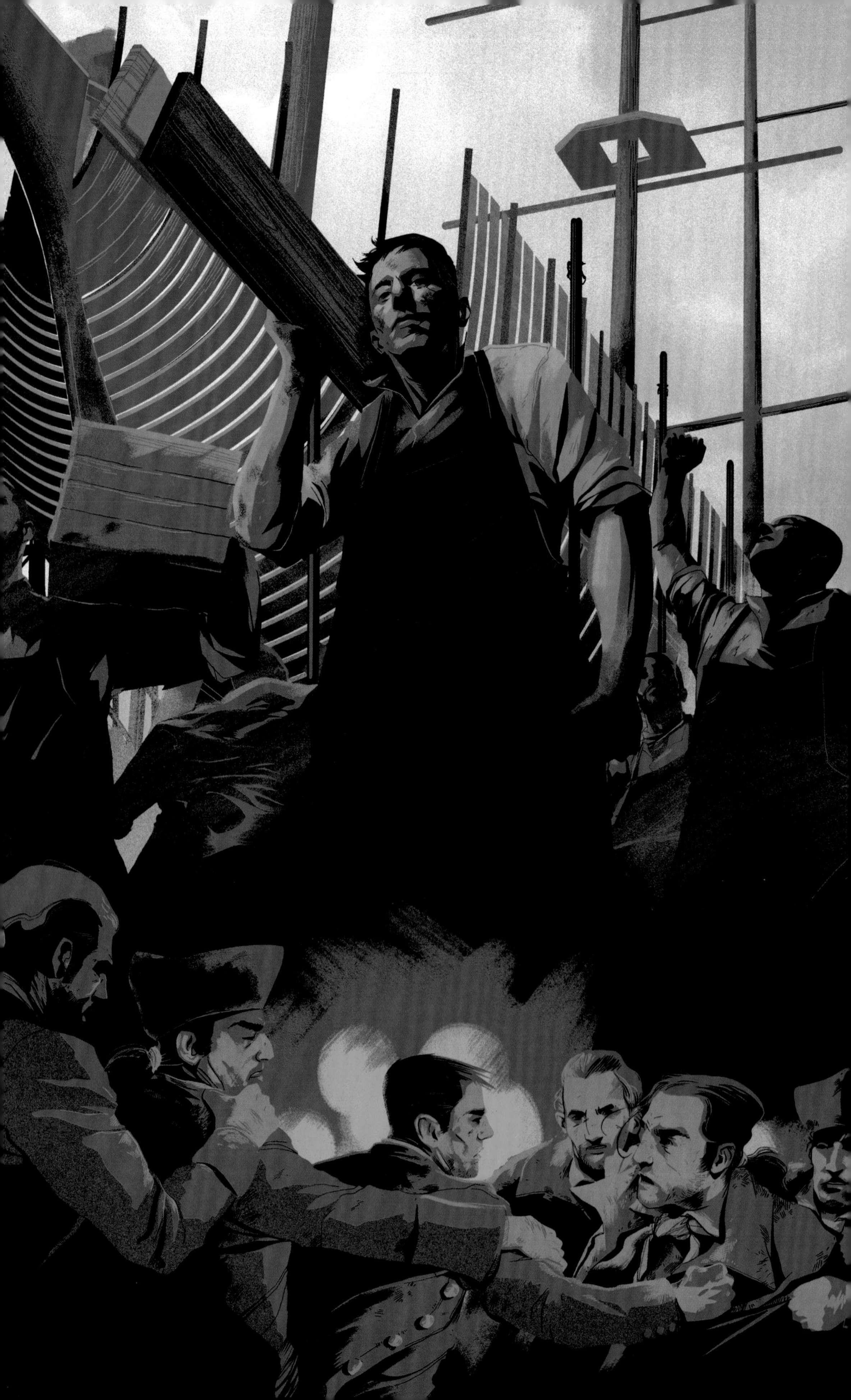

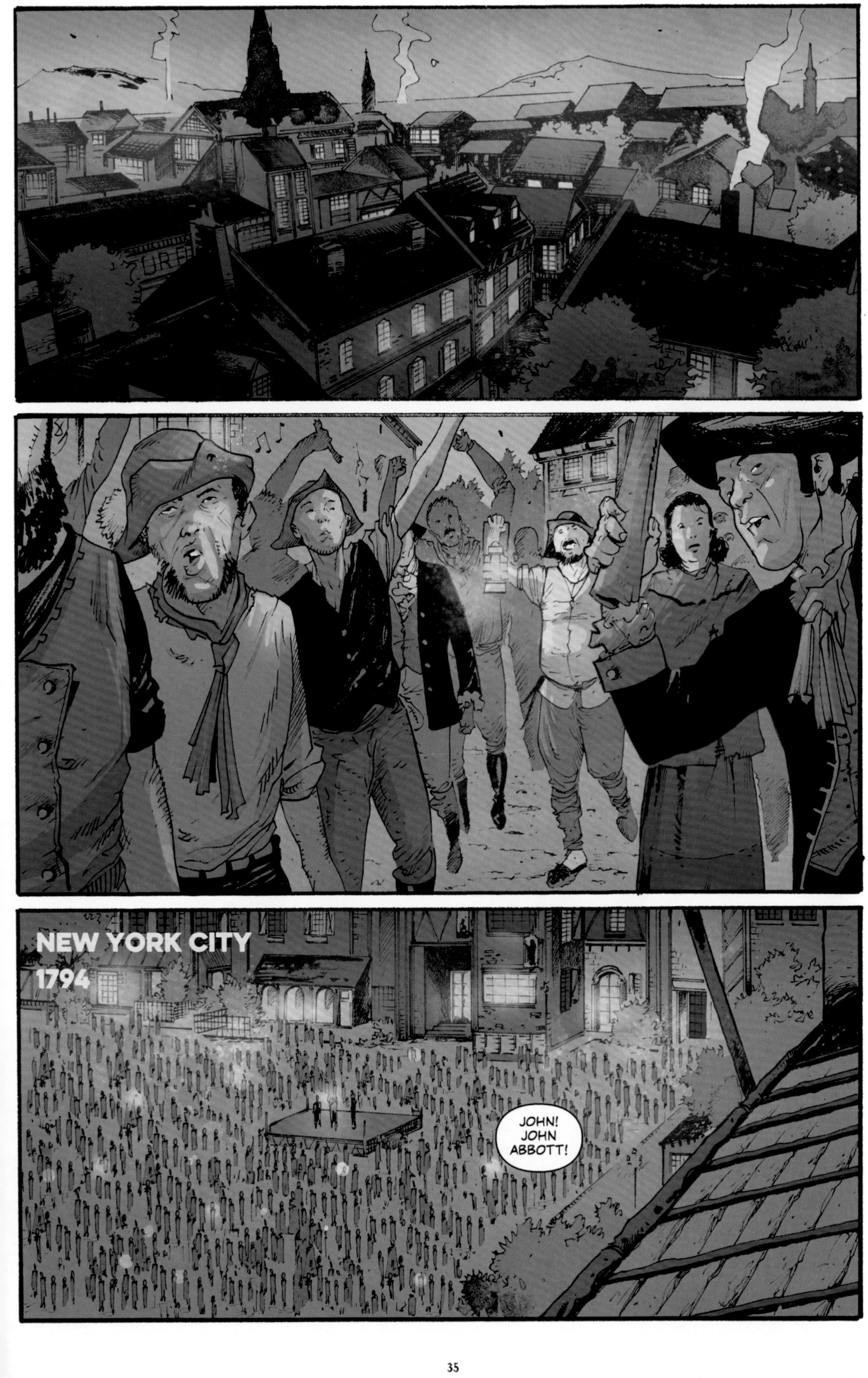
NEW YORK CITY
1794
JOHN!
JOHN
ABBOTT!

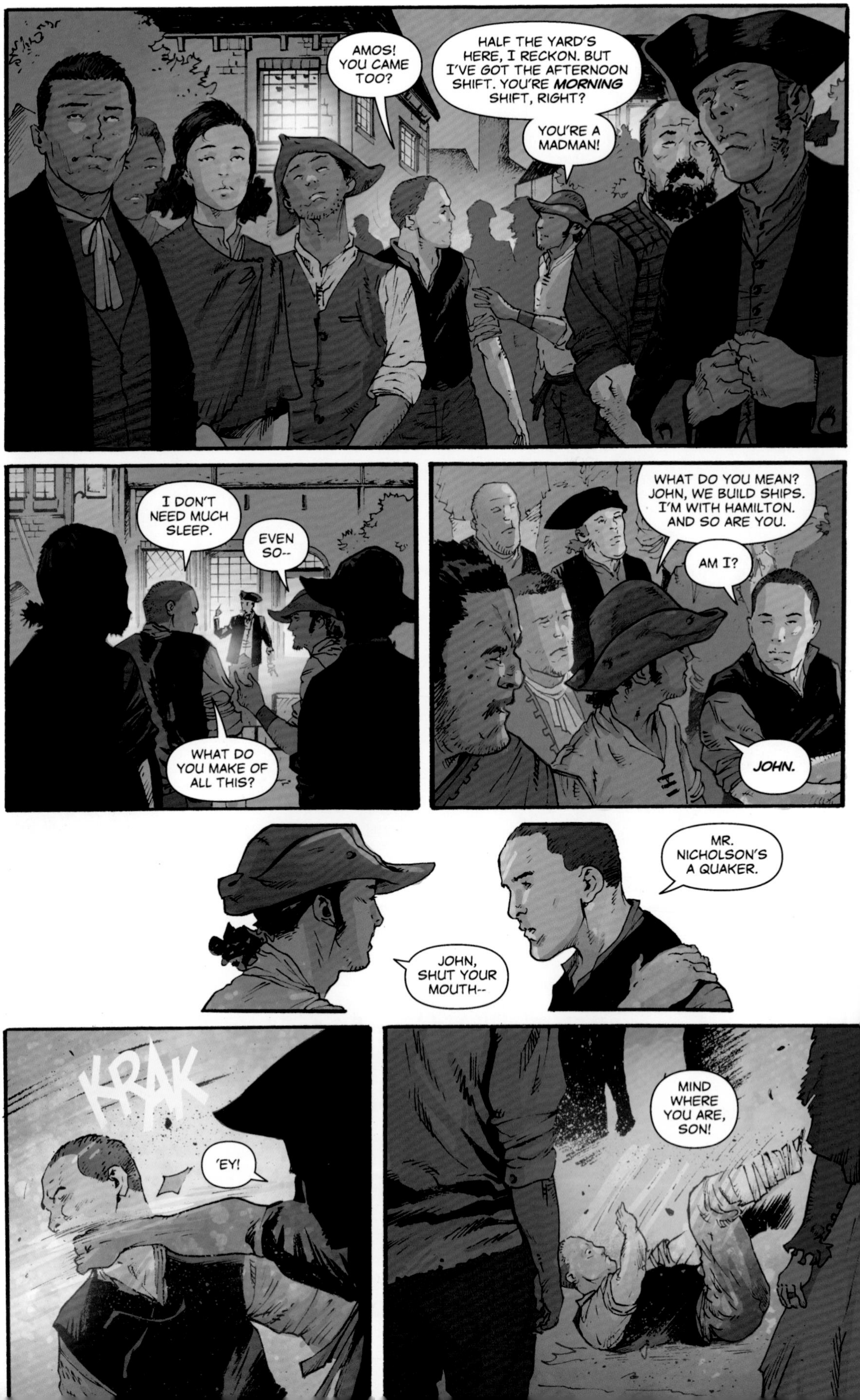
AMOS! YOU CAME TOO?
HALF THE YARD'S HERE, I RECKON. BUT I'VE GOT THE AFTERNOON SHIFT. YOU'RE MORNING SHIFT, RIGHT?
YOU'RE A MADMAN!
I DON'T NEED MUCH SLEEP.
EVEN SO--
WHAT DO YOU MAKE OF ALL THIS?
WHAT DO YOU MEAN? JOHN, WE BUILD SHIPS. I'M WITH HAMILTON. AND SO ARE YOU.
AM I?
JOHN.
MR. NICHOLSON'S A QUAKER.
JOHN, SHUT YOUR MOUTH--
KRAK
'EY!
MIND WHERE YOU ARE, SON!

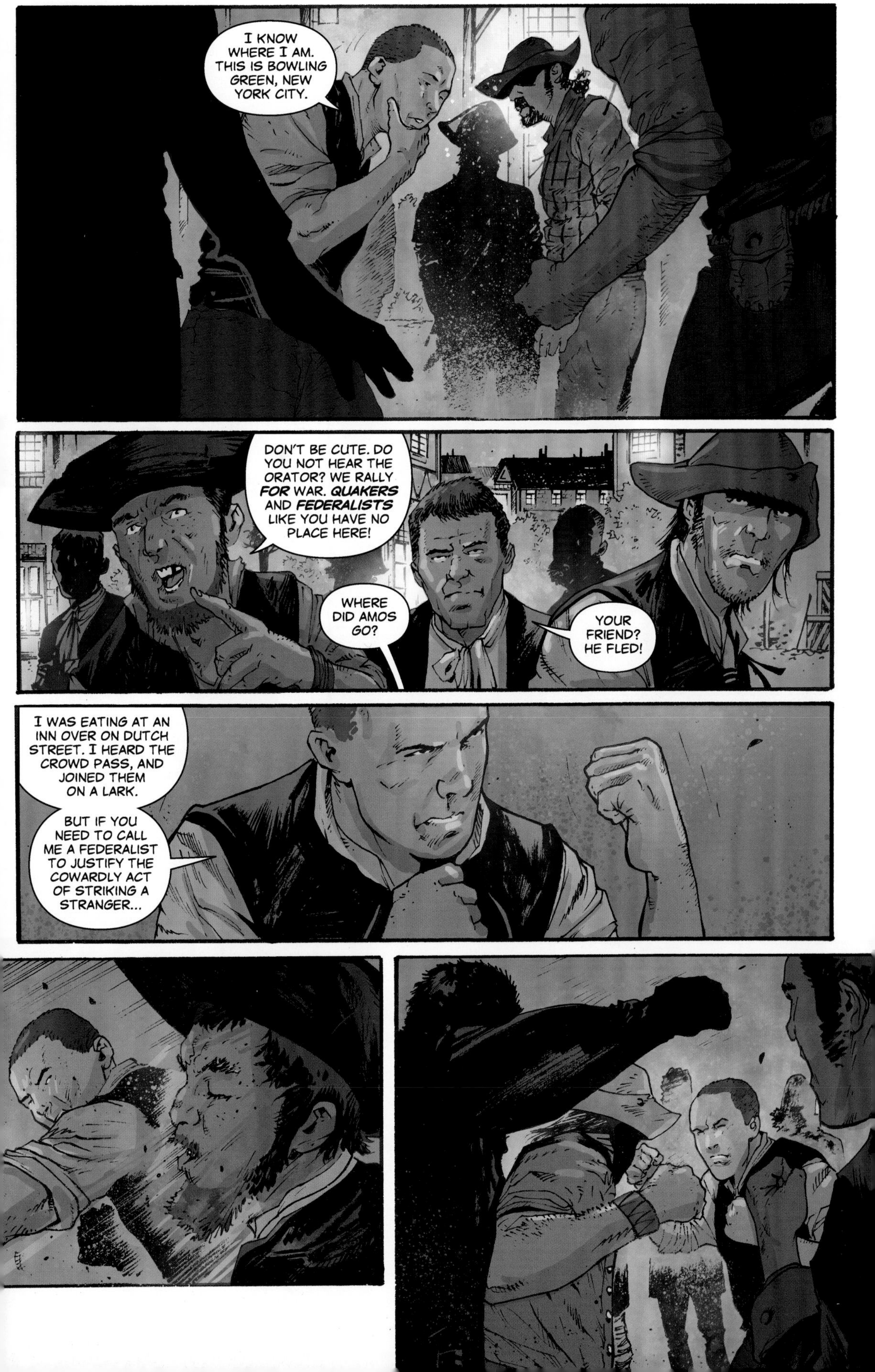

I KNOW WHERE I AM. THIS IS BOWLING GREEN, NEW YORK CITY.
DON'T BE CUTE. DO YOU NOT HEAR THE ORATOR? WE RALLY ***FOR*** WAR. ***QUAKERS*** AND ***FEDERALISTS*** LIKE YOU HAVE NO PLACE HERE!
WHERE DID AMOS GO?
YOUR FRIEND? HE FLED!
I WAS EATING AT AN INN OVER ON DUTCH STREET. I HEARD THE CROWD PASS, AND JOINED THEM ON A LARK.
BUT IF YOU NEED TO CALL ME A FEDERALIST TO JUSTIFY THE COWARDLY ACT OF STRIKING A STRANGER...

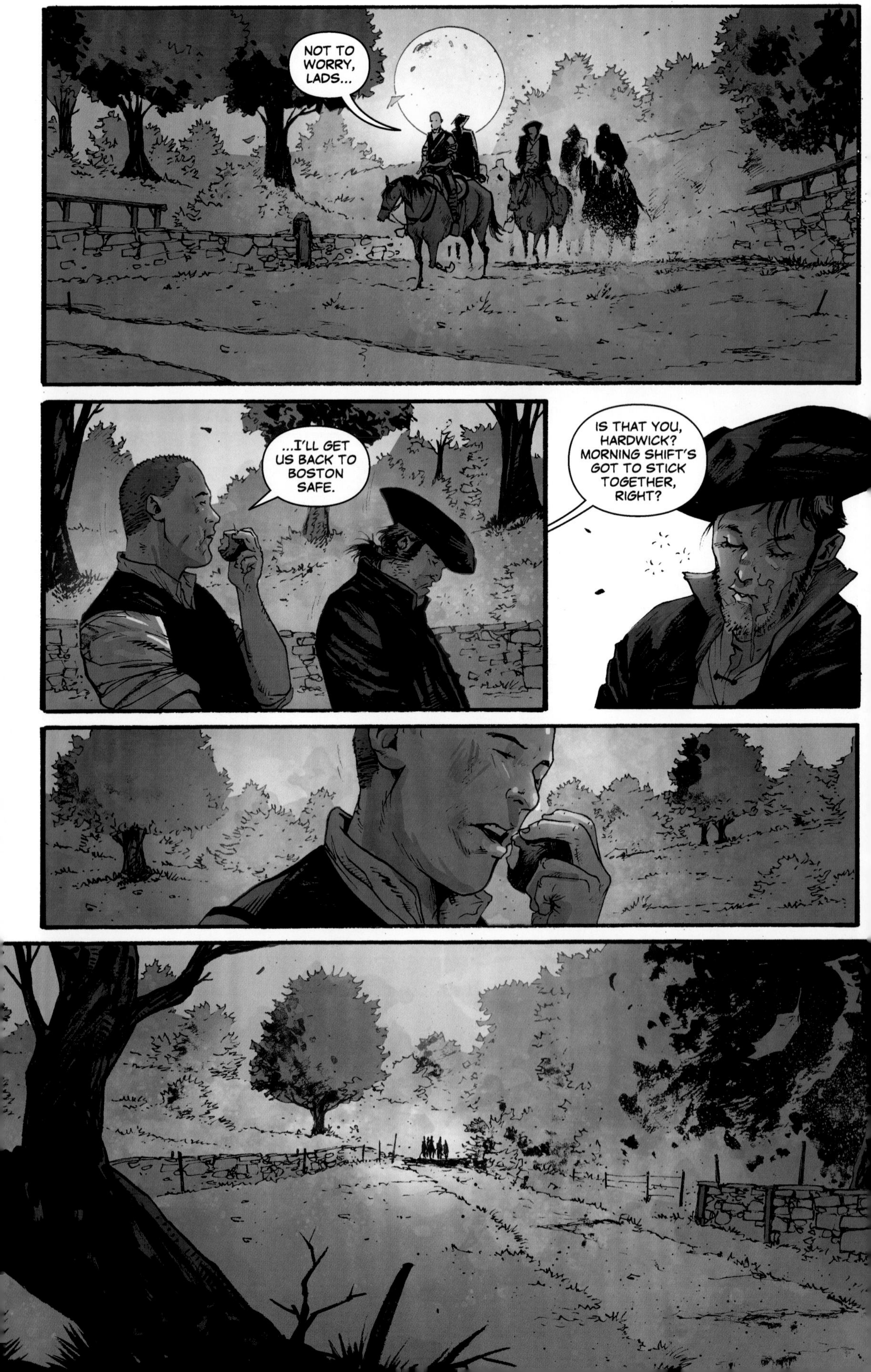
NOT TO WORRY, LADS...
...I'LL GET US BACK TO BOSTON SAFE.
IS THAT YOU, HARDWICK? MORNING SHIFT'S GOT TO STICK TOGETHER, RIGHT?

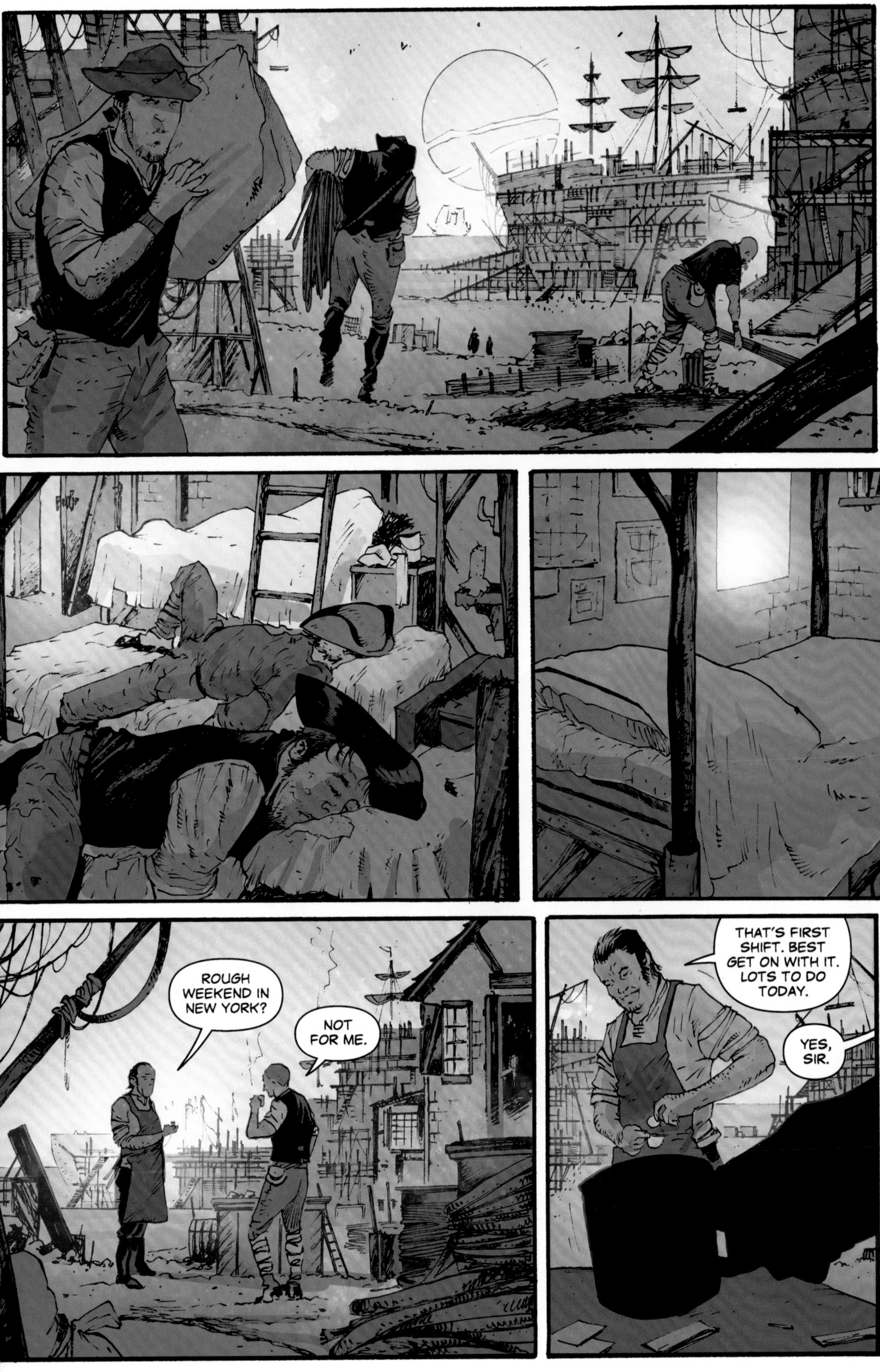
ROUGH WEEKEND IN NEW YORK?
NOT FOR ME.
THAT'S FIRST SHIFT. BEST GET ON WITH IT. LOTS TO DO TODAY.
YES, SIR.

DONT
THE

REBELS

"THESE FREE AND INDEPENDENT STATES"   PART 2 OF 5

IN WHICH THE GOVERNMENT DECIDES TO BUILD A NAVY, AND JOHN ABBOTT FALLS IN WITH ABOLITIONISTS.

BRIAN WOOD · ANDREA MUTTI · LAUREN AFFE · MATT TAYLOR

MR. PRESIDENT.

hmm?

MR. PRESIDENT, I HAVE THE LIST OF PROPOSED NAMES.

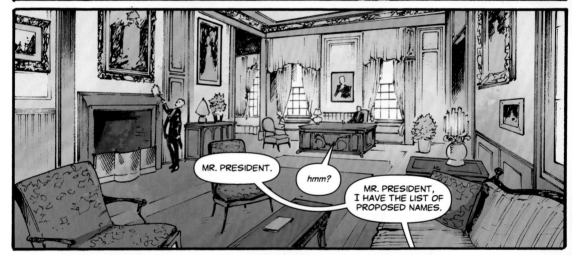

AH, THE FRIGATES WE AGREED TO. THIS IS QUITE A LIST.

THE COMMITTEE ARE PROPOSING NEARLY *FORTY* NAMES, MR. PRESIDENT. YOU CAN SEE THERE ARE SEVERAL ANNOTATIONS AND CONSIDERATIONS, AND CERTAIN MEMBERS OF THE COMMITTEE HAVE REQUESTED--

HOW MANY FRIGATES ARE WE BUILDING, AGAIN?

SIX, SIR.

USE THE FIRST SIX NAMES ON THE LIST.

THANK YOU, MR. KNOX.

THE NAVAL ACT OF 1794
CHAPTER XII

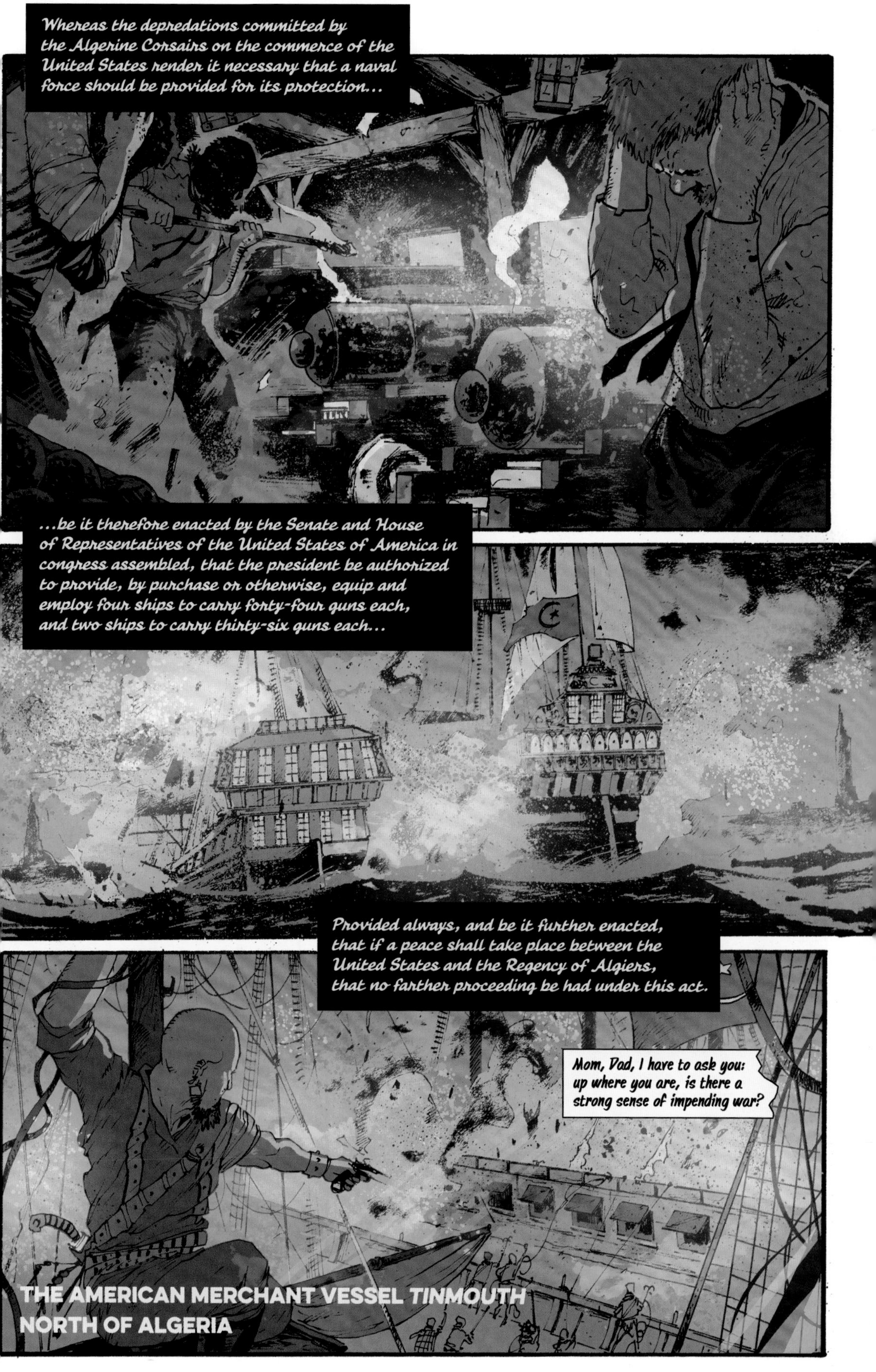
Whereas the depredations committed by the Algerine Corsairs on the commerce of the United States render it necessary that a naval force should be provided for its protection...
...be it therefore enacted by the Senate and House of Representatives of the United States of America in congress assembled, that the president be authorized to provide, by purchase or otherwise, equip and employ four ships to carry forty-four guns each, and two ships to carry thirty-six guns each...
Provided always, and be it further enacted, that if a peace shall take place between the United States and the Regency of Algiers, that no farther proceeding be had under this act.
Mom, Dad, I have to ask you: up where you are, is there a strong sense of impending war?
THE AMERICAN MERCHANT VESSEL *TINMOUTH*
NORTH OF ALGERIA

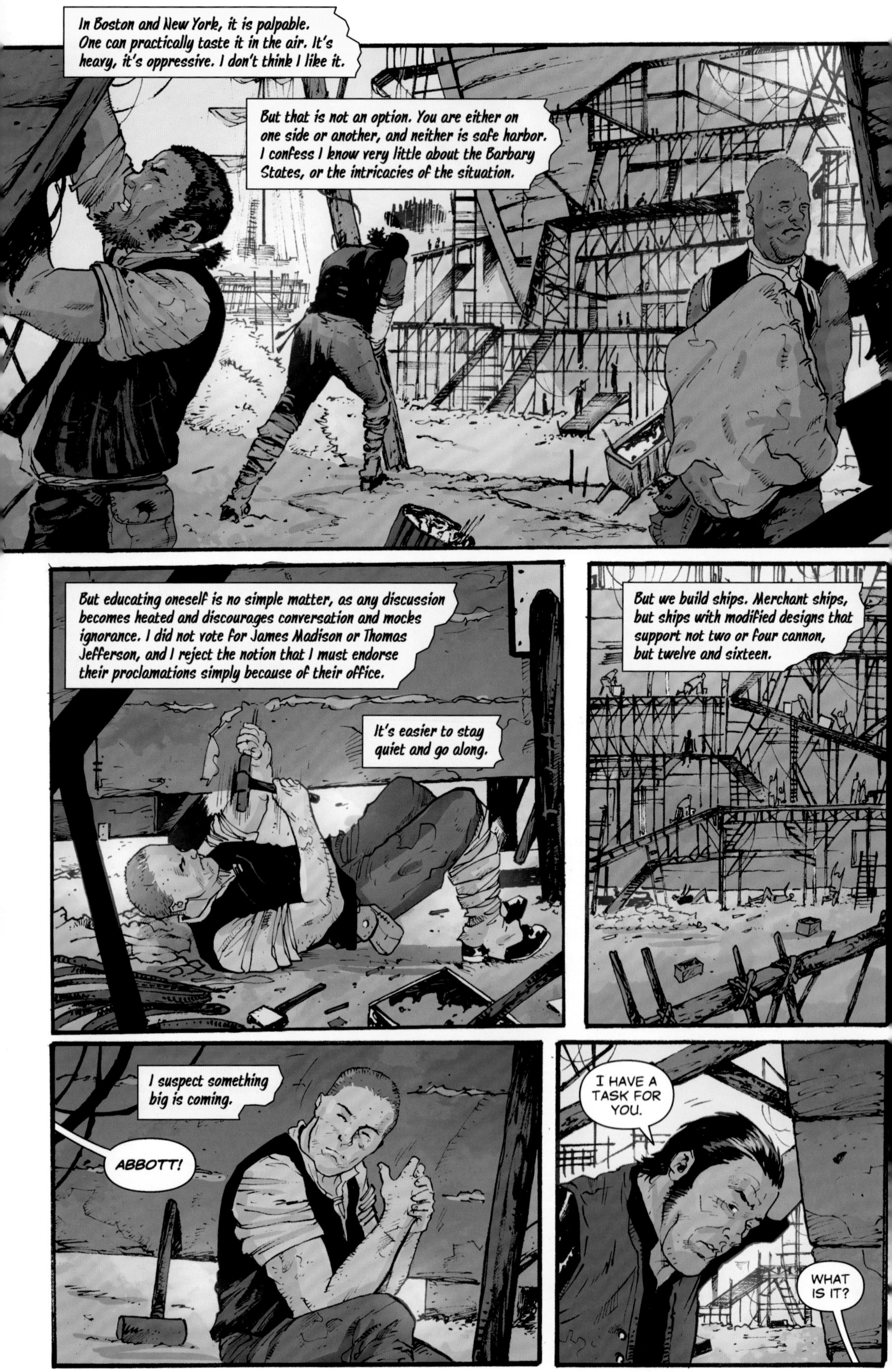
In Boston and New York, it is palpable. One can practically taste it in the air. It's heavy, it's oppressive. I don't think I like it.
But that is not an option. You are either on one side or another, and neither is safe harbor. I confess I know very little about the Barbary States, or the intricacies of the situation.
But educating oneself is no simple matter, as any discussion becomes heated and discourages conversation and mocks ignorance. I did not vote for James Madison or Thomas Jefferson, and I reject the notion that I must endorse their proclamations simply because of their office.
It's easier to stay quiet and go along.
But we build ships. Merchant ships, but ships with modified designs that support not two or four cannon, but twelve and sixteen.
I suspect something big is coming.
ABBOTT!
I HAVE A TASK FOR YOU.
WHAT IS IT?

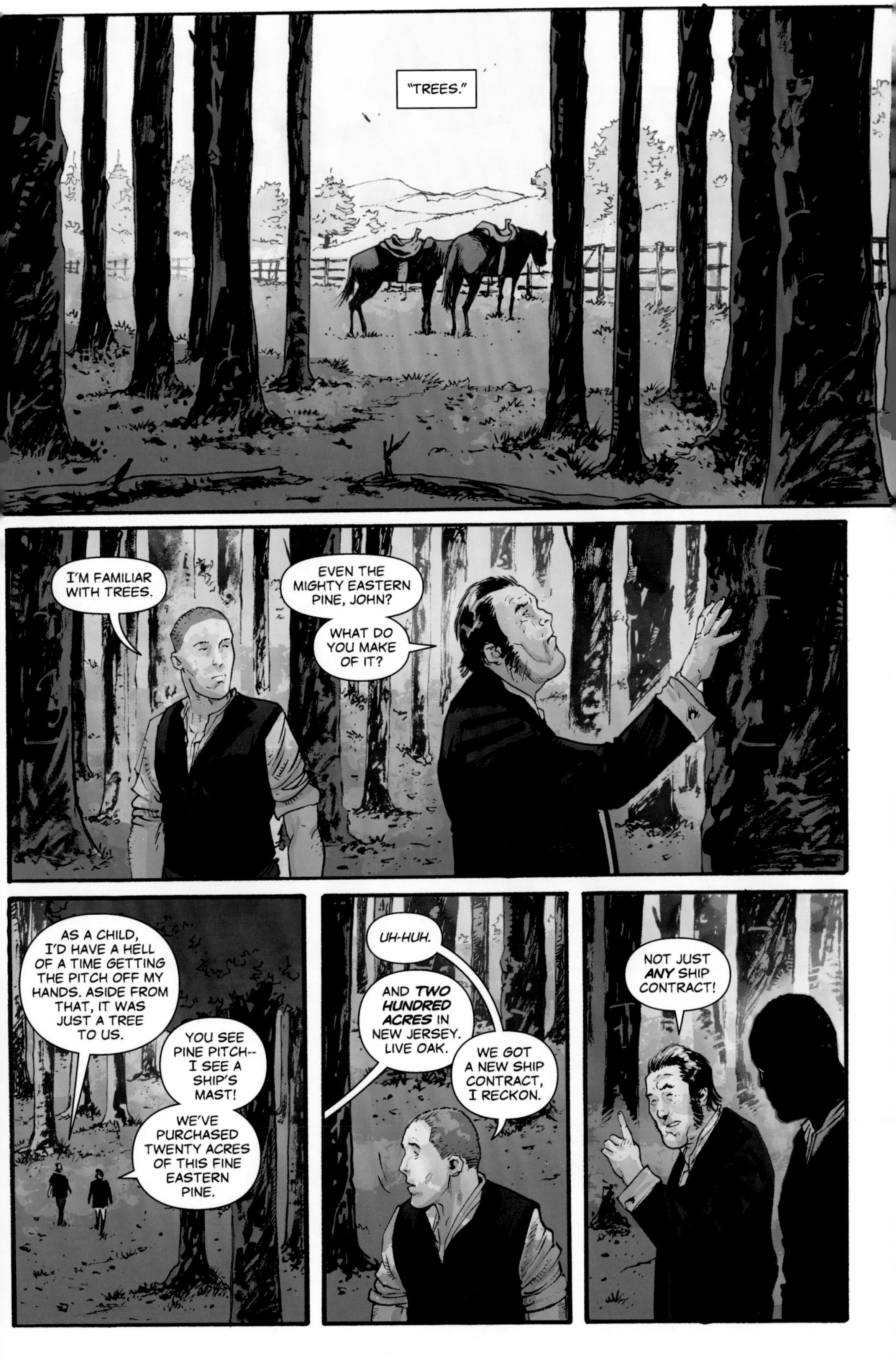
"TREES."
I'M FAMILIAR WITH TREES.
EVEN THE MIGHTY EASTERN PINE, JOHN?
WHAT DO YOU MAKE OF IT?
AS A CHILD, I'D HAVE A HELL OF A TIME GETTING THE PITCH OFF MY HANDS. ASIDE FROM THAT, IT WAS JUST A TREE TO US.
YOU SEE PINE PITCH-- I SEE A SHIP'S MAST!
WE'VE PURCHASED TWENTY ACRES OF THIS FINE EASTERN PINE.
UH-HUH.
AND TWO HUNDRED ACRES IN NEW JERSEY. LIVE OAK.
WE GOT A NEW SHIP CONTRACT, I RECKON.
NOT JUST ANY SHIP CONTRACT!

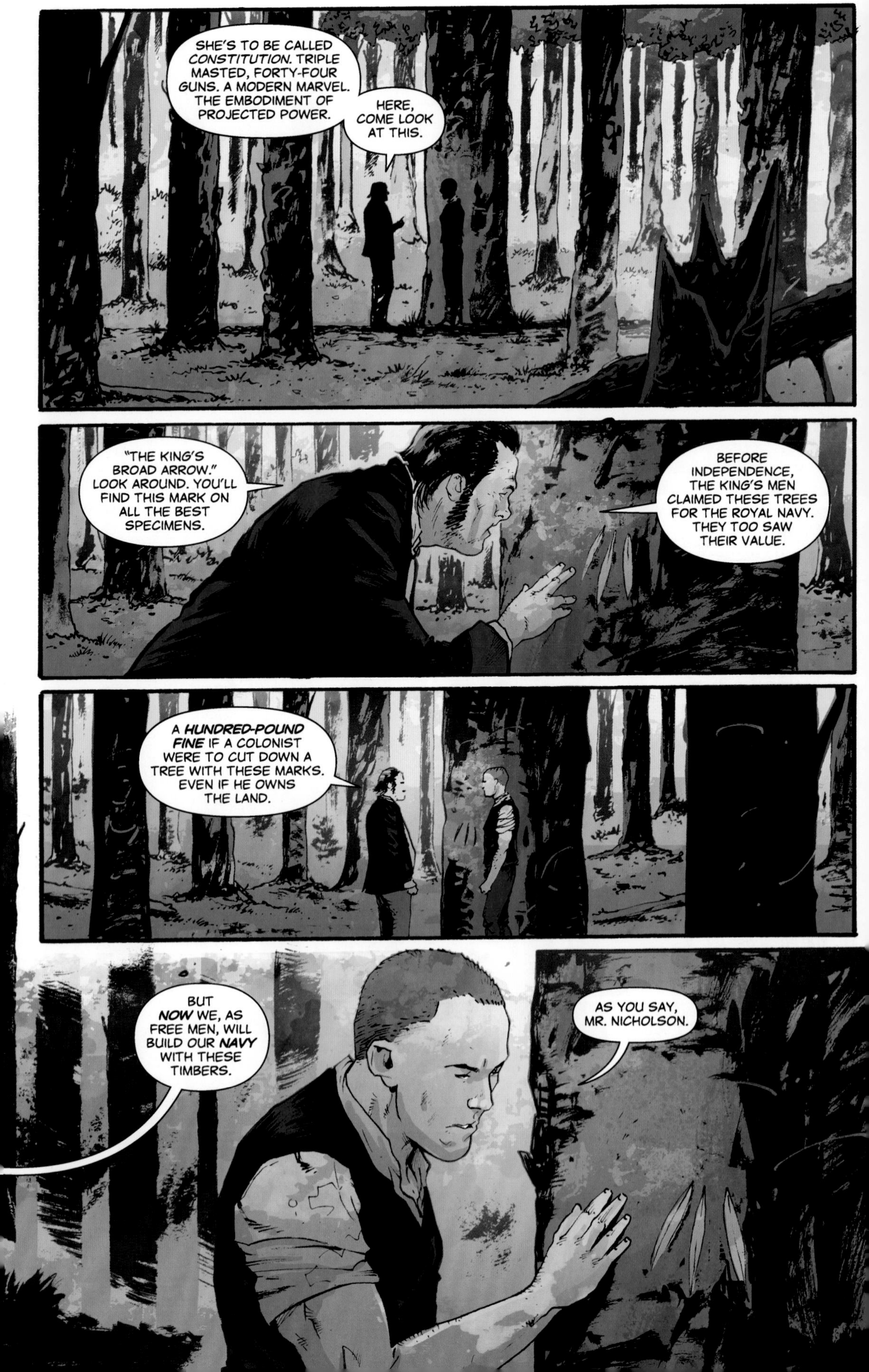

SHE'S TO BE CALLED CONSTITUTION. TRIPLE MASTED, FORTY-FOUR GUNS. A MODERN MARVEL. THE EMBODIMENT OF PROJECTED POWER.
HERE, COME LOOK AT THIS.
"THE KING'S BROAD ARROW." LOOK AROUND. YOU'LL FIND THIS MARK ON ALL THE BEST SPECIMENS.
BEFORE INDEPENDENCE, THE KING'S MEN CLAIMED THESE TREES FOR THE ROYAL NAVY. THEY TOO SAW THEIR VALUE.
A HUNDRED-POUND FINE IF A COLONIST WERE TO CUT DOWN A TREE WITH THESE MARKS. EVEN IF HE OWNS THE LAND.
BUT NOW WE, AS FREE MEN, WILL BUILD OUR NAVY WITH THESE TIMBERS.
AS YOU SAY, MR. NICHOLSON.

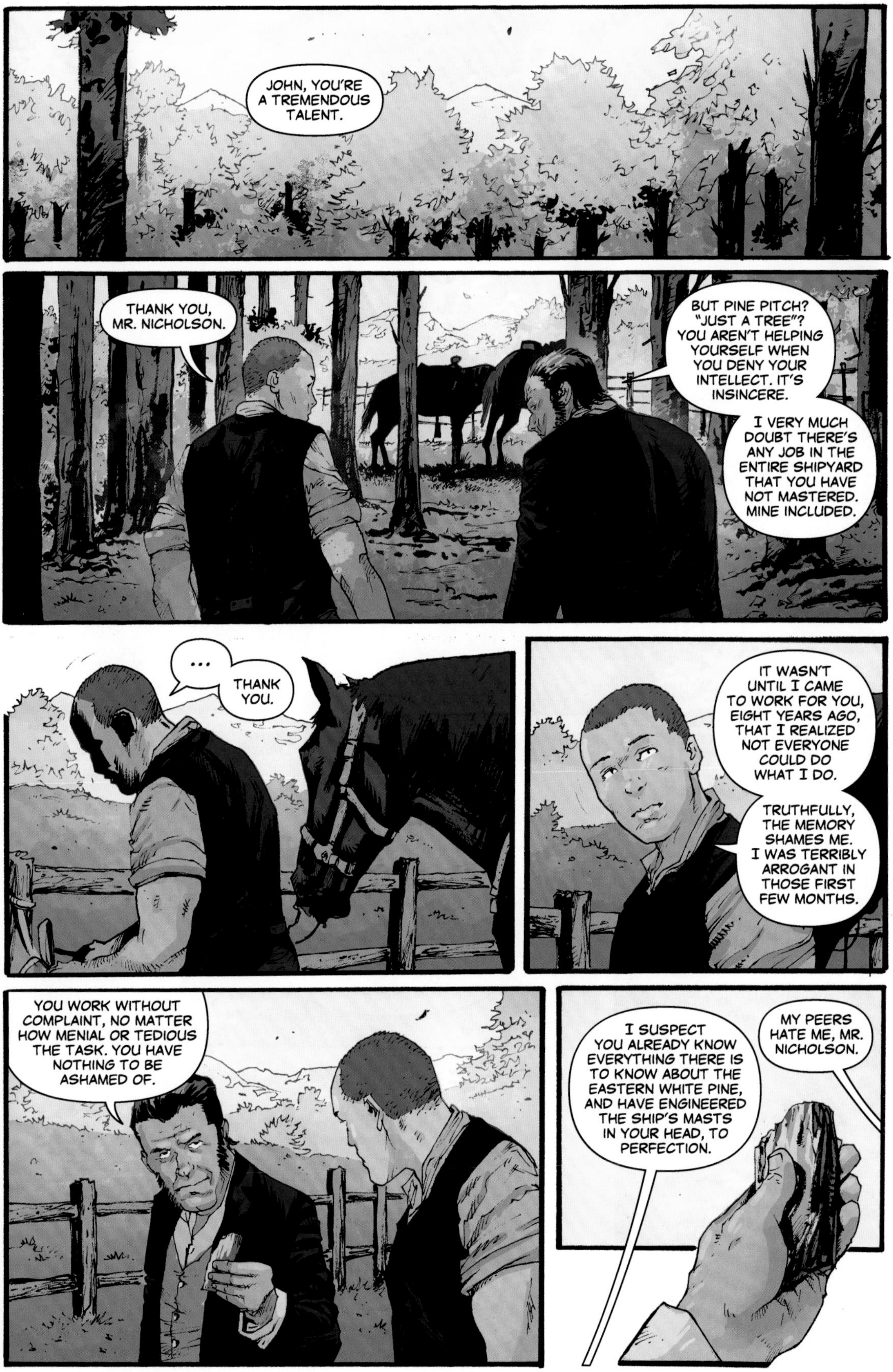
JOHN, YOU'RE A TREMENDOUS TALENT.
THANK YOU, MR. NICHOLSON.
BUT PINE PITCH? "JUST A TREE"? YOU AREN'T HELPING YOURSELF WHEN YOU DENY YOUR INTELLECT. IT'S INSINCERE.
I VERY MUCH DOUBT THERE'S ANY JOB IN THE ENTIRE SHIPYARD THAT YOU HAVE NOT MASTERED. MINE INCLUDED.
...
THANK YOU.
IT WASN'T UNTIL I CAME TO WORK FOR YOU, EIGHT YEARS AGO, THAT I REALIZED NOT EVERYONE COULD DO WHAT I DO.
TRUTHFULLY, THE MEMORY SHAMES ME. I WAS TERRIBLY ARROGANT IN THOSE FIRST FEW MONTHS.
YOU WORK WITHOUT COMPLAINT, NO MATTER HOW MENIAL OR TEDIOUS THE TASK. YOU HAVE NOTHING TO BE ASHAMED OF.
MY PEERS HATE ME, MR. NICHOLSON.
I SUSPECT YOU ALREADY KNOW EVERYTHING THERE IS TO KNOW ABOUT THE EASTERN WHITE PINE, AND HAVE ENGINEERED THE SHIP'S MASTS IN YOUR HEAD, TO PERFECTION.

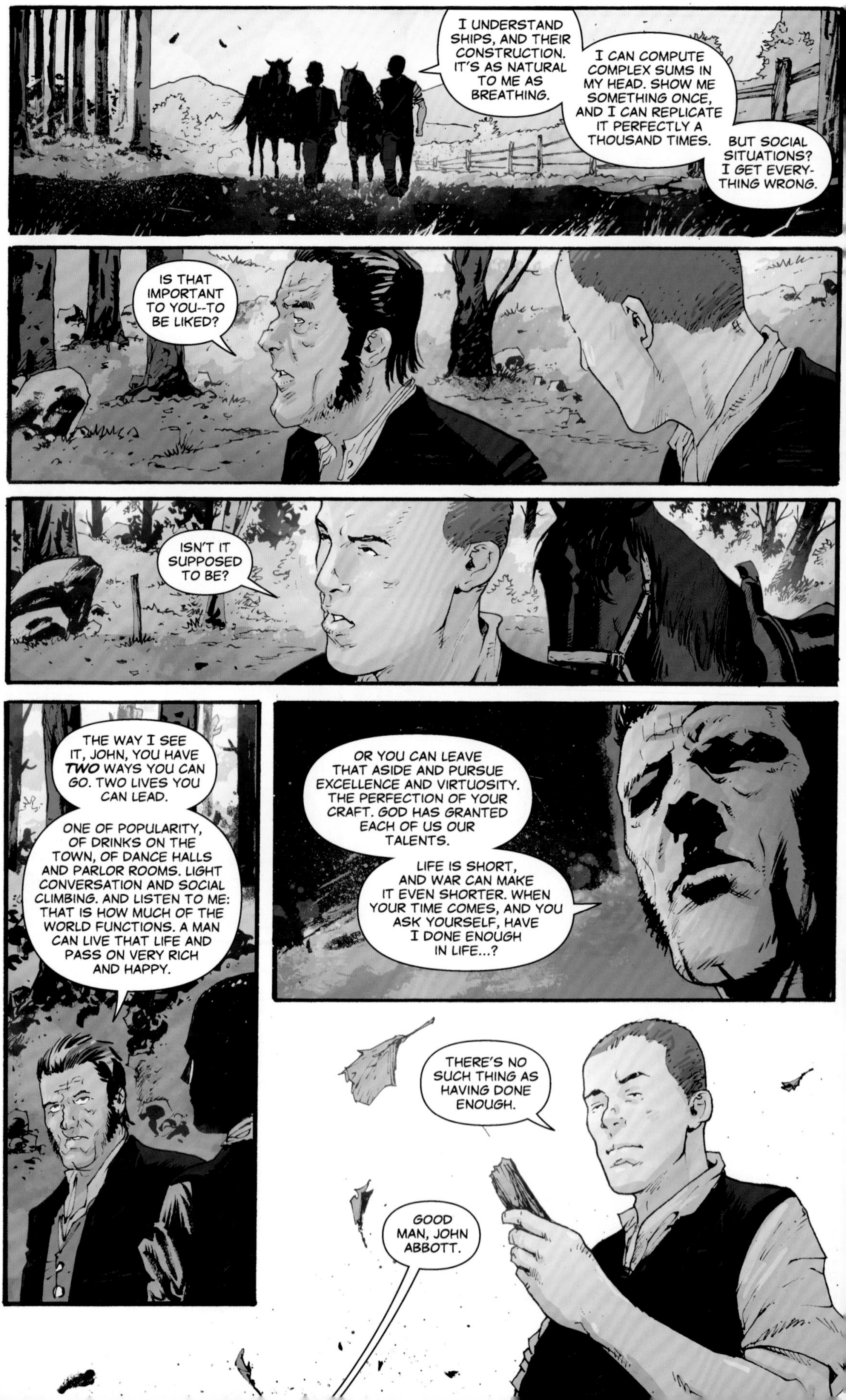
I UNDERSTAND SHIPS, AND THEIR CONSTRUCTION. IT'S AS NATURAL TO ME AS BREATHING.
I CAN COMPUTE COMPLEX SUMS IN MY HEAD. SHOW ME SOMETHING ONCE, AND I CAN REPLICATE IT PERFECTLY A THOUSAND TIMES.
BUT SOCIAL SITUATIONS? I GET EVERY-THING WRONG.
IS THAT IMPORTANT TO YOU--TO BE LIKED?
ISN'T IT SUPPOSED TO BE?
THE WAY I SEE IT, JOHN, YOU HAVE *TWO* WAYS YOU CAN GO. TWO LIVES YOU CAN LEAD.
ONE OF POPULARITY, OF DRINKS ON THE TOWN, OF DANCE HALLS AND PARLOR ROOMS. LIGHT CONVERSATION AND SOCIAL CLIMBING. AND LISTEN TO ME: THAT IS HOW MUCH OF THE WORLD FUNCTIONS. A MAN CAN LIVE THAT LIFE AND PASS ON VERY RICH AND HAPPY.
OR YOU CAN LEAVE THAT ASIDE AND PURSUE EXCELLENCE AND VIRTUOSITY. THE PERFECTION OF YOUR CRAFT. GOD HAS GRANTED EACH OF US OUR TALENTS.
LIFE IS SHORT, AND WAR CAN MAKE IT EVEN SHORTER. WHEN YOUR TIME COMES, AND YOU ASK YOURSELF, HAVE I DONE ENOUGH IN LIFE...?
THERE'S NO SUCH THING AS HAVING DONE ENOUGH.
GOOD MAN, JOHN ABBOTT.

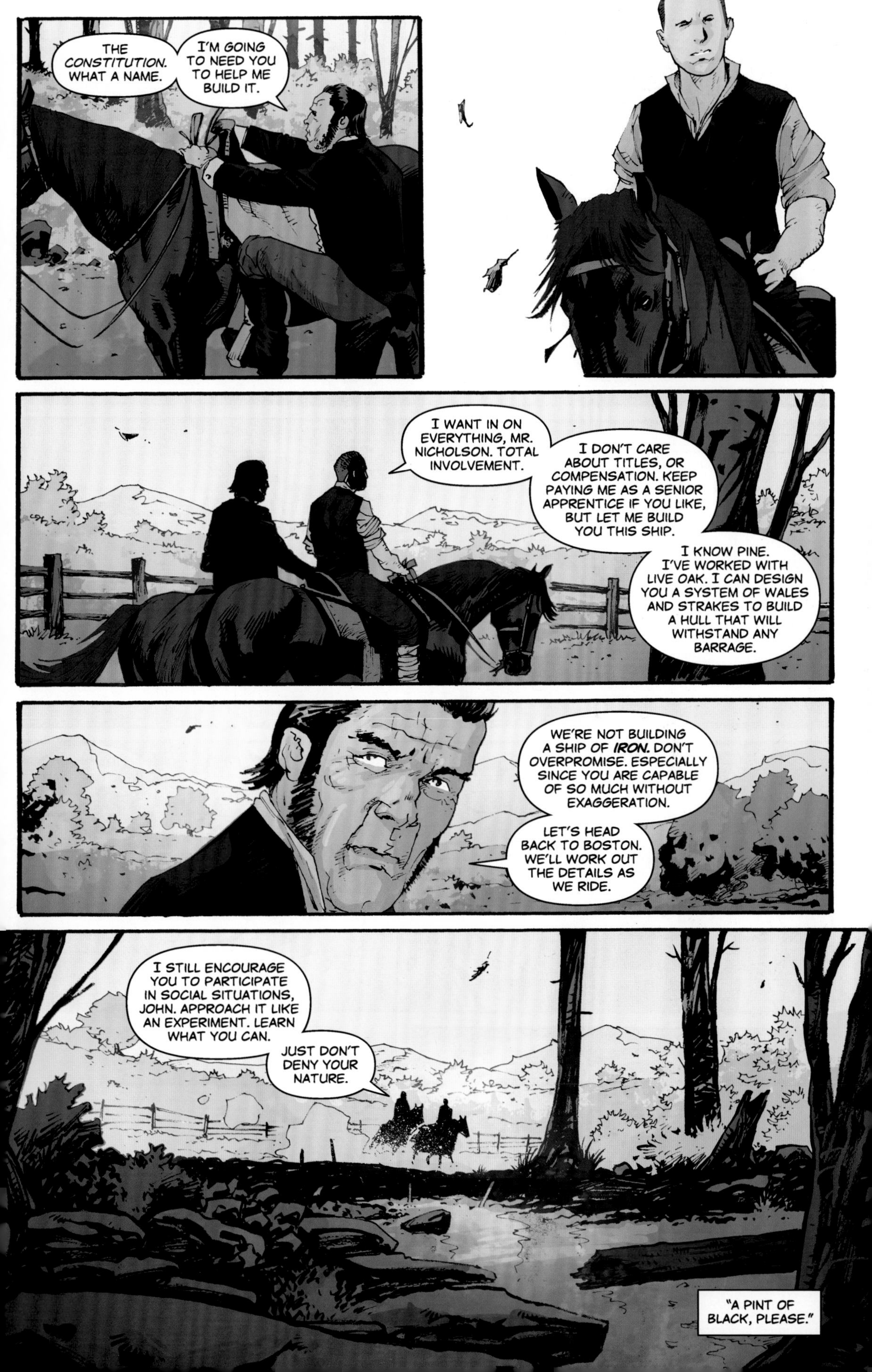
THE *CONSTITUTION.* WHAT A NAME.
I'M GOING TO NEED YOU TO HELP ME BUILD IT.
I WANT IN ON EVERYTHING, MR. NICHOLSON. TOTAL INVOLVEMENT.
I DON'T CARE ABOUT TITLES, OR COMPENSATION. KEEP PAYING ME AS A SENIOR APPRENTICE IF YOU LIKE, BUT LET ME BUILD YOU THIS SHIP.
I KNOW PINE. I'VE WORKED WITH LIVE OAK. I CAN DESIGN YOU A SYSTEM OF WALES AND STRAKES TO BUILD A HULL THAT WILL WITHSTAND ANY BARRAGE.
WE'RE NOT BUILDING A SHIP OF ***IRON.*** DON'T OVERPROMISE. ESPECIALLY SINCE YOU ARE CAPABLE OF SO MUCH WITHOUT EXAGGERATION.
LET'S HEAD BACK TO BOSTON. WE'LL WORK OUT THE DETAILS AS WE RIDE.
I STILL ENCOURAGE YOU TO PARTICIPATE IN SOCIAL SITUATIONS, JOHN. APPROACH IT LIKE AN EXPERIMENT. LEARN WHAT YOU CAN.
JUST DON'T DENY YOUR NATURE.
"A PINT OF BLACK, PLEASE."

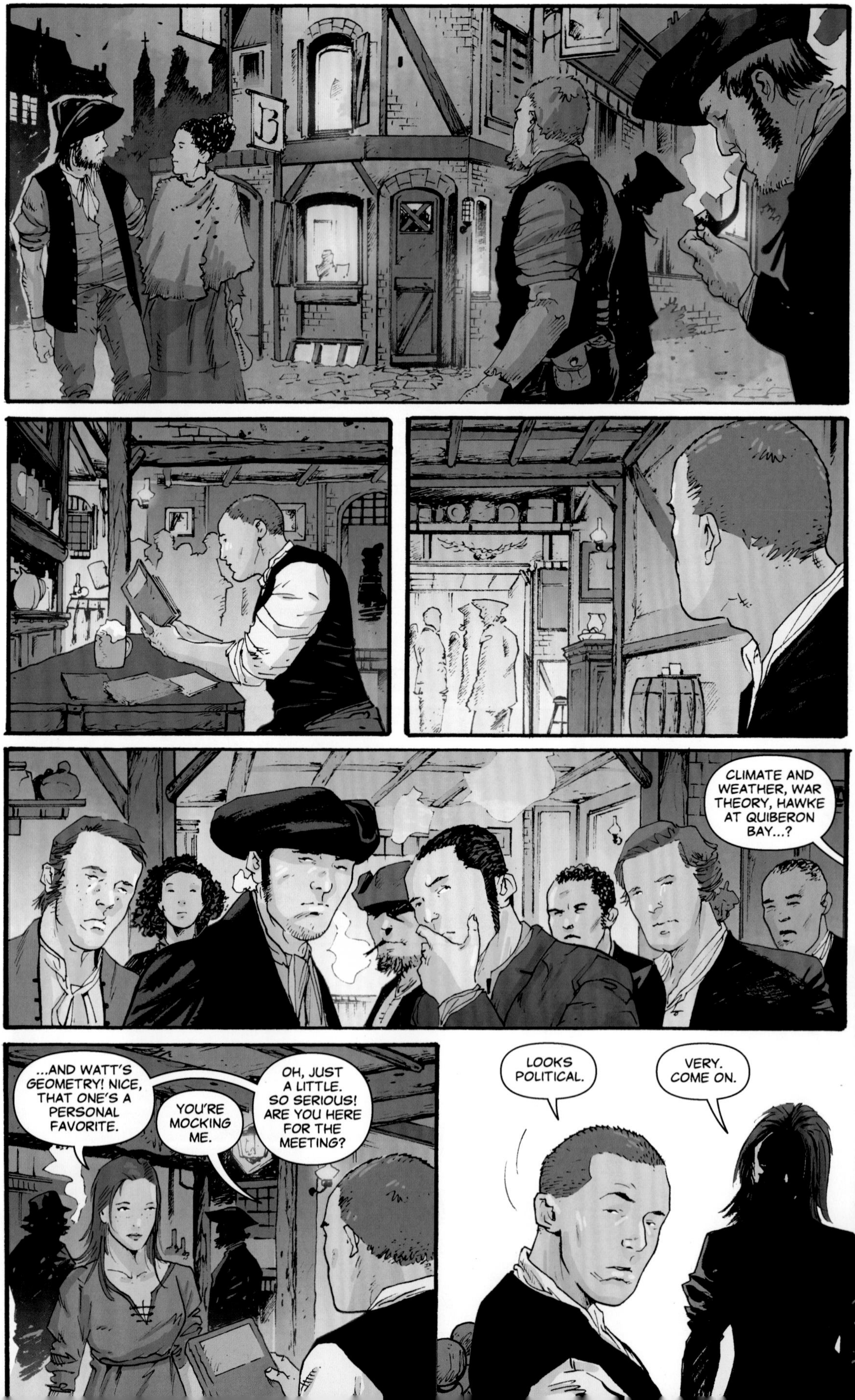
CLIMATE AND WEATHER, WAR THEORY, HAWKE AT QUIBERON BAY...?
...AND WATT'S GEOMETRY! NICE, THAT ONE'S A PERSONAL FAVORITE.
YOU'RE MOCKING ME.
OH, JUST A LITTLE. SO SERIOUS! ARE YOU HERE FOR THE MEETING?
LOOKS POLITICAL.
VERY. COME ON.

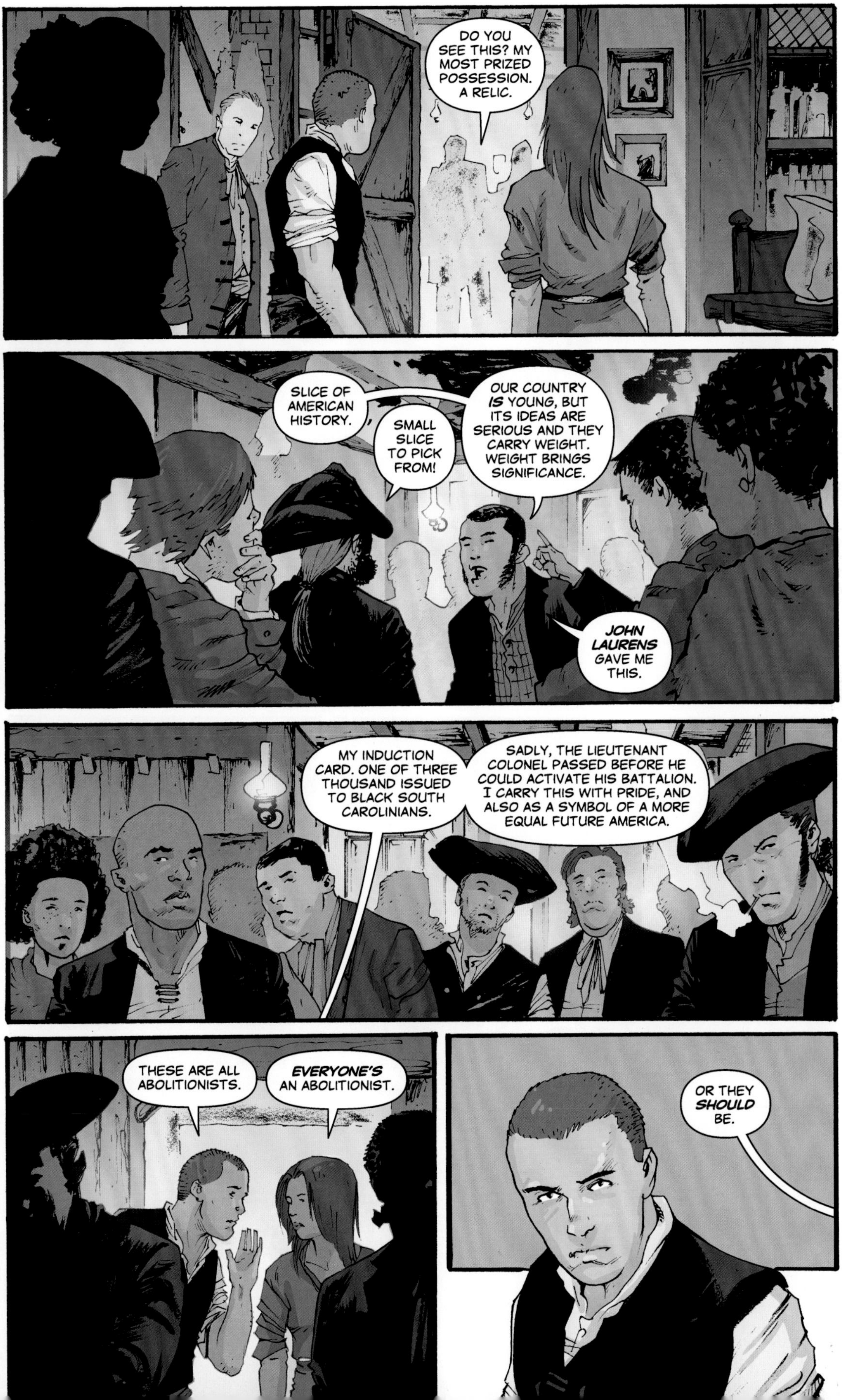
DO YOU SEE THIS? MY MOST PRIZED POSSESSION. A RELIC.
SLICE OF AMERICAN HISTORY.
SMALL SLICE TO PICK FROM!
OUR COUNTRY *IS* YOUNG, BUT ITS IDEAS ARE SERIOUS AND THEY CARRY WEIGHT. WEIGHT BRINGS SIGNIFICANCE.
JOHN LAURENS GAVE ME THIS.
MY INDUCTION CARD. ONE OF THREE THOUSAND ISSUED TO BLACK SOUTH CAROLINIANS.
SADLY, THE LIEUTENANT COLONEL PASSED BEFORE HE COULD ACTIVATE HIS BATTALION. I CARRY THIS WITH PRIDE, AND ALSO AS A SYMBOL OF A MORE EQUAL FUTURE AMERICA.
THESE ARE ALL ABOLITIONISTS.
EVERYONE'S AN ABOLITIONIST.
OR THEY *SHOULD* BE.

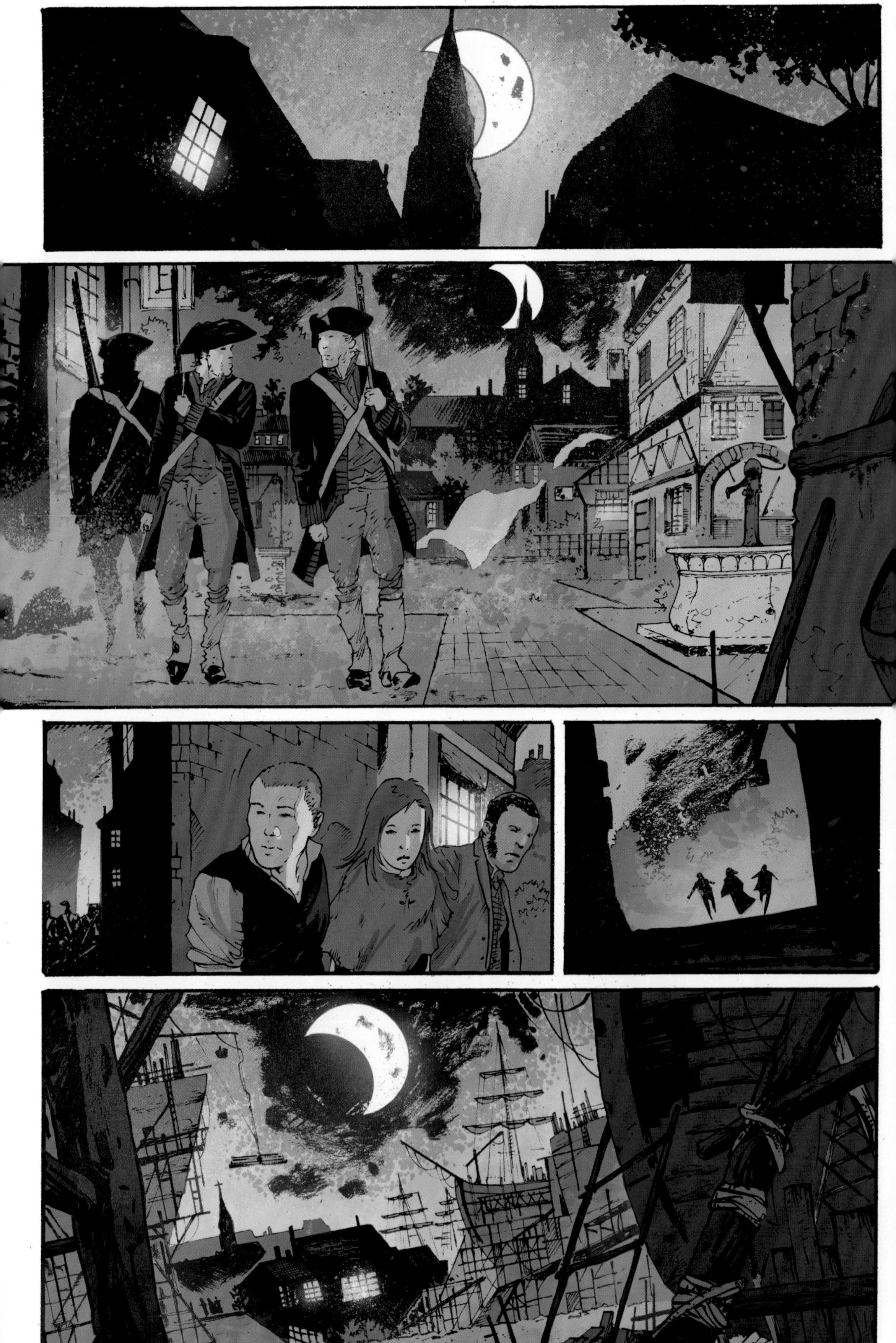

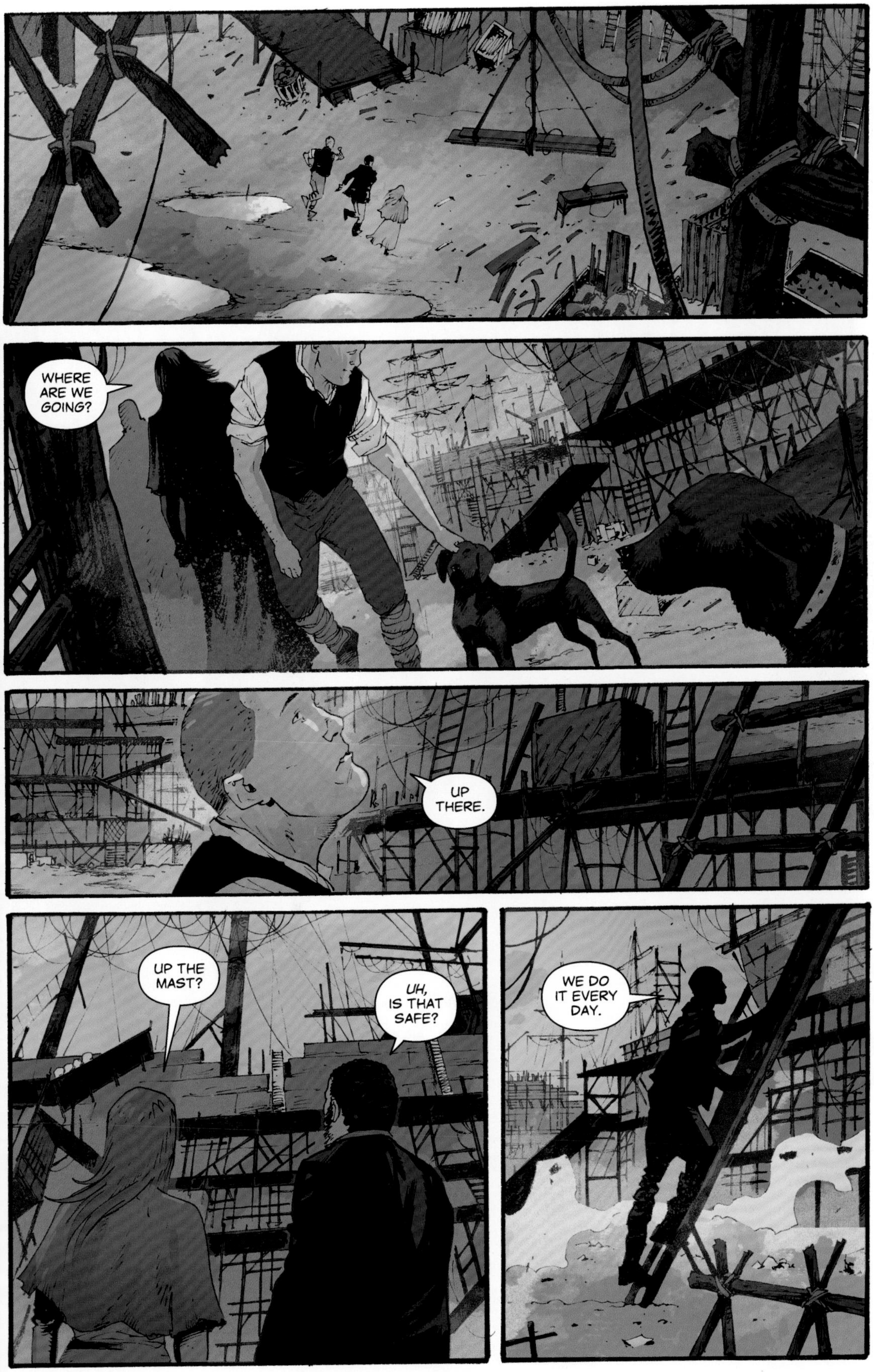
WHERE ARE WE GOING?
UP THERE.
UP THE MAST?
UH, IS THAT SAFE?
WE DO IT EVERY DAY.

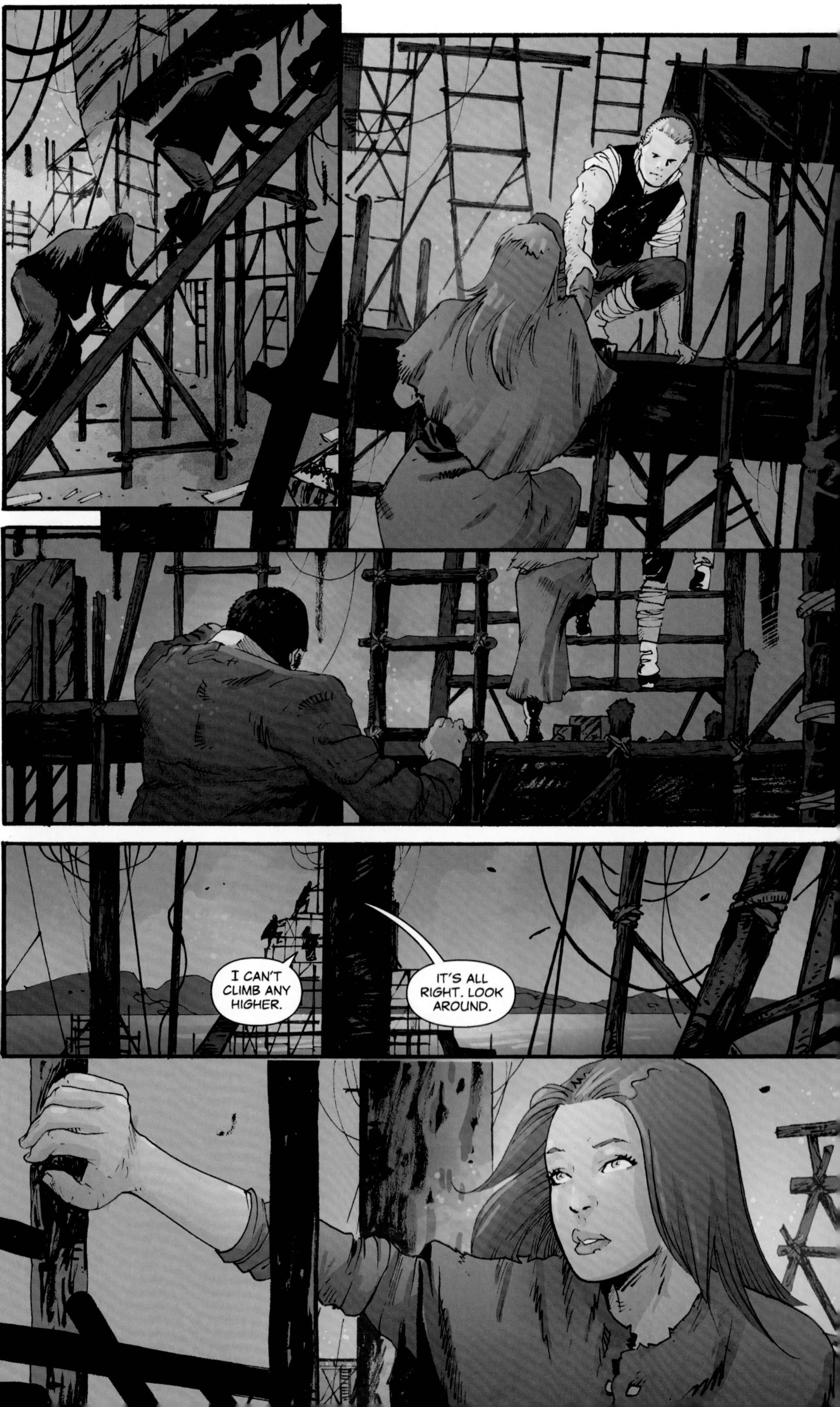
I CAN'T CLIMB ANY HIGHER.
IT'S ALL RIGHT. LOOK AROUND.

AMAZING.

I'VE CLIMBED TREES BEFORE, BUT NOTHING LIKE THIS. I FEEL LIKE I'M SEEING WHAT THE BIRDS SEE.

AND YOU BUILT THIS?

I'VE BEEN BUILDING SHIPS SINCE I WAS LITTLE.

I CAN'T TELL IF IT'S JUST ME, OR IF WE'RE SWAYING.

IT'S MEANT TO SWAY. IT'S MEANT TO BE LIGHT AND FLEXIBLE.

I GET IT, JOHN.

GET WHAT?

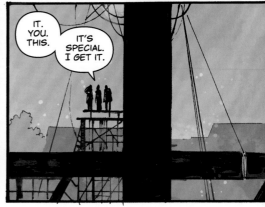

IT. YOU. THIS.

IT'S SPECIAL. I GET IT.

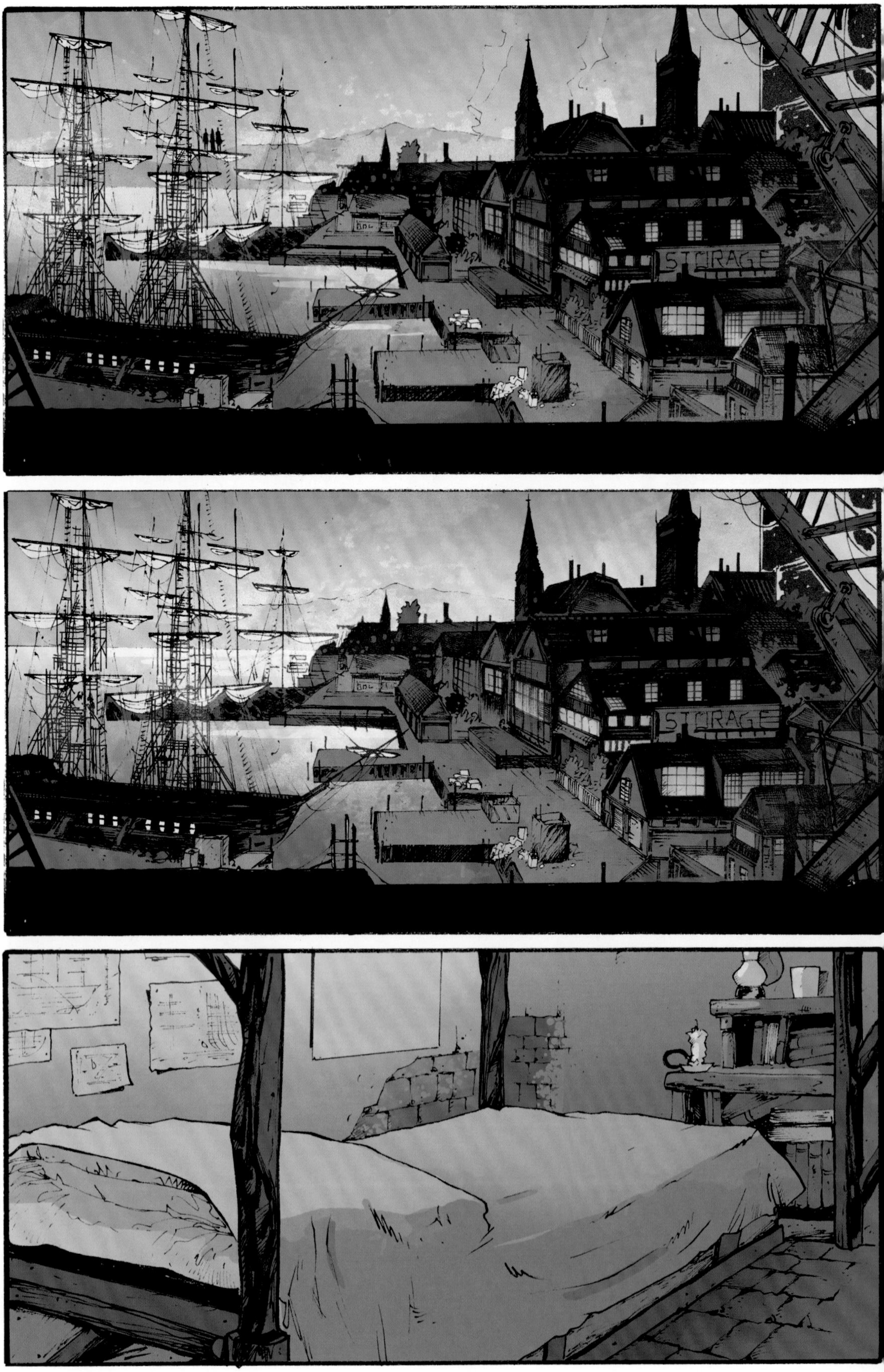
STORAGE
STORAGE

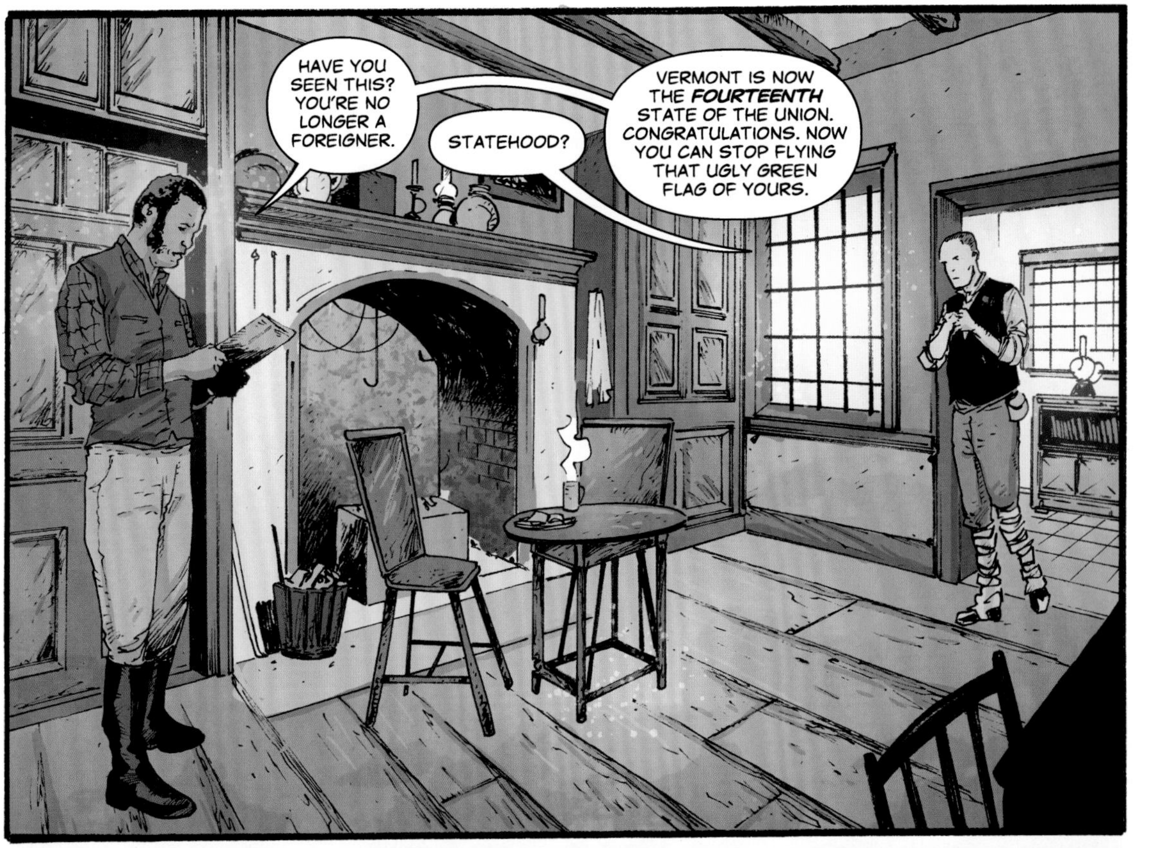
HAVE YOU SEEN THIS? YOU'RE NO LONGER A FOREIGNER.
STATEHOOD?
VERMONT IS NOW THE **FOURTEENTH** STATE OF THE UNION. CONGRATULATIONS. NOW YOU CAN STOP FLYING THAT UGLY GREEN FLAG OF YOURS.

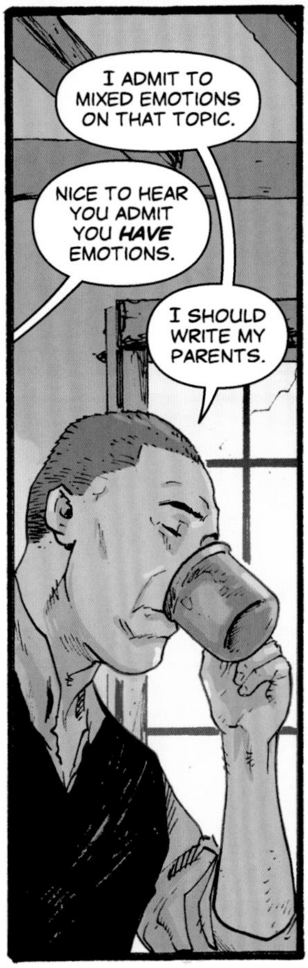
I ADMIT TO MIXED EMOTIONS ON THAT TOPIC.
NICE TO HEAR YOU ADMIT YOU ***HAVE*** EMOTIONS.
I SHOULD WRITE MY PARENTS.

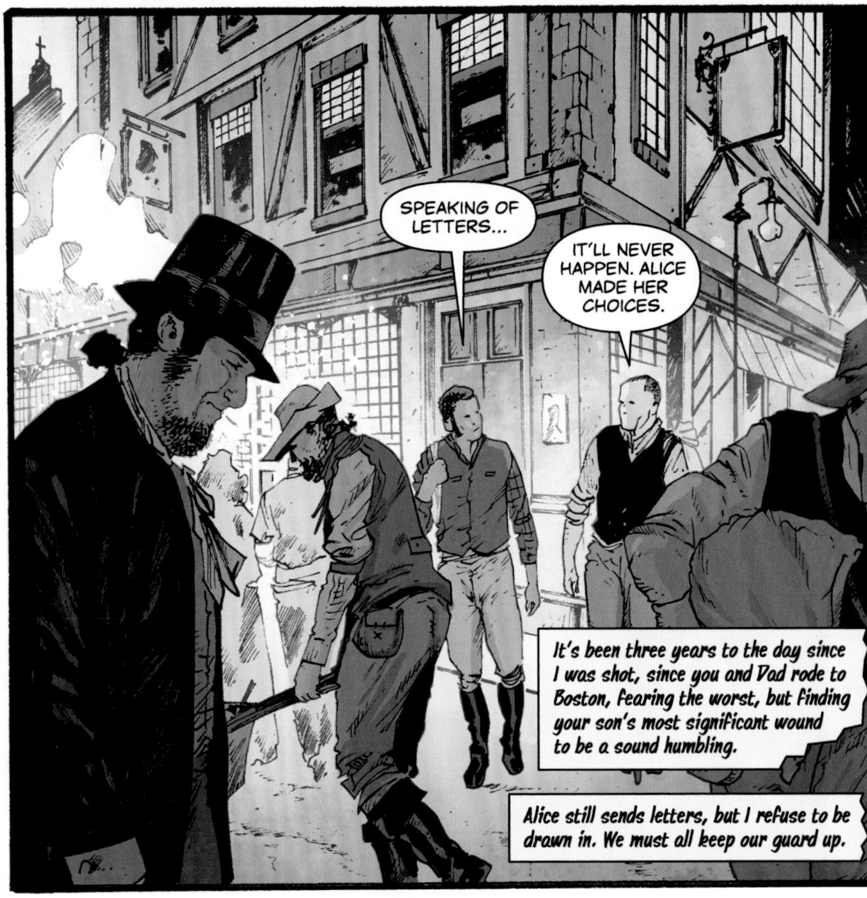
SPEAKING OF LETTERS...
IT'LL NEVER HAPPEN. ALICE MADE HER CHOICES.
It's been three years to the day since I was shot, since you and Dad rode to Boston, fearing the worst, but finding your son's most significant wound to be a sound humbling.
Alice still sends letters, but I refuse to be drawn in. We must all keep our guard up.

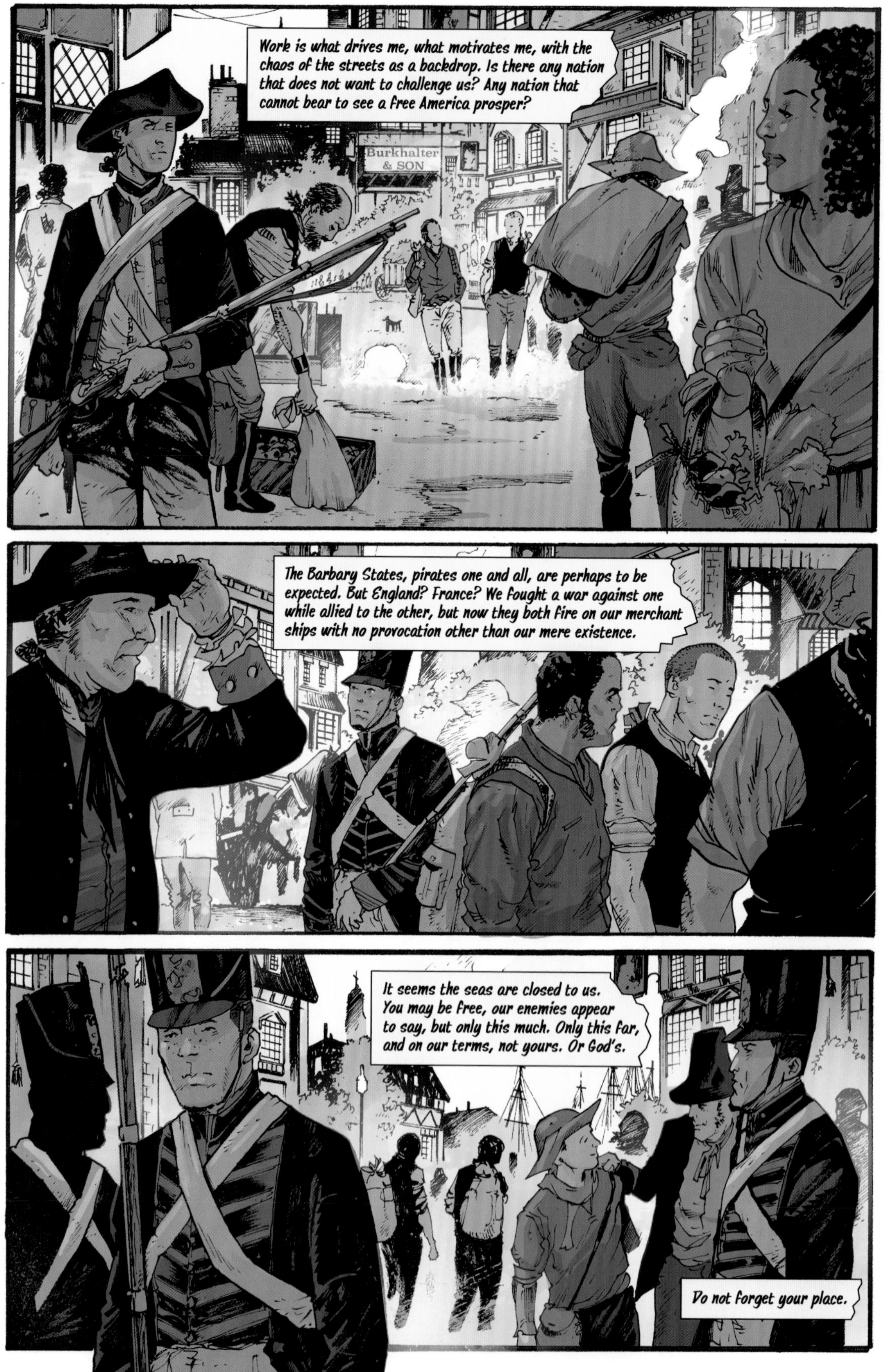
Work is what drives me, what motivates me, with the chaos of the streets as a backdrop. Is there any nation that does not want to challenge us? Any nation that cannot bear to see a free America prosper?
Burkhalter & SON
The Barbary States, pirates one and all, are perhaps to be expected. But England? France? We fought a war against one while allied to the other, but now they both fire on our merchant ships with no provocation other than our mere existence.
It seems the seas are closed to us. You may be free, our enemies appear to say, but only this much. Only this far, and on our terms, not yours. Or God's.
Do not forget your place.

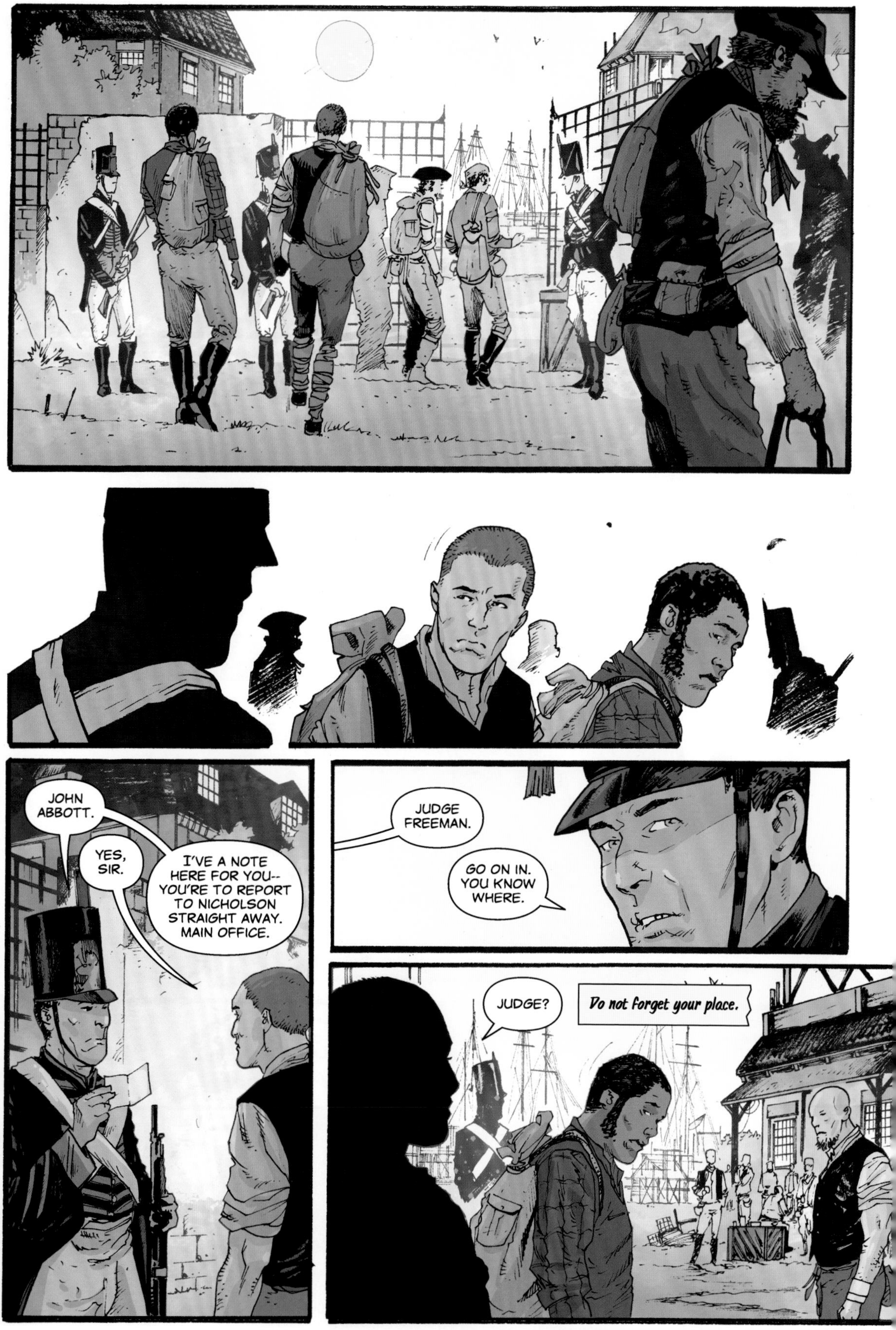
JOHN ABBOTT.
YES, SIR.
I'VE A NOTE HERE FOR YOU-- YOU'RE TO REPORT TO NICHOLSON STRAIGHT AWAY. MAIN OFFICE.
JUDGE FREEMAN.
GO ON IN. YOU KNOW WHERE.
JUDGE?
Do not forget your place.

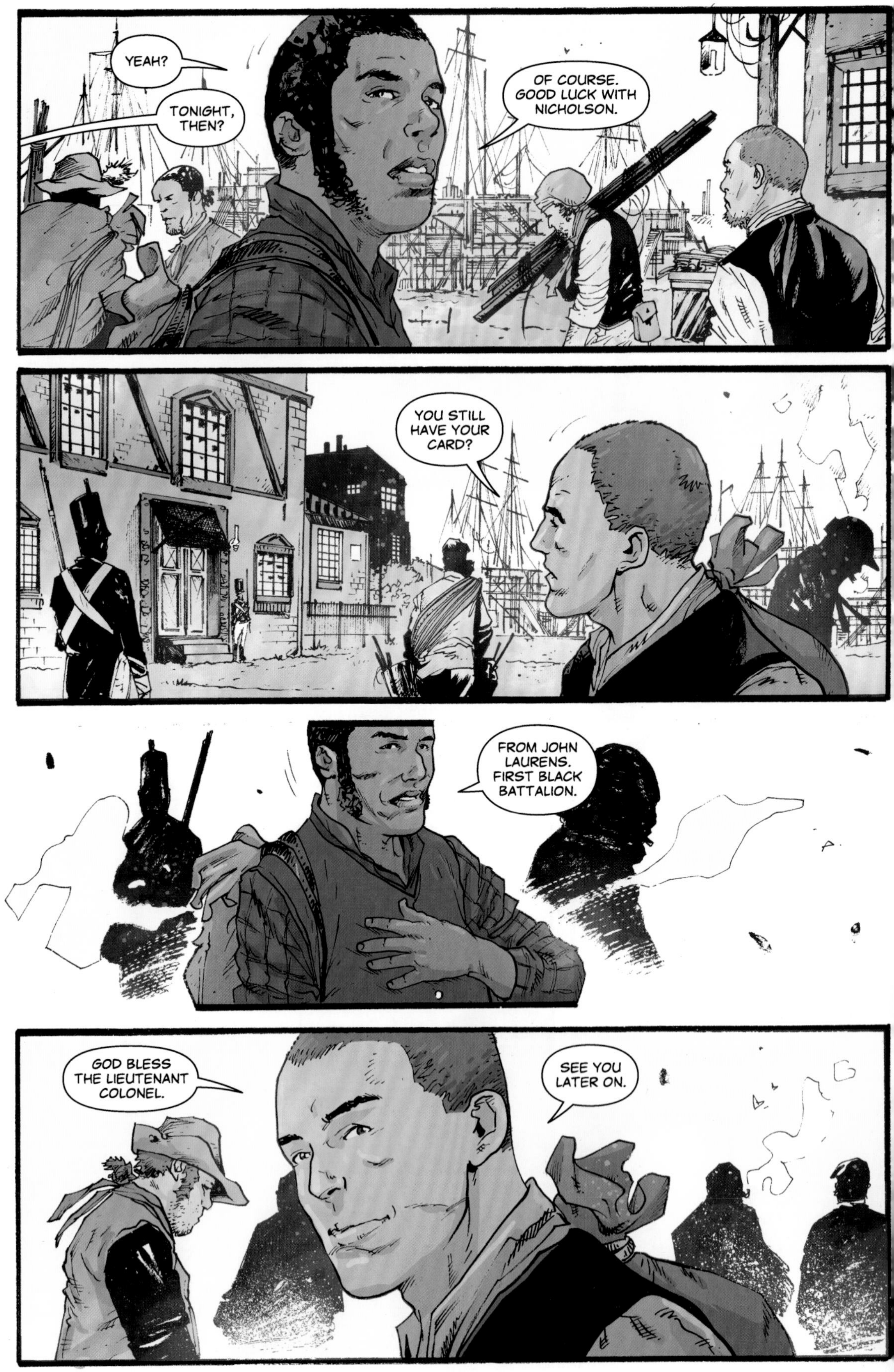
YEAH?
TONIGHT, THEN?
OF COURSE. GOOD LUCK WITH NICHOLSON.
YOU STILL HAVE YOUR CARD?
FROM JOHN LAURENS. FIRST BLACK BATTALION.
GOD BLESS THE LIEUTENANT COLONEL.
SEE YOU LATER ON.

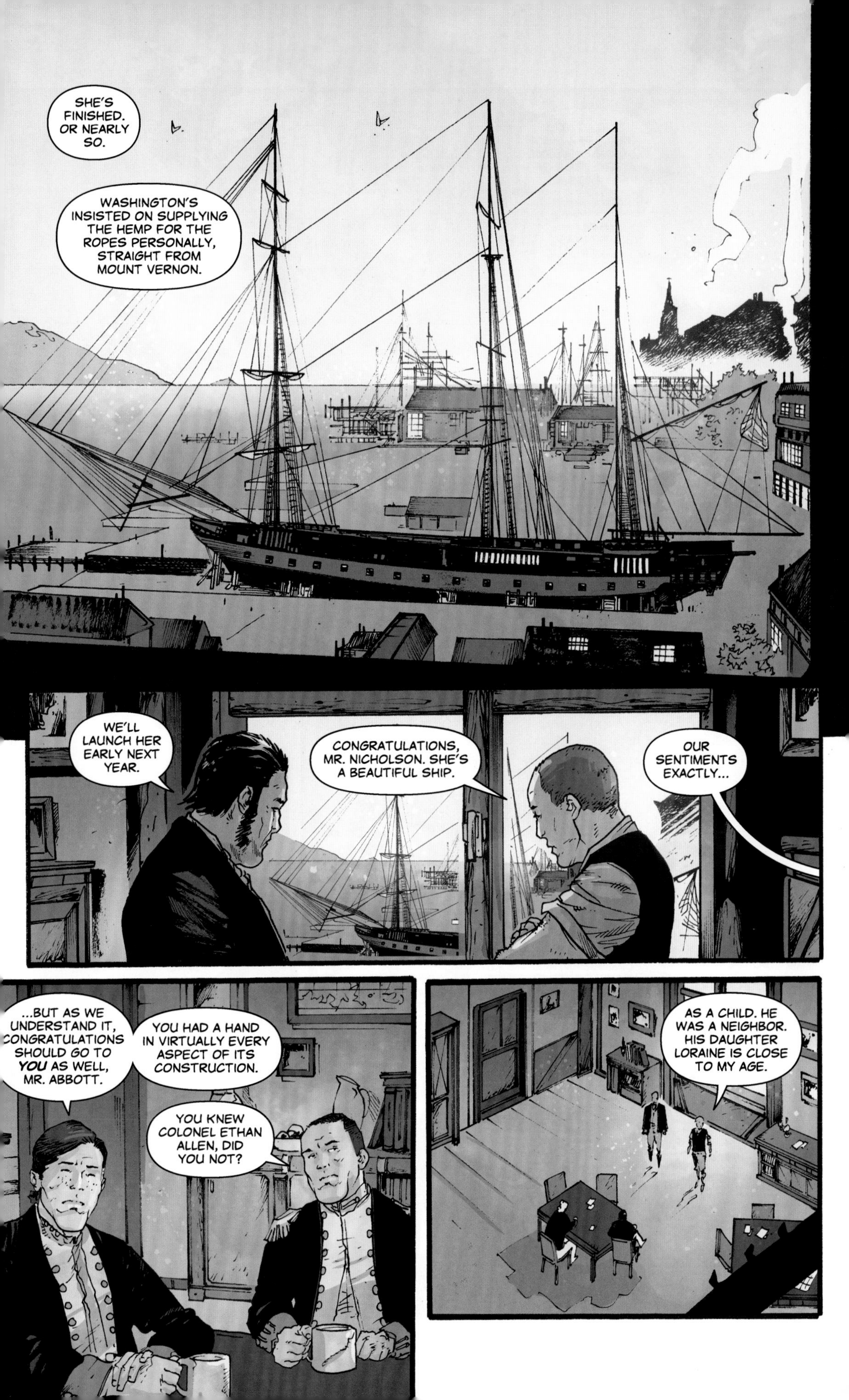
SHE'S FINISHED. OR NEARLY SO.
WASHINGTON'S INSISTED ON SUPPLYING THE HEMP FOR THE ROPES PERSONALLY, STRAIGHT FROM MOUNT VERNON.
WE'LL LAUNCH HER EARLY NEXT YEAR.
CONGRATULATIONS, MR. NICHOLSON. SHE'S A BEAUTIFUL SHIP.
OUR SENTIMENTS EXACTLY...
...BUT AS WE UNDERSTAND IT, CONGRATULATIONS SHOULD GO TO *YOU* AS WELL, MR. ABBOTT.
YOU HAD A HAND IN VIRTUALLY EVERY ASPECT OF ITS CONSTRUCTION.
YOU KNEW COLONEL ETHAN ALLEN, DID YOU NOT?
AS A CHILD. HE WAS A NEIGHBOR. HIS DAUGHTER LORAINE IS CLOSE TO MY AGE.

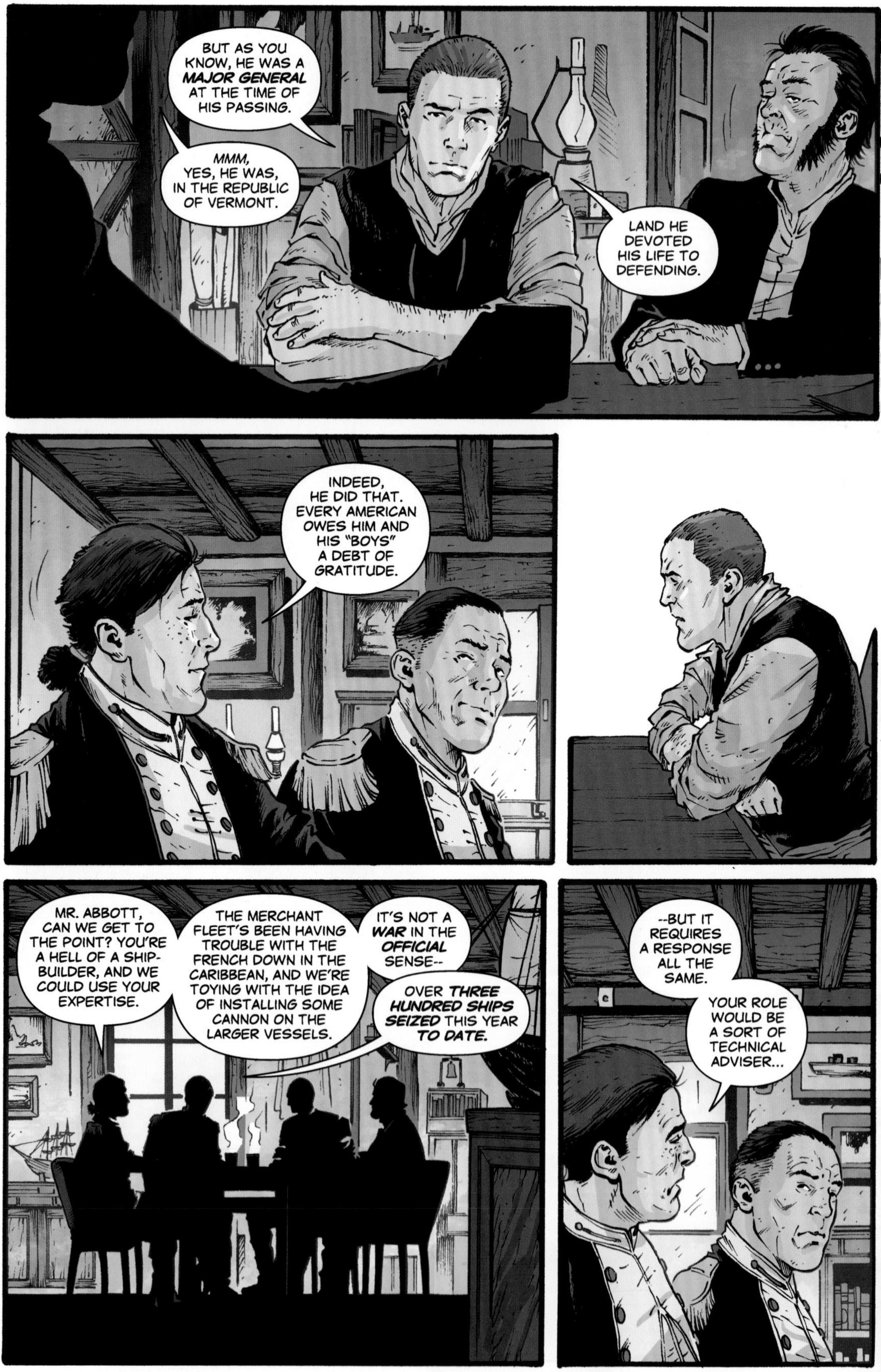

BUT AS YOU KNOW, HE WAS A MAJOR GENERAL AT THE TIME OF HIS PASSING.
MMM, YES, HE WAS, IN THE REPUBLIC OF VERMONT.
LAND HE DEVOTED HIS LIFE TO DEFENDING.
INDEED, HE DID THAT. EVERY AMERICAN OWES HIM AND HIS "BOYS" A DEBT OF GRATITUDE.
MR. ABBOTT, CAN WE GET TO THE POINT? YOU'RE A HELL OF A SHIP-BUILDER, AND WE COULD USE YOUR EXPERTISE.
THE MERCHANT FLEET'S BEEN HAVING TROUBLE WITH THE FRENCH DOWN IN THE CARIBBEAN, AND WE'RE TOYING WITH THE IDEA OF INSTALLING SOME CANNON ON THE LARGER VESSELS.
IT'S NOT A WAR IN THE OFFICIAL SENSE--
OVER THREE HUNDRED SHIPS SEIZED THIS YEAR TO DATE.
--BUT IT REQUIRES A RESPONSE ALL THE SAME.
YOUR ROLE WOULD BE A SORT OF TECHNICAL ADVISER...

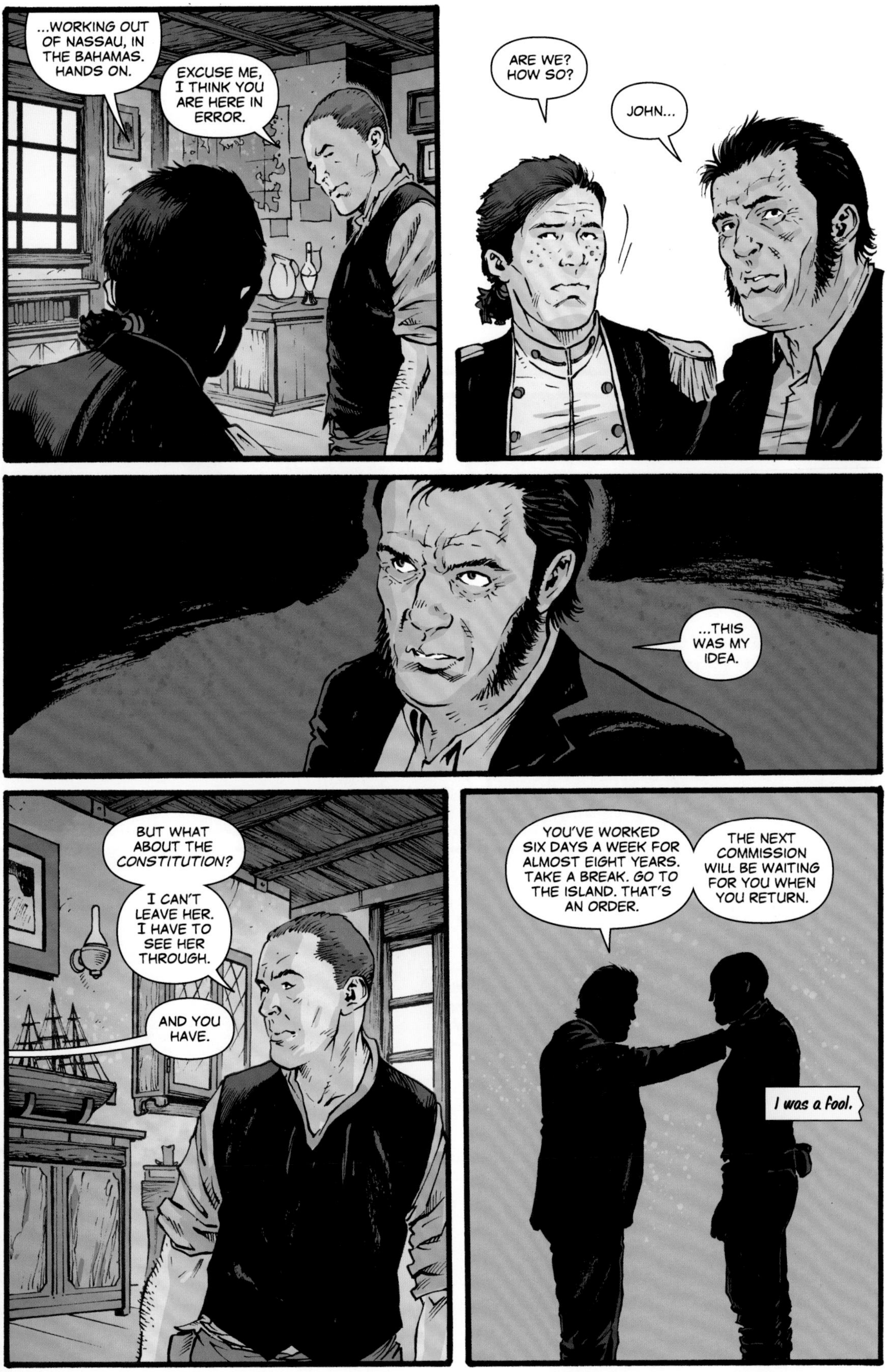
...WORKING OUT OF NASSAU, IN THE BAHAMAS. HANDS ON.
EXCUSE ME, I THINK YOU ARE HERE IN ERROR.
ARE WE? HOW SO?
JOHN...
...THIS WAS MY IDEA.
BUT WHAT ABOUT THE *CONSTITUTION*?
I CAN'T LEAVE HER. I HAVE TO SEE HER THROUGH.
AND YOU HAVE.
YOU'VE WORKED SIX DAYS A WEEK FOR ALMOST EIGHT YEARS. TAKE A BREAK. GO TO THE ISLAND. THAT'S AN ORDER.
THE NEXT COMMISSION WILL BE WAITING FOR YOU WHEN YOU RETURN.
I was a fool.

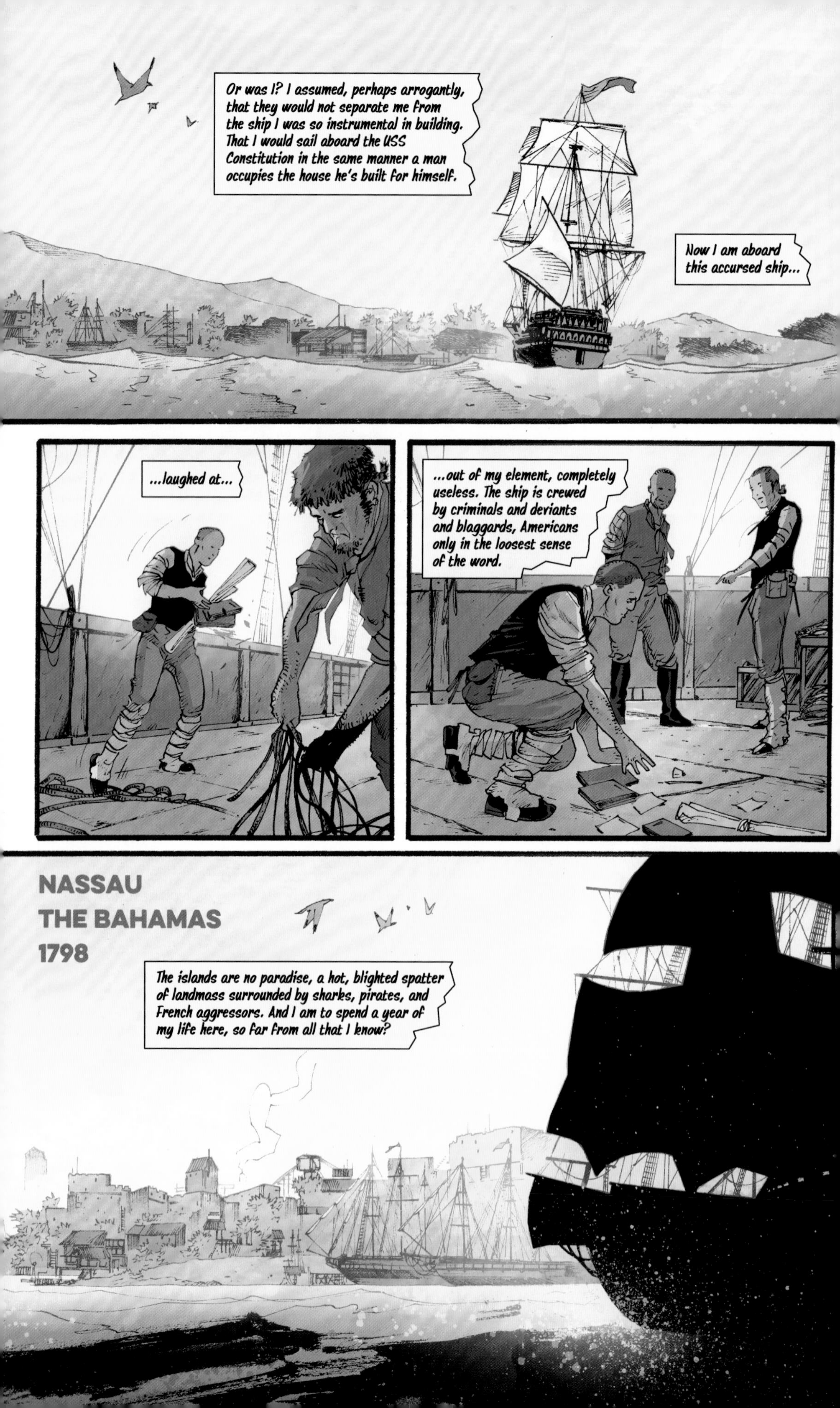
Or was I? I assumed, perhaps arrogantly, that they would not separate me from the ship I was so instrumental in building. That I would sail aboard the USS Constitution in the same manner a man occupies the house he's built for himself.
Now I am aboard this accursed ship...
...laughed at...
...out of my element, completely useless. The ship is crewed by criminals and deviants and blaggards, Americans only in the loosest sense of the word.
NASSAU
THE BAHAMAS
1798
The islands are no paradise, a hot, blighted spatter of landmass surrounded by sharks, pirates, and French aggressors. And I am to spend a year of my life here, so far from all that I know?

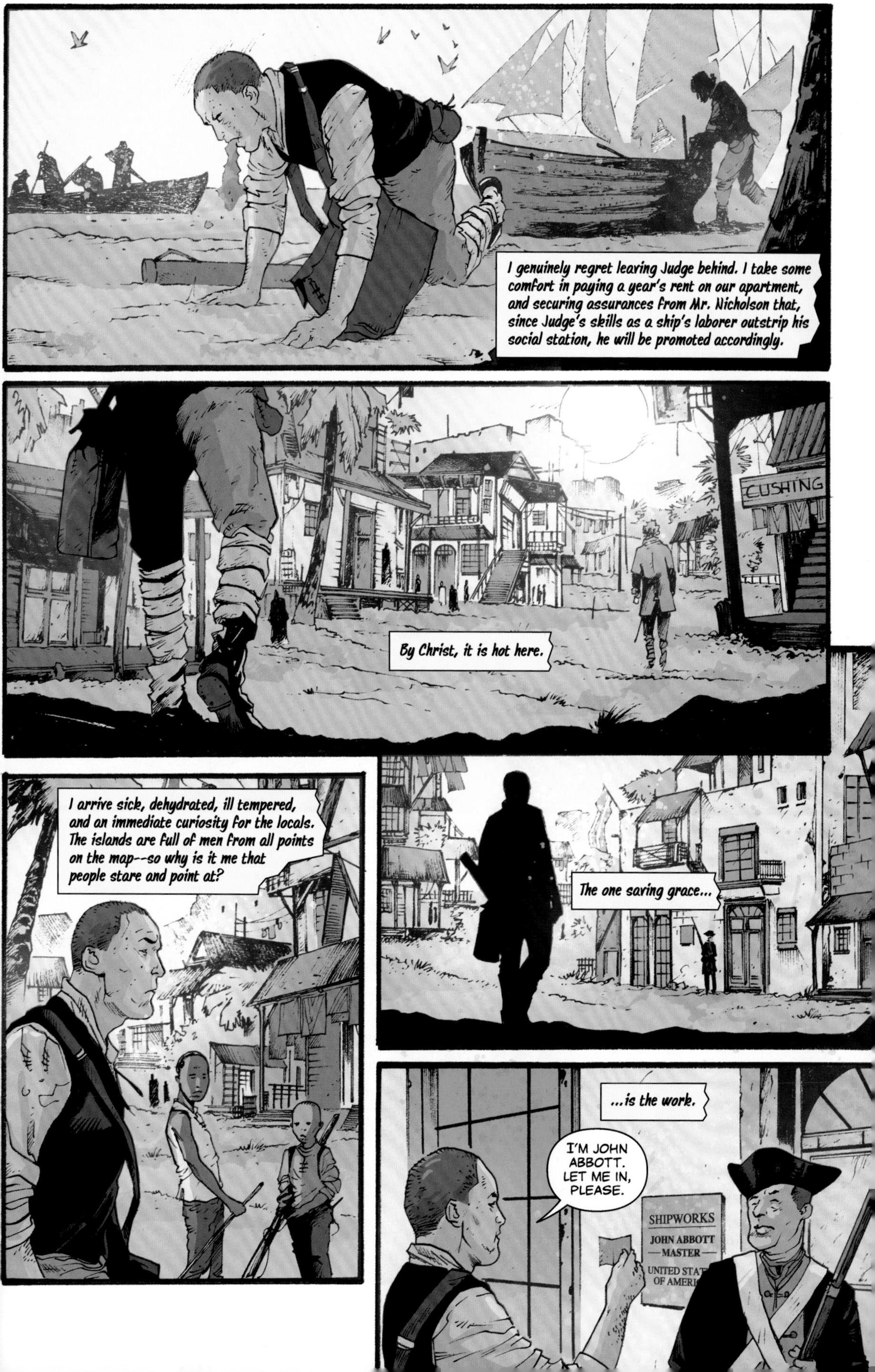
I genuinely regret leaving Judge behind. I take some comfort in paying a year's rent on our apartment, and securing assurances from Mr. Nicholson that, since Judge's skills as a ship's laborer outstrip his social station, he will be promoted accordingly.
CUSHING
By Christ, it is hot here.
I arrive sick, dehydrated, ill tempered, and an immediate curiosity for the locals. The islands are full of men from all points on the map--so why is it me that people stare and point at?
The one saving grace...
...is the work.
I'M JOHN ABBOTT. LET ME IN, PLEASE.
SHIPWORKS
JOHN ABBOTT
MASTER

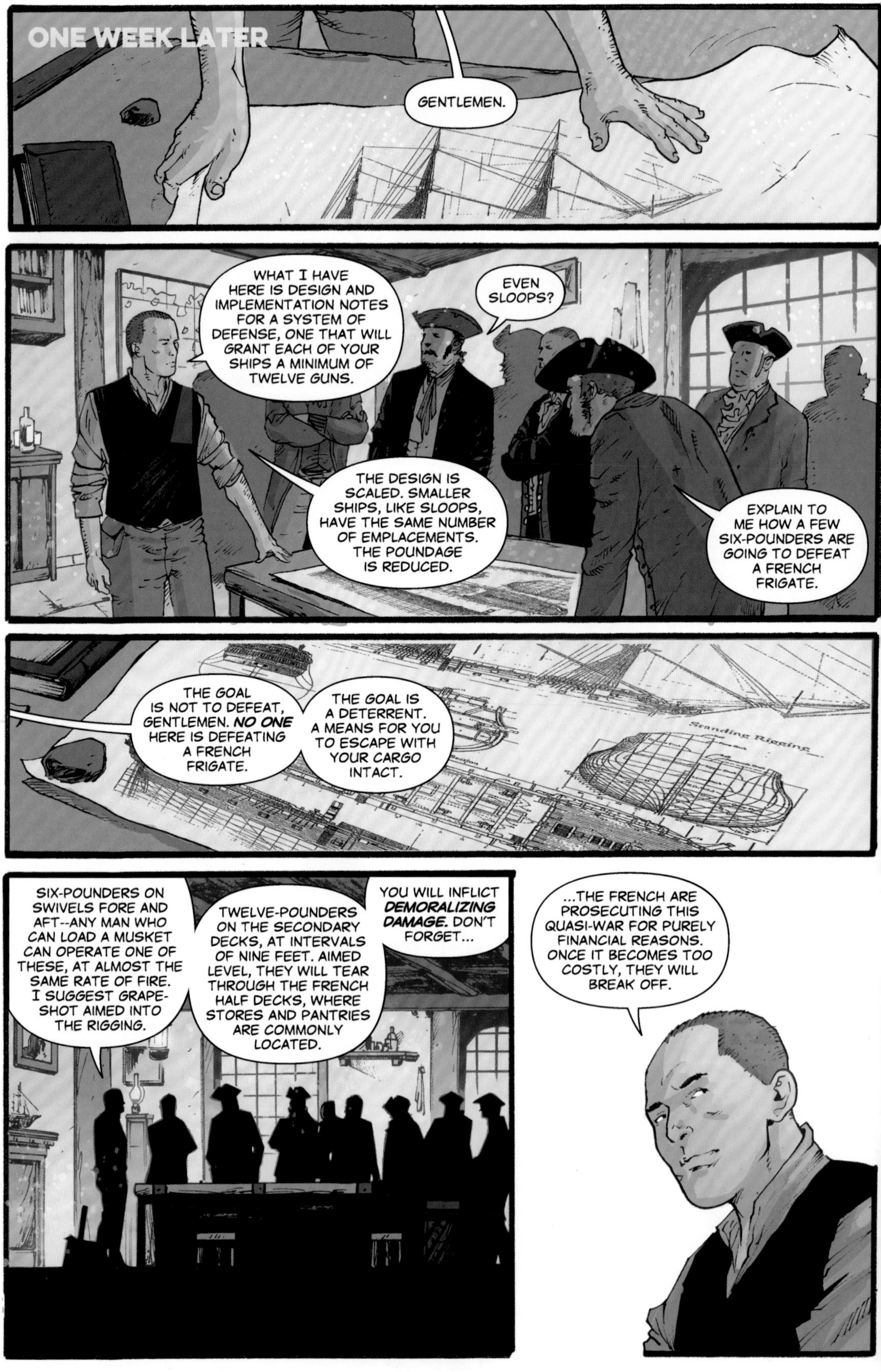
ONE WEEK LATER
GENTLEMEN.
WHAT I HAVE HERE IS DESIGN AND IMPLEMENTATION NOTES FOR A SYSTEM OF DEFENSE, ONE THAT WILL GRANT EACH OF YOUR SHIPS A MINIMUM OF TWELVE GUNS.
EVEN SLOOPS?
THE DESIGN IS SCALED. SMALLER SHIPS, LIKE SLOOPS, HAVE THE SAME NUMBER OF EMPLACEMENTS. THE POUNDAGE IS REDUCED.
EXPLAIN TO ME HOW A FEW SIX-POUNDERS ARE GOING TO DEFEAT A FRENCH FRIGATE.
THE GOAL IS NOT TO DEFEAT, GENTLEMEN. ***NO ONE*** HERE IS DEFEATING A FRENCH FRIGATE.
THE GOAL IS A DETERRENT. A MEANS FOR YOU TO ESCAPE WITH YOUR CARGO INTACT.
Standing Rigging
SIX-POUNDERS ON SWIVELS FORE AND AFT--ANY MAN WHO CAN LOAD A MUSKET CAN OPERATE ONE OF THESE, AT ALMOST THE SAME RATE OF FIRE. I SUGGEST GRAPE-SHOT AIMED INTO THE RIGGING.
TWELVE-POUNDERS ON THE SECONDARY DECKS, AT INTERVALS OF NINE FEET. AIMED LEVEL, THEY WILL TEAR THROUGH THE FRENCH HALF DECKS, WHERE STORES AND PANTRIES ARE COMMONLY LOCATED.
YOU WILL INFLICT ***DEMORALIZING DAMAGE.*** DON'T FORGET...
...THE FRENCH ARE PROSECUTING THIS QUASI-WAR FOR PURELY FINANCIAL REASONS. ONCE IT BECOMES TOO COSTLY, THEY WILL BREAK OFF.

LET'S DRINK TO GOVERNMENT SUBSIDIES.

AND MR. ABBOTT OF BOSTON.

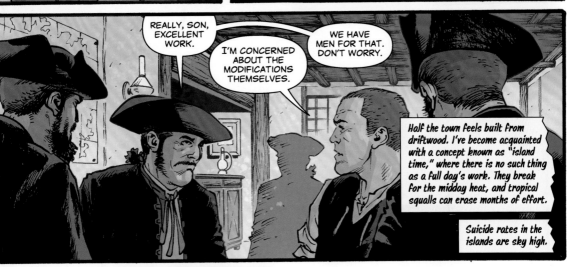

REALLY, SON, EXCELLENT WORK.

I'M CONCERNED ABOUT THE MODIFICATIONS THEMSELVES.

WE HAVE MEN FOR THAT. DON'T WORRY.

Half the town feels built from driftwood. I've become acquainted with a concept known as "island time," where there is no such thing as a full day's work. They break for the midday heat, and tropical squalls can erase months of effort.

Suicide rates in the islands are sky high.

LISTEN, I HAVE A HOUSE IN FREETOWN. COME WITH ME TOMORROW--HAVE A PROPER MEAL. MEET MY FAMILY BEFORE YOU HEAD BACK TO THE STATES.

THIS WILL TAKE THEM EIGHTEEN MONTHS, WITH NO ASSURANCES OF QUALITY. OR SUCCESS.

PARDON?

I hate it here to the extent that words fail me. But my duty is clear.

THANK YOU, BUT I DECLINE THE INVITATION.

TELL YOUR PURSER, MASTER, AND CHIEF TO EXPECT ME AT DAWN.

"RESET!"

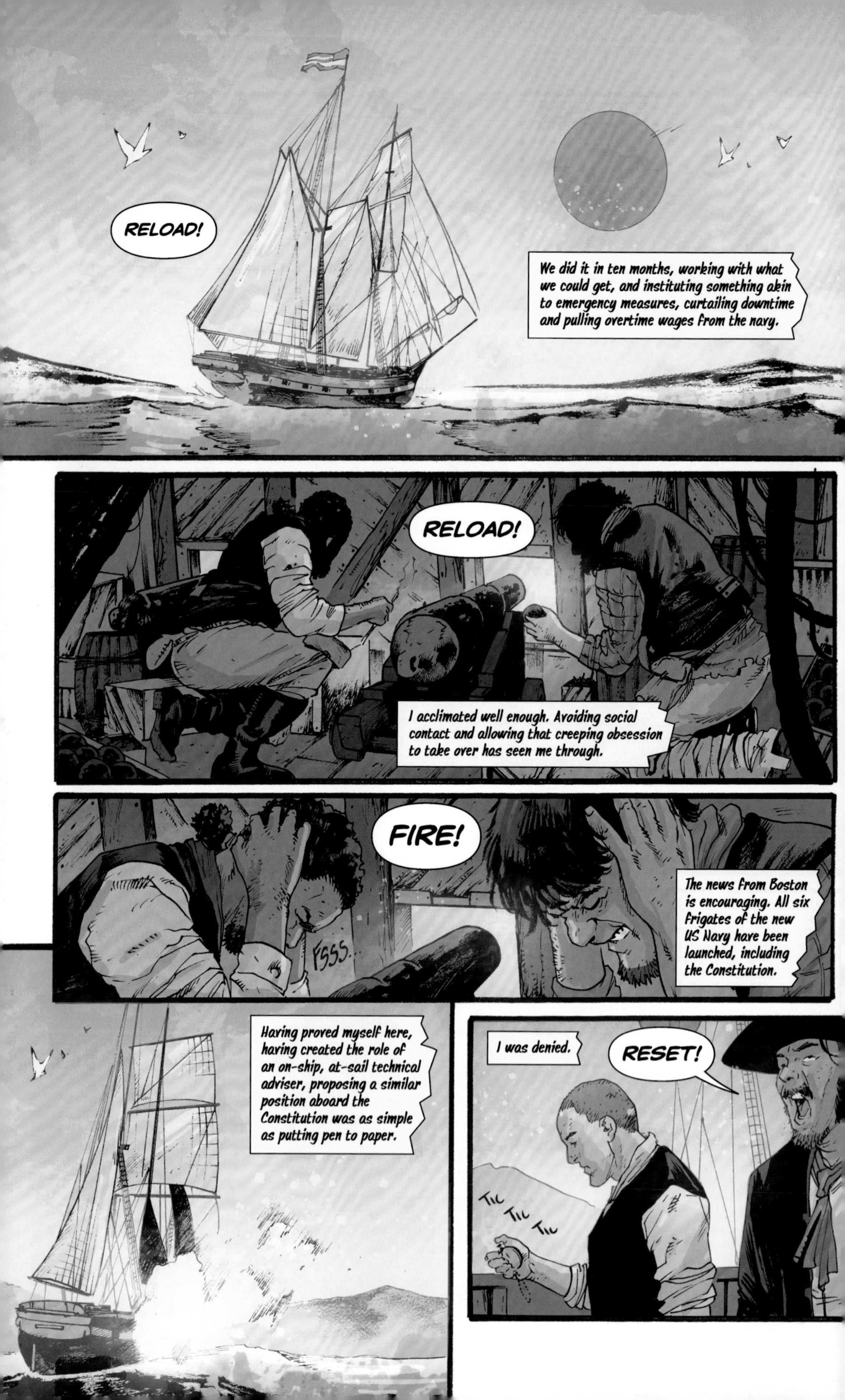
RELOAD!
We did it in ten months, working with what we could get, and instituting something akin to emergency measures, curtailing downtime and pulling overtime wages from the navy.
RELOAD!
I acclimated well enough. Avoiding social contact and allowing that creeping obsession to take over has seen me through.
FIRE!
The news from Boston is encouraging. All six frigates of the new US Navy have been launched, including the Constitution.
FSSS.
Having proved myself here, having created the role of an on-ship, at-sail technical adviser, proposing a similar position aboard the Constitution was as simple as putting pen to paper.
I was denied.
RESET!
TIC
TIC
TIC

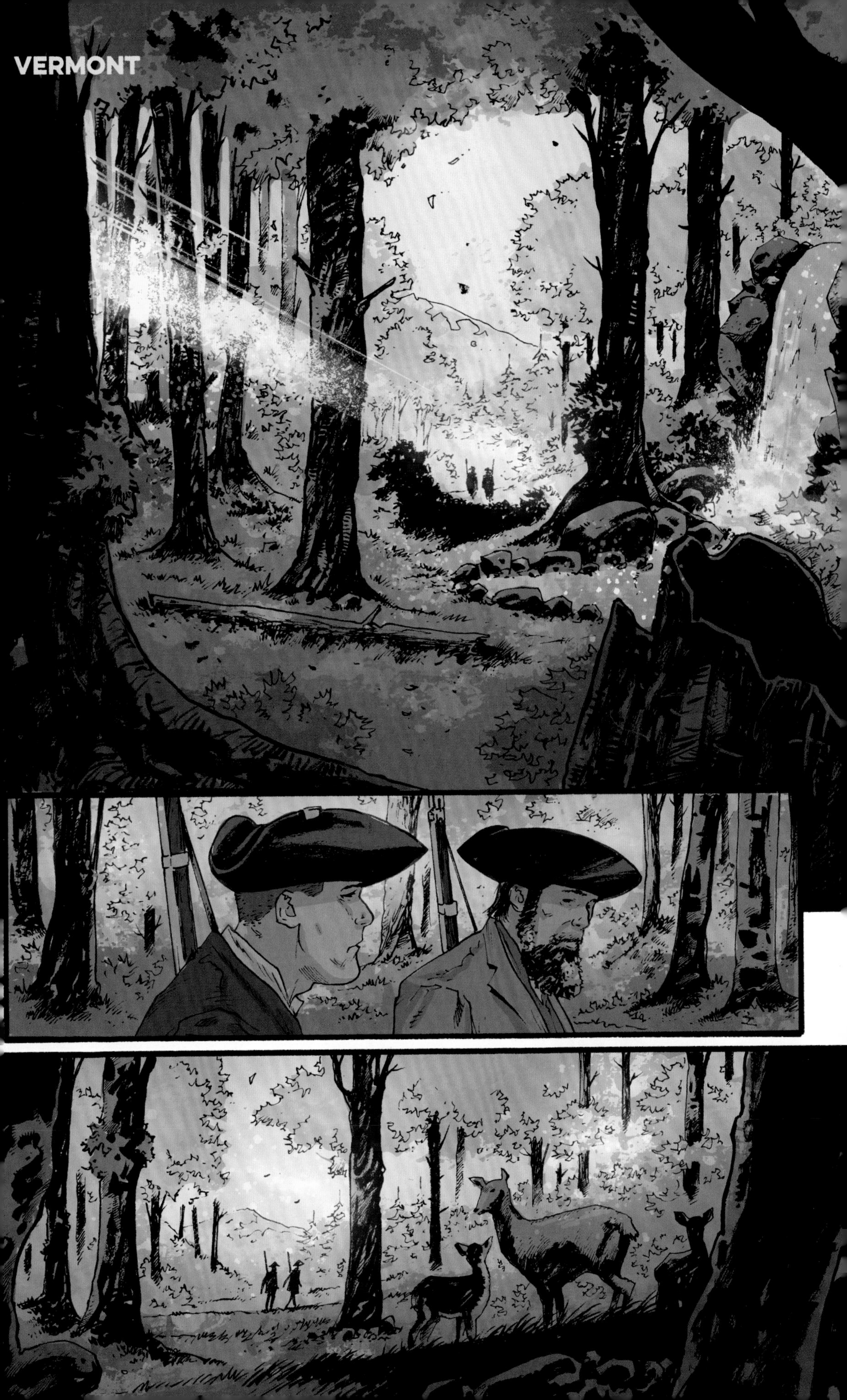
VERMONT

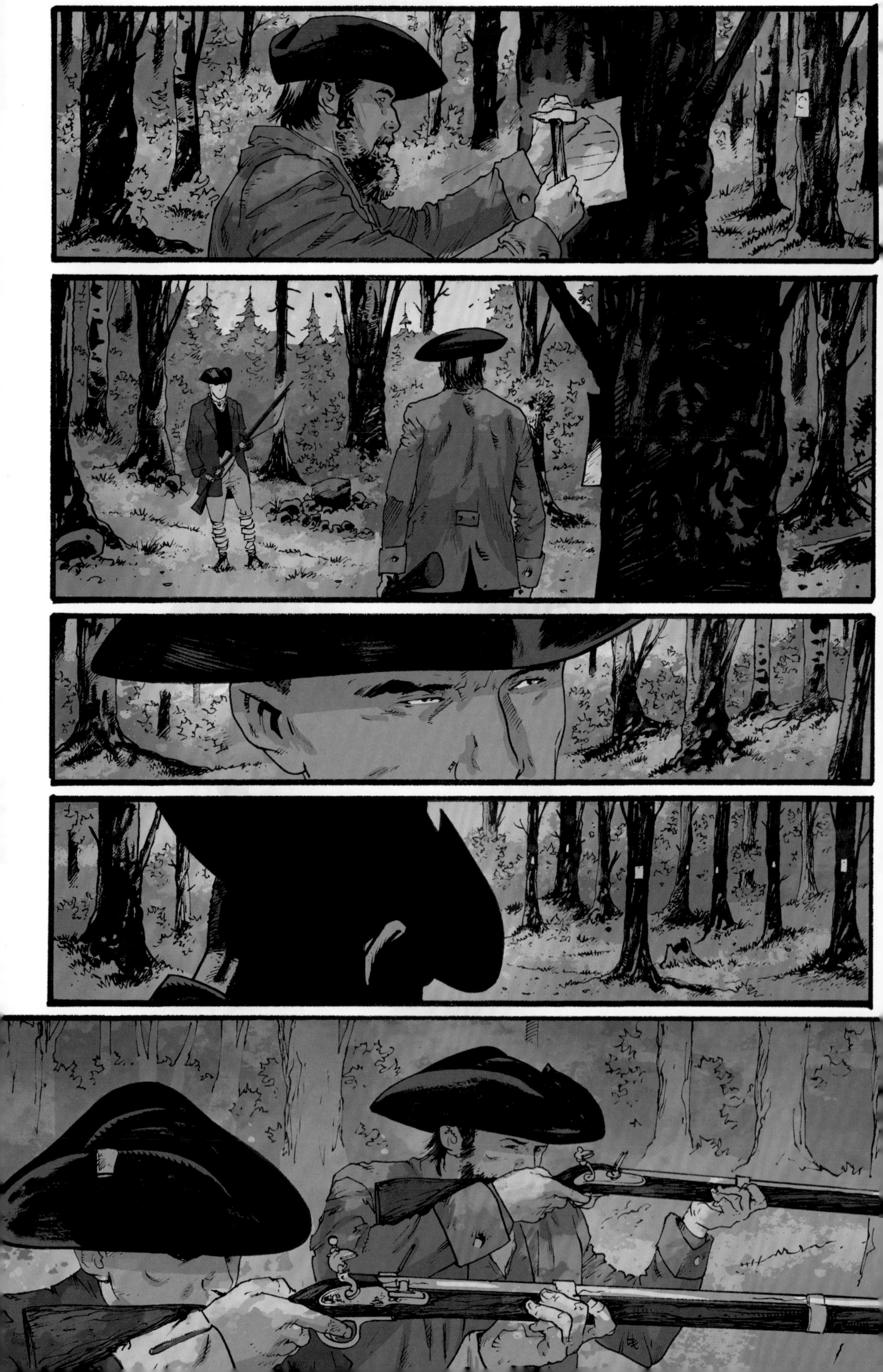

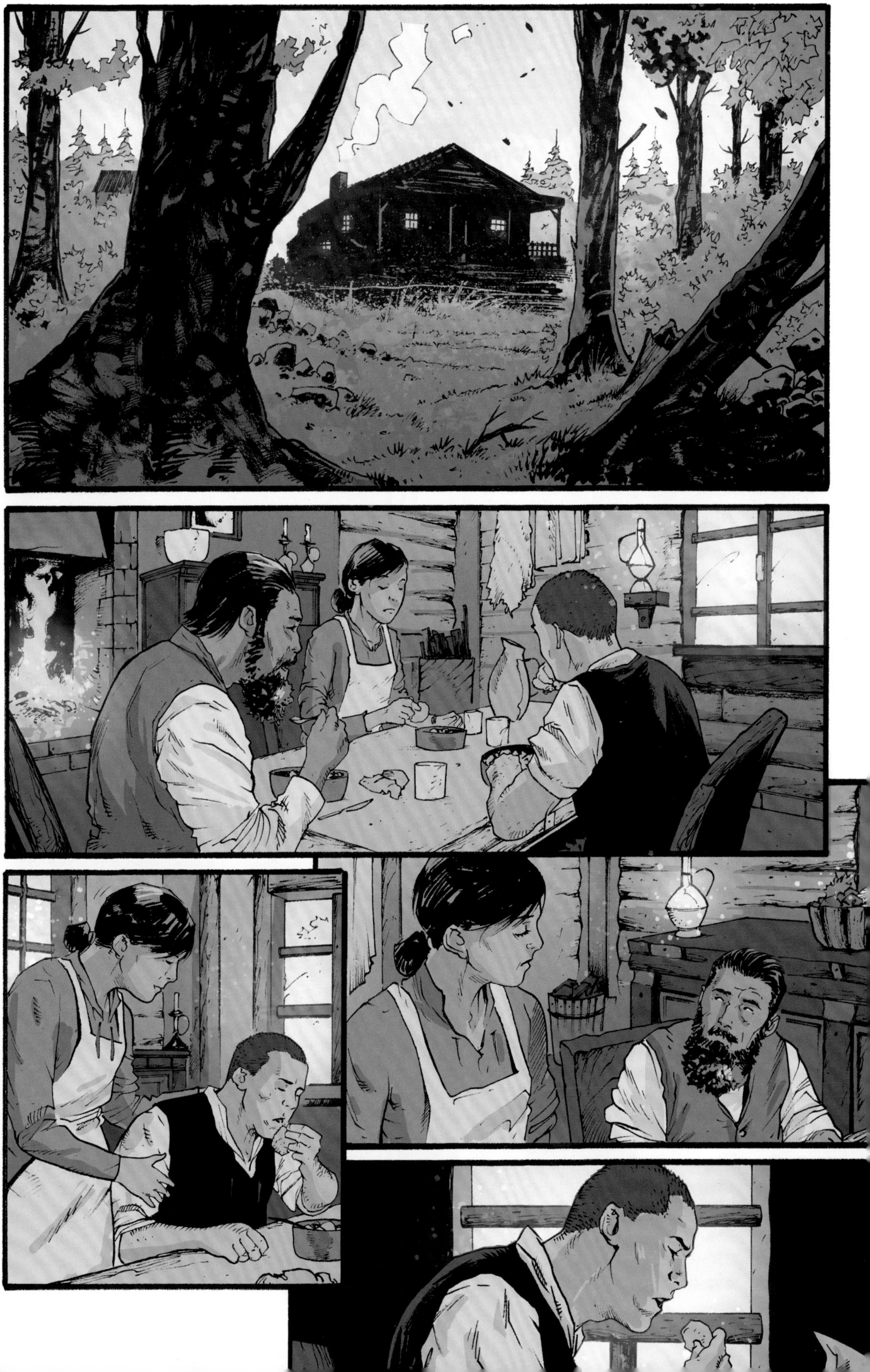

BOSTON

LOOKING FOR SOMETHING IN PARTICULAR?

I AM.

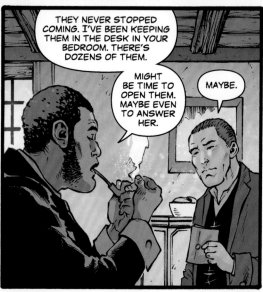

THEY NEVER STOPPED COMING. I'VE BEEN KEEPING THEM IN THE DESK IN YOUR BEDROOM. THERE'S DOZENS OF THEM.

MIGHT BE TIME TO OPEN THEM. MAYBE EVEN TO ANSWER HER.

MAYBE.

BUT *THIS* IS THE ONE I NEED TO READ TODAY.

Don't say it's like starting over. It's not. I got such an early start in life, and accomplished so much. I have no regrets.

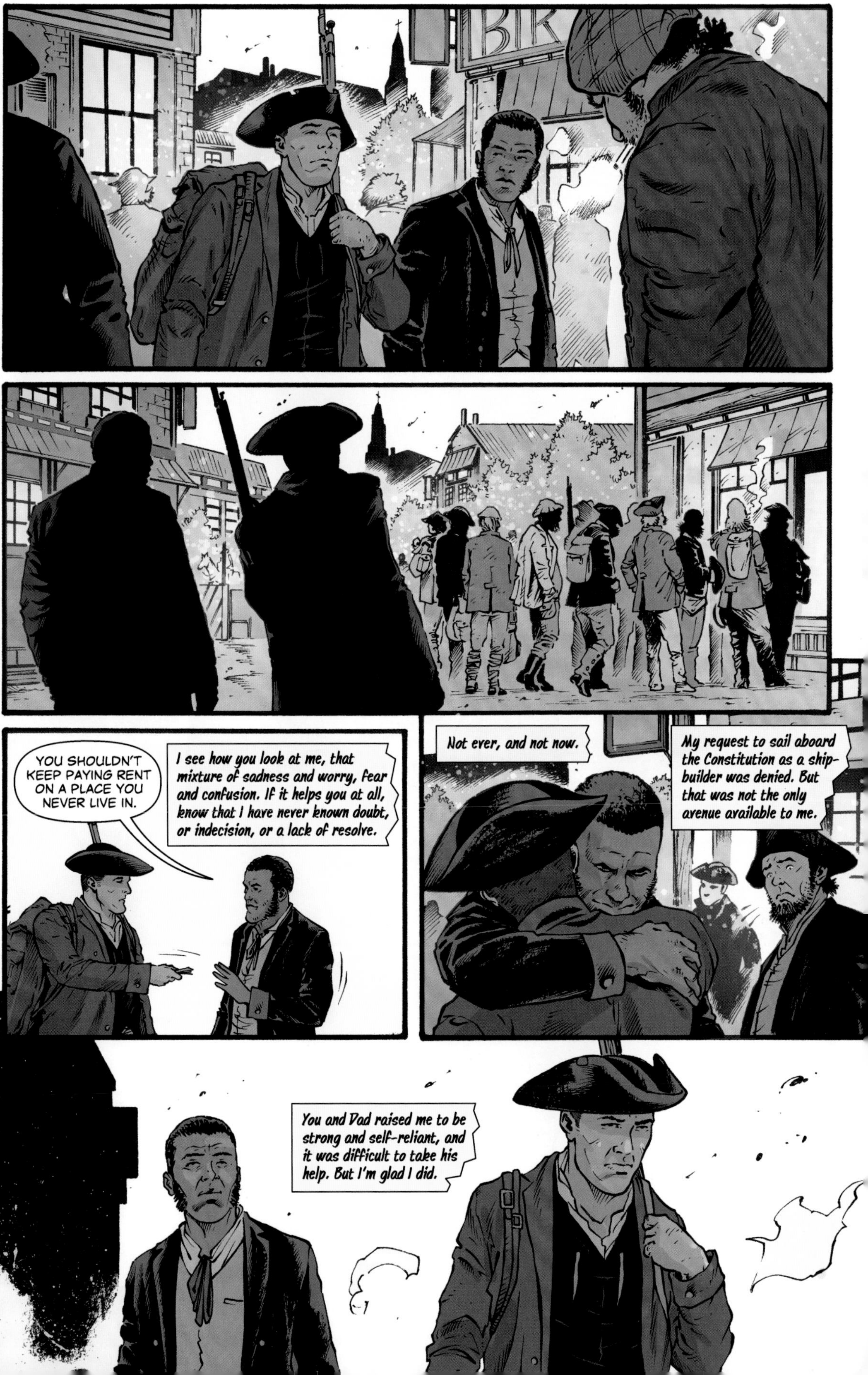
YOU SHOULDN'T KEEP PAYING RENT ON A PLACE YOU NEVER LIVE IN.
I see how you look at me, that mixture of sadness and worry, fear and confusion. If it helps you at all, know that I have never known doubt, or indecision, or a lack of resolve.
Not ever, and not now.
My request to sail aboard the Constitution as a ship-builder was denied. But that was not the only avenue available to me.
You and Dad raised me to be strong and self-reliant, and it was difficult to take his help. But I'm glad I did.

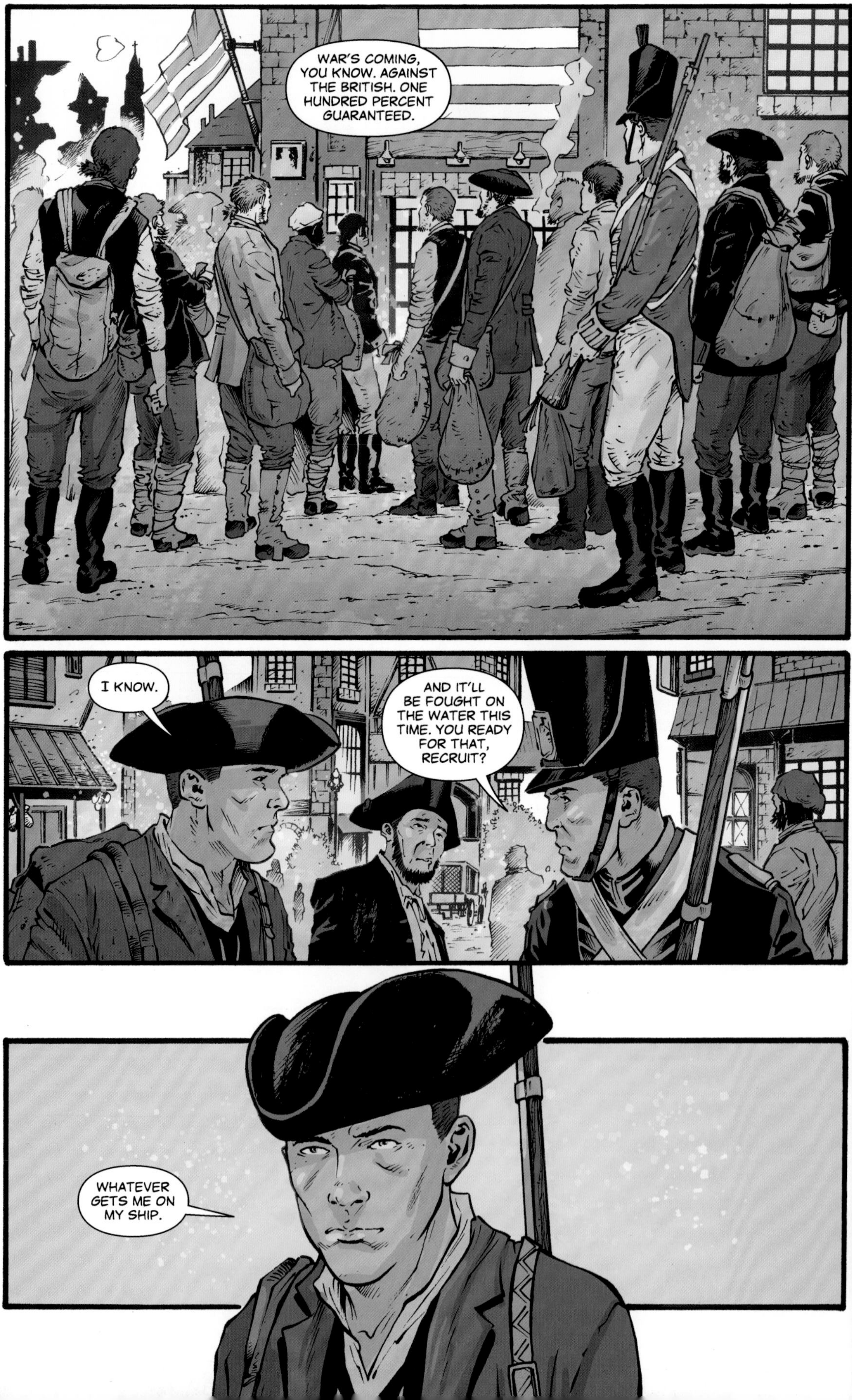
WAR'S COMING, YOU KNOW. AGAINST THE BRITISH. ONE HUNDRED PERCENT GUARANTEED.
I KNOW.
AND IT'LL BE FOUGHT ON THE WATER THIS TIME. YOU READY FOR THAT, RECRUIT?
WHATEVER GETS ME ON MY SHIP.

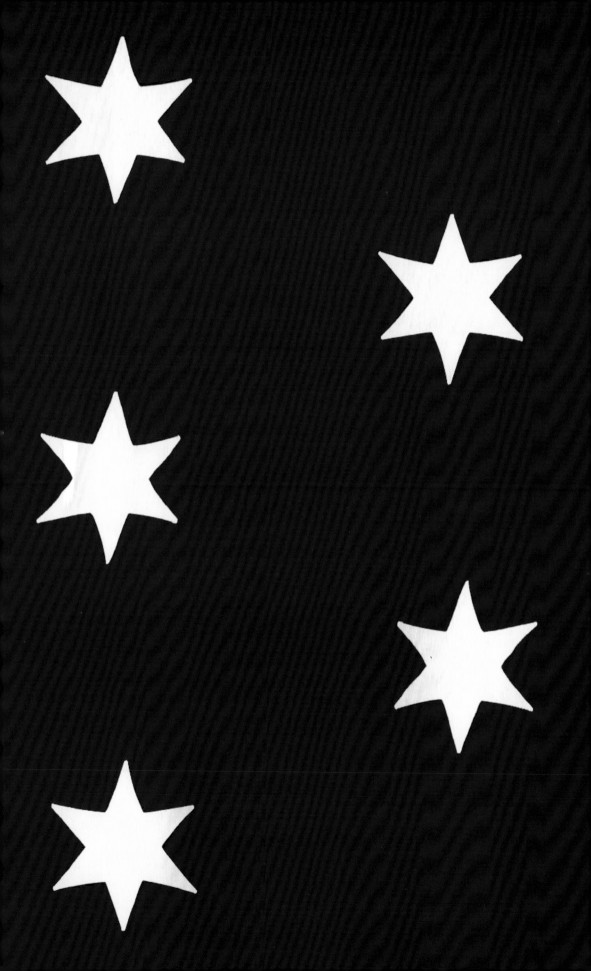

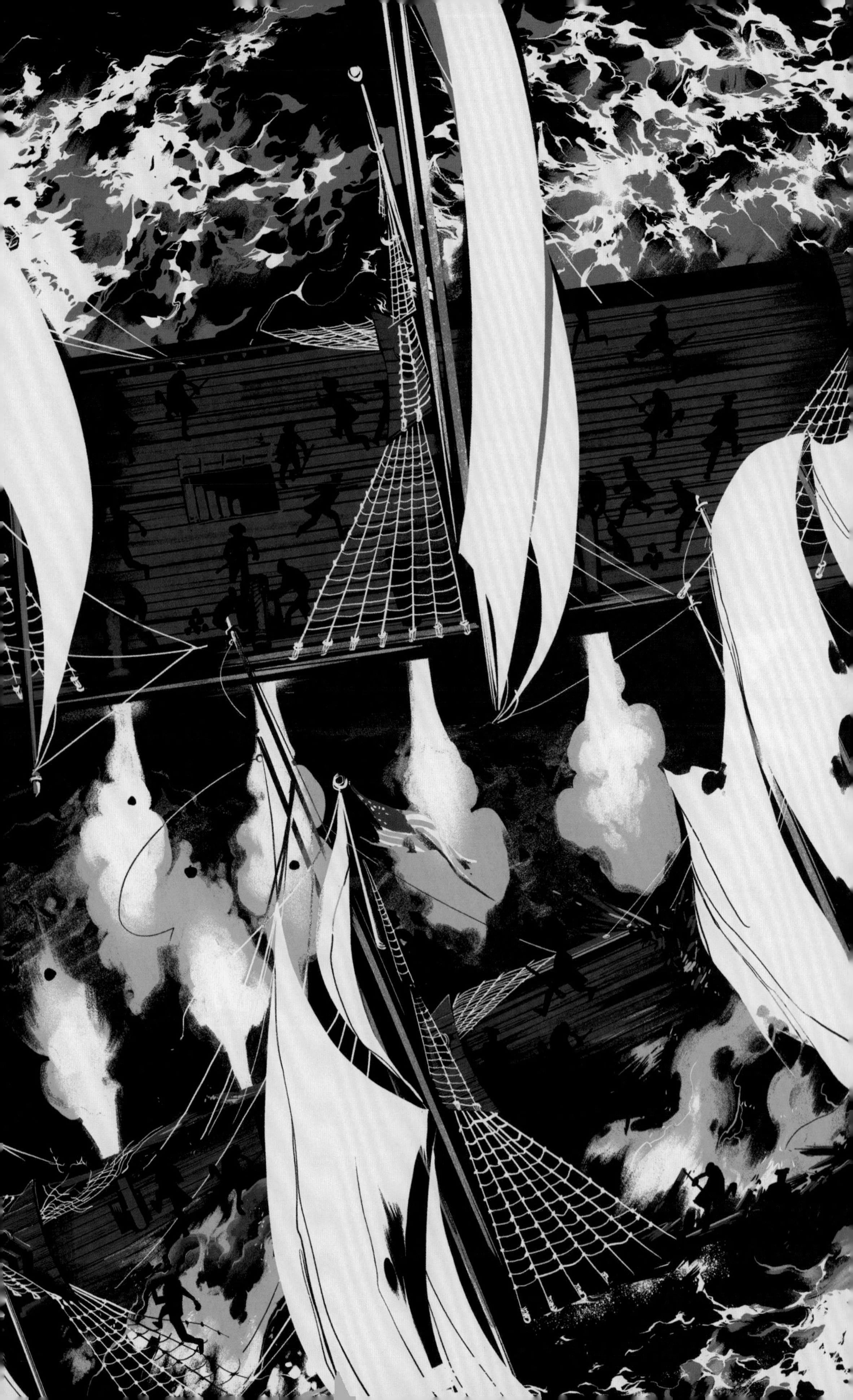

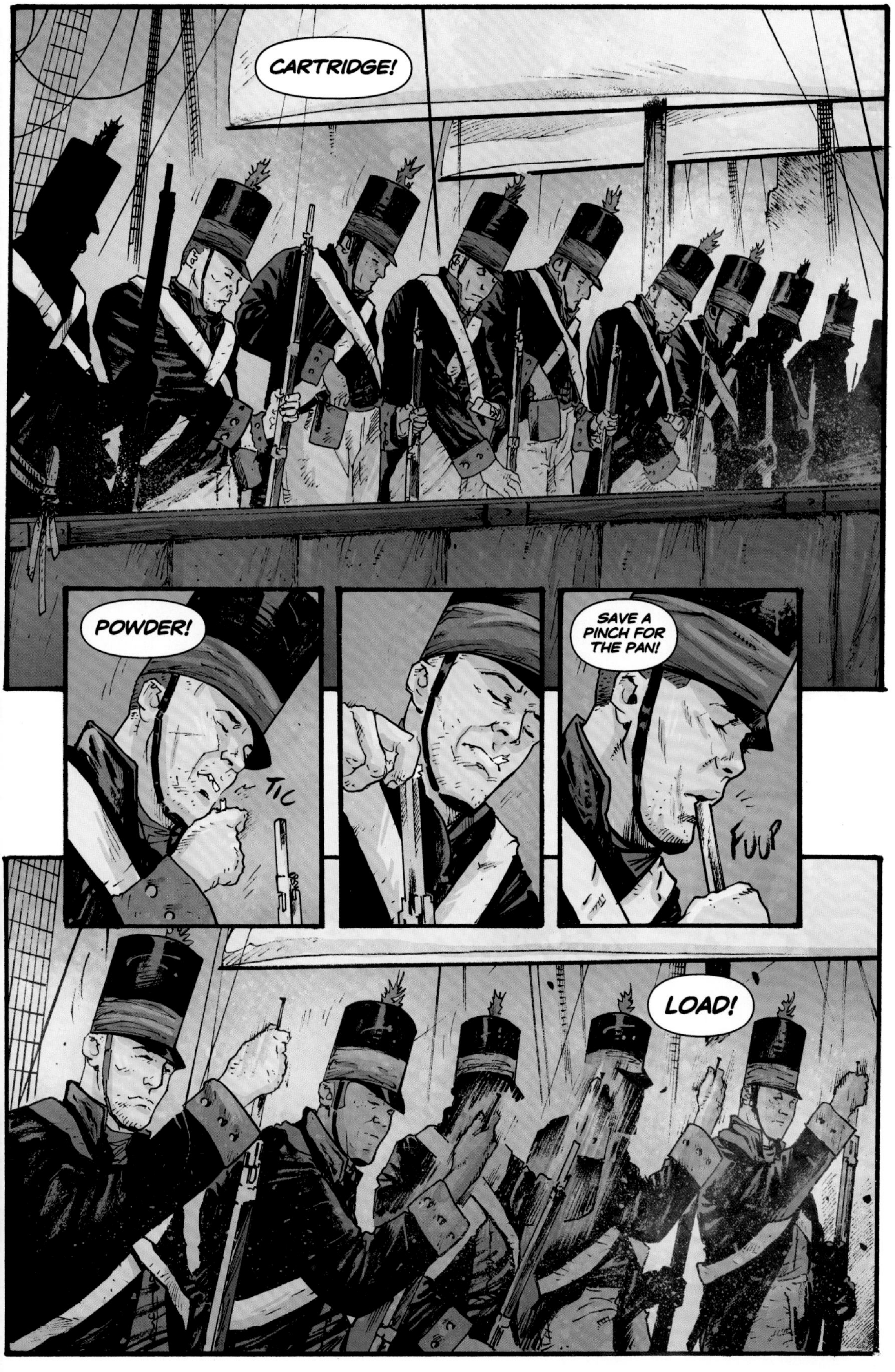
CARTRIDGE!
POWDER!
TIC
SAVE A PINCH FOR THE PAN!
FUUP
LOAD!

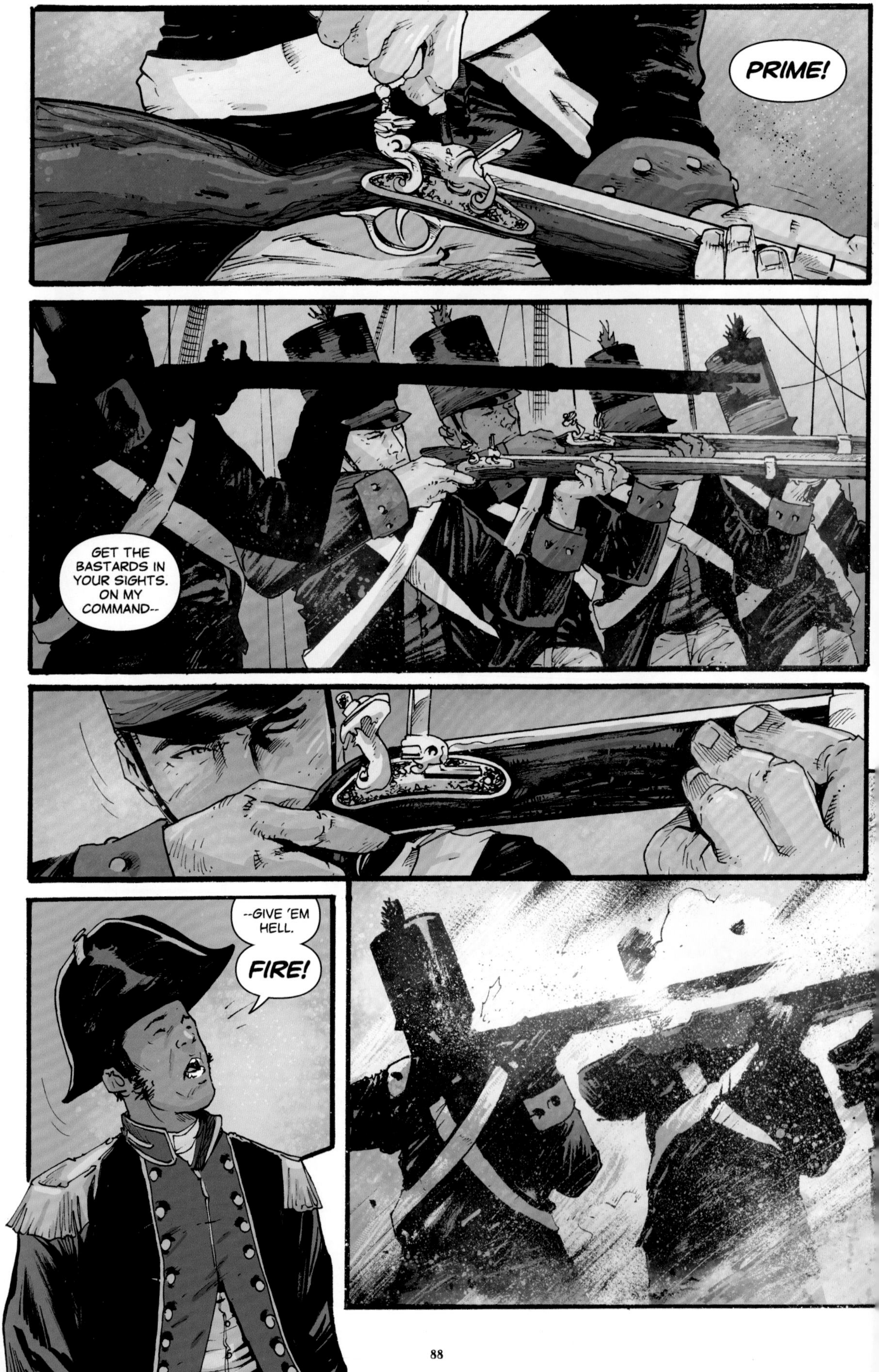
PRIME!
GET THE BASTARDS IN YOUR SIGHTS. ON MY COMMAND--
--GIVE 'EM HELL.
FIRE!

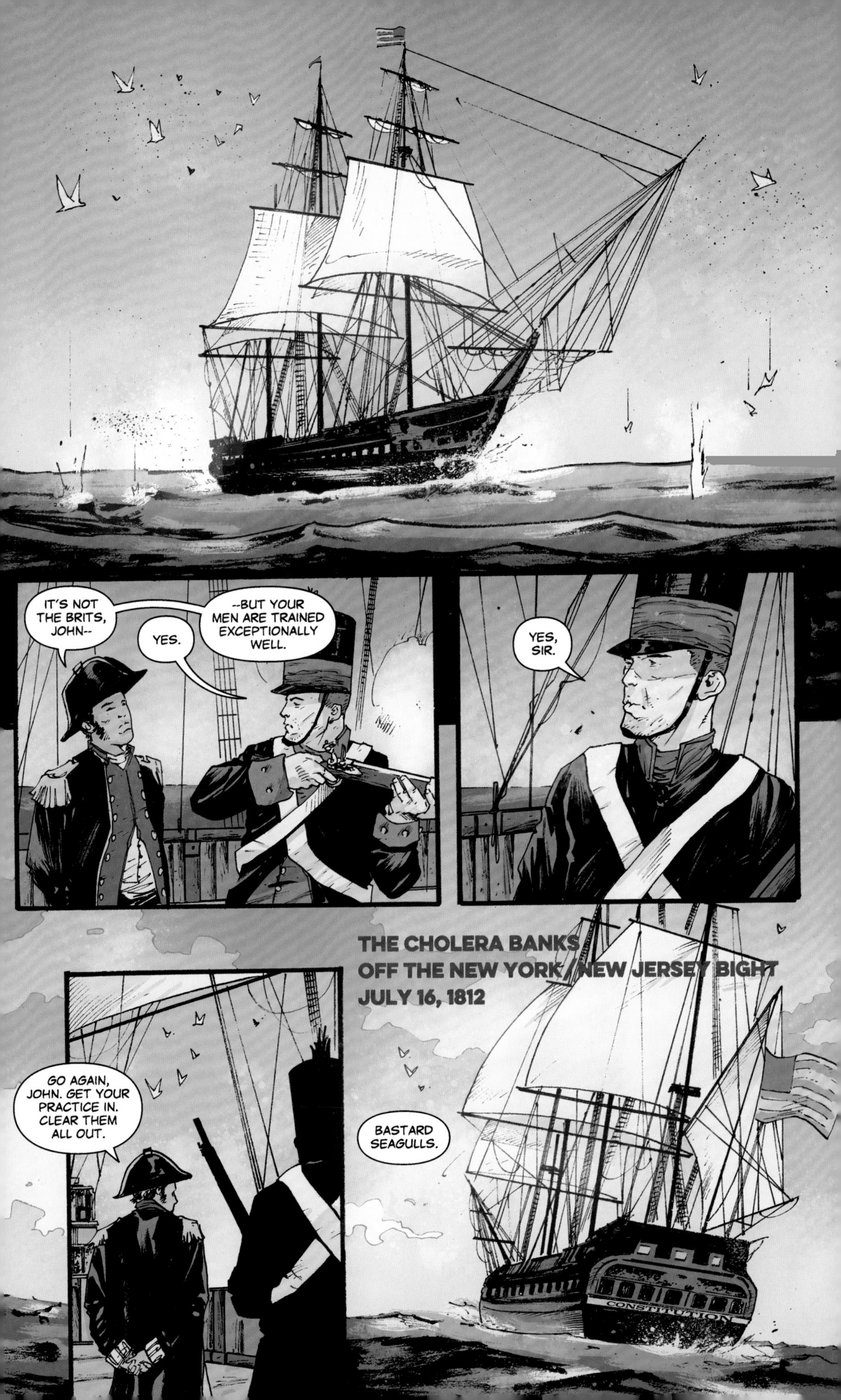

IT'S NOT THE BRITS, JOHN--
YES.
--BUT YOUR MEN ARE TRAINED EXCEPTIONALLY WELL.
YES, SIR.
THE CHOLERA BANKS
OFF THE NEW YORK/NEW JERSEY BIGHT
JULY 16, 1812
GO AGAIN, JOHN. GET YOUR PRACTICE IN. CLEAR THEM ALL OUT.
BASTARD SEAGULLS.
CONSTITUTION

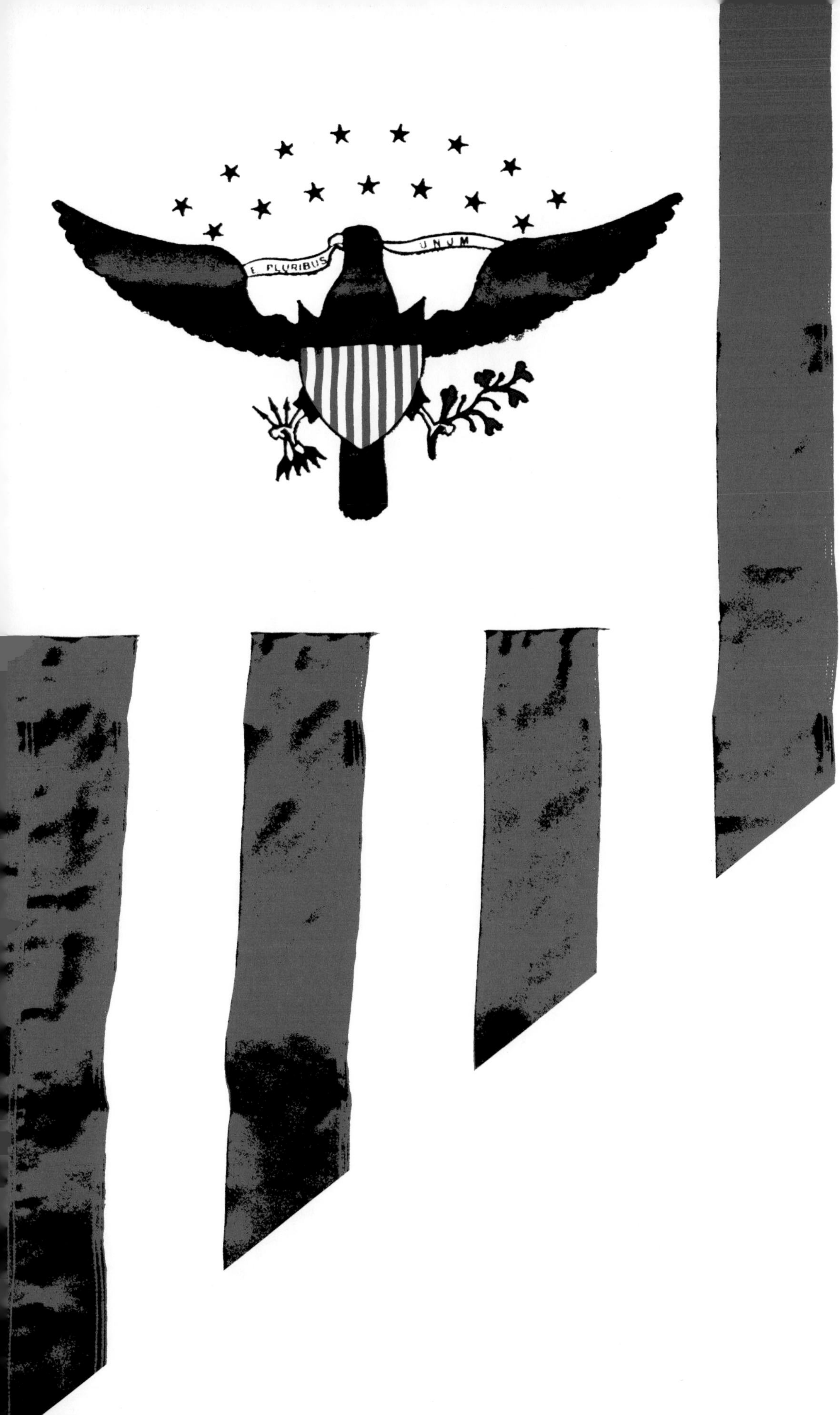
E PLURIBUS UNUM

REBELS

"THESE FREE AND INDEPENDENT STATES" - PART 4 OF 5

IN WHICH JOHN ABBOTT GETS HIS WAR.

BRIAN WOOD · ANDREA MUTTI · LAUREN AFFE · MATT TAYLOR

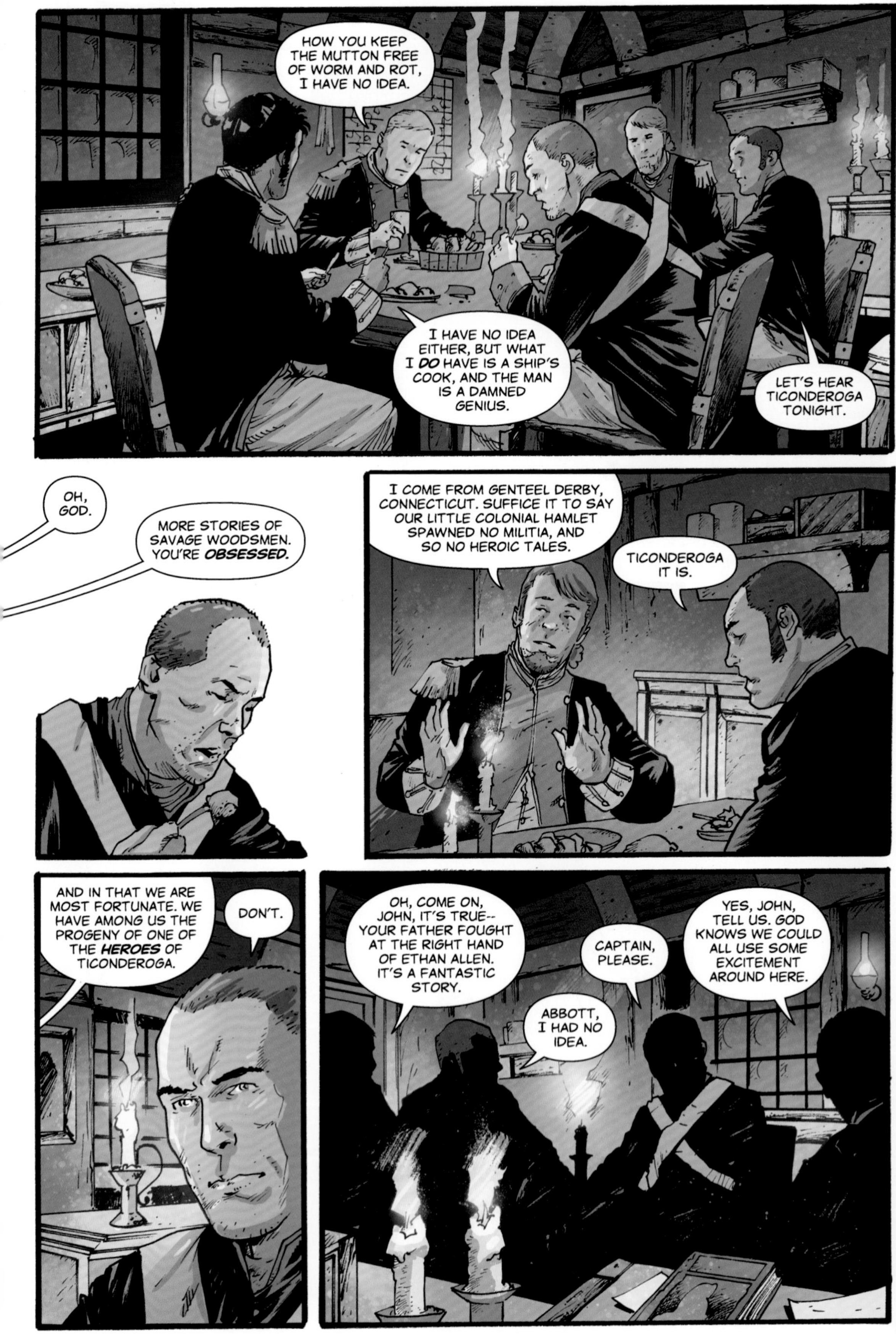
HOW YOU KEEP THE MUTTON FREE OF WORM AND ROT, I HAVE NO IDEA.
I HAVE NO IDEA EITHER, BUT WHAT I *DO* HAVE IS A SHIP'S COOK, AND THE MAN IS A DAMNED GENIUS.
LET'S HEAR TICONDEROGA TONIGHT.
OH, GOD.
MORE STORIES OF SAVAGE WOODSMEN. YOU'RE ***OBSESSED.***
I COME FROM GENTEEL DERBY, CONNECTICUT. SUFFICE IT TO SAY OUR LITTLE COLONIAL HAMLET SPAWNED NO MILITIA, AND SO NO HEROIC TALES.
TICONDEROGA IT IS.
AND IN THAT WE ARE MOST FORTUNATE. WE HAVE AMONG US THE PROGENY OF ONE OF THE ***HEROES*** OF TICONDEROGA.
DON'T.
OH, COME ON, JOHN, IT'S TRUE-- YOUR FATHER FOUGHT AT THE RIGHT HAND OF ETHAN ALLEN. IT'S A FANTASTIC STORY.
CAPTAIN, PLEASE.
ABBOTT, I HAD NO IDEA.
YES, JOHN, TELL US. GOD KNOWS WE COULD ALL USE SOME EXCITEMENT AROUND HERE.

GENTLEMEN. IF YOU FEEL A LACK OF EXCITEMENT IN YOUR LIVES, DON'T SEEK OUT NOSTALGIC STORIES TOLD OVER YOUR WINE.

MAYBE CONSIDER, INSTEAD, THE FACT WE SAIL POINTLESSLY AROUND NEW YORK HARBOR, AVOIDING THE BRITISH FLEET AND WASTING OUR AMMUNITION ON BIRDS. THERE'S A WAR ON.

ABBOTT--

HERE'S YOUR TICONDEROGA STORY.

BRAVE MEN LIKE MY FATHER-- PATRIOTS, EVERY SINGLE ONE OF THEM--PICKED UP THEIR RIFLES AND PUT DOWN A TYRANNY. THESE WERE NOT MEN WITH A CONSTITUTION TO GUIDE THEM, A FLAG TO RALLY UNDER, OR A CHAIN OF COMMAND TO CONSULT.

AND I STAND HERE, AN AMERICAN, BECAUSE MY FATHER CHOSE TO ACT RATHER THAN LISTEN TO STORIES.

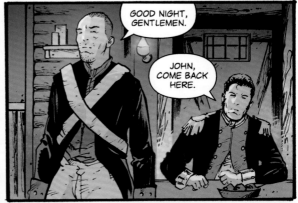

GOOD NIGHT, GENTLEMEN.

JOHN, COME BACK HERE.

...

WELL, HE'S A HELL OF A SOLDIER.

WITH SETH ABBOTT AS A FATHER, HOW COULD HE NOT BE?

BUT TICONDEROGA WAS CAPTURED WITHOUT A SINGLE SHOT BEING FIRED. IT'S AN AMAZING STORY.

WAIT, SO *YOU* KNOW THE STORY AS WELL? HELL, OUT WITH IT!

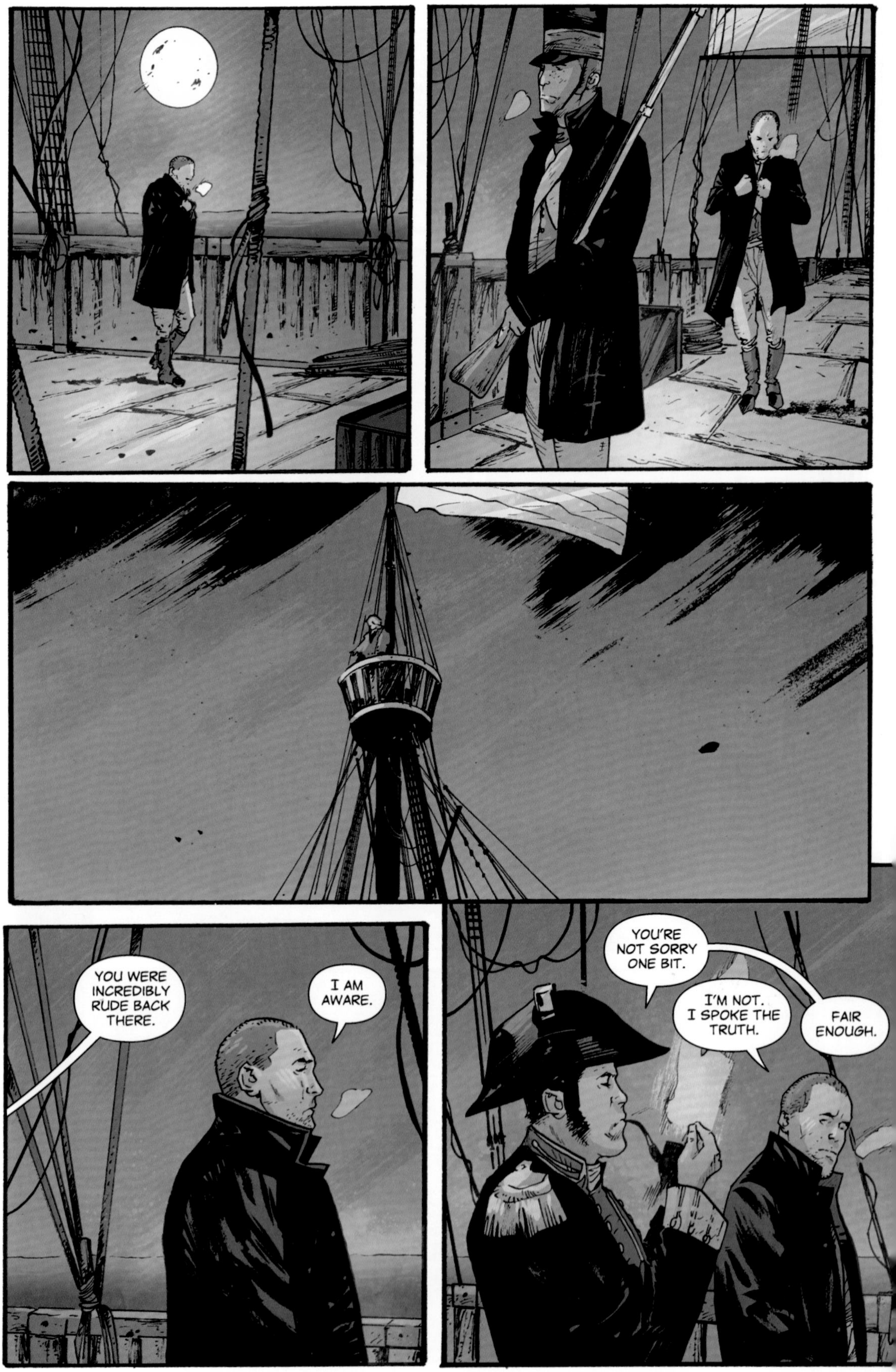
YOU WERE INCREDIBLY RUDE BACK THERE.
I AM AWARE.
YOU'RE NOT SORRY ONE BIT.
I'M NOT. I SPOKE THE TRUTH.
FAIR ENOUGH.

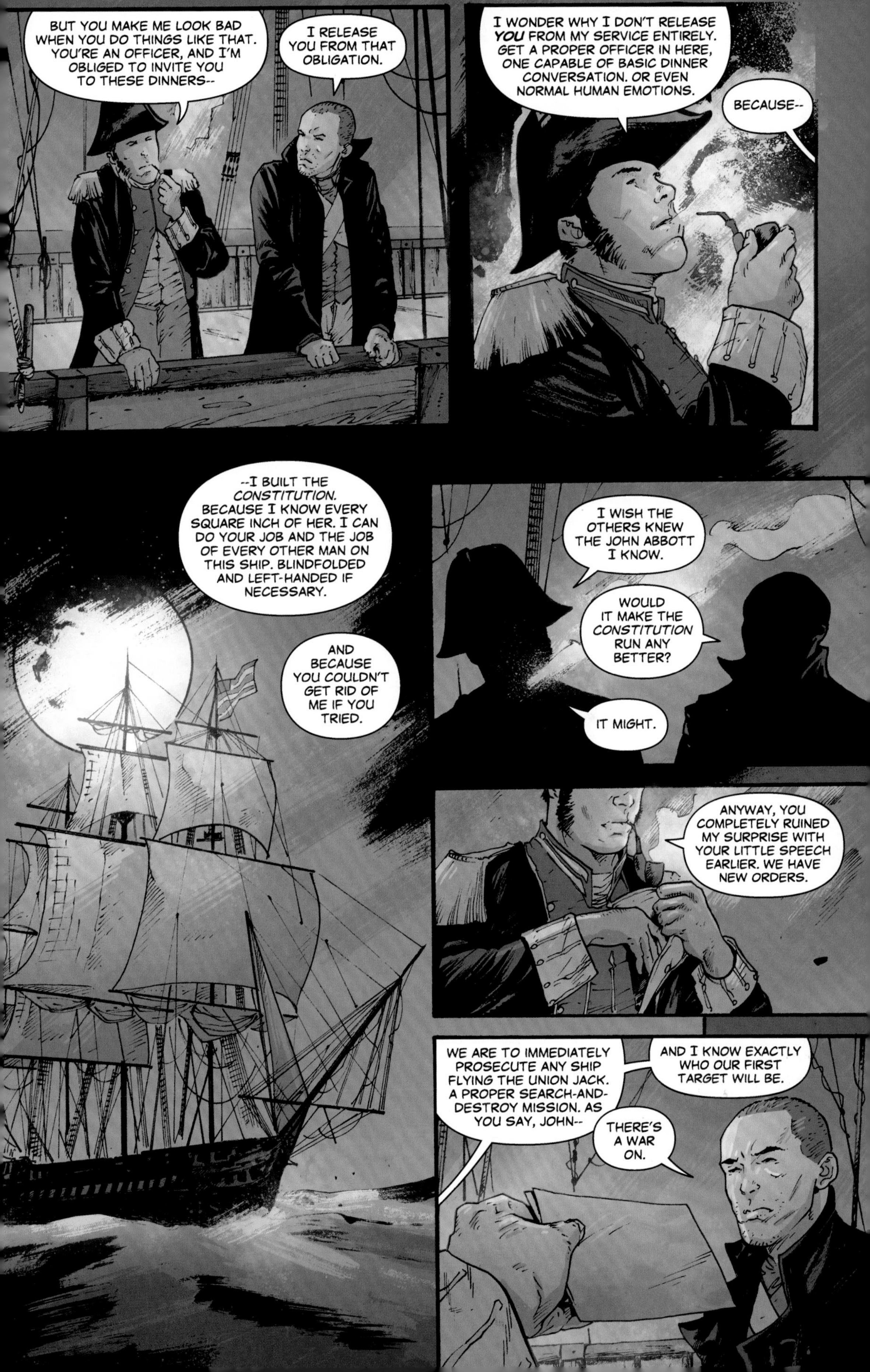
BUT YOU MAKE ME LOOK BAD WHEN YOU DO THINGS LIKE THAT. YOU'RE AN OFFICER, AND I'M OBLIGED TO INVITE YOU TO THESE DINNERS--
I RELEASE YOU FROM THAT OBLIGATION.
I WONDER WHY I DON'T RELEASE *YOU* FROM MY SERVICE ENTIRELY. GET A PROPER OFFICER IN HERE, ONE CAPABLE OF BASIC DINNER CONVERSATION. OR EVEN NORMAL HUMAN EMOTIONS.
BECAUSE--
--I BUILT THE *CONSTITUTION*. BECAUSE I KNOW EVERY SQUARE INCH OF HER. I CAN DO YOUR JOB AND THE JOB OF EVERY OTHER MAN ON THIS SHIP. BLINDFOLDED AND LEFT-HANDED IF NECESSARY.
AND BECAUSE YOU COULDN'T GET RID OF ME IF YOU TRIED.
I WISH THE OTHERS KNEW THE JOHN ABBOTT I KNOW.
WOULD IT MAKE THE *CONSTITUTION* RUN ANY BETTER?
IT MIGHT.
ANYWAY, YOU COMPLETELY RUINED MY SURPRISE WITH YOUR LITTLE SPEECH EARLIER. WE HAVE NEW ORDERS.
WE ARE TO IMMEDIATELY PROSECUTE ANY SHIP FLYING THE UNION JACK. A PROPER SEARCH-AND-DESTROY MISSION. AS YOU SAY, JOHN--
THERE'S A WAR ON.
AND I KNOW EXACTLY WHO OUR FIRST TARGET WILL BE.

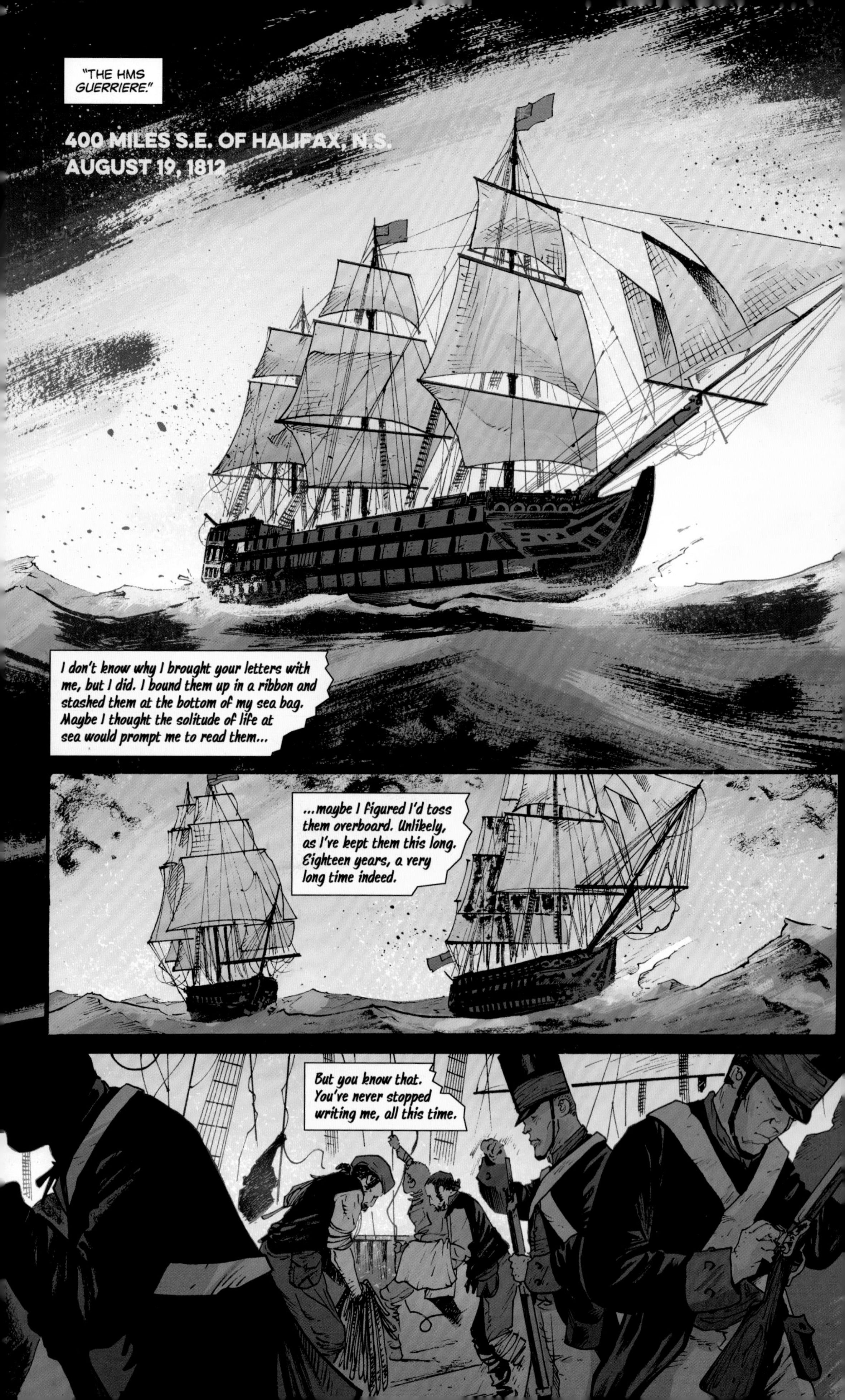
"THE HMS GUERRIERE."
400 MILES S.E. OF HALIFAX, N.S.
AUGUST 19, 1812
I don't know why I brought your letters with me, but I did. I bound them up in a ribbon and stashed them at the bottom of my sea bag. Maybe I thought the solitude of life at sea would prompt me to read them...
...maybe I figured I'd toss them overboard. Unlikely, as I've kept them this long. Eighteen years, a very long time indeed.
But you know that. You've never stopped writing me, all this time.

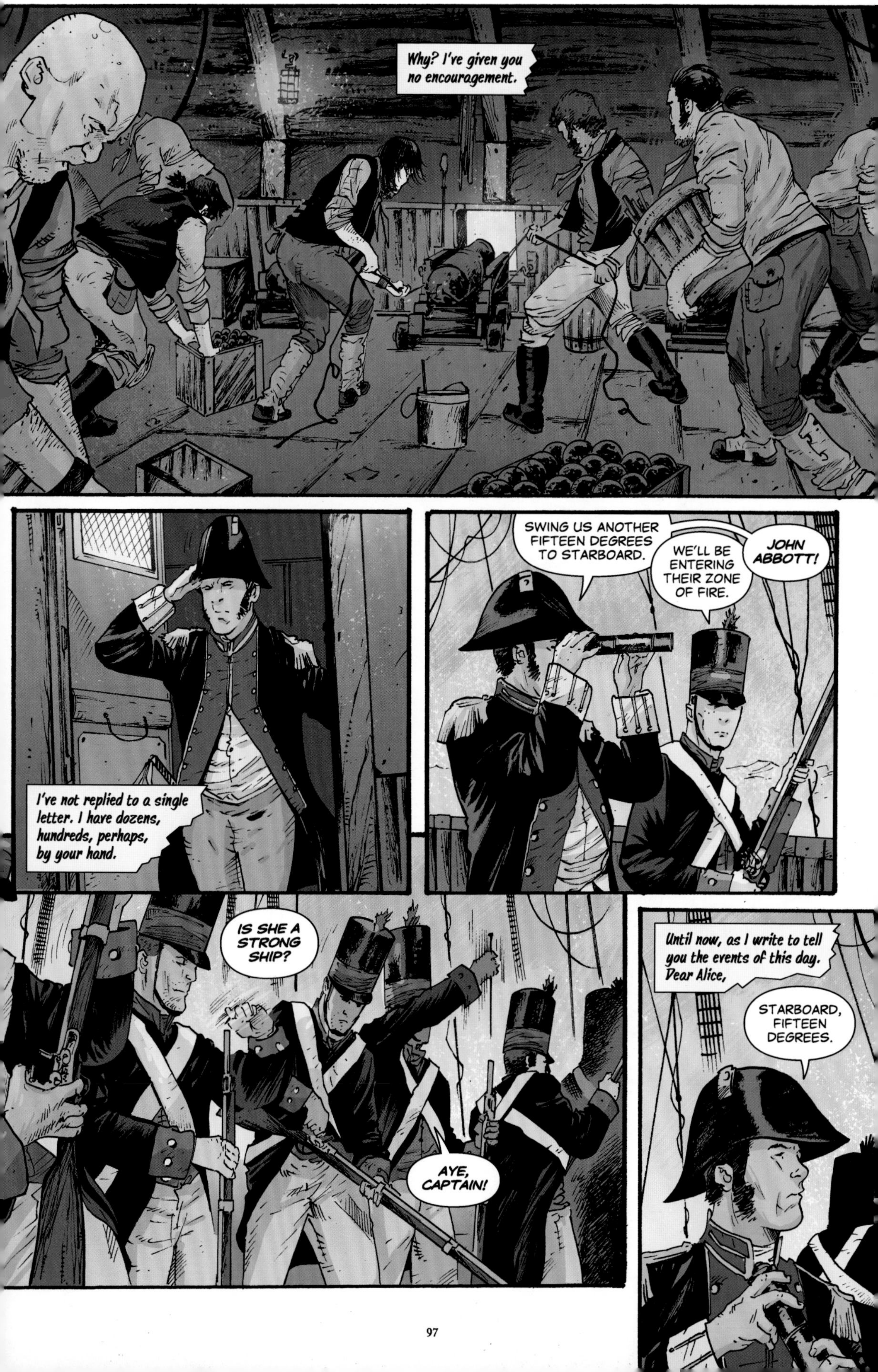
Why? I've given you no encouragement.
I've not replied to a single letter. I have dozens, hundreds, perhaps, by your hand.
SWING US ANOTHER FIFTEEN DEGREES TO STARBOARD.
WE'LL BE ENTERING THEIR ZONE OF FIRE.
JOHN ABBOTT!
IS SHE A STRONG SHIP?
AYE, CAPTAIN!
Until now, as I write to tell you the events of this day. Dear Alice,
STARBOARD, FIFTEEN DEGREES.

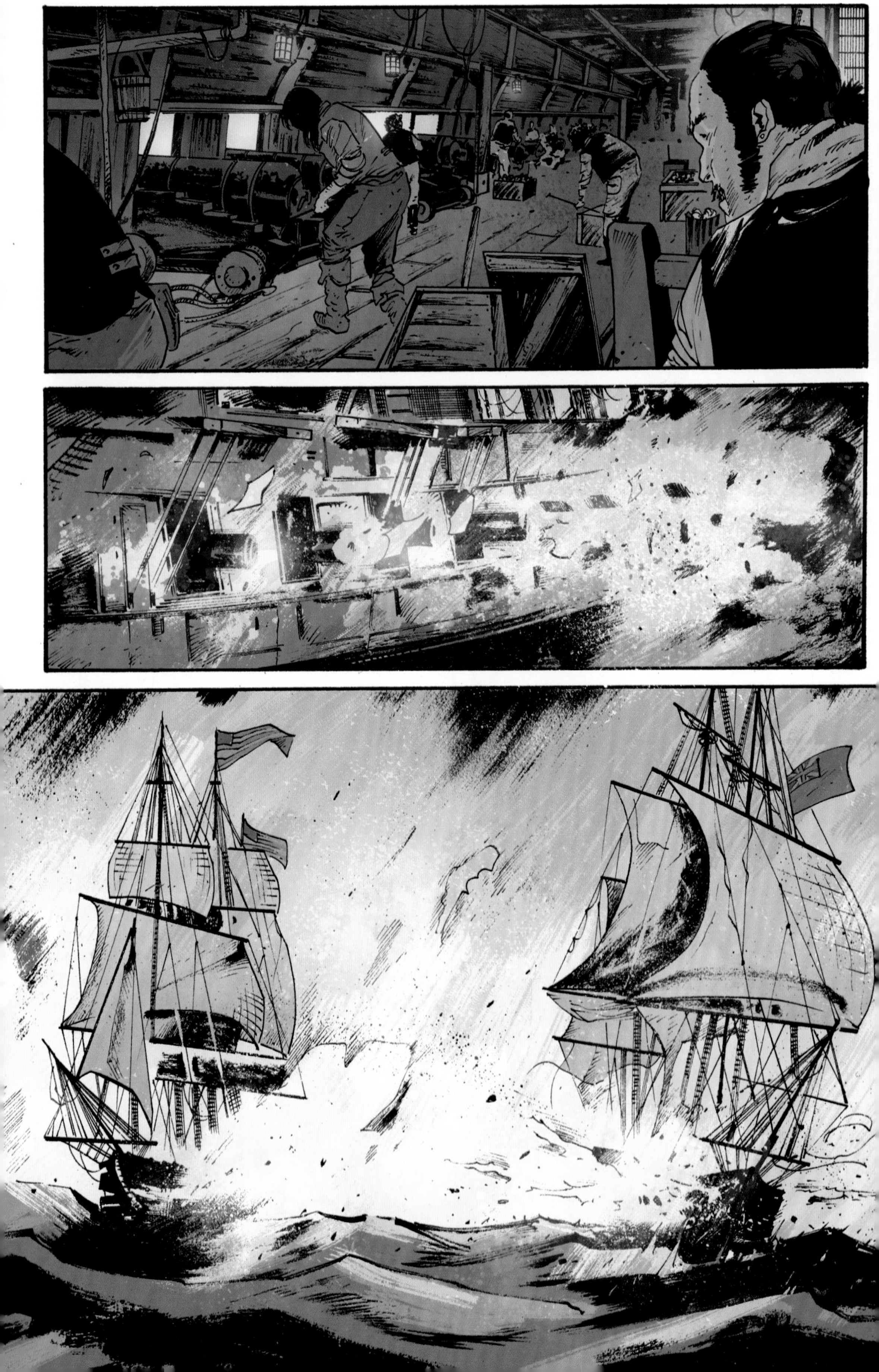

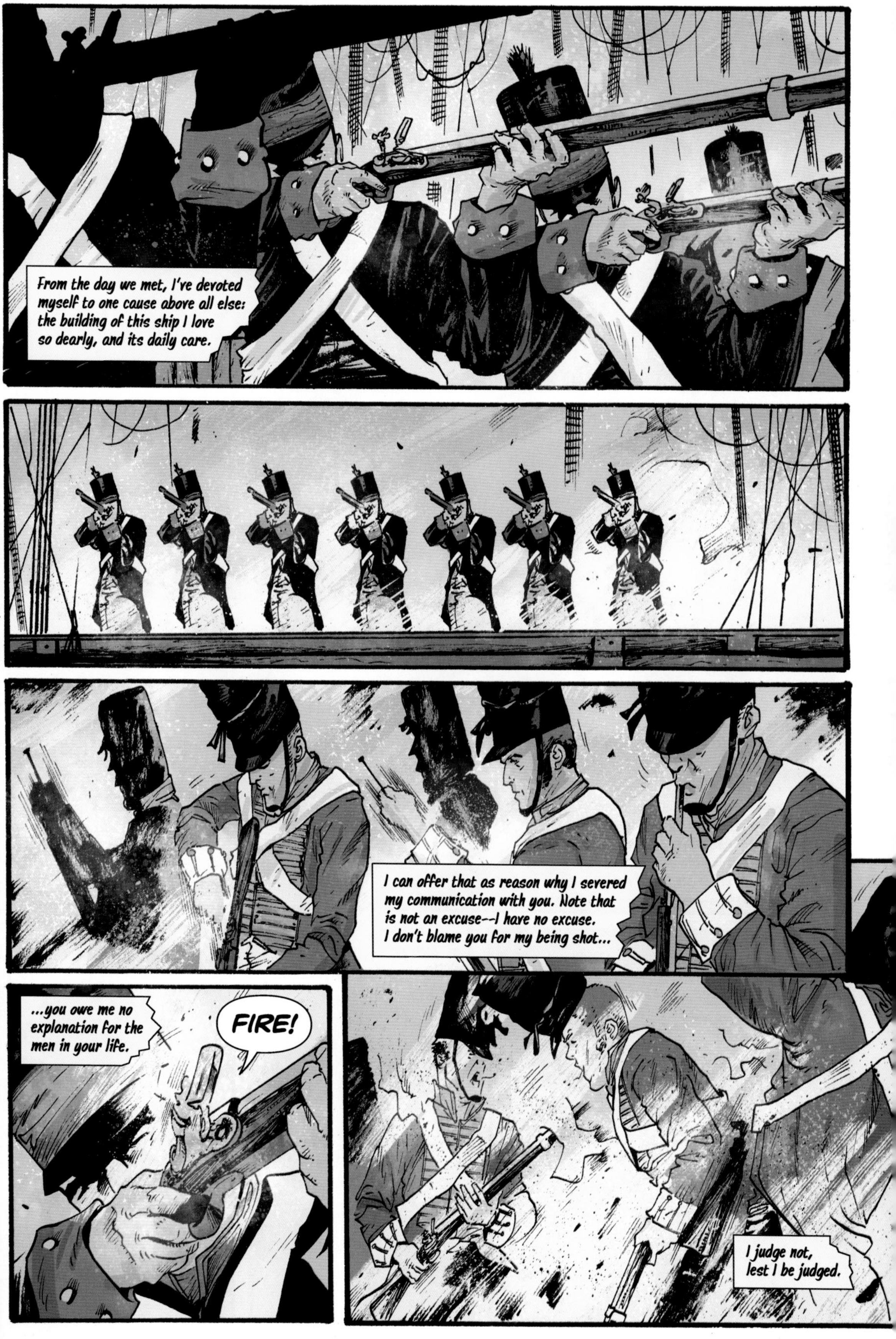
From the day we met, I've devoted myself to one cause above all else: the building of this ship I love so dearly, and its daily care.
I can offer that as reason why I severed my communication with you. Note that is not an excuse--I have no excuse. I don't blame you for my being shot...
...you owe me no explanation for the men in your life.
FIRE!
I judge not, lest I be judged.

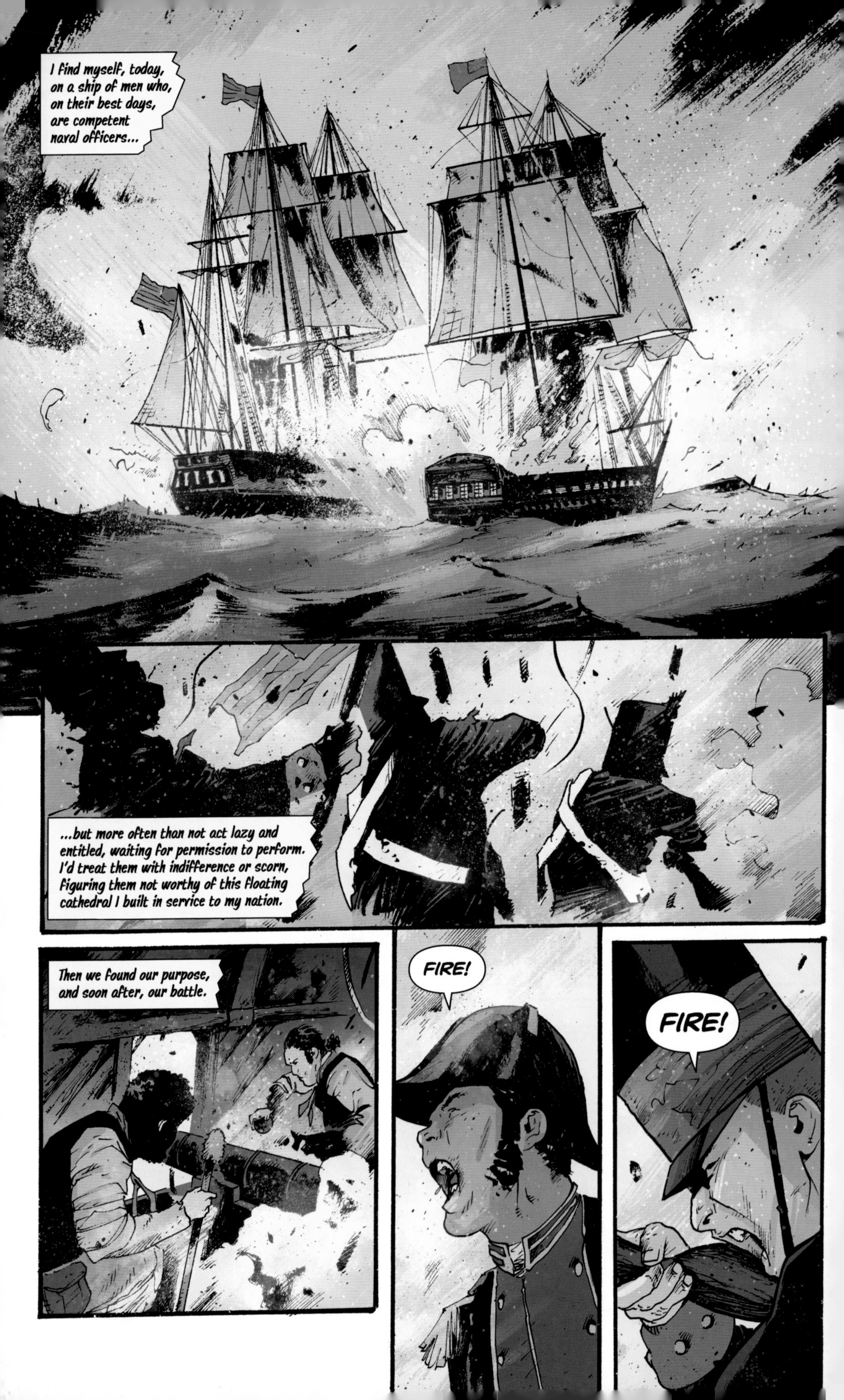
I find myself, today, on a ship of men who, on their best days, are competent naval officers...
...but more often than not act lazy and entitled, waiting for permission to perform. I'd treat them with indifference or scorn, figuring them not worthy of this floating cathedral I built in service to my nation.
Then we found our purpose, and soon after, our battle.
FIRE!
FIRE!

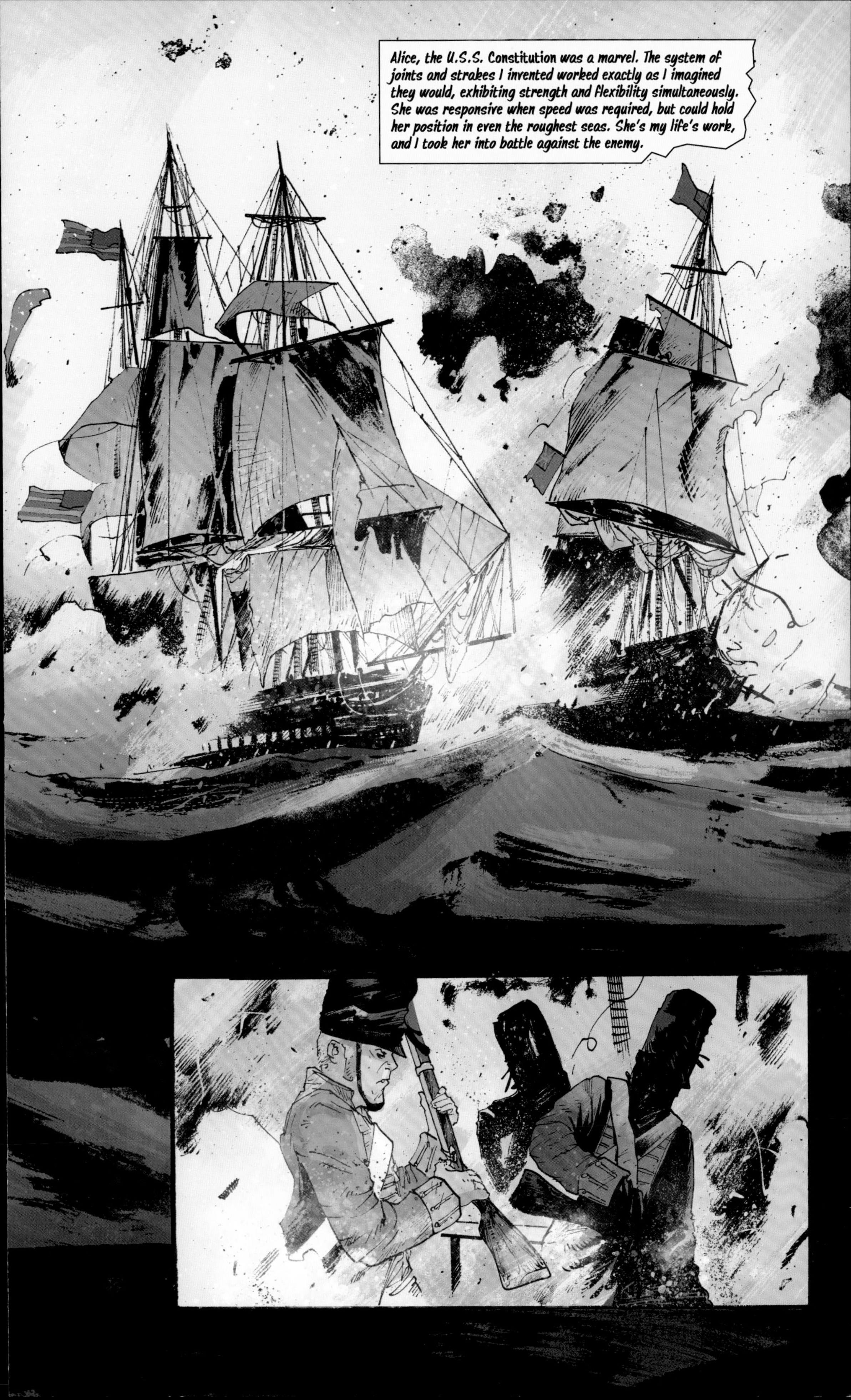
Alice, the U.S.S. Constitution was a marvel. The system of joints and strakes I invented worked exactly as I imagined they would, exhibiting strength and flexibility simultaneously. She was responsive when speed was required, but could hold her position in even the roughest seas. She's my life's work, and I took her into battle against the enemy.

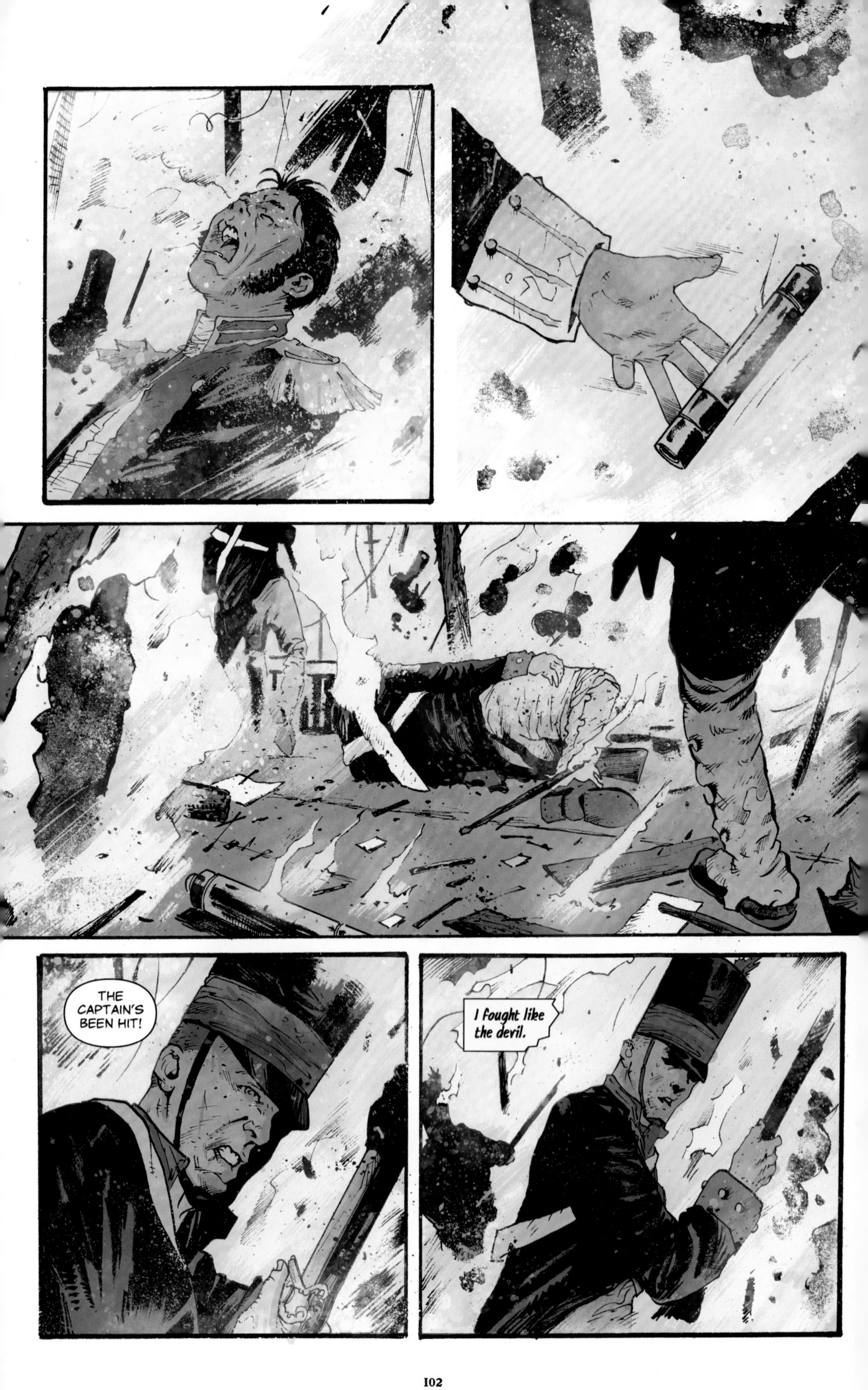
THE CAPTAIN'S BEEN HIT!
I fought like the devil.

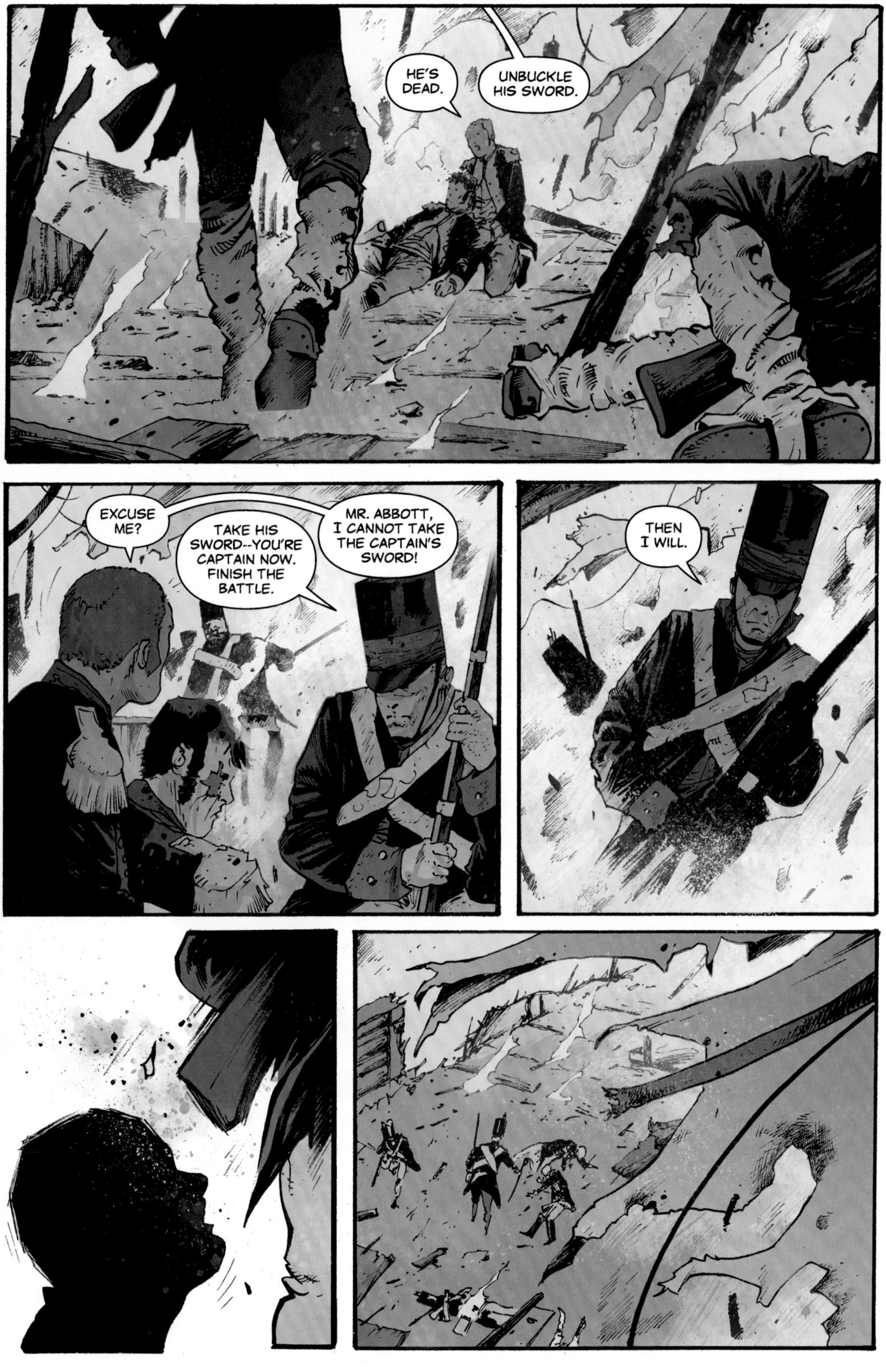
HE'S DEAD.
UNBUCKLE HIS SWORD.
EXCUSE ME?
TAKE HIS SWORD--YOU'RE CAPTAIN NOW. FINISH THE BATTLE.
MR. ABBOTT, I CANNOT TAKE THE CAPTAIN'S SWORD!
THEN I WILL.

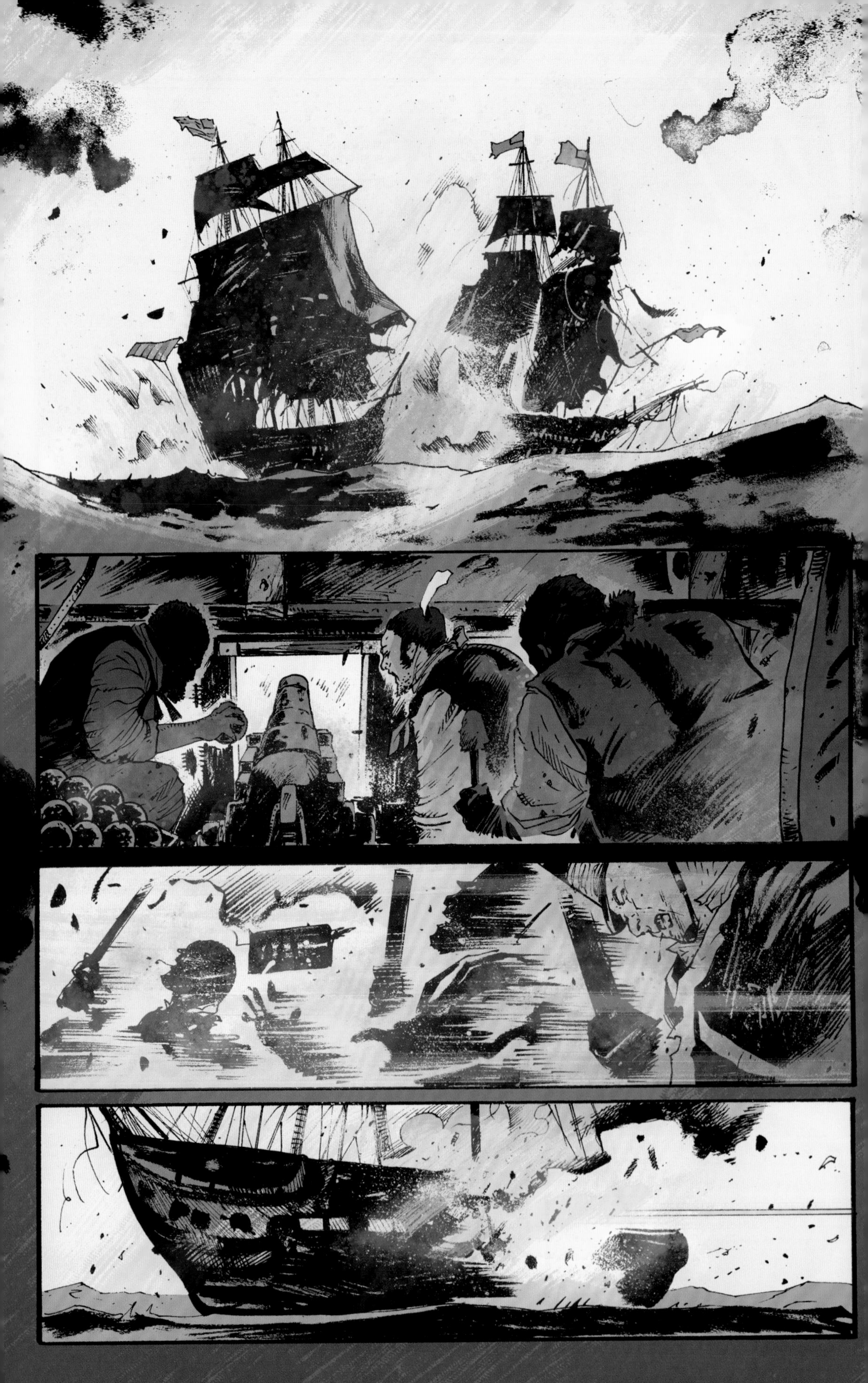

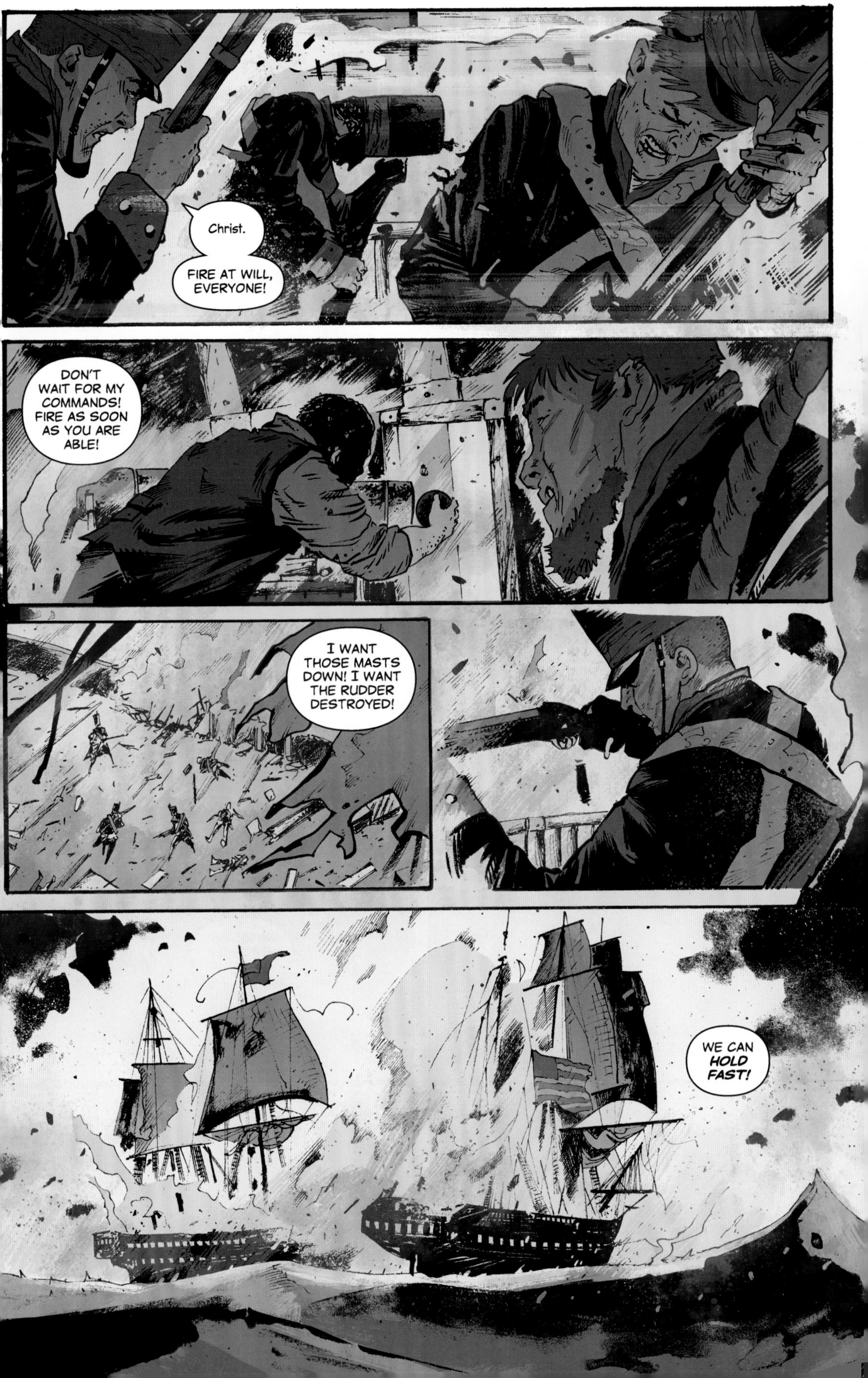
Christ.
FIRE AT WILL, EVERYONE!
DON'T WAIT FOR MY COMMANDS! FIRE AS SOON AS YOU ARE ABLE!
I WANT THOSE MASTS DOWN! I WANT THE RUDDER DESTROYED!
WE CAN *HOLD FAST!*

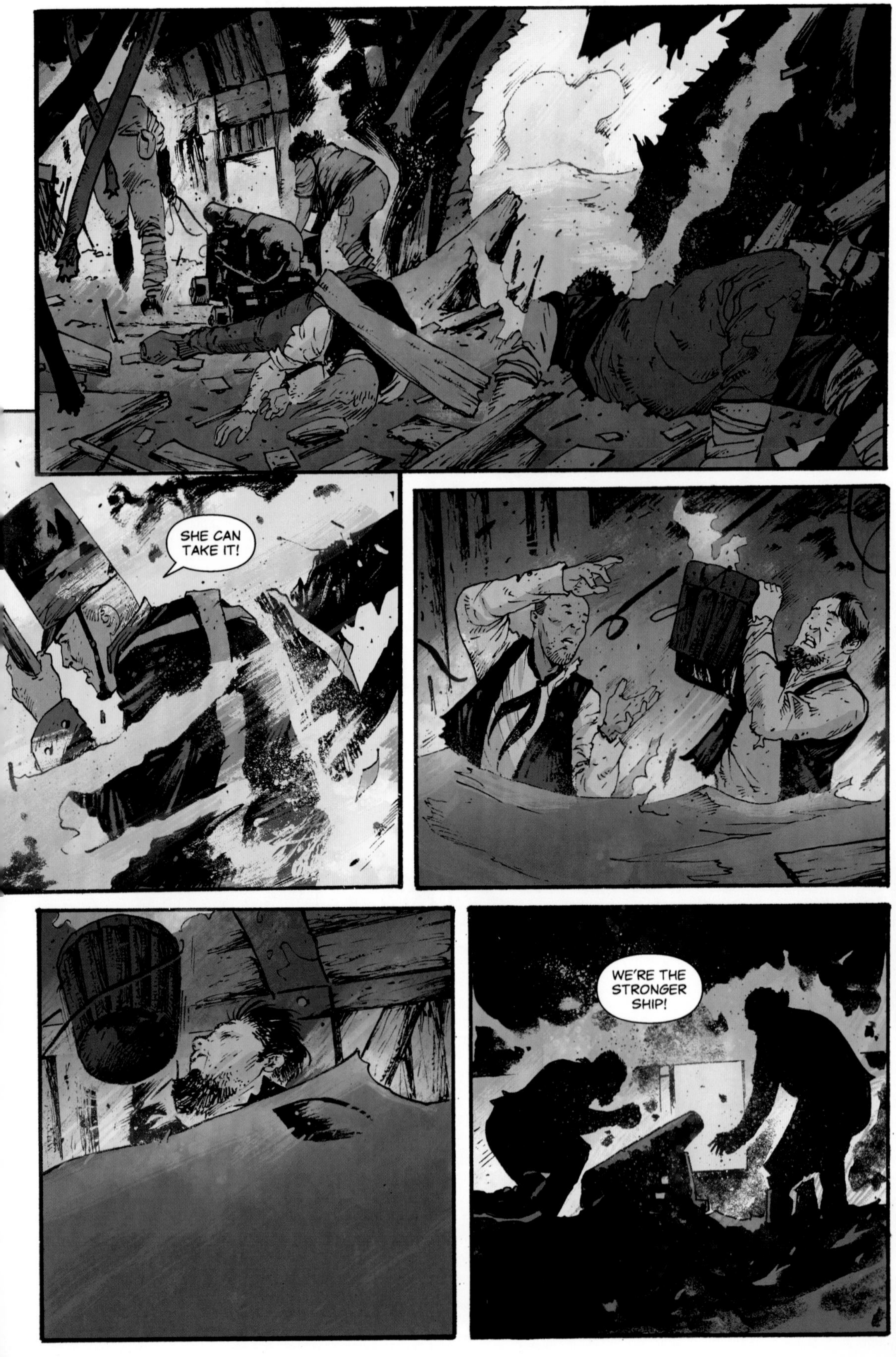
SHE CAN
TAKE IT!
WE'RE THE
STRONGER
SHIP!

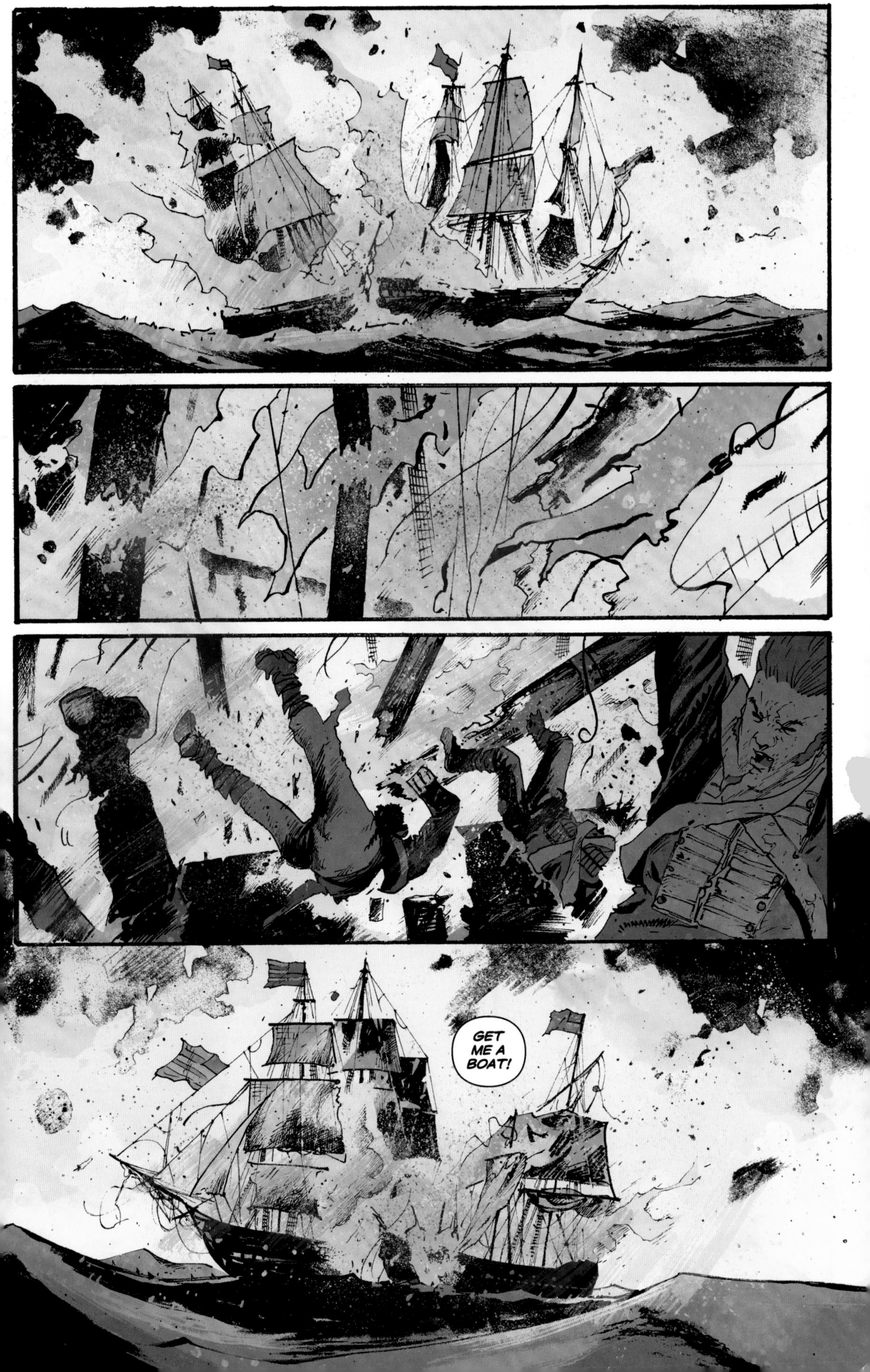
GET ME A BOAT!

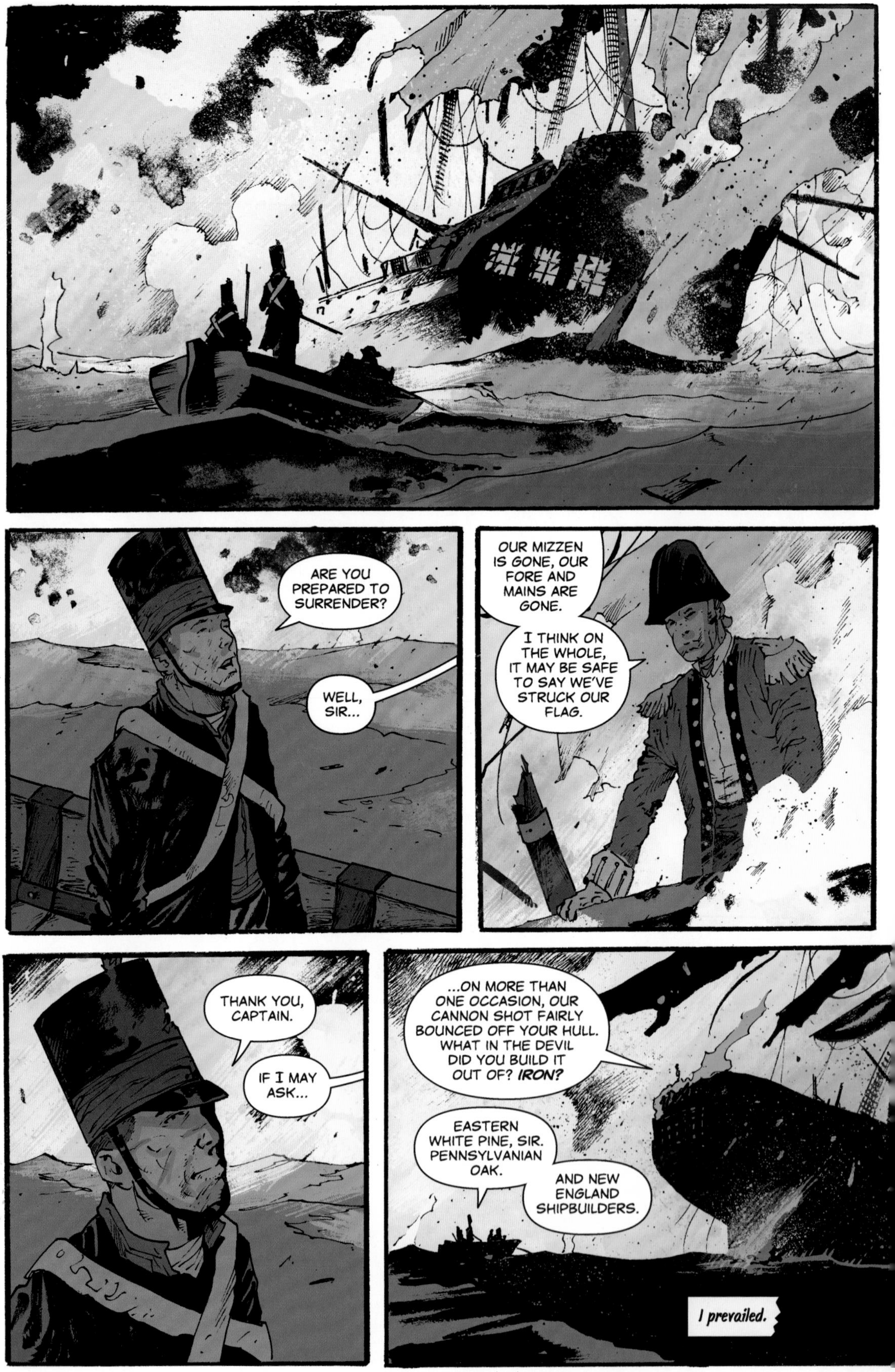
ARE YOU PREPARED TO SURRENDER?
WELL, SIR...
OUR MIZZEN IS GONE, OUR FORE AND MAINS ARE GONE.
I THINK ON THE WHOLE, IT MAY BE SAFE TO SAY WE'VE STRUCK OUR FLAG.
THANK YOU, CAPTAIN.
IF I MAY ASK...
...ON MORE THAN ONE OCCASION, OUR CANNON SHOT FAIRLY BOUNCED OFF YOUR HULL. WHAT IN THE DEVIL DID YOU BUILD IT OUT OF? ***IRON?***
EASTERN WHITE PINE, SIR. PENNSYLVANIAN OAK.
AND NEW ENGLAND SHIPBUILDERS.
I prevailed.

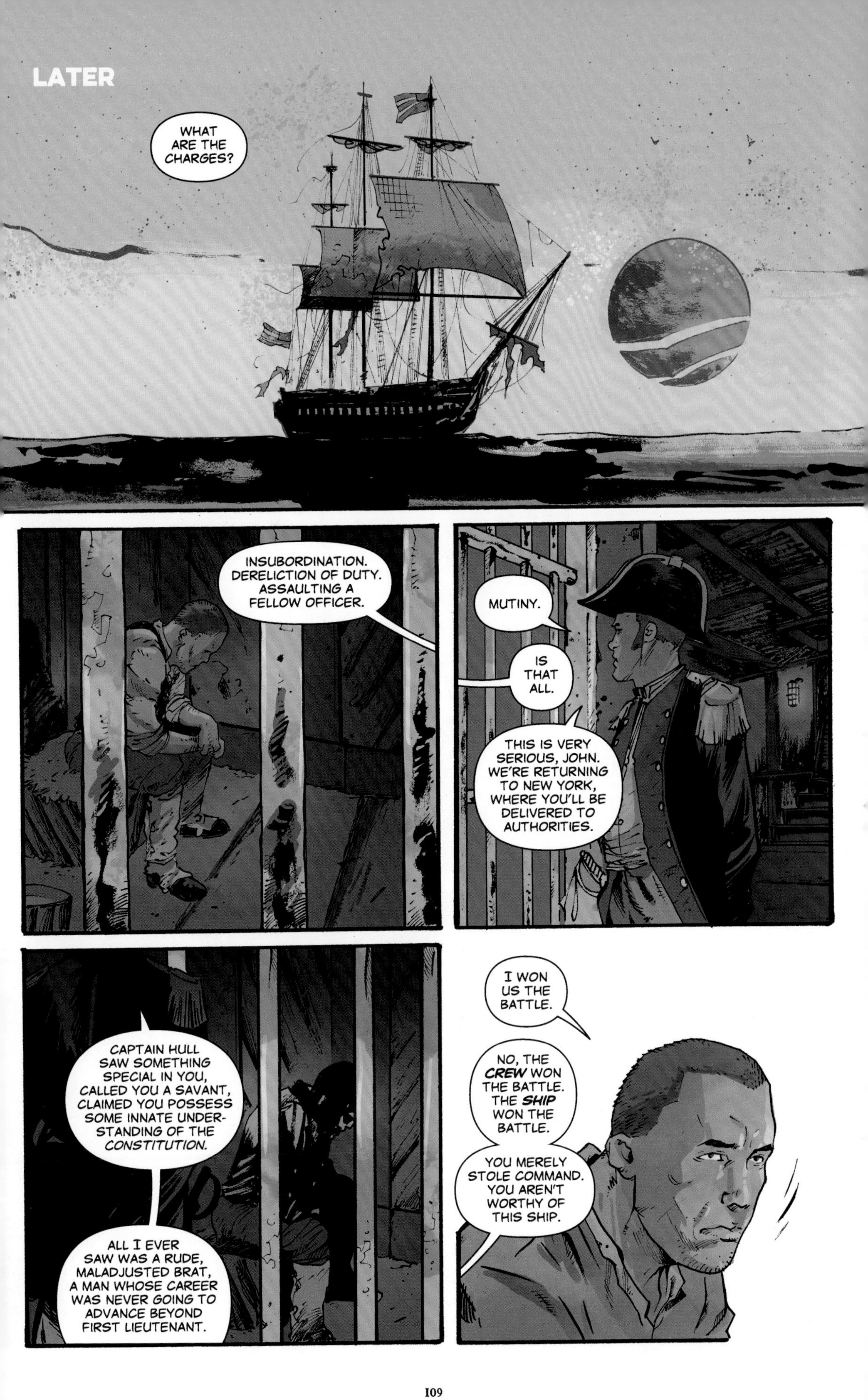
LATER
WHAT ARE THE CHARGES?
INSUBORDINATION. DERELICTION OF DUTY. ASSAULTING A FELLOW OFFICER.
MUTINY.
IS THAT ALL.
THIS IS VERY SERIOUS, JOHN. WE'RE RETURNING TO NEW YORK, WHERE YOU'LL BE DELIVERED TO AUTHORITIES.
CAPTAIN HULL SAW SOMETHING SPECIAL IN YOU, CALLED YOU A SAVANT, CLAIMED YOU POSSESS SOME INNATE UNDER-STANDING OF THE CONSTITUTION.
ALL I EVER SAW WAS A RUDE, MALADJUSTED BRAT, A MAN WHOSE CAREER WAS NEVER GOING TO ADVANCE BEYOND FIRST LIEUTENANT.
I WON US THE BATTLE.
NO, THE CREW WON THE BATTLE. THE SHIP WON THE BATTLE.
YOU MERELY STOLE COMMAND. YOU AREN'T WORTHY OF THIS SHIP.

I AM THE **SHIP!**

Good God...

DID YOU **HEAR ME?**

I HEARD. YOU SHOULD BE VERY COMFORTABLE DOWN HERE, THEN.

Now, with no career left, I find myself for the first time in three decades without a clear image in my head of who I'm meant to be. I am adrift, subject to the whims of forces beyond my control.

Then I see from your letters that you live in New York.

And so I dare to imagine a new future. One I have not earned and do not deserve.

But I am not beyond redemption.

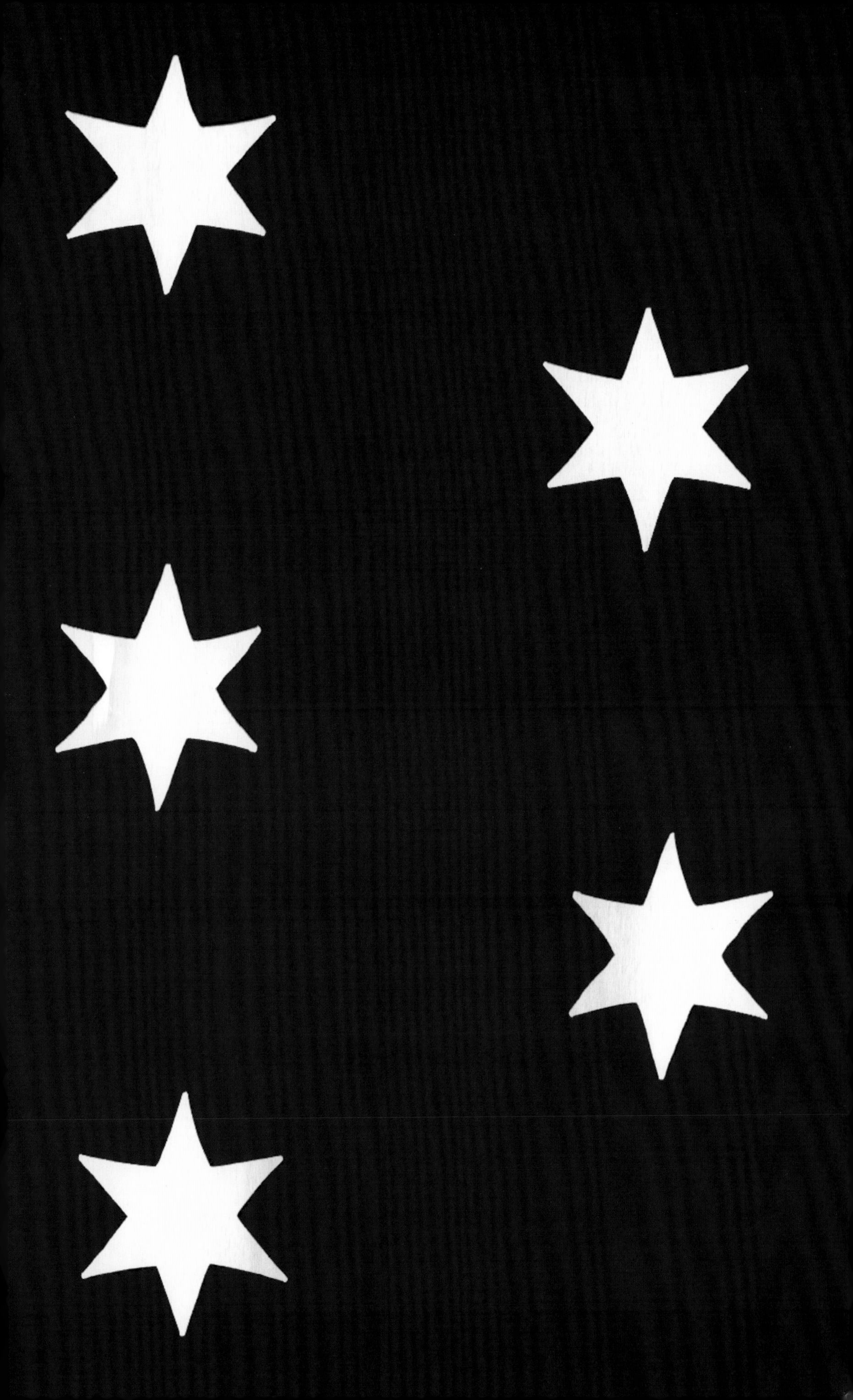

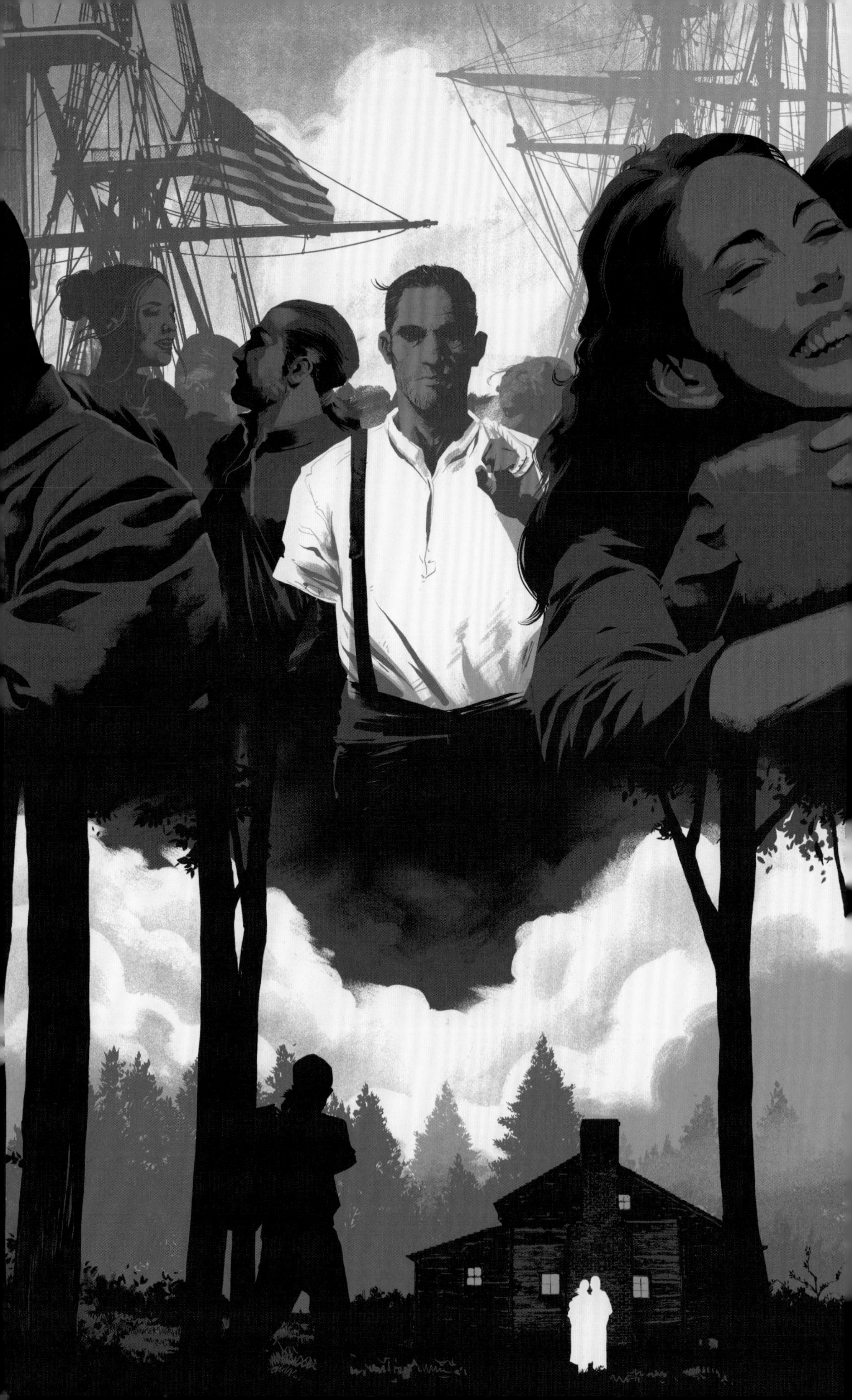

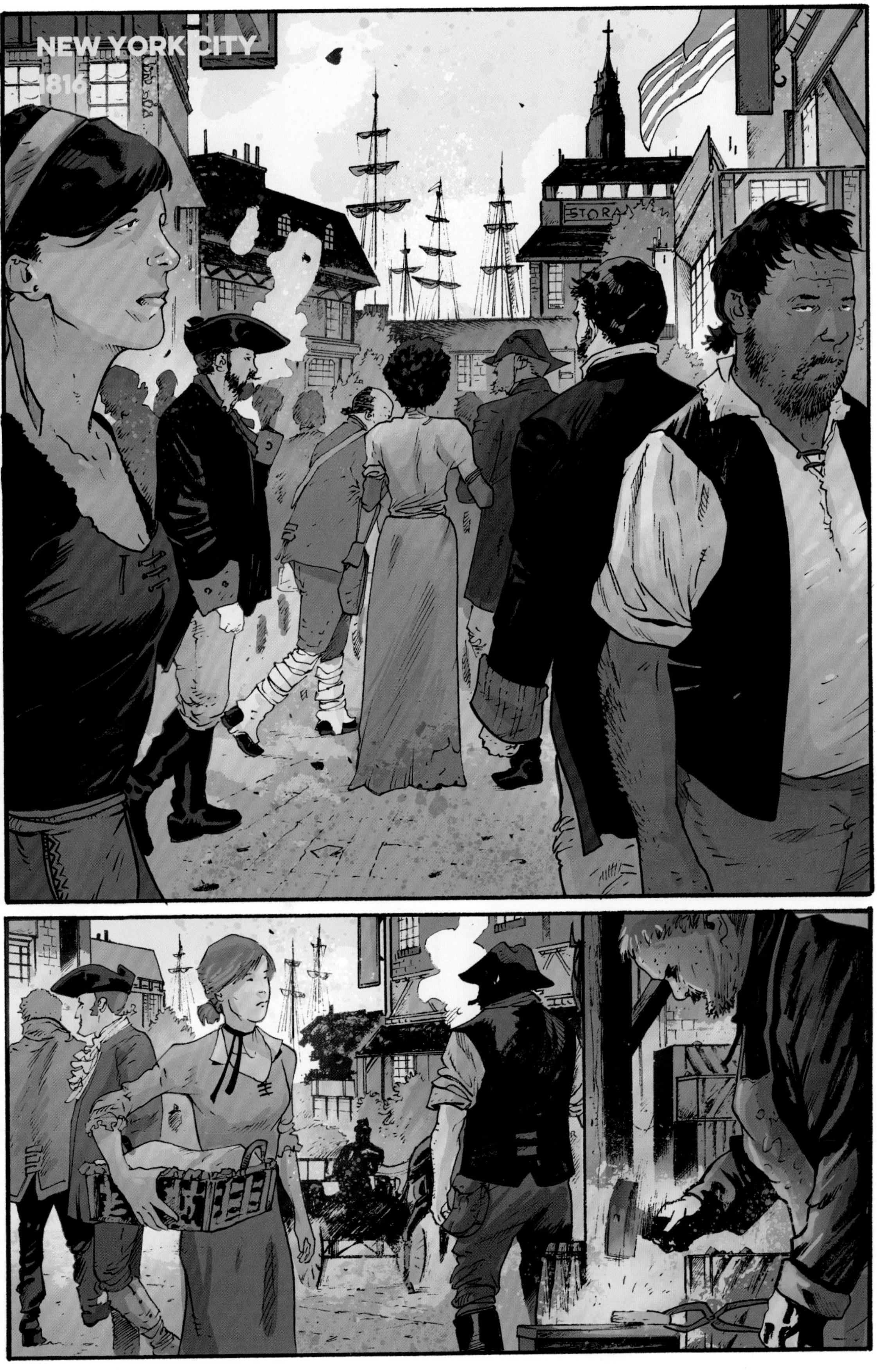
NEW YORK CITY
1816
STORA

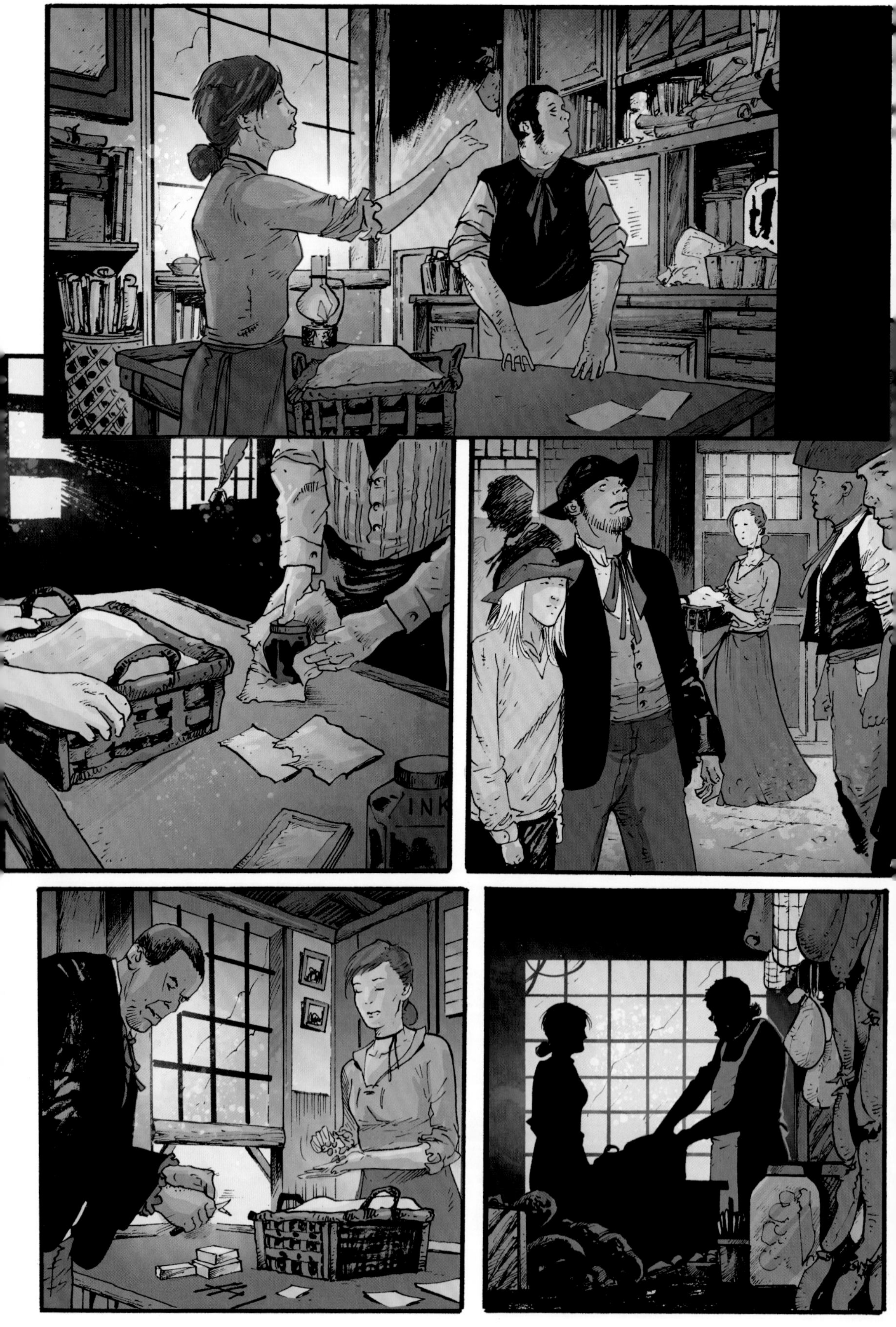
INK

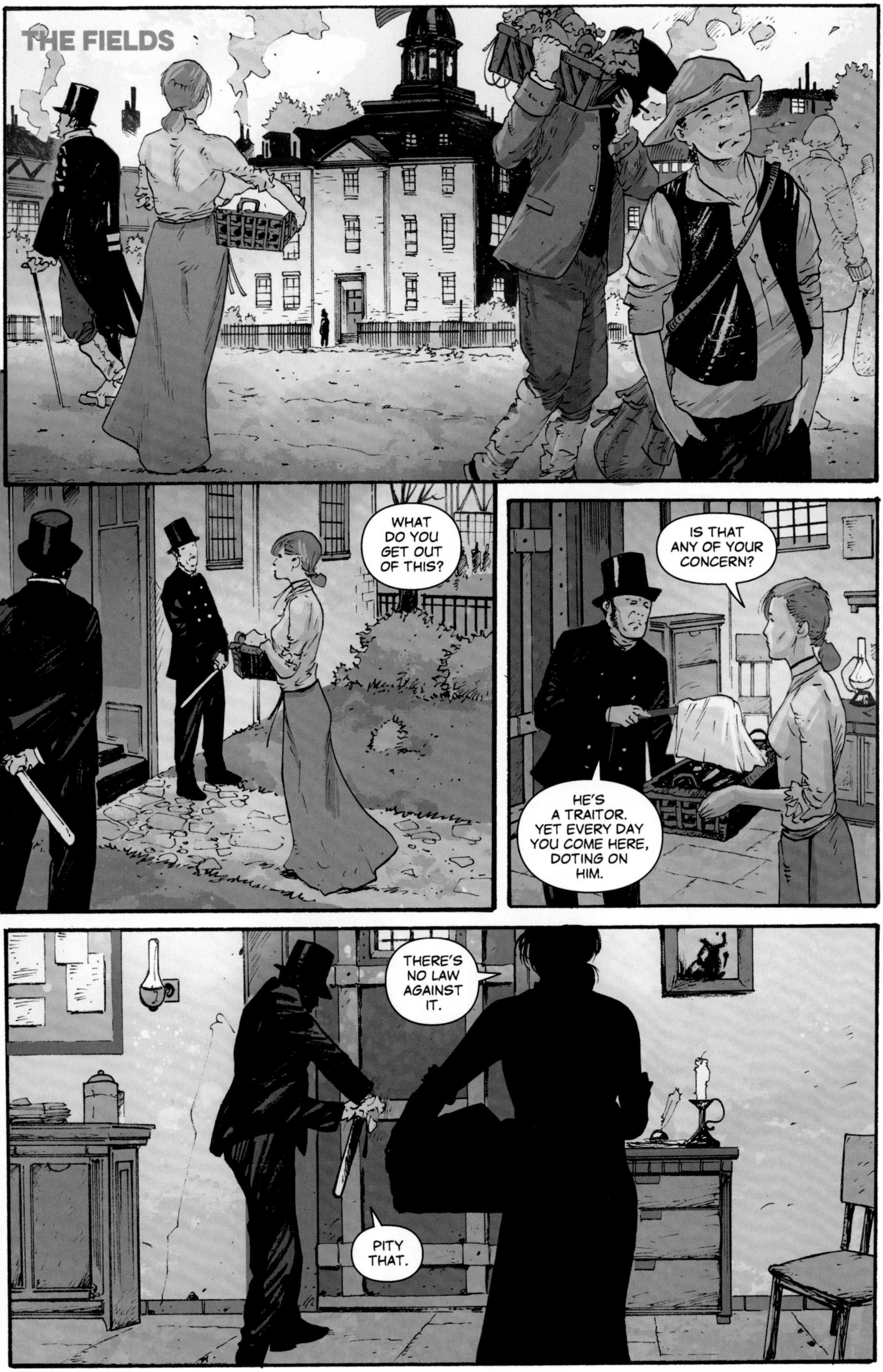
THE FIELDS
WHAT DO YOU GET OUT OF THIS?
IS THAT ANY OF YOUR CONCERN?
HE'S A TRAITOR. YET EVERY DAY YOU COME HERE, DOTING ON HIM.
THERE'S NO LAW AGAINST IT.
PITY THAT.

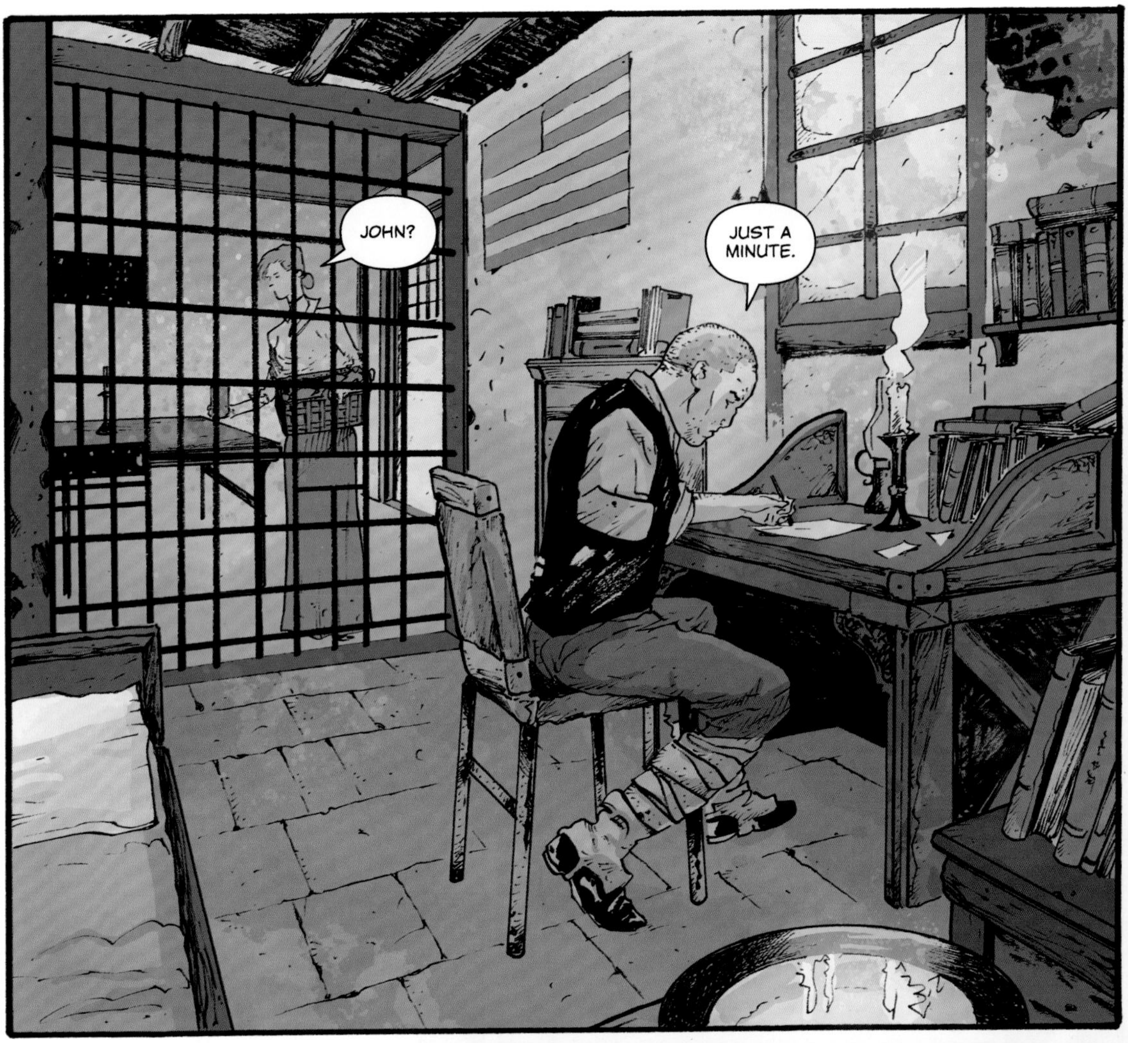
JOHN?
JUST A MINUTE.

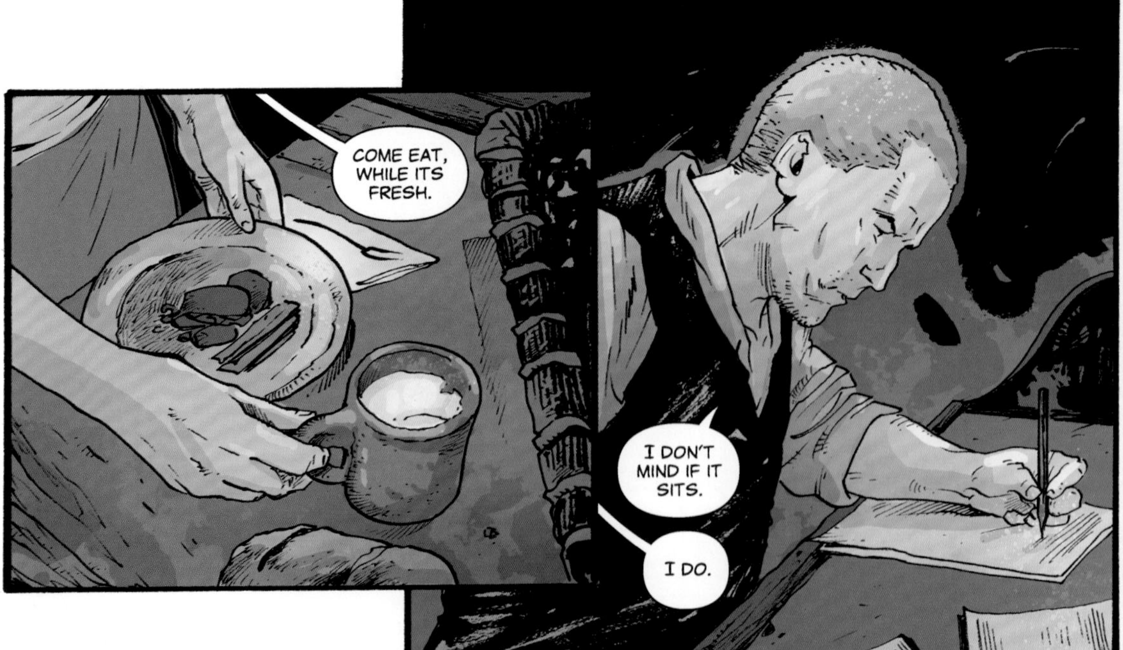
COME EAT, WHILE ITS FRESH.
I DON'T MIND IF IT SITS.
I DO.

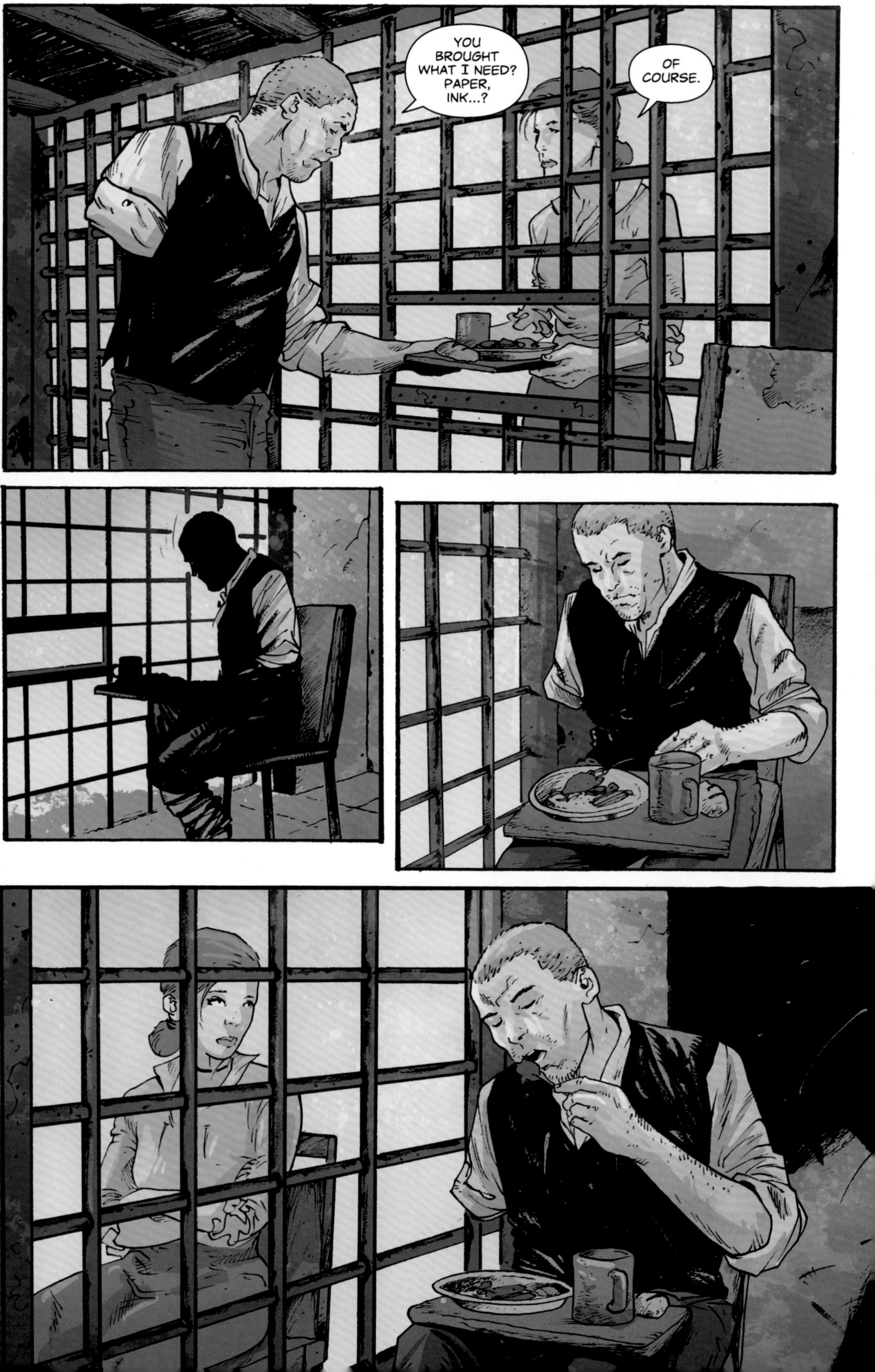
YOU BROUGHT WHAT I NEED? PAPER, INK...?
OF COURSE.

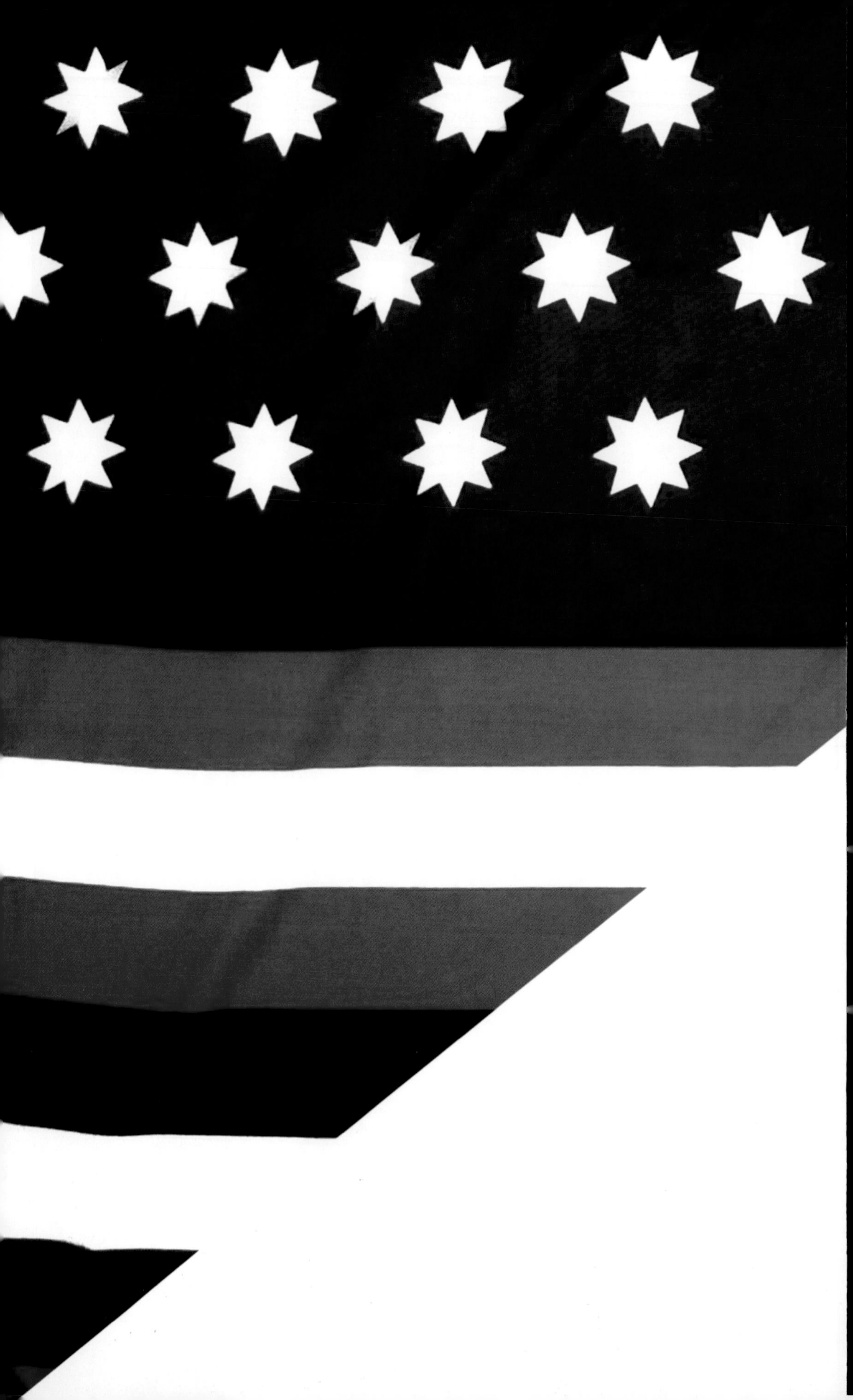

REBELS

"THESE FREE AND INDEPENDENT STATES" - PART 5 OF 5

IN WHICH AMERICA WINS ITS SECOND WAR AGAINST BRITAIN, AND JOHN ABBOTT GOES HOME.

BRIAN WOOD · ANDREA MUTTI · LAUREN AFFE · MATT TAYLOR

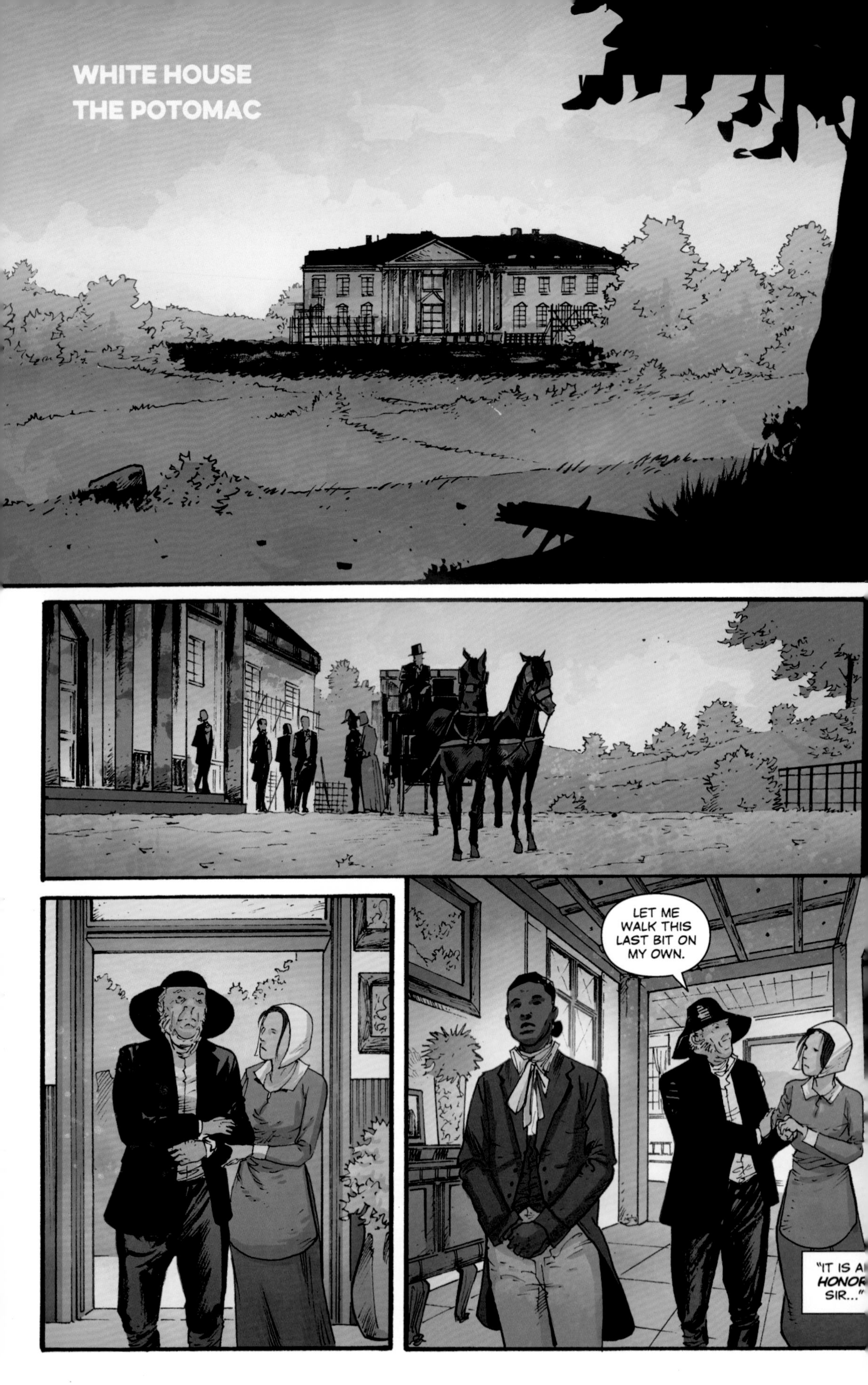
WHITE HOUSE
THE POTOMAC
LET ME WALK THIS LAST BIT ON MY OWN.
"IT IS A
HONOR
SIR..."

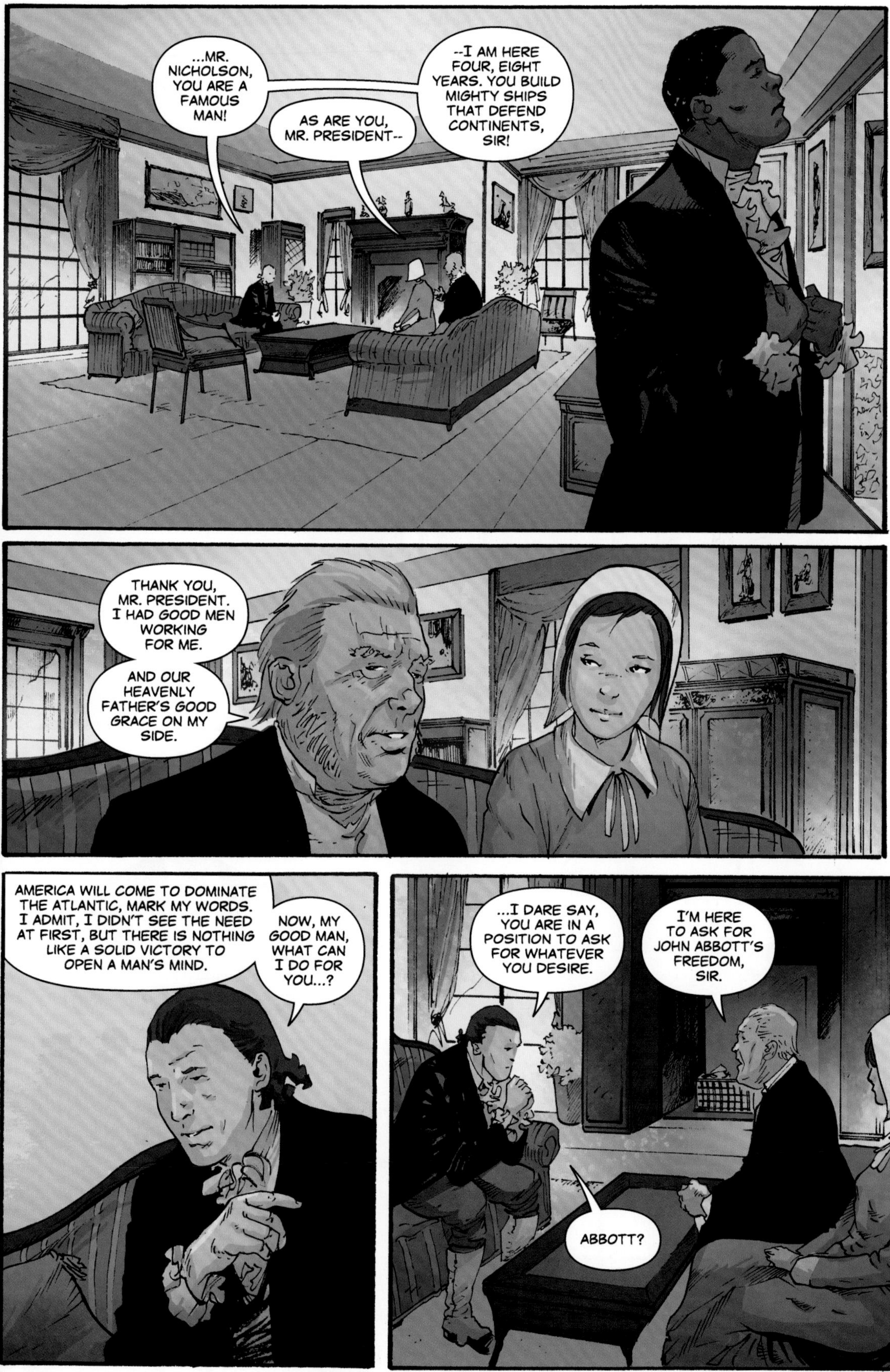
...MR. NICHOLSON, YOU ARE A FAMOUS MAN!
AS ARE YOU, MR. PRESIDENT--
--I AM HERE FOUR, EIGHT YEARS. YOU BUILD MIGHTY SHIPS THAT DEFEND CONTINENTS, SIR!
THANK YOU, MR. PRESIDENT. I HAD GOOD MEN WORKING FOR ME.
AND OUR HEAVENLY FATHER'S GOOD GRACE ON MY SIDE.
AMERICA WILL COME TO DOMINATE THE ATLANTIC, MARK MY WORDS. I ADMIT, I DIDN'T SEE THE NEED AT FIRST, BUT THERE IS NOTHING LIKE A SOLID VICTORY TO OPEN A MAN'S MIND.
NOW, MY GOOD MAN, WHAT CAN I DO FOR YOU...?
...I DARE SAY, YOU ARE IN A POSITION TO ASK FOR WHATEVER YOU DESIRE.
I'M HERE TO ASK FOR JOHN ABBOTT'S FREEDOM, SIR.
ABBOTT?

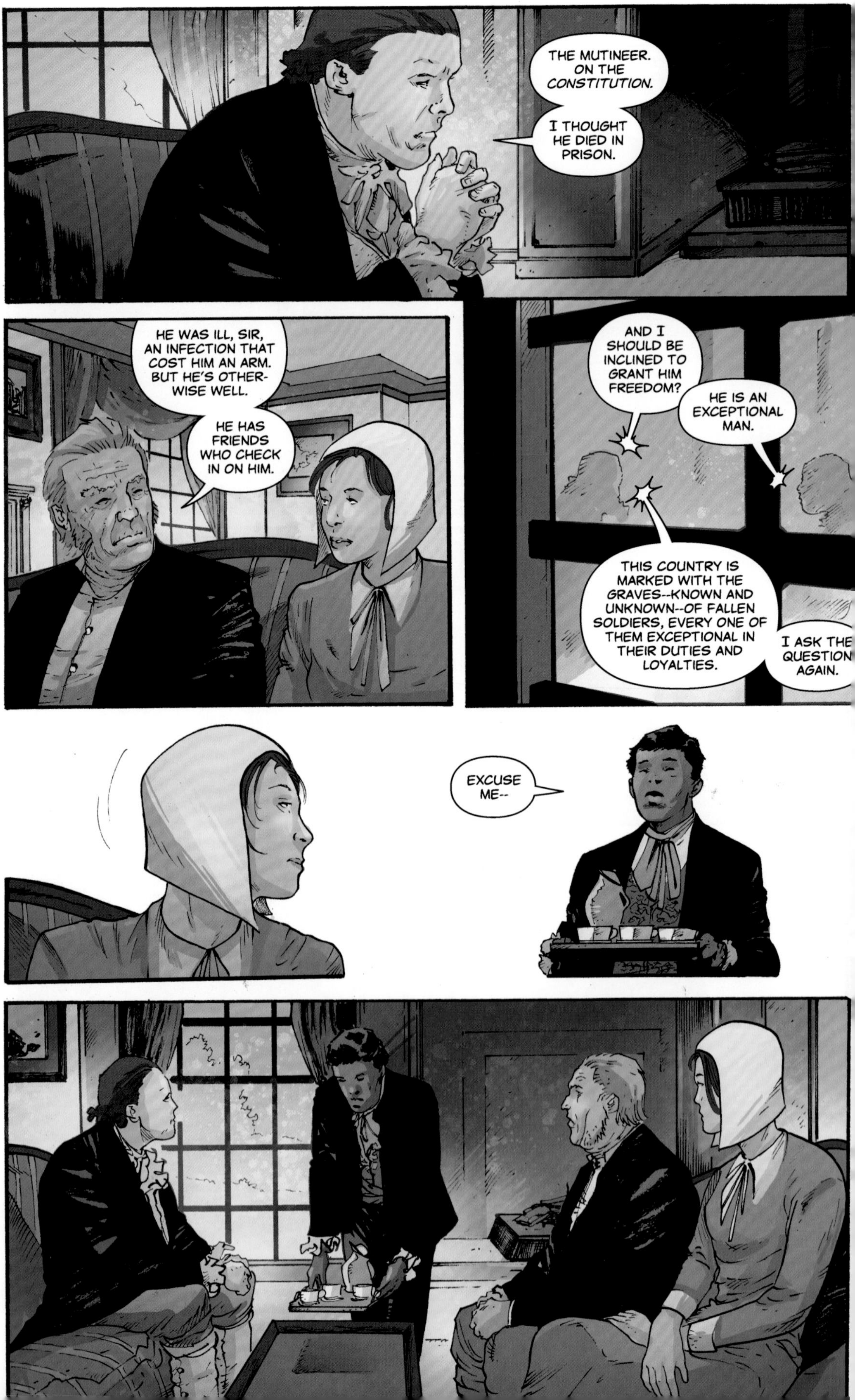
THE MUTINEER. ON THE CONSTITUTION.
I THOUGHT HE DIED IN PRISON.
HE WAS ILL, SIR, AN INFECTION THAT COST HIM AN ARM. BUT HE'S OTHERWISE WELL.
HE HAS FRIENDS WHO CHECK IN ON HIM.
AND I SHOULD BE INCLINED TO GRANT HIM FREEDOM?
HE IS AN EXCEPTIONAL MAN.
THIS COUNTRY IS MARKED WITH THE GRAVES--KNOWN AND UNKNOWN--OF FALLEN SOLDIERS, EVERY ONE OF THEM EXCEPTIONAL IN THEIR DUTIES AND LOYALTIES.
I ASK THE QUESTION AGAIN.
EXCUSE ME--

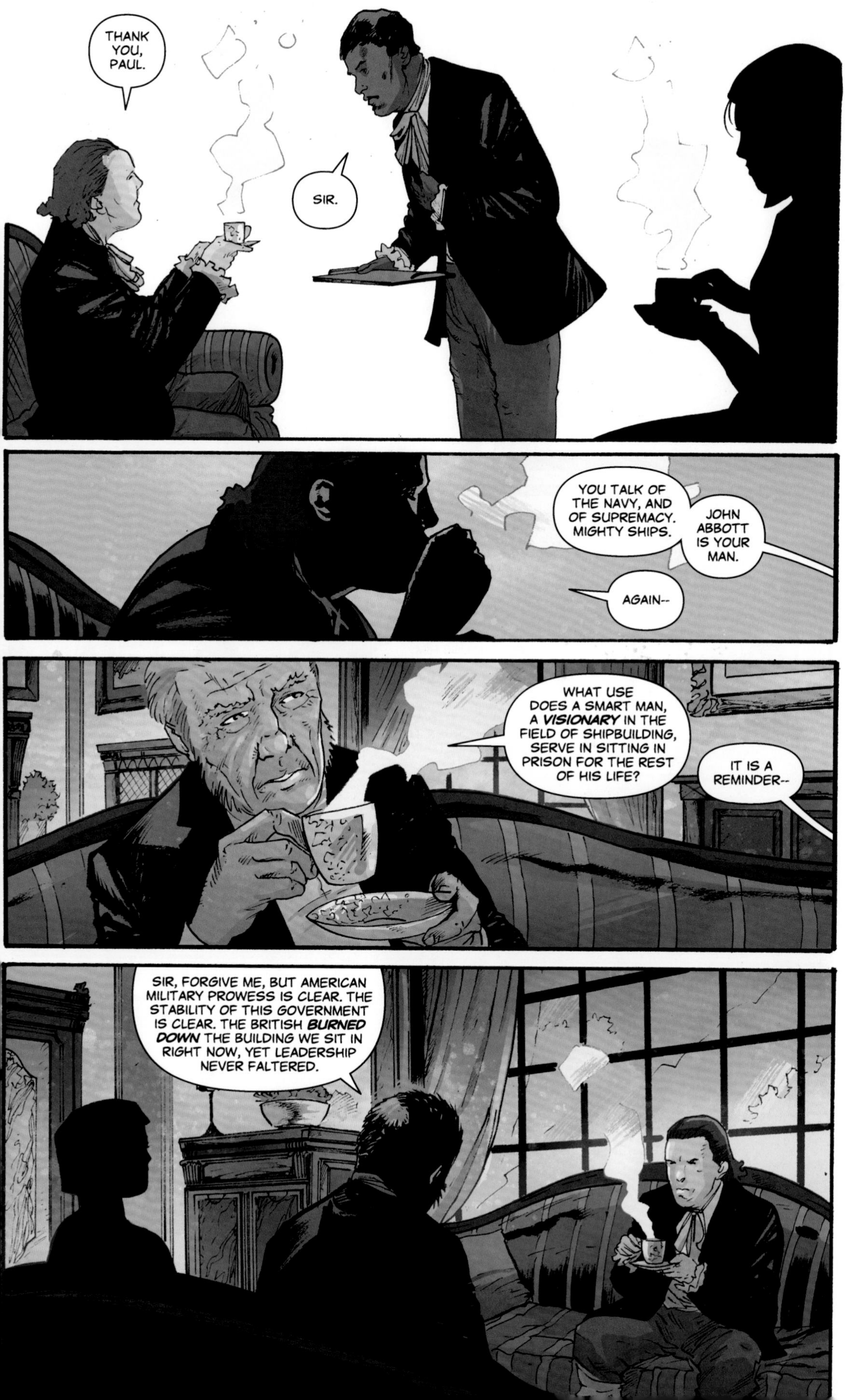
THANK YOU, PAUL.
SIR.
YOU TALK OF THE NAVY, AND OF SUPREMACY. MIGHTY SHIPS.
JOHN ABBOTT IS YOUR MAN.
AGAIN--
WHAT USE DOES A SMART MAN, A VISIONARY IN THE FIELD OF SHIPBUILDING, SERVE IN SITTING IN PRISON FOR THE REST OF HIS LIFE?
IT IS A REMINDER--
SIR, FORGIVE ME, BUT AMERICAN MILITARY PROWESS IS CLEAR. THE STABILITY OF THIS GOVERNMENT IS CLEAR. THE BRITISH BURNED DOWN THE BUILDING WE SIT IN RIGHT NOW, YET LEADERSHIP NEVER FALTERED.

MR. PRESIDENT, YOU WORRY ABOUT THE MESSAGE IT WOULD SIGNAL TO FREE A MAN CONVICTED OF MUTINY.

PERHAPS INSTEAD CONSIDER THE IDEA THAT THIS NATION IS STRONG AND SECURE ENOUGH TO DEMONSTRATE THIS ONE SMALL MERCY.

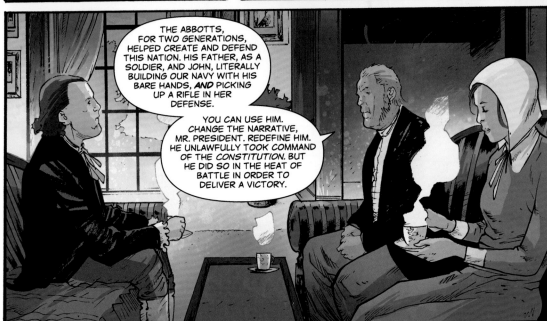

THE ABBOTTS, FOR TWO GENERATIONS, HELPED CREATE AND DEFEND THIS NATION. HIS FATHER, AS A SOLDIER, AND JOHN, LITERALLY BUILDING OUR NAVY WITH HIS BARE HANDS, *AND* PICKING UP A RIFLE IN HER DEFENSE.

YOU CAN USE HIM. CHANGE THE NARRATIVE, MR. PRESIDENT. REDEFINE HIM. HE UNLAWFULLY TOOK COMMAND OF THE *CONSTITUTION.* BUT HE DID SO IN THE HEAT OF BATTLE IN ORDER TO DELIVER A VICTORY.

HE STILL WANTS TO SERVE.

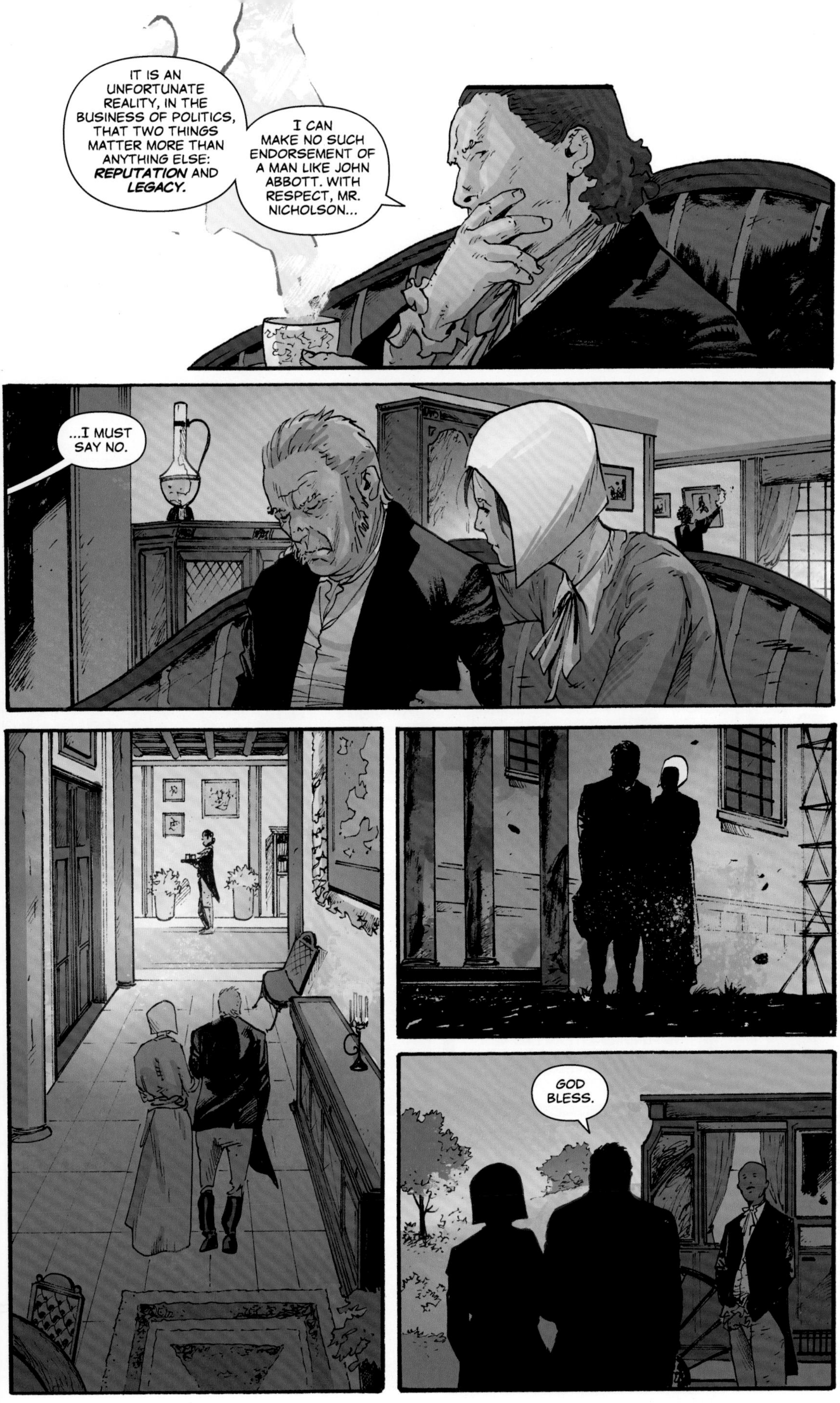
IT IS AN UNFORTUNATE REALITY, IN THE BUSINESS OF POLITICS, THAT TWO THINGS MATTER MORE THAN ANYTHING ELSE: REPUTATION AND LEGACY.
I CAN MAKE NO SUCH ENDORSEMENT OF A MAN LIKE JOHN ABBOTT. WITH RESPECT, MR. NICHOLSON...
...I MUST SAY NO.
GOD BLESS.

MR. NICHOLSON!

STOP THE CARRIAGE, PLEASE!

EH?

MR. NICHOLSON!

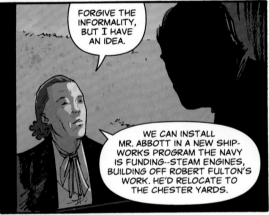

FORGIVE THE INFORMALITY, BUT I HAVE AN IDEA.

WE CAN INSTALL MR. ABBOTT IN A NEW SHIP-WORKS PROGRAM THE NAVY IS FUNDING--STEAM ENGINES, BUILDING OFF ROBERT FULTON'S WORK. HE'D RELOCATE TO THE CHESTER YARDS.

WOULD HE BE UP TO IT?

THERE'S A CATCH.

ABSOLUTELY.

NO ONE CAN KNOW.

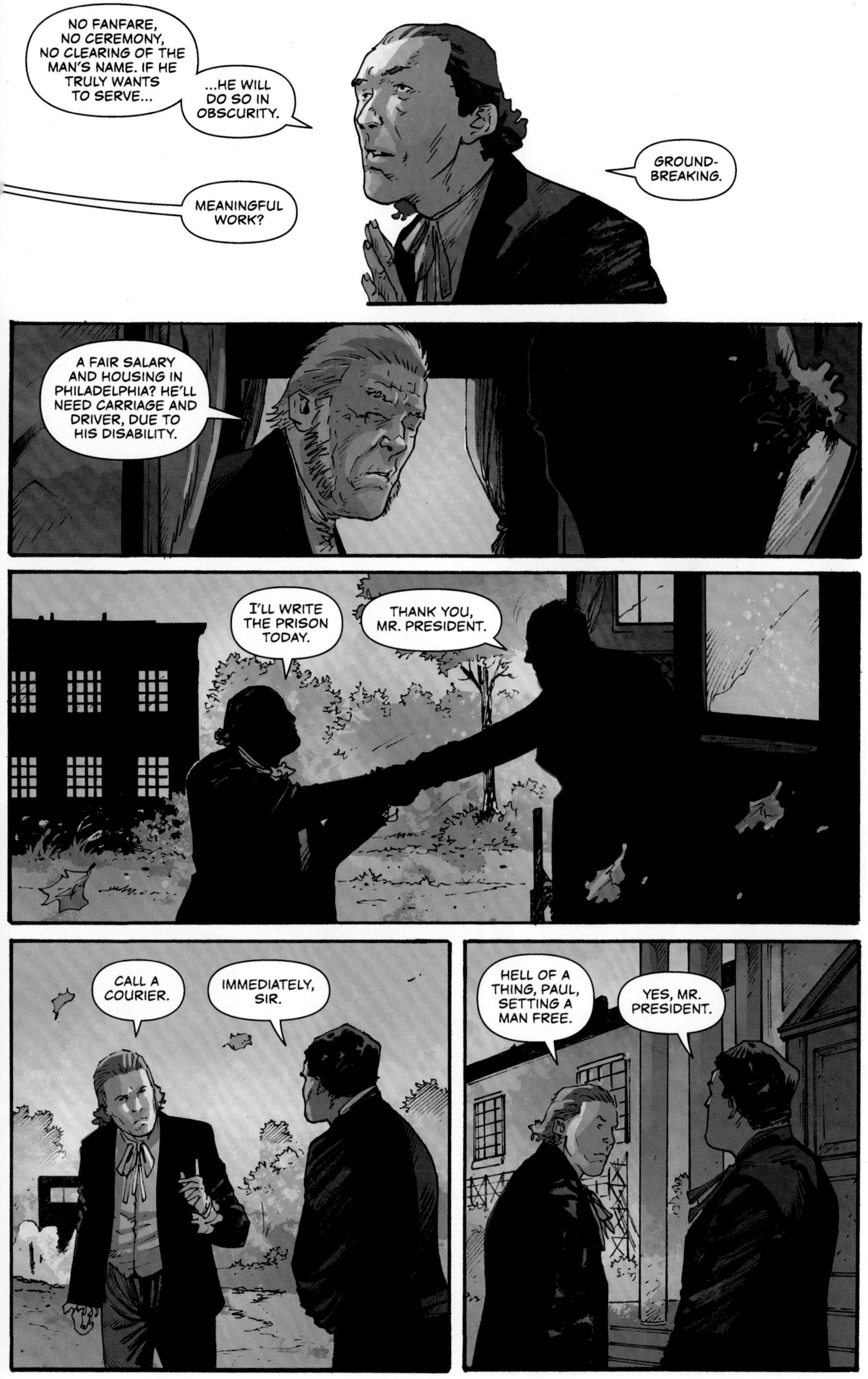
NO FANFARE, NO CEREMONY, NO CLEARING OF THE MAN'S NAME. IF HE TRULY WANTS TO SERVE...
...HE WILL DO SO IN OBSCURITY.
MEANINGFUL WORK?
GROUND-BREAKING.
A FAIR SALARY AND HOUSING IN PHILADELPHIA? HE'LL NEED CARRIAGE AND DRIVER, DUE TO HIS DISABILITY.
I'LL WRITE THE PRISON TODAY.
THANK YOU, MR. PRESIDENT.
CALL A COURIER.
IMMEDIATELY, SIR.
HELL OF A THING, PAUL, SETTING A MAN FREE.
YES, MR. PRESIDENT.

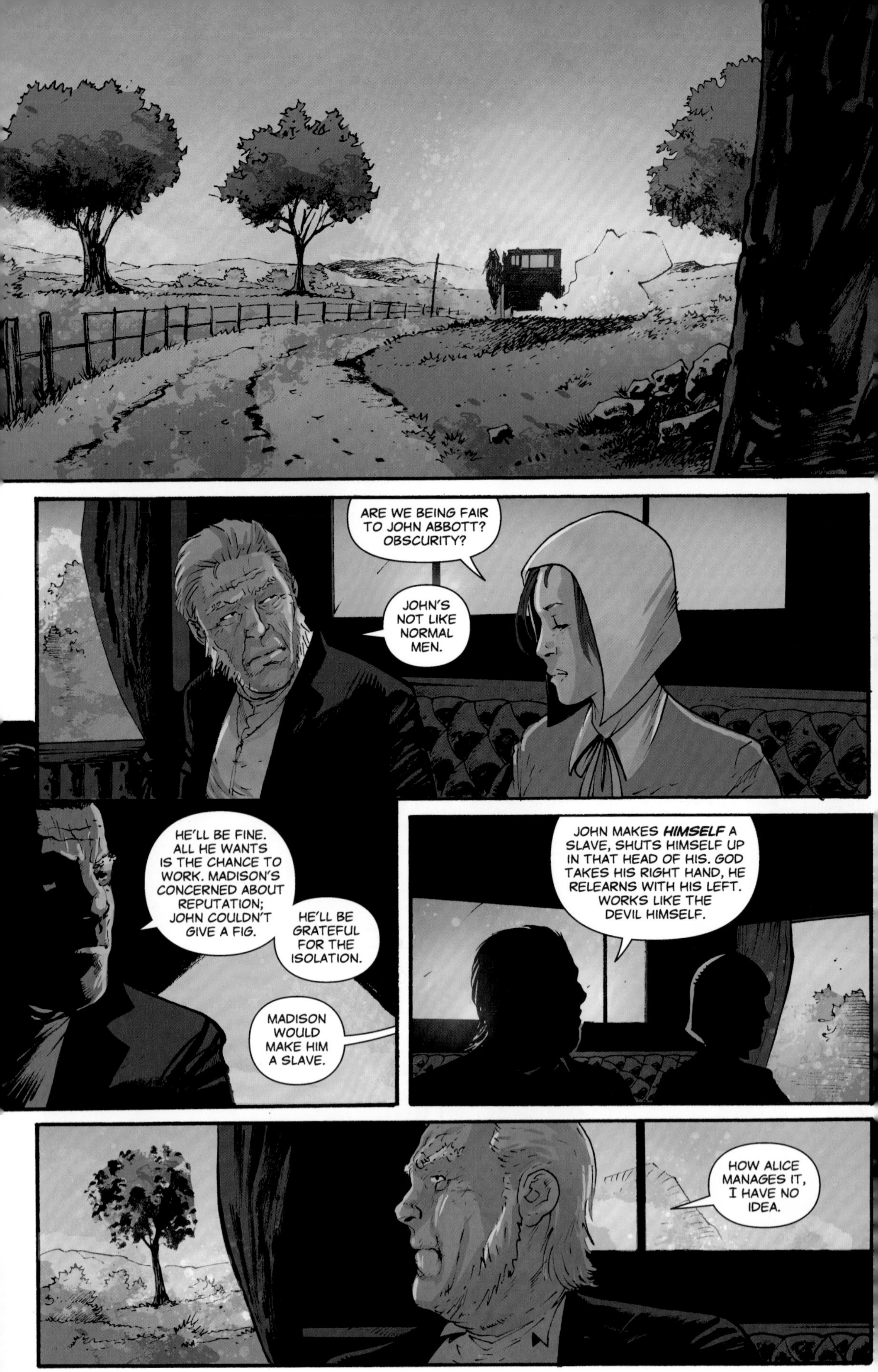
ARE WE BEING FAIR TO JOHN ABBOTT? OBSCURITY?
JOHN'S NOT LIKE NORMAL MEN.
HE'LL BE FINE. ALL HE WANTS IS THE CHANCE TO WORK. MADISON'S CONCERNED ABOUT REPUTATION; JOHN COULDN'T GIVE A FIG.
HE'LL BE GRATEFUL FOR THE ISOLATION.
MADISON WOULD MAKE HIM A SLAVE.
JOHN MAKES *HIMSELF* A SLAVE, SHUTS HIMSELF UP IN THAT HEAD OF HIS. GOD TAKES HIS RIGHT HAND, HE RELEARNS WITH HIS LEFT. WORKS LIKE THE DEVIL HIMSELF.
HOW ALICE MANAGES IT, I HAVE NO IDEA.

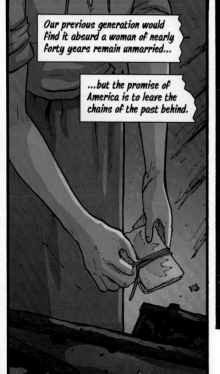

Our previous generation would find it absurd a woman of nearly forty years remain unmarried...

...but the promise of America is to leave the chains of the past behind.

And I make the choices I make as a woman, free to ally myself with the man I love.

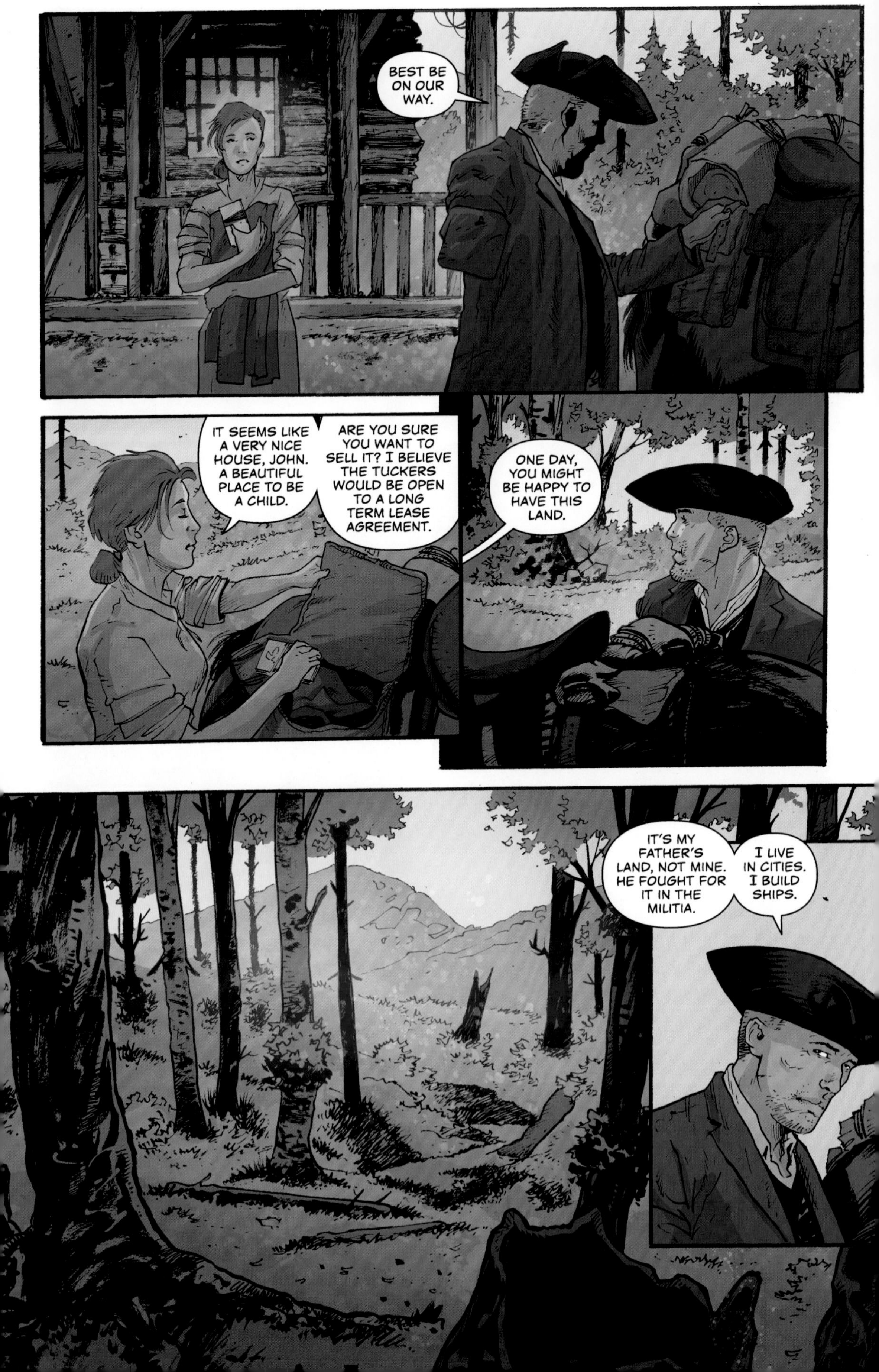
BEST BE ON OUR WAY.
IT SEEMS LIKE A VERY NICE HOUSE, JOHN. A BEAUTIFUL PLACE TO BE A CHILD.
ARE YOU SURE YOU WANT TO SELL IT? I BELIEVE THE TUCKERS WOULD BE OPEN TO A LONG TERM LEASE AGREEMENT.
ONE DAY, YOU MIGHT BE HAPPY TO HAVE THIS LAND.
IT'S MY FATHER'S LAND, NOT MINE. HE FOUGHT FOR IT IN THE MILITIA.
I LIVE IN CITIES. I BUILD SHIPS.

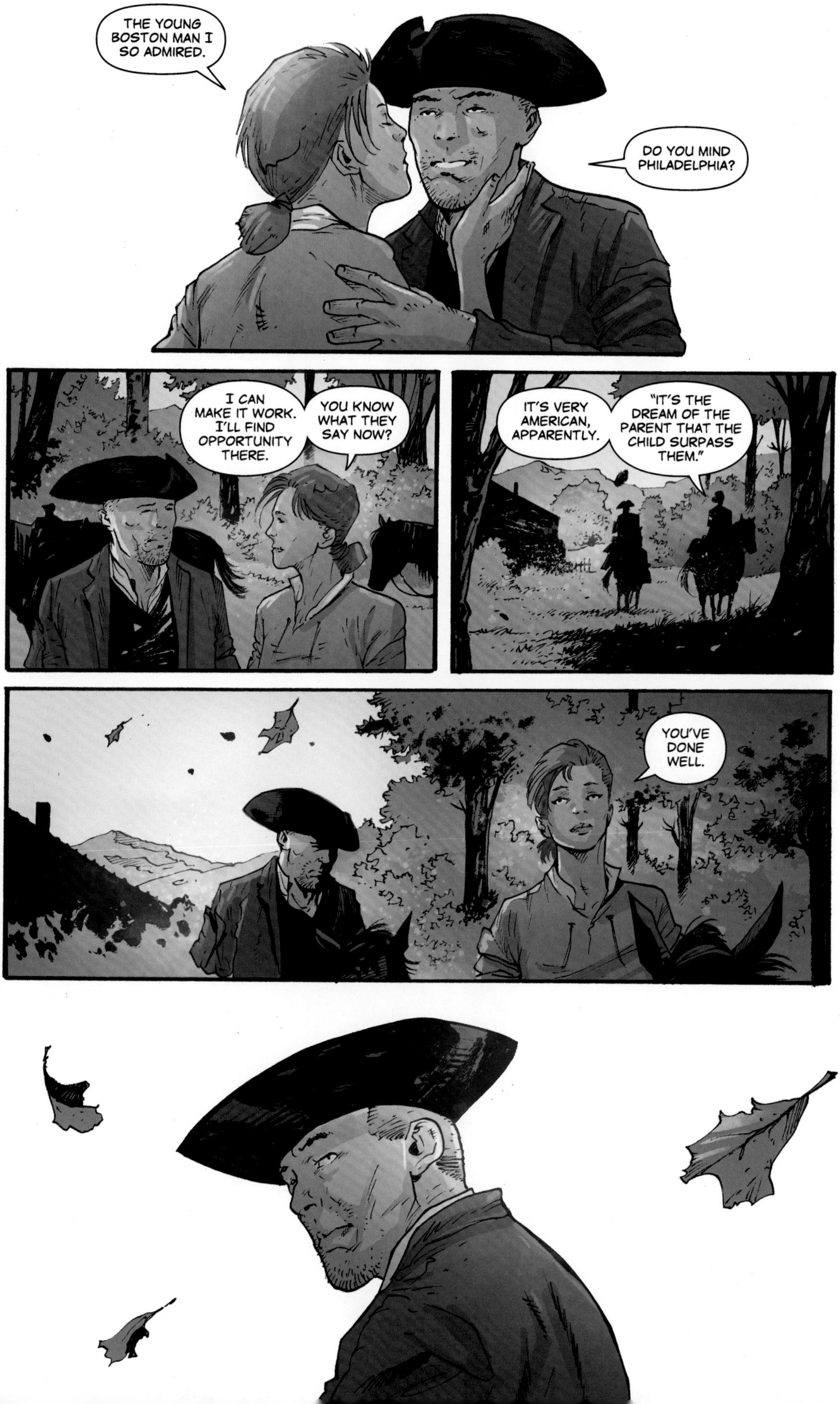
THE YOUNG BOSTON MAN I SO ADMIRED.
DO YOU MIND PHILADELPHIA?
I CAN MAKE IT WORK. I'LL FIND OPPORTUNITY THERE.
YOU KNOW WHAT THEY SAY NOW?
IT'S VERY AMERICAN, APPARENTLY.
"IT'S THE DREAM OF THE PARENT THAT THE CHILD SURPASS THEM."
YOU'VE DONE WELL.

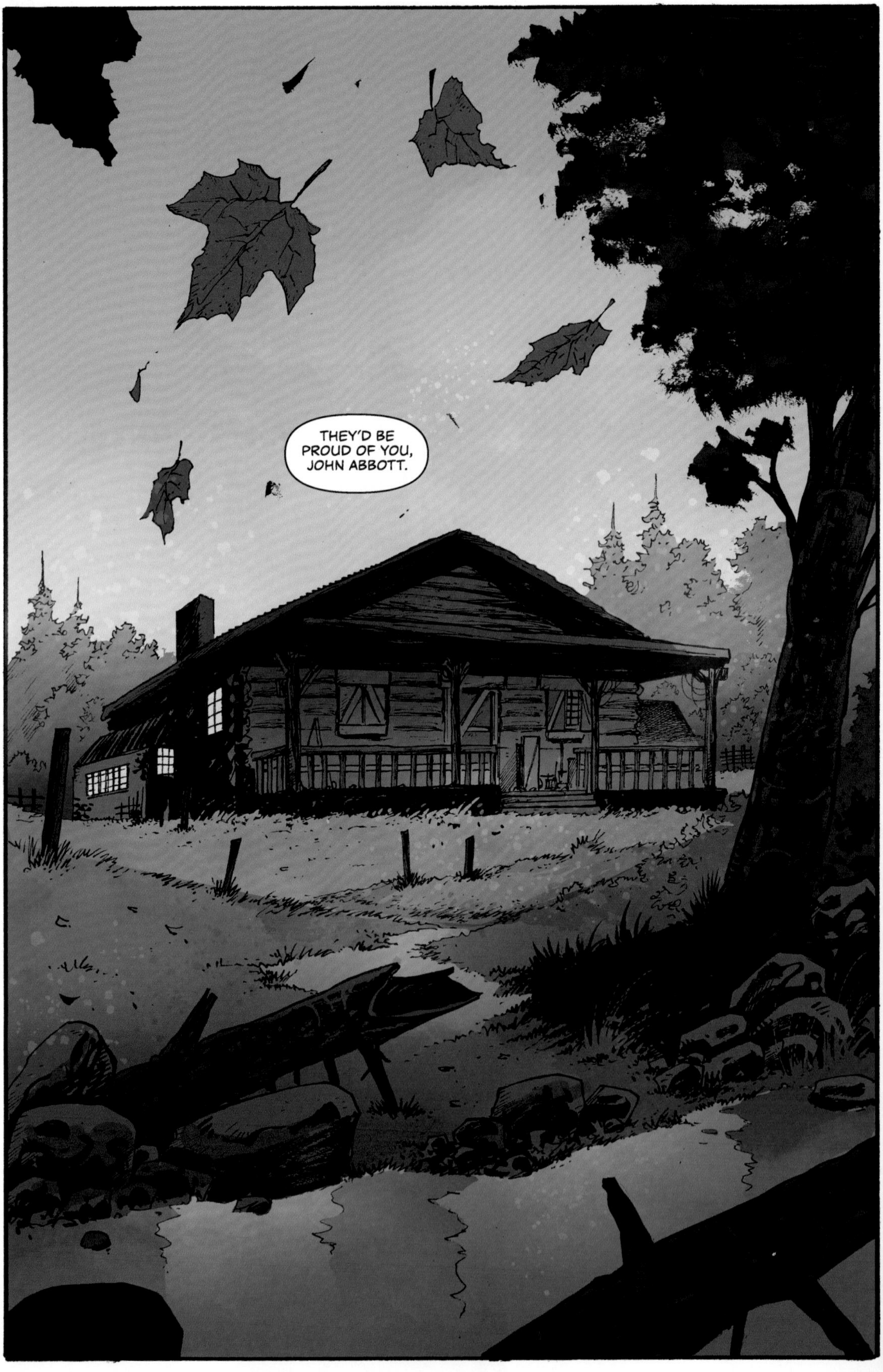
THEY'D BE PROUD OF YOU, JOHN ABBOTT.

THE END

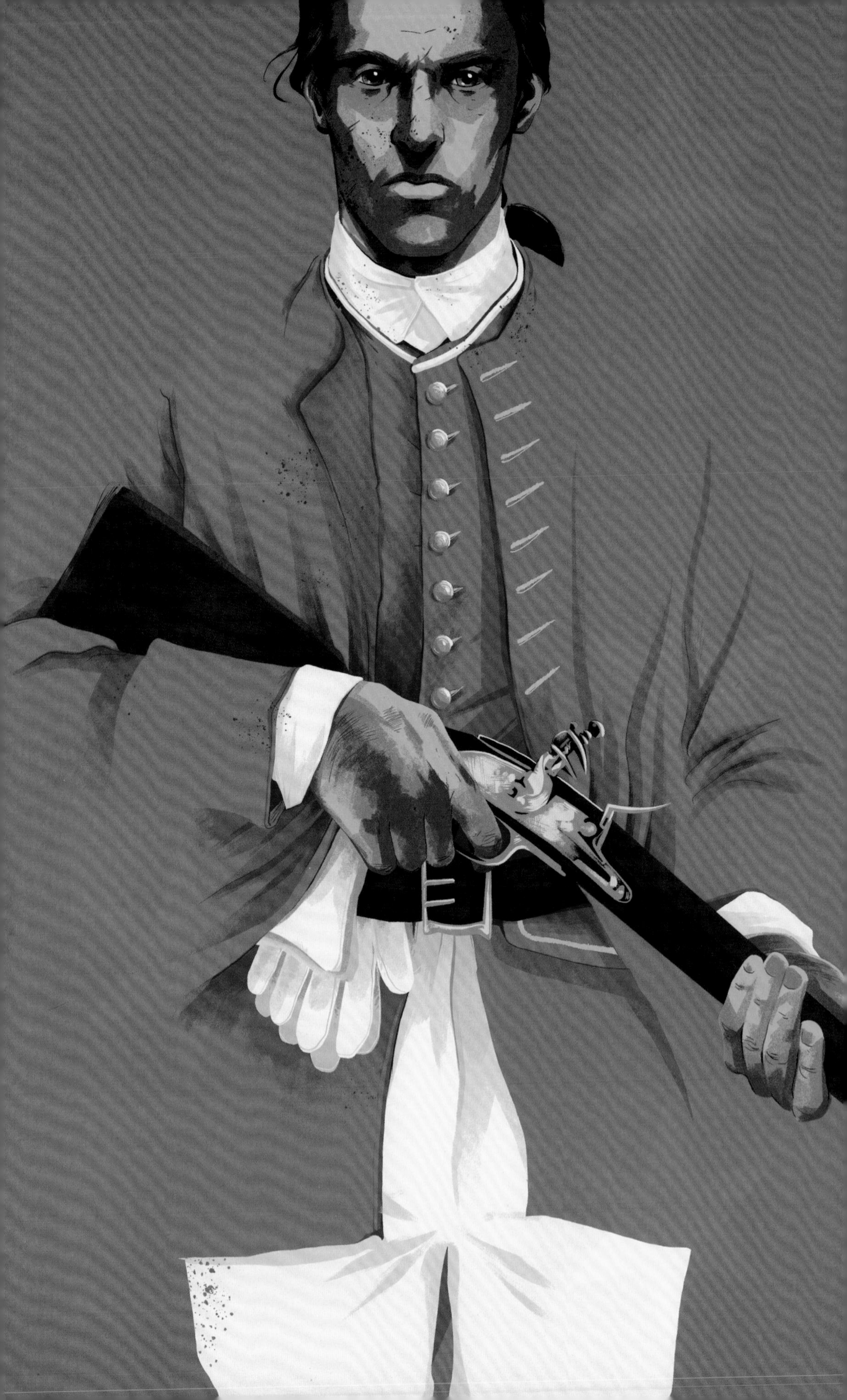

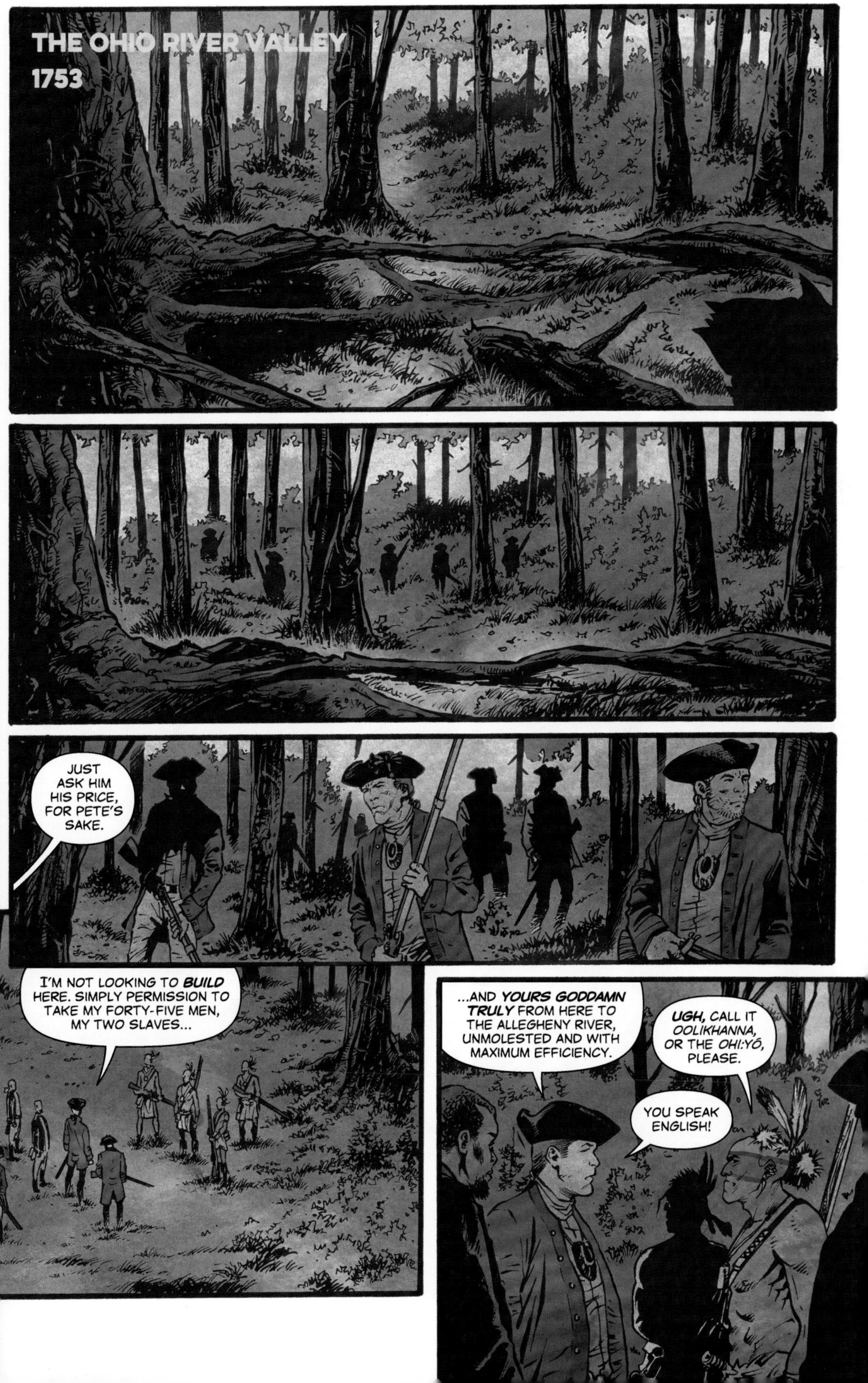

THE OHIO RIVER VALLEY
1753
JUST ASK HIM HIS PRICE, FOR PETE'S SAKE.
I'M NOT LOOKING TO *BUILD* HERE. SIMPLY PERMISSION TO TAKE MY FORTY-FIVE MEN, MY TWO SLAVES...
...AND *YOURS GODDAMN TRULY* FROM HERE TO THE ALLEGHENY RIVER, UNMOLESTED AND WITH MAXIMUM EFFICIENCY.
UGH, CALL IT *OOLIKHANNA,* OR THE *OHI:YÓ,* PLEASE.
YOU SPEAK ENGLISH!

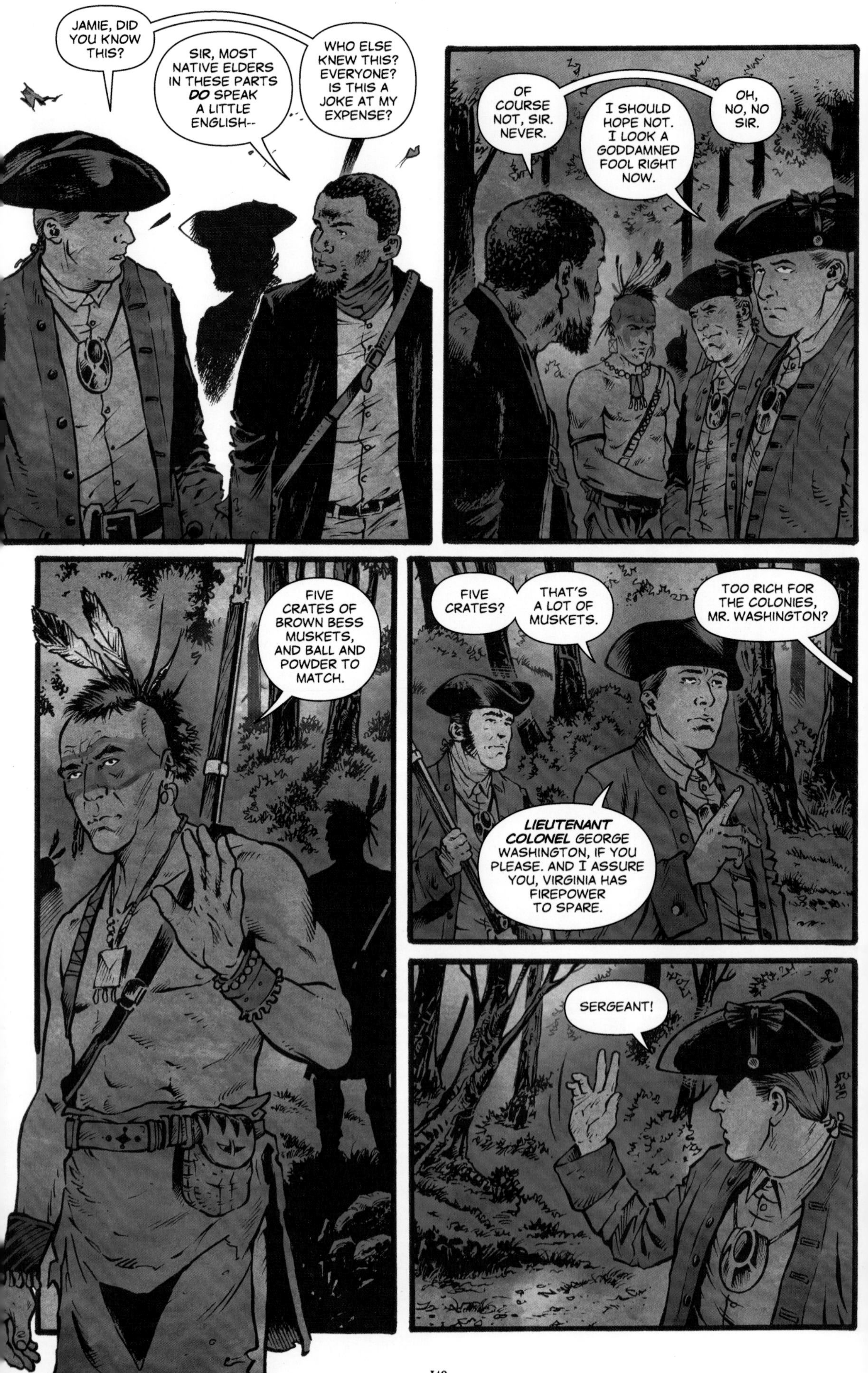
JAMIE, DID YOU KNOW THIS?
SIR, MOST NATIVE ELDERS IN THESE PARTS **DO** SPEAK A LITTLE ENGLISH--
WHO ELSE KNEW THIS? EVERYONE? IS THIS A JOKE AT MY EXPENSE?
OF COURSE NOT, SIR. NEVER.
I SHOULD HOPE NOT. I LOOK A GODDAMNED FOOL RIGHT NOW.
OH, NO, NO SIR.
FIVE CRATES OF BROWN BESS MUSKETS, AND BALL AND POWDER TO MATCH.
FIVE CRATES?
THAT'S A LOT OF MUSKETS.
TOO RICH FOR THE COLONIES, MR. WASHINGTON?
LIEUTENANT COLONEL GEORGE WASHINGTON, IF YOU PLEASE. AND I ASSURE YOU, VIRGINIA HAS FIREPOWER TO SPARE.
SERGEANT!

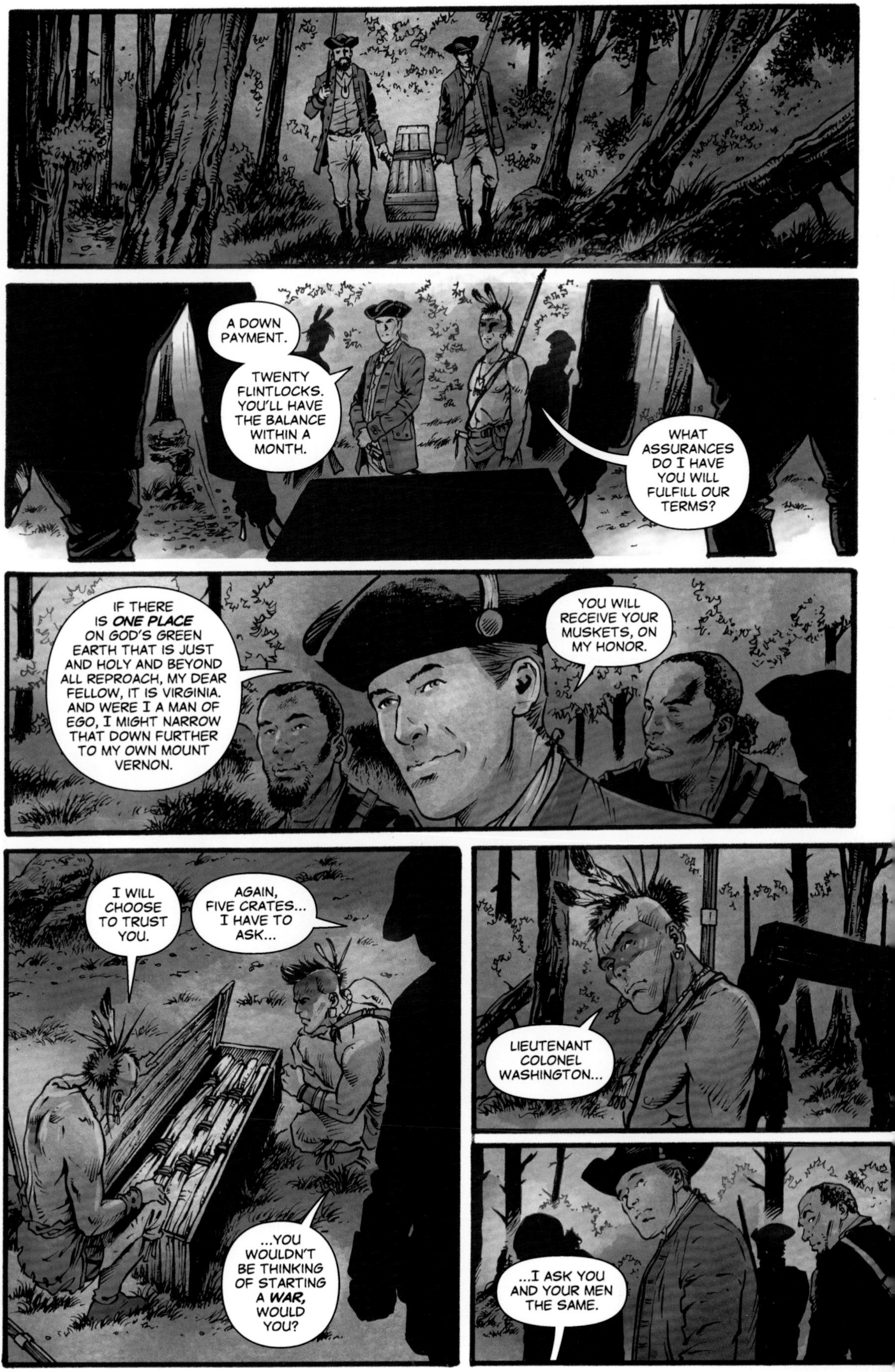
A DOWN PAYMENT.
TWENTY FLINTLOCKS. YOU'LL HAVE THE BALANCE WITHIN A MONTH.
WHAT ASSURANCES DO I HAVE YOU WILL FULFILL OUR TERMS?
IF THERE IS ONE PLACE ON GOD'S GREEN EARTH THAT IS JUST AND HOLY AND BEYOND ALL REPROACH, MY DEAR FELLOW, IT IS VIRGINIA. AND WERE I A MAN OF EGO, I MIGHT NARROW THAT DOWN FURTHER TO MY OWN MOUNT VERNON.
YOU WILL RECEIVE YOUR MUSKETS, ON MY HONOR.
I WILL CHOOSE TO TRUST YOU.
AGAIN, FIVE CRATES... I HAVE TO ASK...
...YOU WOULDN'T BE THINKING OF STARTING A WAR, WOULD YOU?
LIEUTENANT COLONEL WASHINGTON...
...I ASK YOU AND YOUR MEN THE SAME.

REBELS

"THE VIRGINIAN"

IN WHICH A YOUNG GEORGE WASHINGTON TESTS THE LIMITS, WITH DIRE CONSEQUENCES.

BRIAN WOOD · ANDREA MUTTI · LAUREN AFFE · MATT TAYLOR

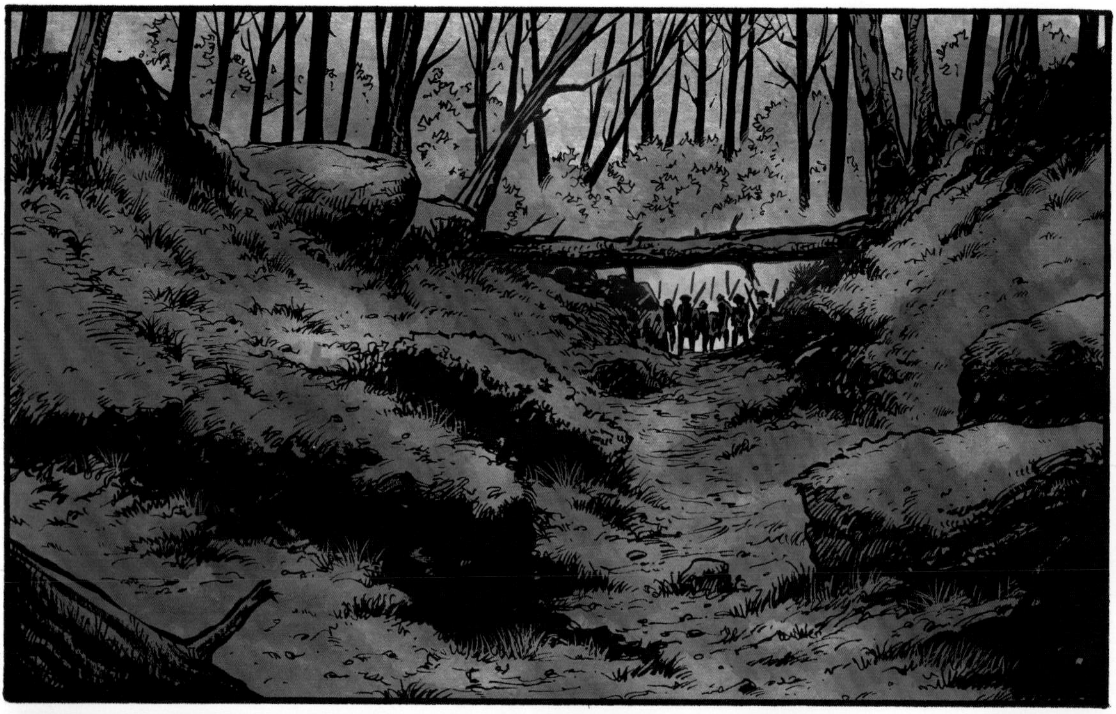

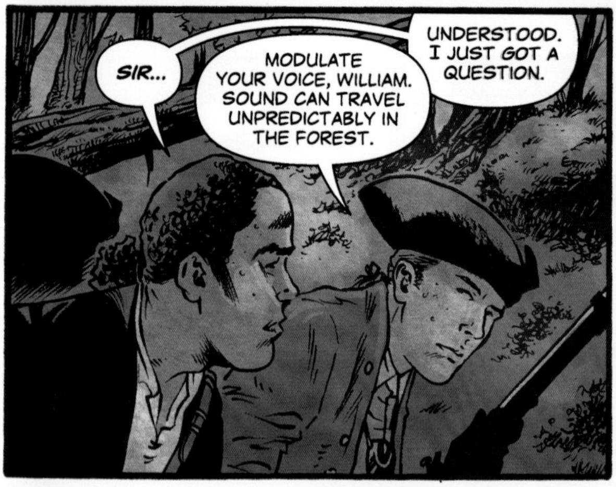
SIR...
MODULATE YOUR VOICE, WILLIAM. SOUND CAN TRAVEL UNPREDICTABLY IN THE FOREST.
UNDERSTOOD. I JUST GOT A QUESTION.

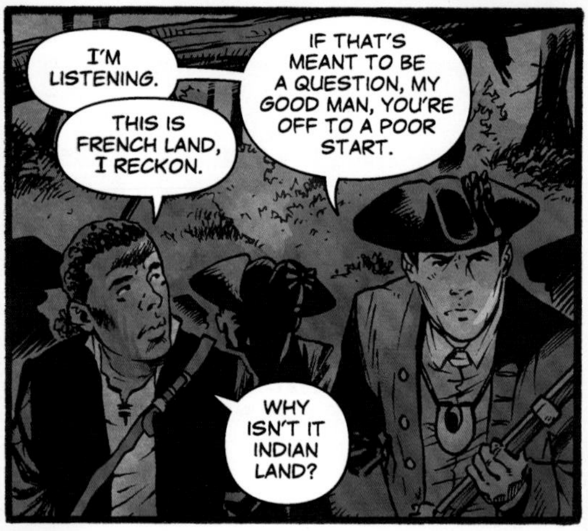
I'M LISTENING.
THIS IS FRENCH LAND, I RECKON.
IF THAT'S MEANT TO BE A QUESTION, MY GOOD MAN, YOU'RE OFF TO A POOR START.
WHY ISN'T IT INDIAN LAND?

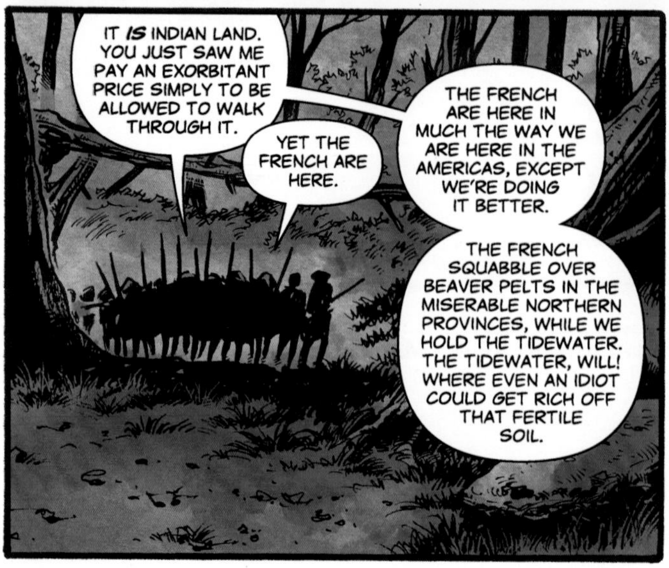
IT *IS* INDIAN LAND. YOU JUST SAW ME PAY AN EXORBITANT PRICE SIMPLY TO BE ALLOWED TO WALK THROUGH IT.
YET THE FRENCH ARE HERE.
THE FRENCH ARE HERE IN MUCH THE WAY WE ARE HERE IN THE AMERICAS, EXCEPT WE'RE DOING IT BETTER.
THE FRENCH SQUABBLE OVER BEAVER PELTS IN THE MISERABLE NORTHERN PROVINCES, WHILE WE HOLD THE TIDEWATER. THE TIDEWATER, WILL! WHERE EVEN AN IDIOT COULD GET RICH OFF THAT FERTILE SOIL.

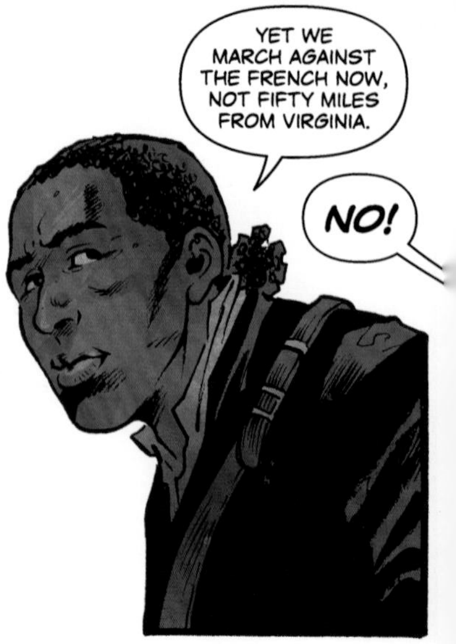
YET WE MARCH AGAINST THE FRENCH NOW, NOT FIFTY MILES FROM VIRGINIA.
NO!

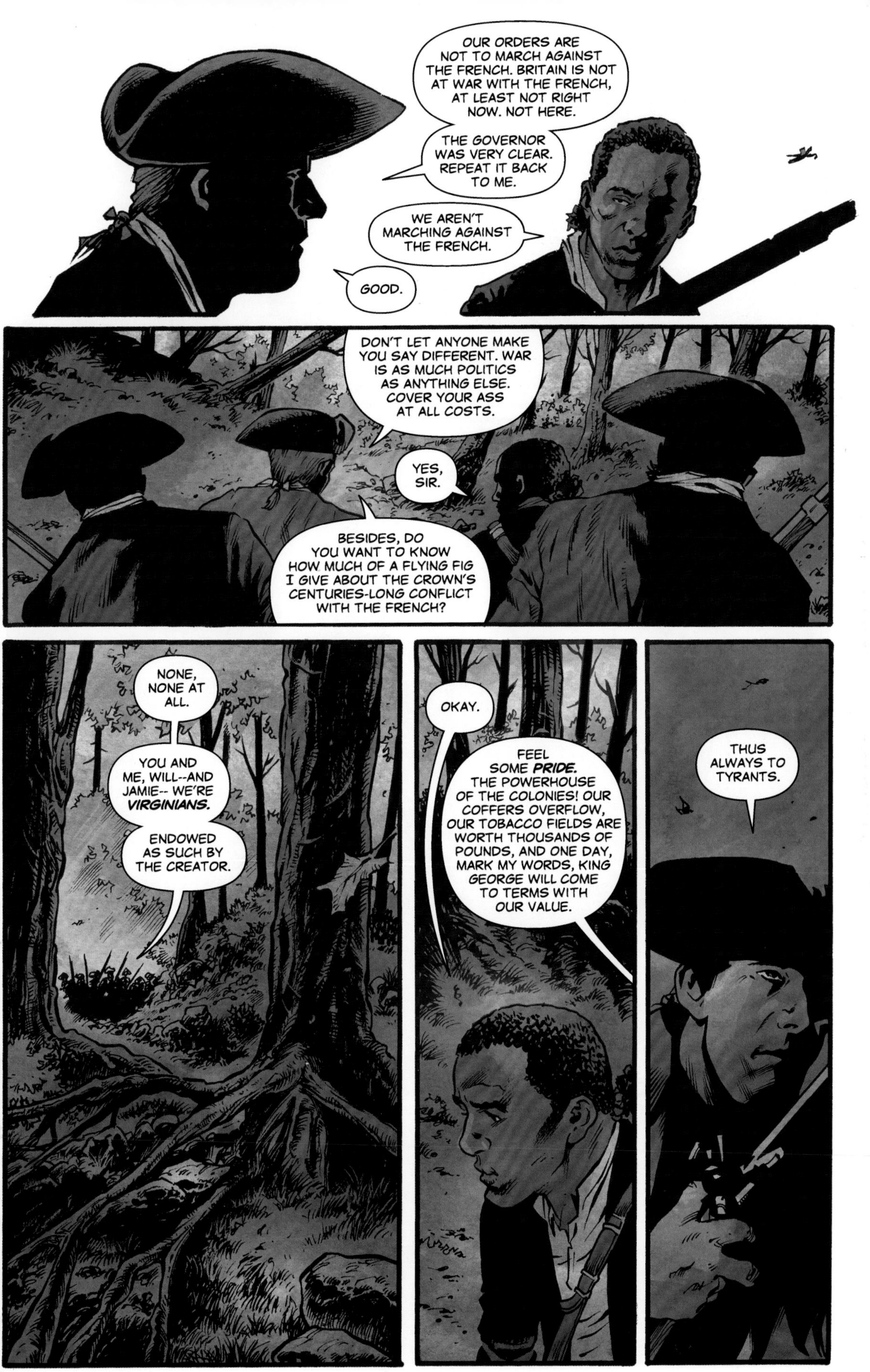
OUR ORDERS ARE NOT TO MARCH AGAINST THE FRENCH. BRITAIN IS NOT AT WAR WITH THE FRENCH, AT LEAST NOT RIGHT NOW. NOT HERE.
THE GOVERNOR WAS VERY CLEAR. REPEAT IT BACK TO ME.
WE AREN'T MARCHING AGAINST THE FRENCH.
GOOD.
DON'T LET ANYONE MAKE YOU SAY DIFFERENT. WAR IS AS MUCH POLITICS AS ANYTHING ELSE. COVER YOUR ASS AT ALL COSTS.
YES, SIR.
BESIDES, DO YOU WANT TO KNOW HOW MUCH OF A FLYING FIG I GIVE ABOUT THE CROWN'S CENTURIES-LONG CONFLICT WITH THE FRENCH?
NONE, NONE AT ALL.
YOU AND ME, WILL--AND JAMIE-- WE'RE ***VIRGINIANS.***
ENDOWED AS SUCH BY THE CREATOR.
OKAY.
FEEL SOME ***PRIDE.*** THE POWERHOUSE OF THE COLONIES! OUR COFFERS OVERFLOW, OUR TOBACCO FIELDS ARE WORTH THOUSANDS OF POUNDS, AND ONE DAY, MARK MY WORDS, KING GEORGE WILL COME TO TERMS WITH OUR VALUE.
THUS ALWAYS TO TYRANTS.

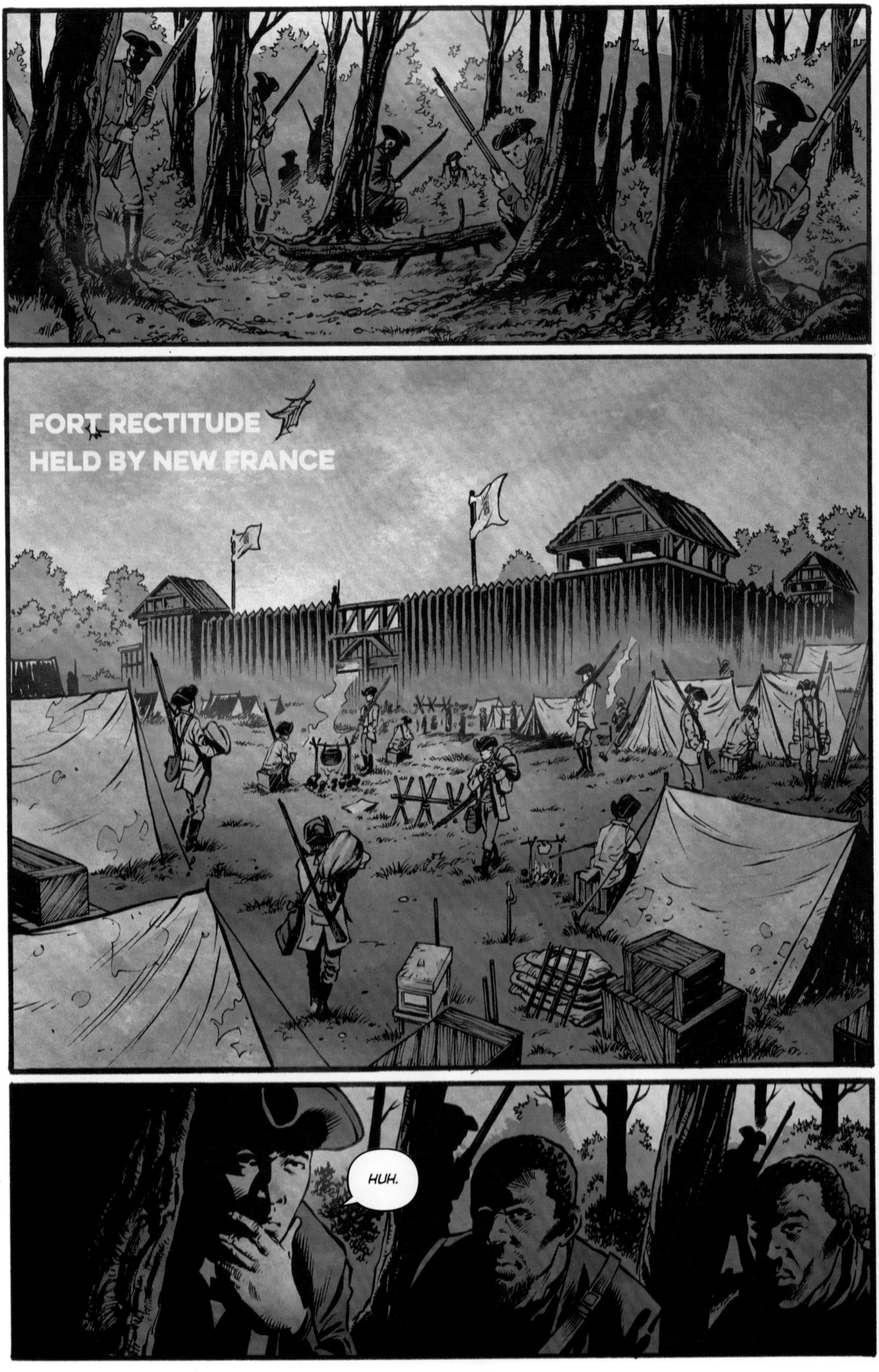
FORT RECTITUDE
HELD BY NEW FRANCE
HUH.

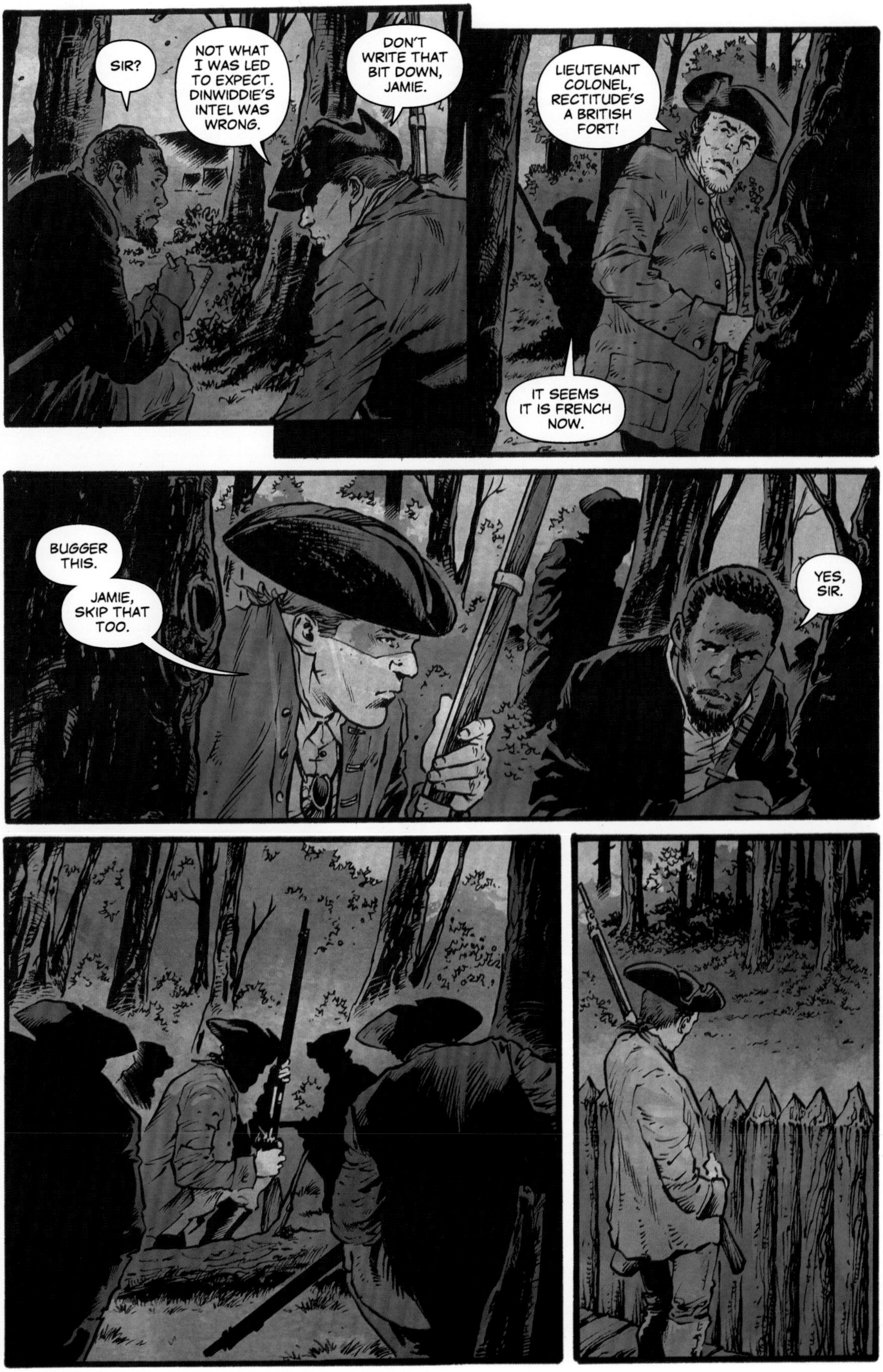
SIR?
NOT WHAT I WAS LED TO EXPECT. DINWIDDIE'S INTEL WAS WRONG.
DON'T WRITE THAT BIT DOWN, JAMIE.
LIEUTENANT COLONEL, RECTITUDE'S A BRITISH FORT!
IT SEEMS IT IS FRENCH NOW.
BUGGER THIS.
JAMIE, SKIP THAT TOO.
YES, SIR.

JAMIE.

YES, SIR.

HOW MANY FRENCHMEN DO YOU RECKON ARE IN THAT FORT?

BASED ON THE TENTS, SIR? TWO DOZEN, PERHAPS THREE.

I'D AGREE WITH THAT. CANNON?

NONE THAT I CAN SEE.

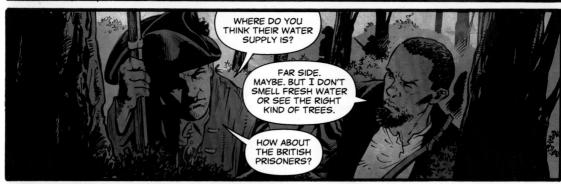

WHERE DO YOU THINK THEIR WATER SUPPLY IS?

FAR SIDE. MAYBE. BUT I DON'T SMELL FRESH WATER OR SEE THE RIGHT KIND OF TREES.

HOW ABOUT THE BRITISH PRISONERS?

SIR.

THEY'LL BE HELD INSIDE THE WALLS, SIR, OBVIOUSLY.

SPEAK YOUR MIND, JAMIE.

THERE ARE NO PRISONERS. THEY MARCHED THEM ELSE-WHERE.

AGREED.

SIR!

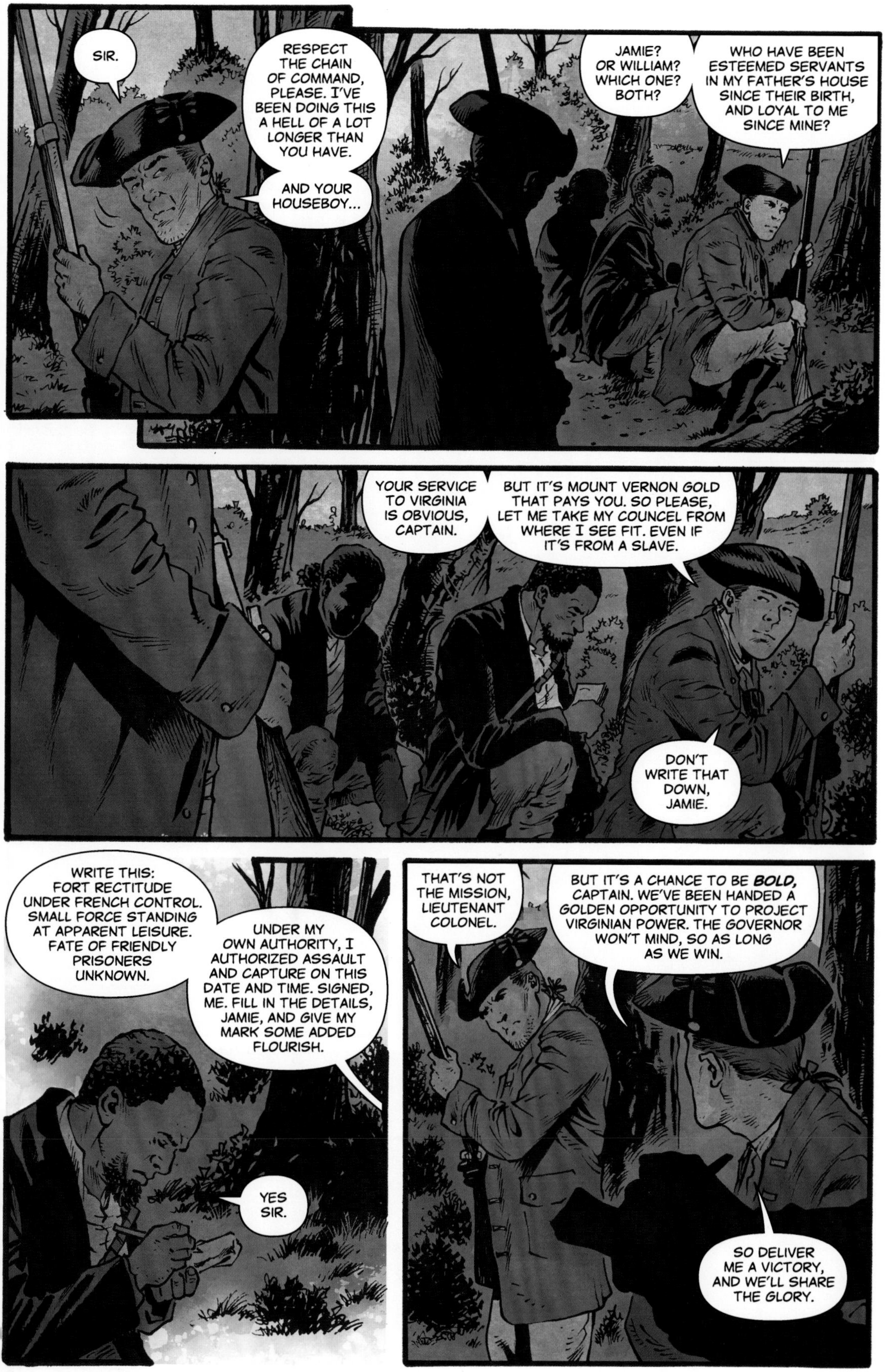
SIR.
RESPECT THE CHAIN OF COMMAND, PLEASE. I'VE BEEN DOING THIS A HELL OF A LOT LONGER THAN YOU HAVE.
AND YOUR HOUSEBOY...
JAMIE? OR WILLIAM? WHICH ONE? BOTH?
WHO HAVE BEEN ESTEEMED SERVANTS IN MY FATHER'S HOUSE SINCE THEIR BIRTH, AND LOYAL TO ME SINCE MINE?
YOUR SERVICE TO VIRGINIA IS OBVIOUS, CAPTAIN.
BUT IT'S MOUNT VERNON GOLD THAT PAYS YOU. SO PLEASE, LET ME TAKE MY COUNCEL FROM WHERE I SEE FIT. EVEN IF IT'S FROM A SLAVE.
DON'T WRITE THAT DOWN, JAMIE.
WRITE THIS: FORT RECTITUDE UNDER FRENCH CONTROL. SMALL FORCE STANDING AT APPARENT LEISURE. FATE OF FRIENDLY PRISONERS UNKNOWN.
UNDER MY OWN AUTHORITY, I AUTHORIZED ASSAULT AND CAPTURE ON THIS DATE AND TIME. SIGNED, ME. FILL IN THE DETAILS, JAMIE, AND GIVE MY MARK SOME ADDED FLOURISH.
YES SIR.
THAT'S NOT THE MISSION, LIEUTENANT COLONEL.
BUT IT'S A CHANCE TO BE ***BOLD,*** CAPTAIN. WE'VE BEEN HANDED A GOLDEN OPPORTUNITY TO PROJECT VIRGINIAN POWER. THE GOVERNOR WON'T MIND, SO AS LONG AS WE WIN.
SO DELIVER ME A VICTORY, AND WE'LL SHARE THE GLORY.

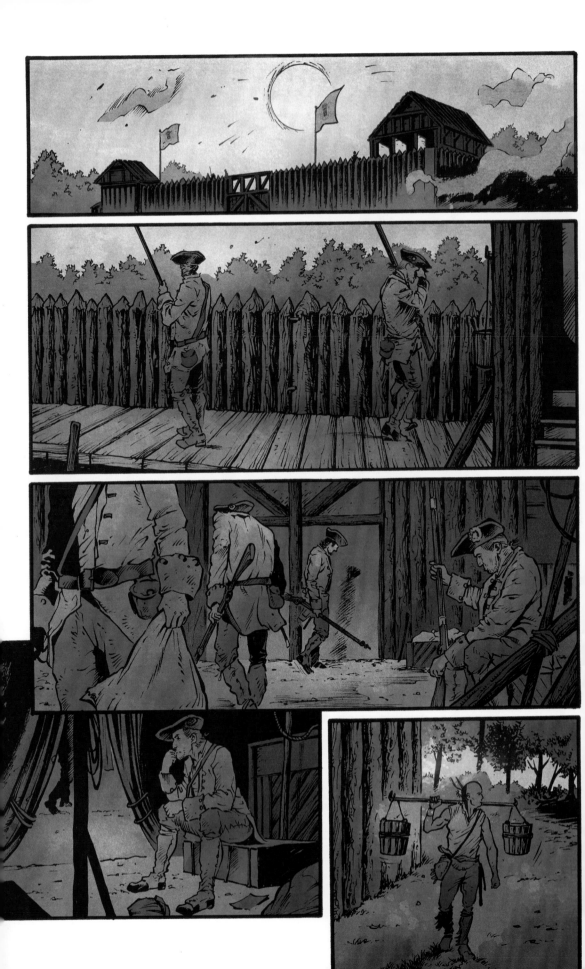

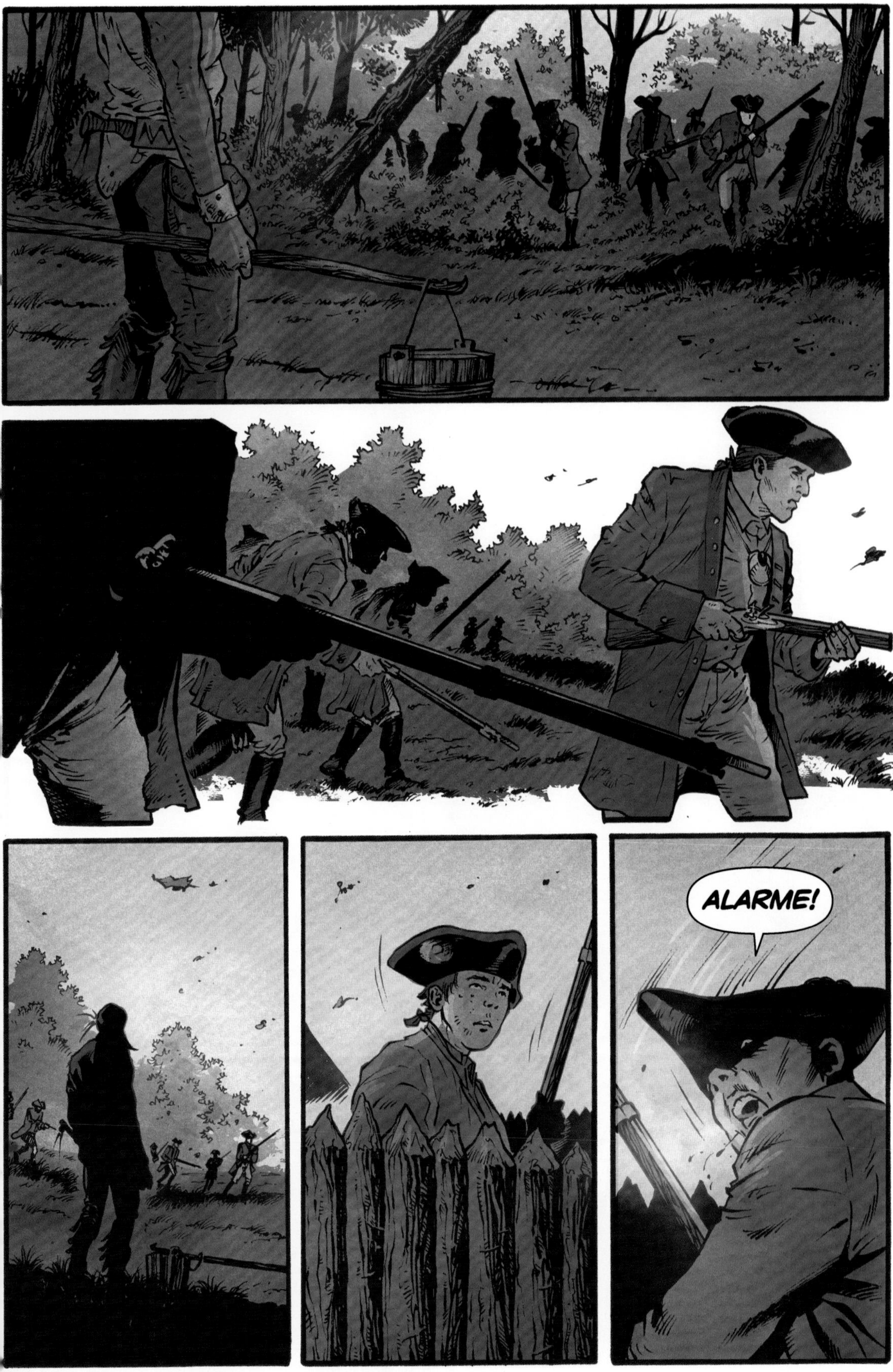
ALARME!

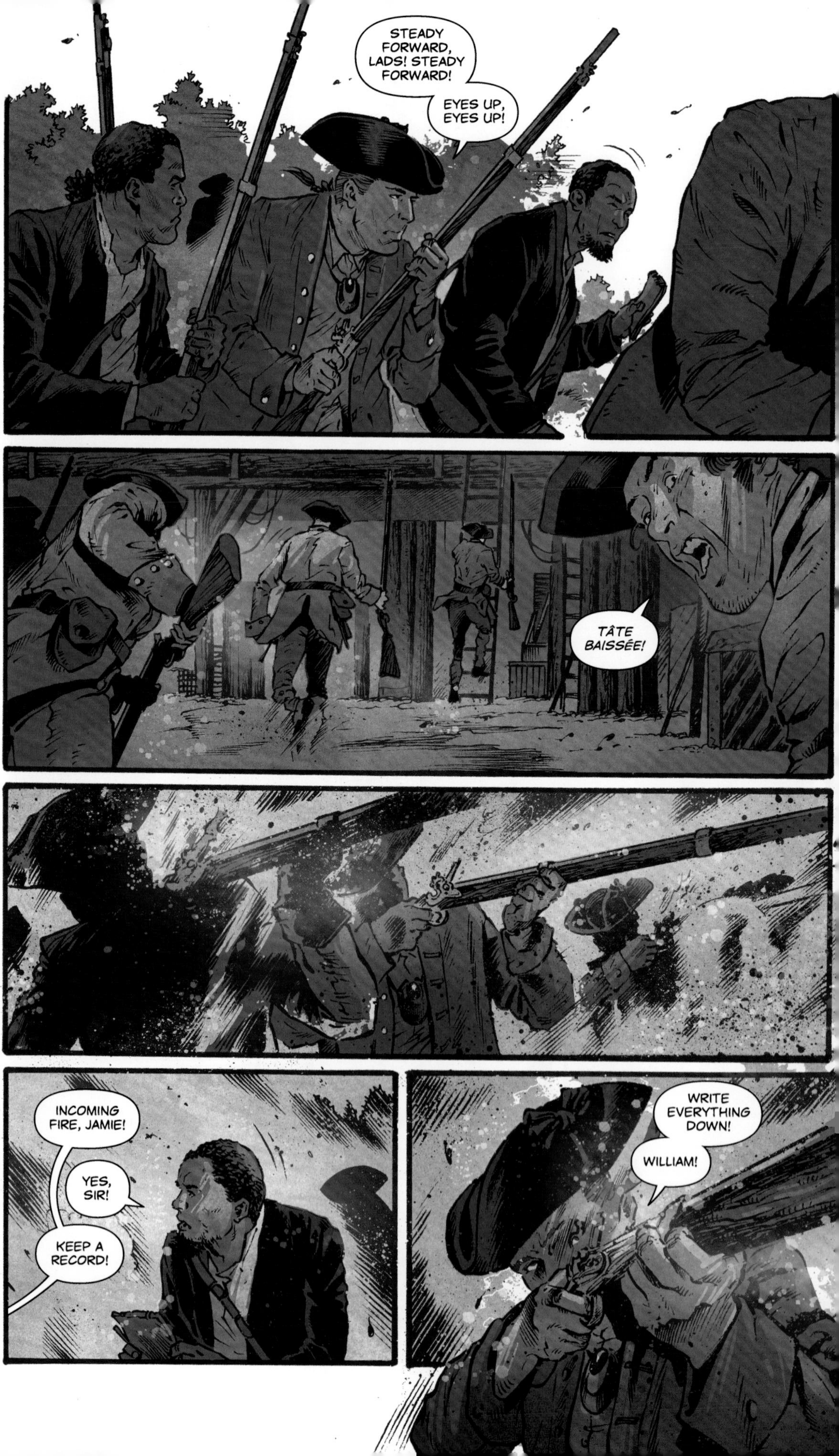
STEADY FORWARD, LADS! STEADY FORWARD!
EYES UP, EYES UP!
TÂTE BAISSÉE!
INCOMING FIRE, JAMIE!
YES, SIR!
KEEP A RECORD!
WRITE EVERYTHING DOWN!
WILLIAM!

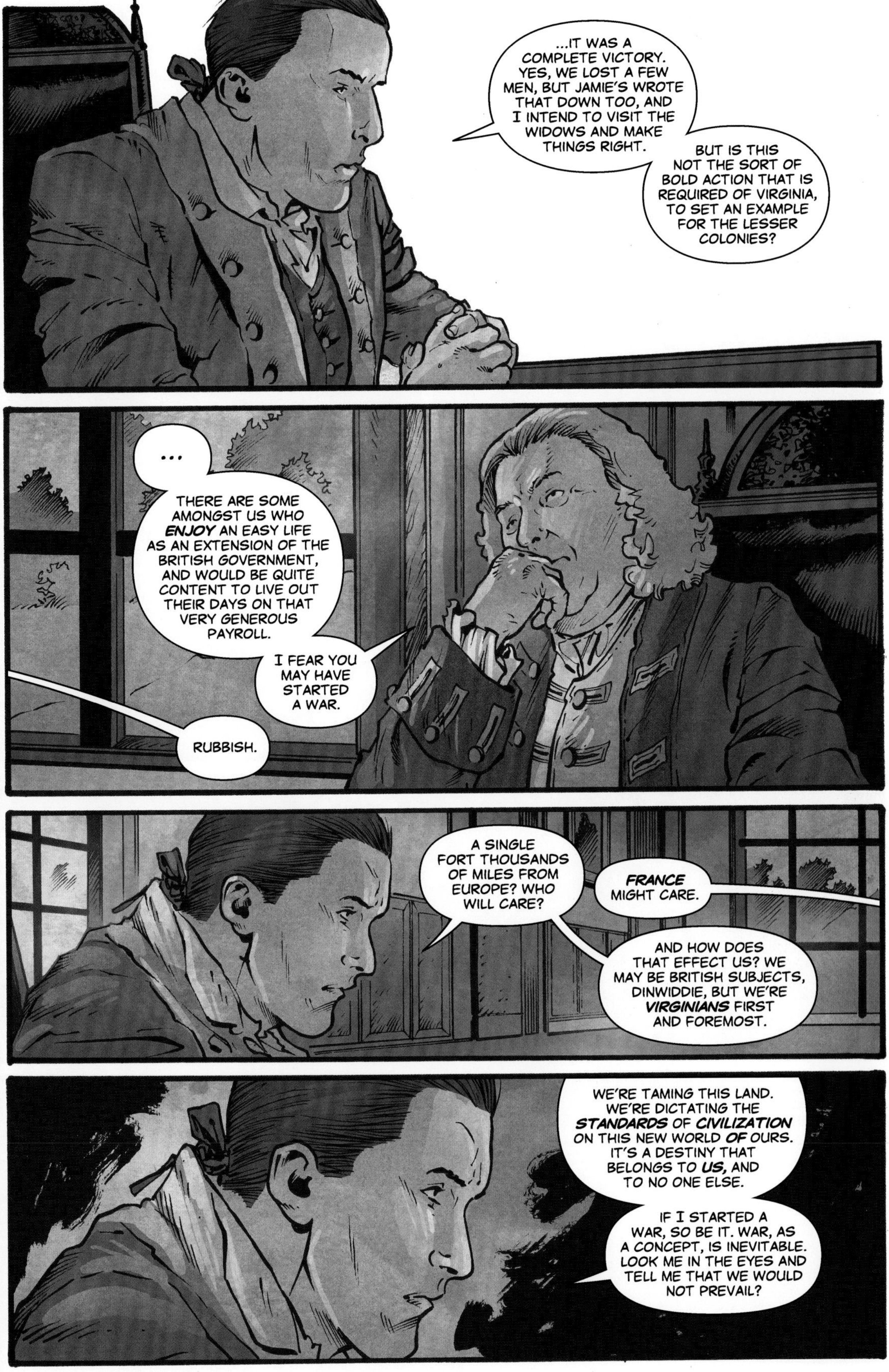
...IT WAS A COMPLETE VICTORY. YES, WE LOST A FEW MEN, BUT JAMIE'S WROTE THAT DOWN TOO, AND I INTEND TO VISIT THE WIDOWS AND MAKE THINGS RIGHT.
BUT IS THIS NOT THE SORT OF BOLD ACTION THAT IS REQUIRED OF VIRGINIA, TO SET AN EXAMPLE FOR THE LESSER COLONIES?
...
THERE ARE SOME AMONGST US WHO ENJOY AN EASY LIFE AS AN EXTENSION OF THE BRITISH GOVERNMENT, AND WOULD BE QUITE CONTENT TO LIVE OUT THEIR DAYS ON THAT VERY GENEROUS PAYROLL.
I FEAR YOU MAY HAVE STARTED A WAR.
RUBBISH.
A SINGLE FORT THOUSANDS OF MILES FROM EUROPE? WHO WILL CARE?
FRANCE MIGHT CARE.
AND HOW DOES THAT EFFECT US? WE MAY BE BRITISH SUBJECTS, DINWIDDIE, BUT WE'RE VIRGINIANS FIRST AND FOREMOST.
WE'RE TAMING THIS LAND. WE'RE DICTATING THE STANDARDS OF CIVILIZATION ON THIS NEW WORLD OF OURS. IT'S A DESTINY THAT BELONGS TO US, AND TO NO ONE ELSE.
IF I STARTED A WAR, SO BE IT. WAR, AS A CONCEPT, IS INEVITABLE. LOOK ME IN THE EYES AND TELL ME THAT WE WOULD NOT PREVAIL?

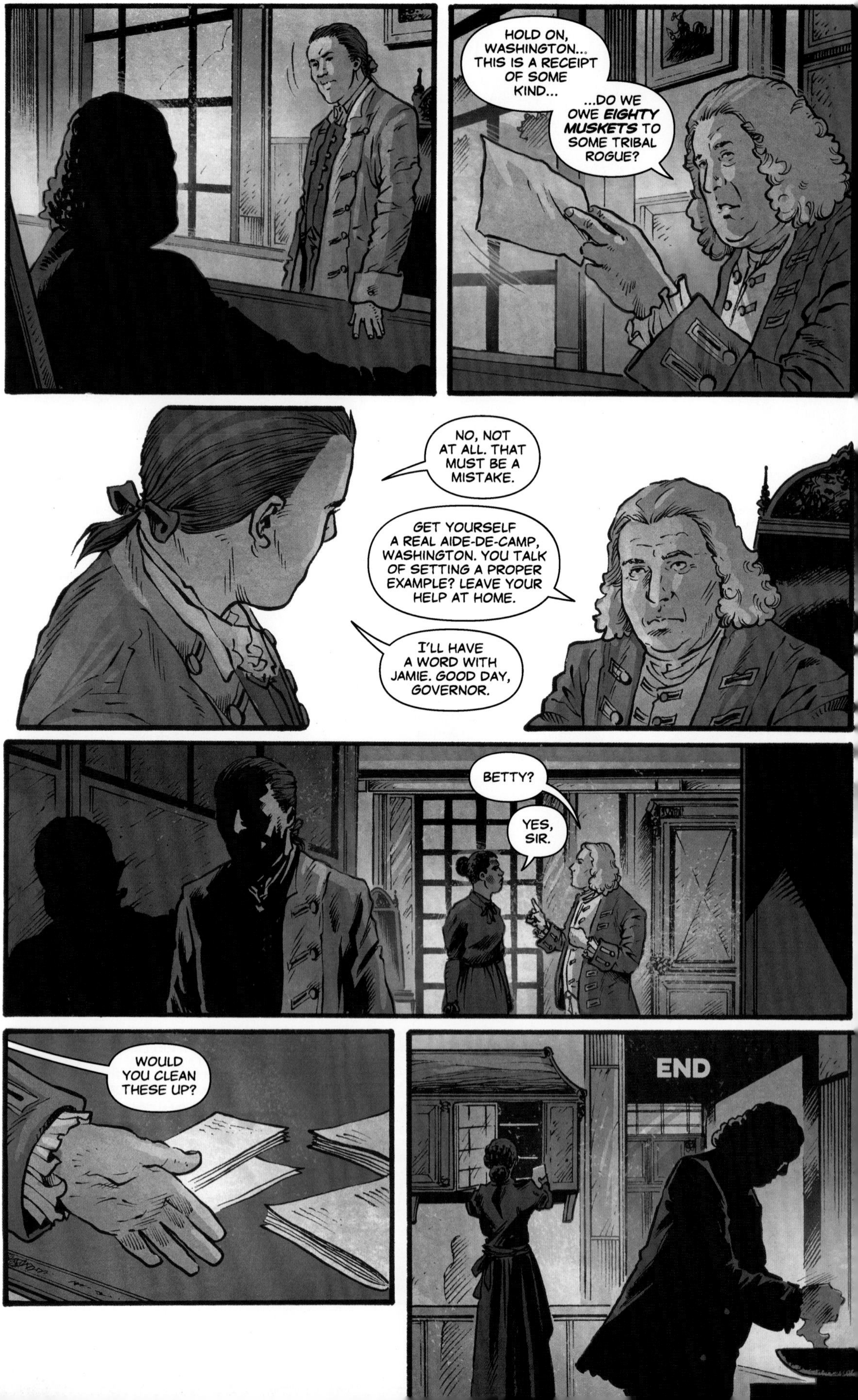
HOLD ON, WASHINGTON... THIS IS A RECEIPT OF SOME KIND...
...DO WE OWE EIGHTY MUSKETS TO SOME TRIBAL ROGUE?
NO, NOT AT ALL. THAT MUST BE A MISTAKE.
GET YOURSELF A REAL AIDE-DE-CAMP, WASHINGTON. YOU TALK OF SETTING A PROPER EXAMPLE? LEAVE YOUR HELP AT HOME.
I'LL HAVE A WORD WITH JAMIE. GOOD DAY, GOVERNOR.
BETTY?
YES, SIR.
WOULD YOU CLEAN THESE UP?
END

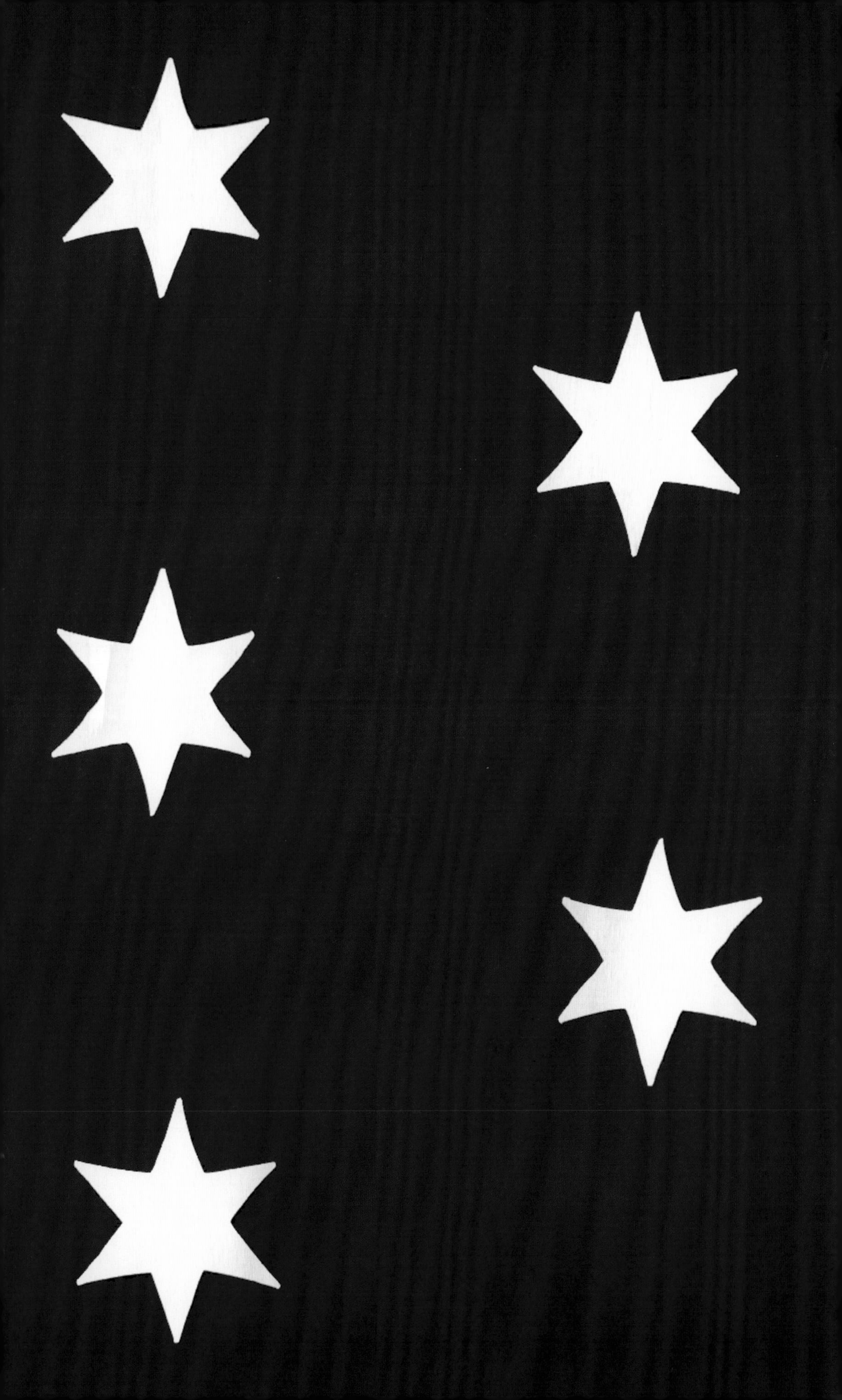

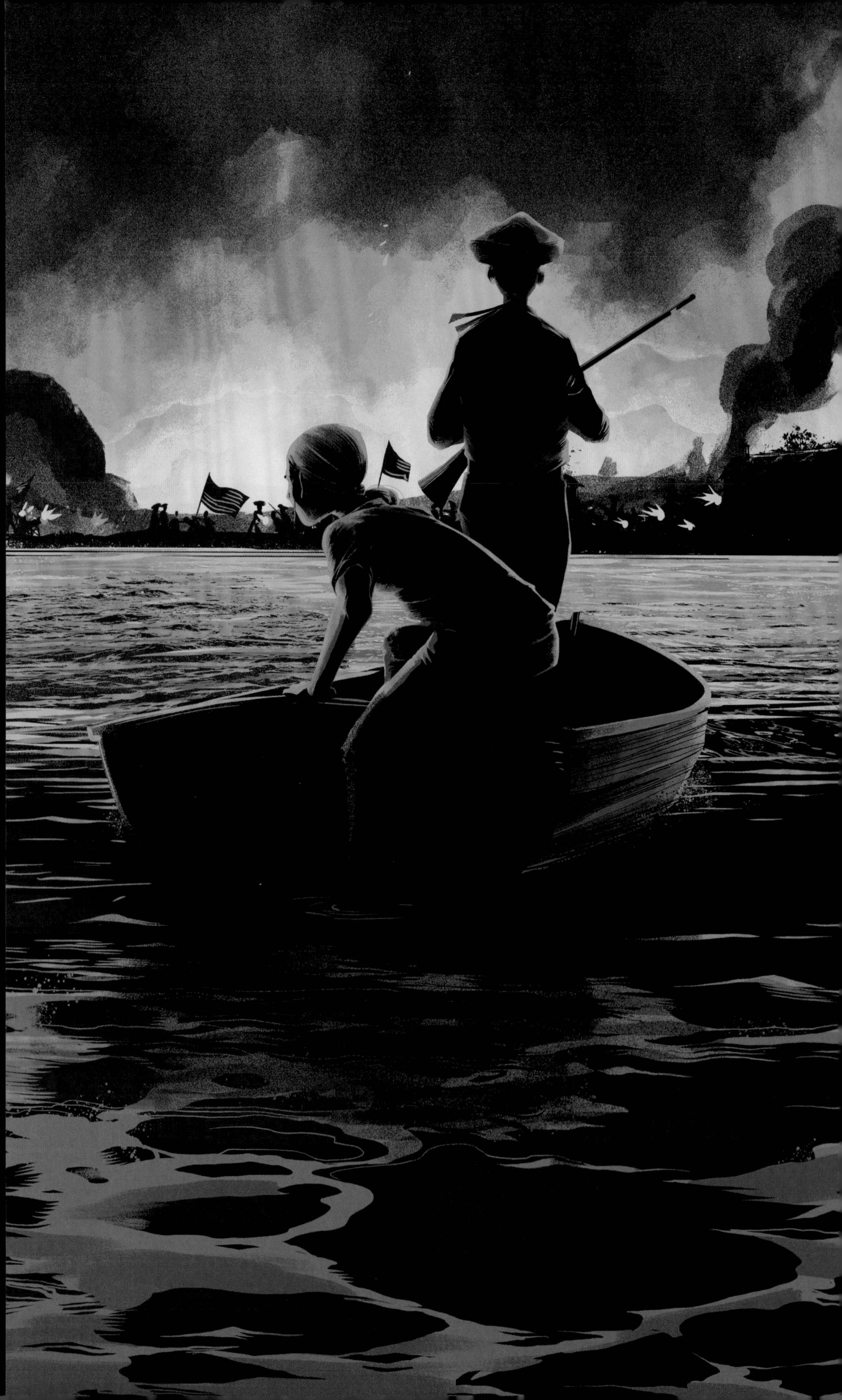

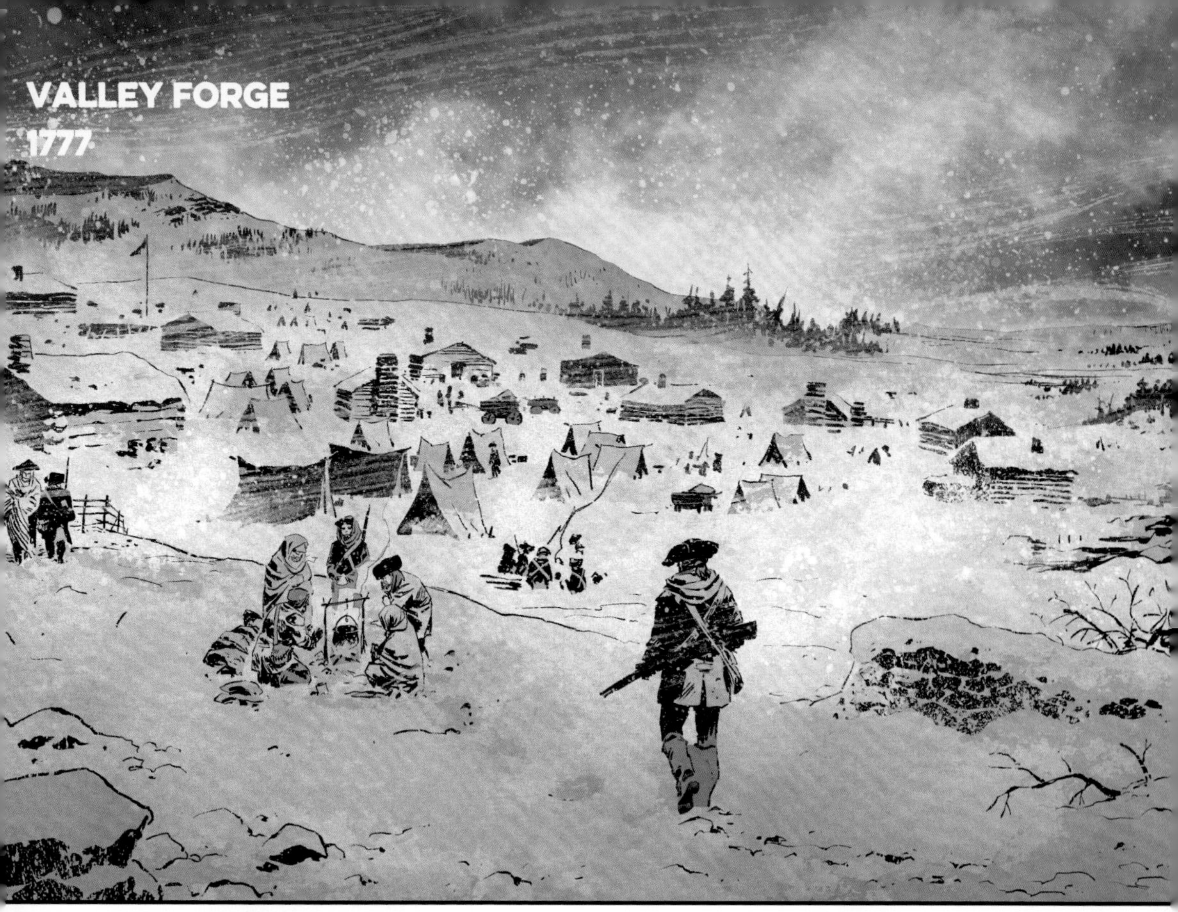
VALLEY FORGE
1777

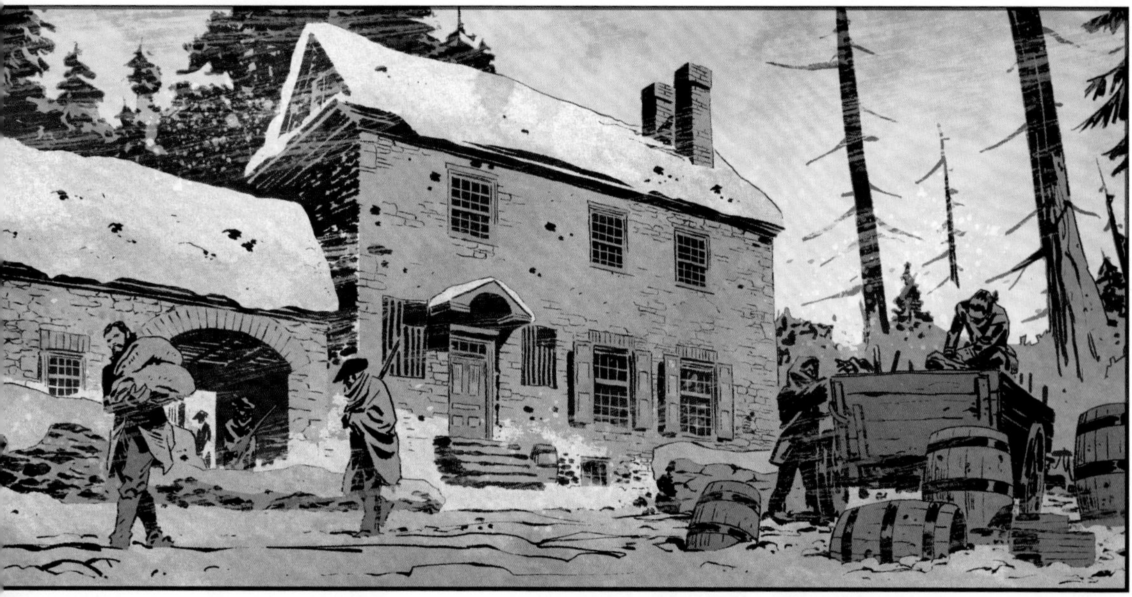

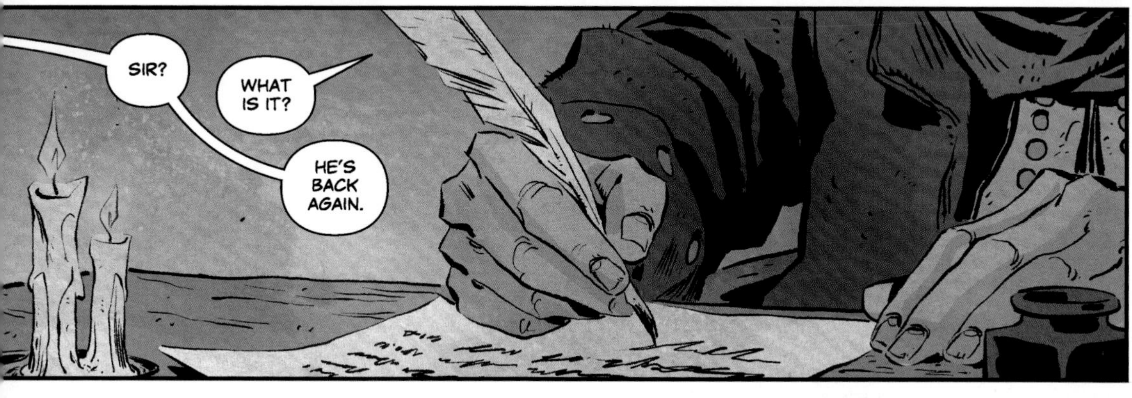
SIR?
WHAT IS IT?
HE'S BACK AGAIN.

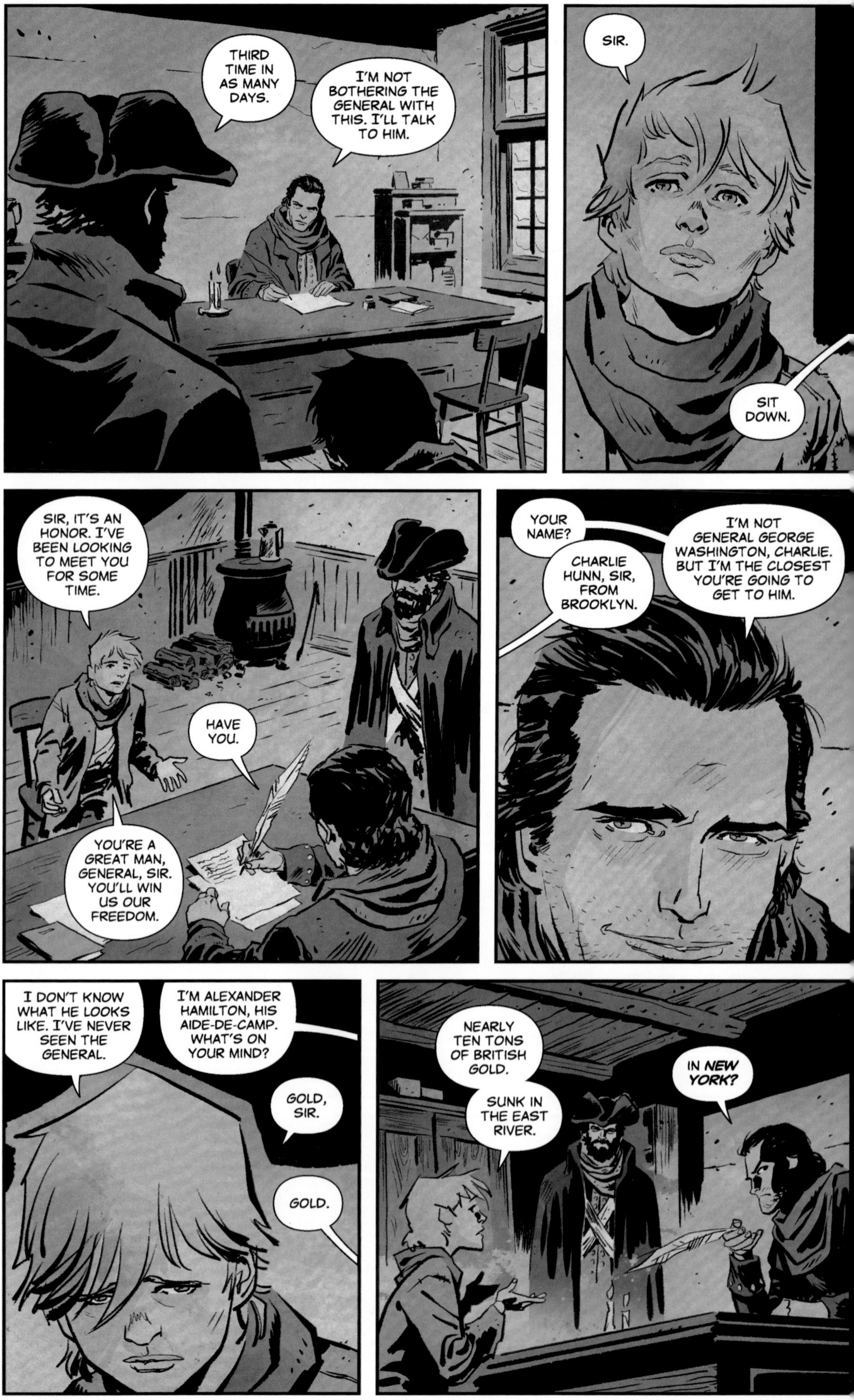
THIRD TIME IN AS MANY DAYS.
I'M NOT BOTHERING THE GENERAL WITH THIS. I'LL TALK TO HIM.
SIR.
SIT DOWN.
SIR, IT'S AN HONOR. I'VE BEEN LOOKING TO MEET YOU FOR SOME TIME.
HAVE YOU.
YOU'RE A GREAT MAN, GENERAL, SIR. YOU'LL WIN US OUR FREEDOM.
YOUR NAME?
CHARLIE HUNN, SIR, FROM BROOKLYN.
I'M NOT GENERAL GEORGE WASHINGTON, CHARLIE. BUT I'M THE CLOSEST YOU'RE GOING TO GET TO HIM.
I DON'T KNOW WHAT HE LOOKS LIKE. I'VE NEVER SEEN THE GENERAL.
I'M ALEXANDER HAMILTON, HIS AIDE-DE-CAMP. WHAT'S ON YOUR MIND?
GOLD, SIR.
GOLD.
NEARLY TEN TONS OF BRITISH GOLD.
SUNK IN THE EAST RIVER.
IN NEW YORK?

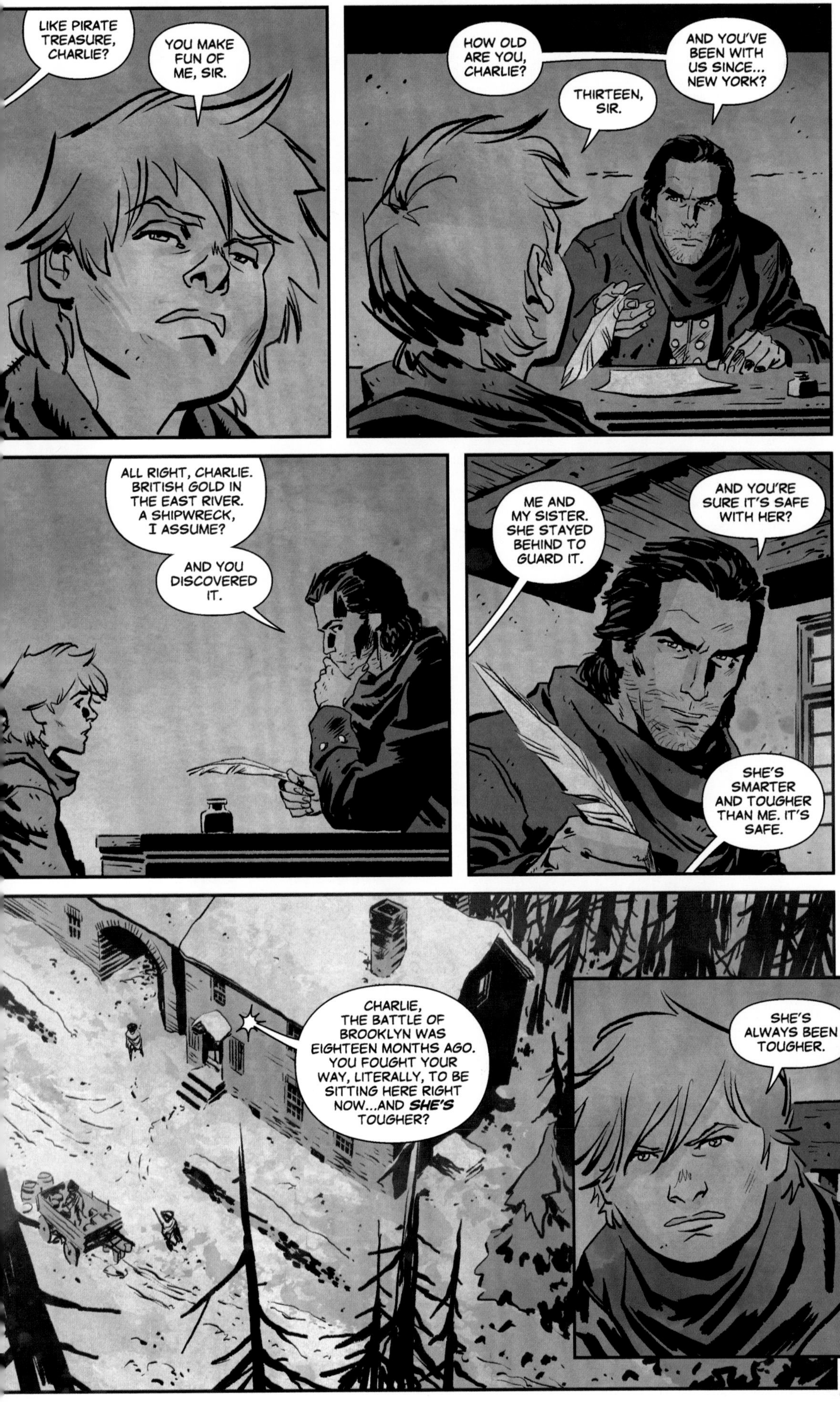
LIKE PIRATE TREASURE, CHARLIE?
YOU MAKE FUN OF ME, SIR.
HOW OLD ARE YOU, CHARLIE?
THIRTEEN, SIR.
AND YOU'VE BEEN WITH US SINCE... NEW YORK?
ALL RIGHT, CHARLIE. BRITISH GOLD IN THE EAST RIVER. A SHIPWRECK, I ASSUME?
AND YOU DISCOVERED IT.
ME AND MY SISTER. SHE STAYED BEHIND TO GUARD IT.
AND YOU'RE SURE IT'S SAFE WITH HER?
SHE'S SMARTER AND TOUGHER THAN ME. IT'S SAFE.
CHARLIE, THE BATTLE OF BROOKLYN WAS EIGHTEEN MONTHS AGO. YOU FOUGHT YOUR WAY, LITERALLY, TO BE SITTING HERE RIGHT NOW...AND *SHE'S* TOUGHER?
SHE'S ALWAYS BEEN TOUGHER.

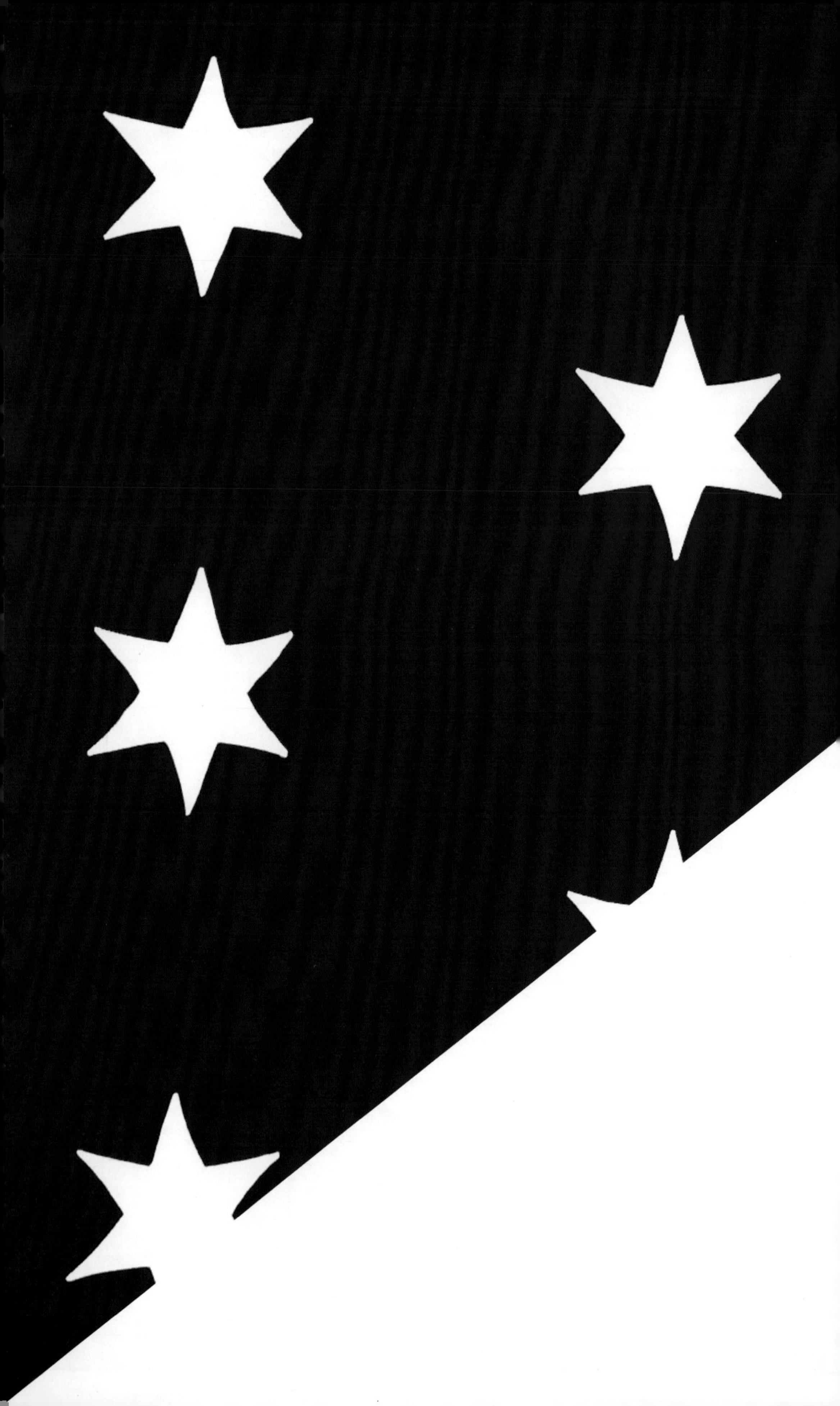

REBELS

"BROOKLYN HEIGHTS"

IN WHICH GEORGE WASHINGTON GIVES UP BROOKLYN, AND TWO SIBLINGS FIGHT TO GET IT BACK.

BRIAN WOOD · LUCA CASALANGUIDA · LAUREN AFFE · MATT TAYLOR

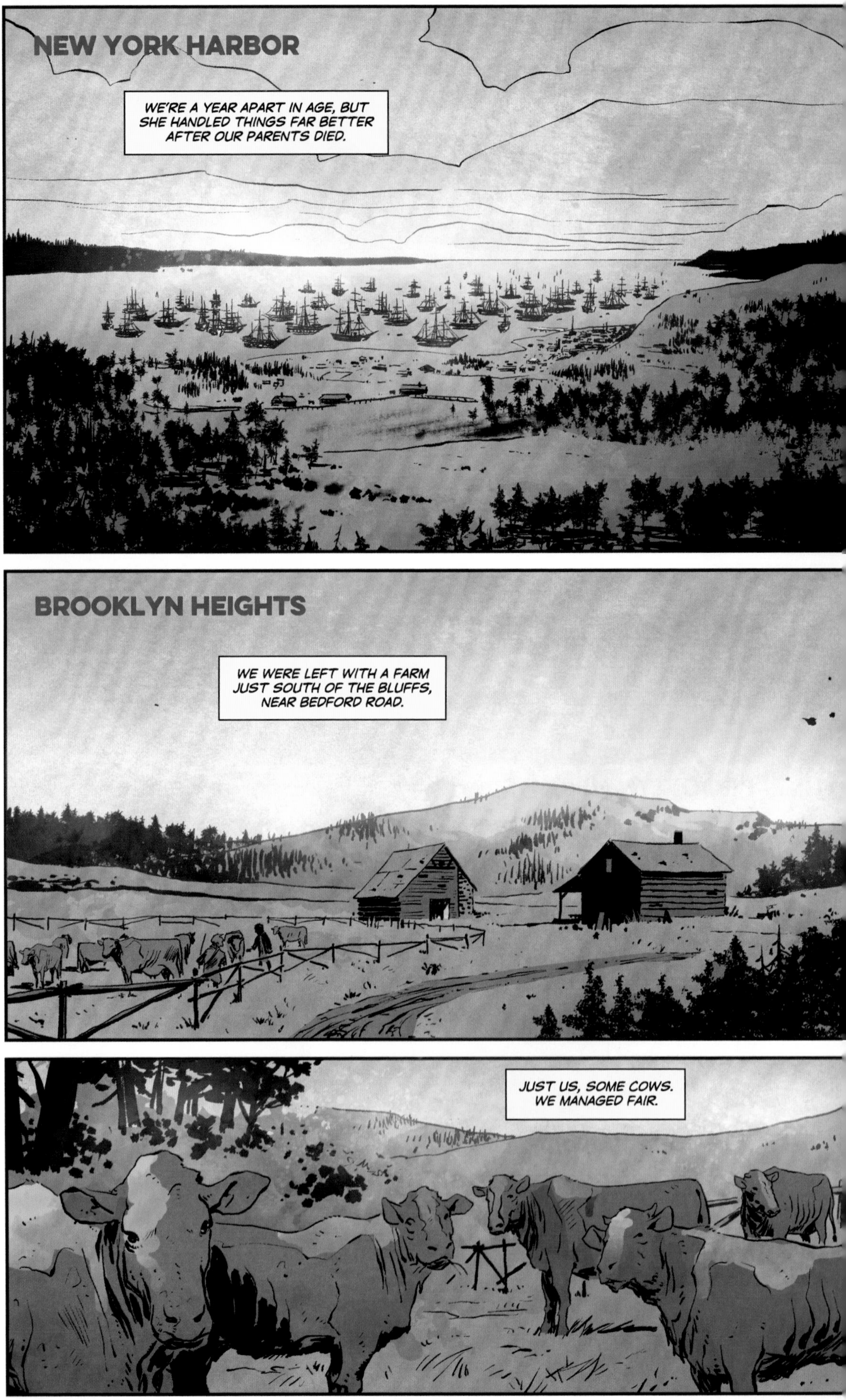
NEW YORK HARBOR
WE'RE A YEAR APART IN AGE, BUT SHE HANDLED THINGS FAR BETTER AFTER OUR PARENTS DIED.
BROOKLYN HEIGHTS
WE WERE LEFT WITH A FARM JUST SOUTH OF THE BLUFFS, NEAR BEDFORD ROAD.
JUST US, SOME COWS. WE MANAGED FAIR.

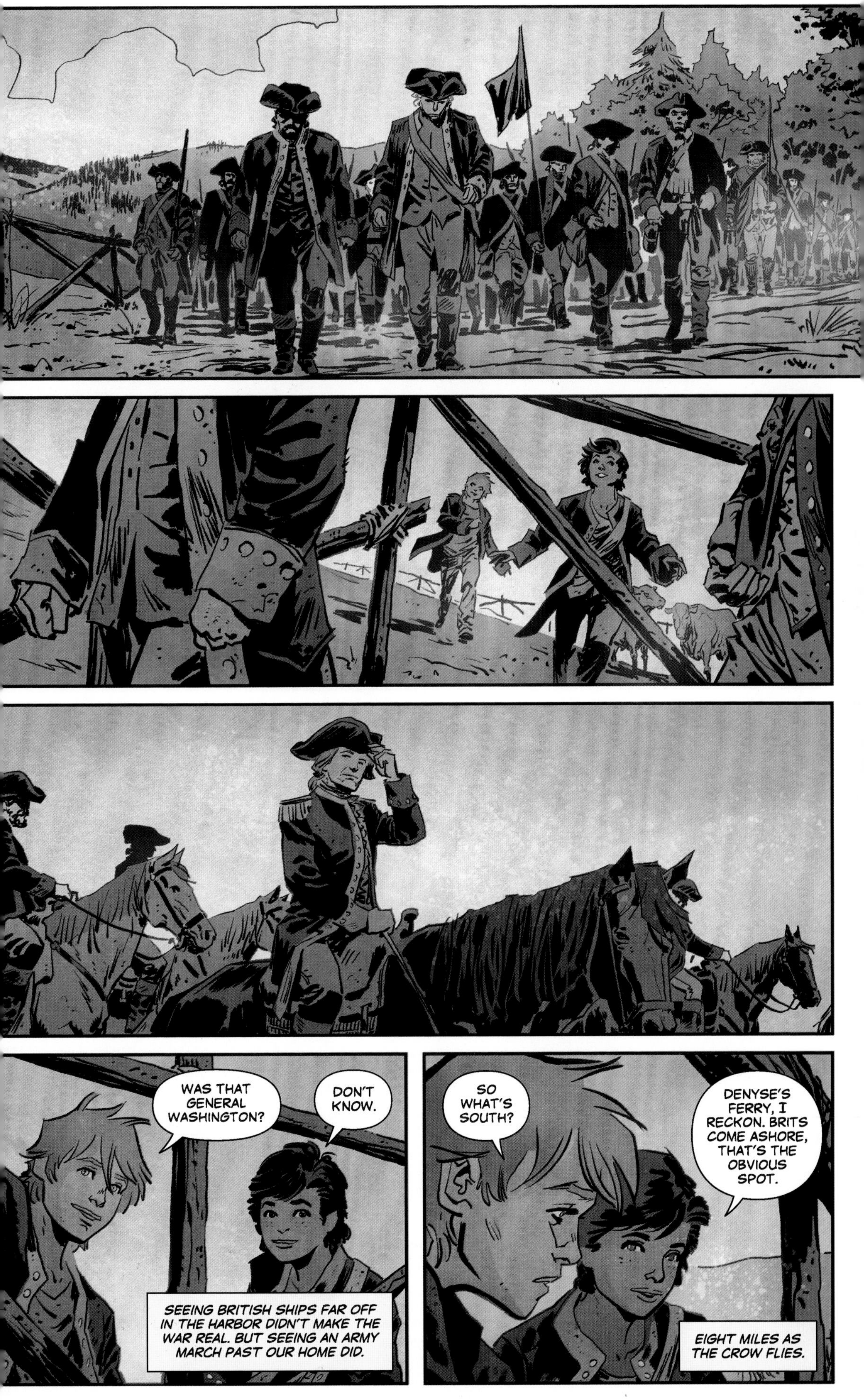

WAS THAT GENERAL WASHINGTON?
DON'T KNOW.
SEEING BRITISH SHIPS FAR OFF IN THE HARBOR DIDN'T MAKE THE WAR REAL. BUT SEEING AN ARMY MARCH PAST OUR HOME DID.
SO WHAT'S SOUTH?
DENYSE'S FERRY, I RECKON. BRITS COME ASHORE, THAT'S THE OBVIOUS SPOT.
EIGHT MILES AS THE CROW FLIES.

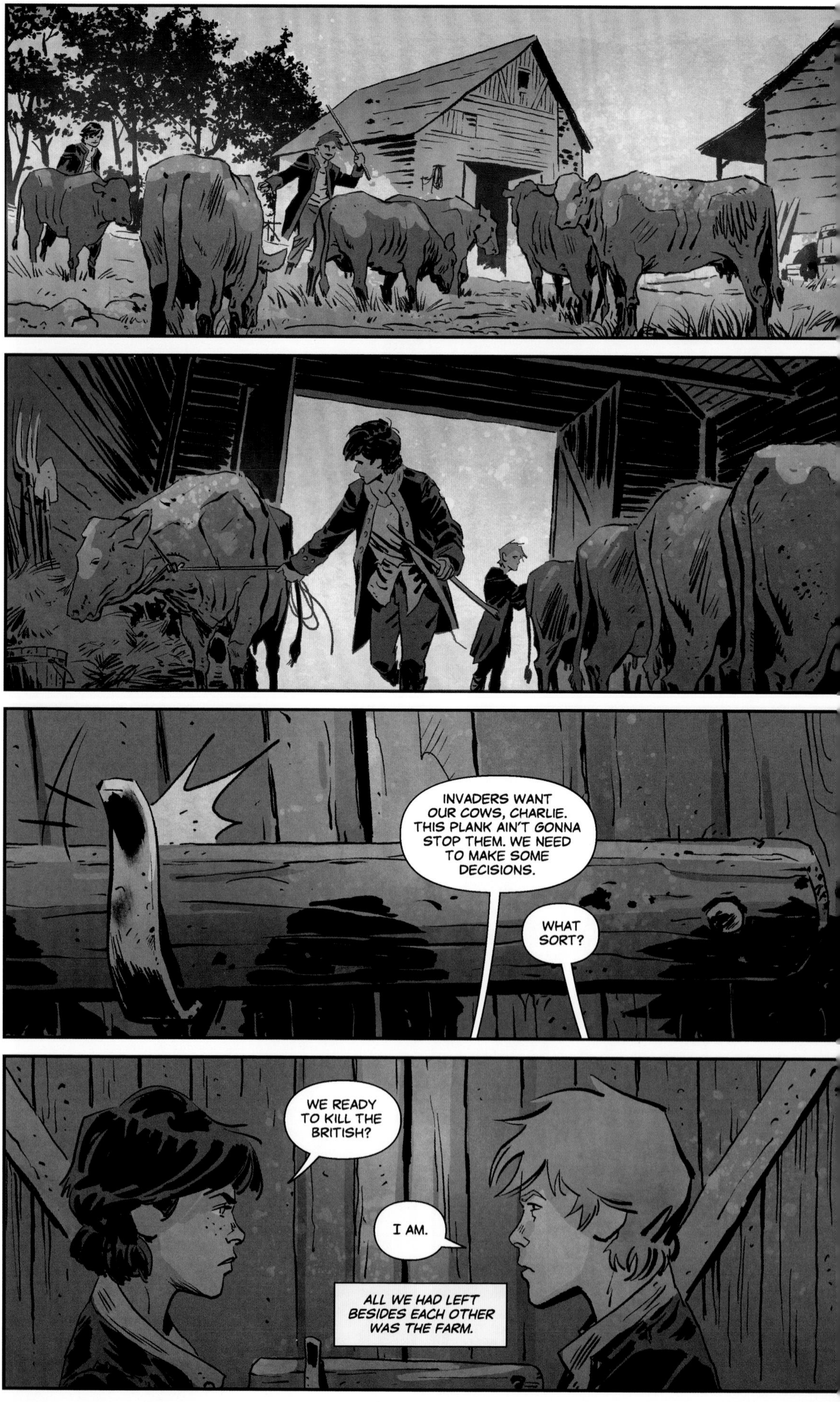
INVADERS WANT OUR COWS, CHARLIE. THIS PLANK AIN'T GONNA STOP THEM. WE NEED TO MAKE SOME DECISIONS.
WHAT SORT?
WE READY TO KILL THE BRITISH?
I AM.
ALL WE HAD LEFT BESIDES EACH OTHER WAS THE FARM.

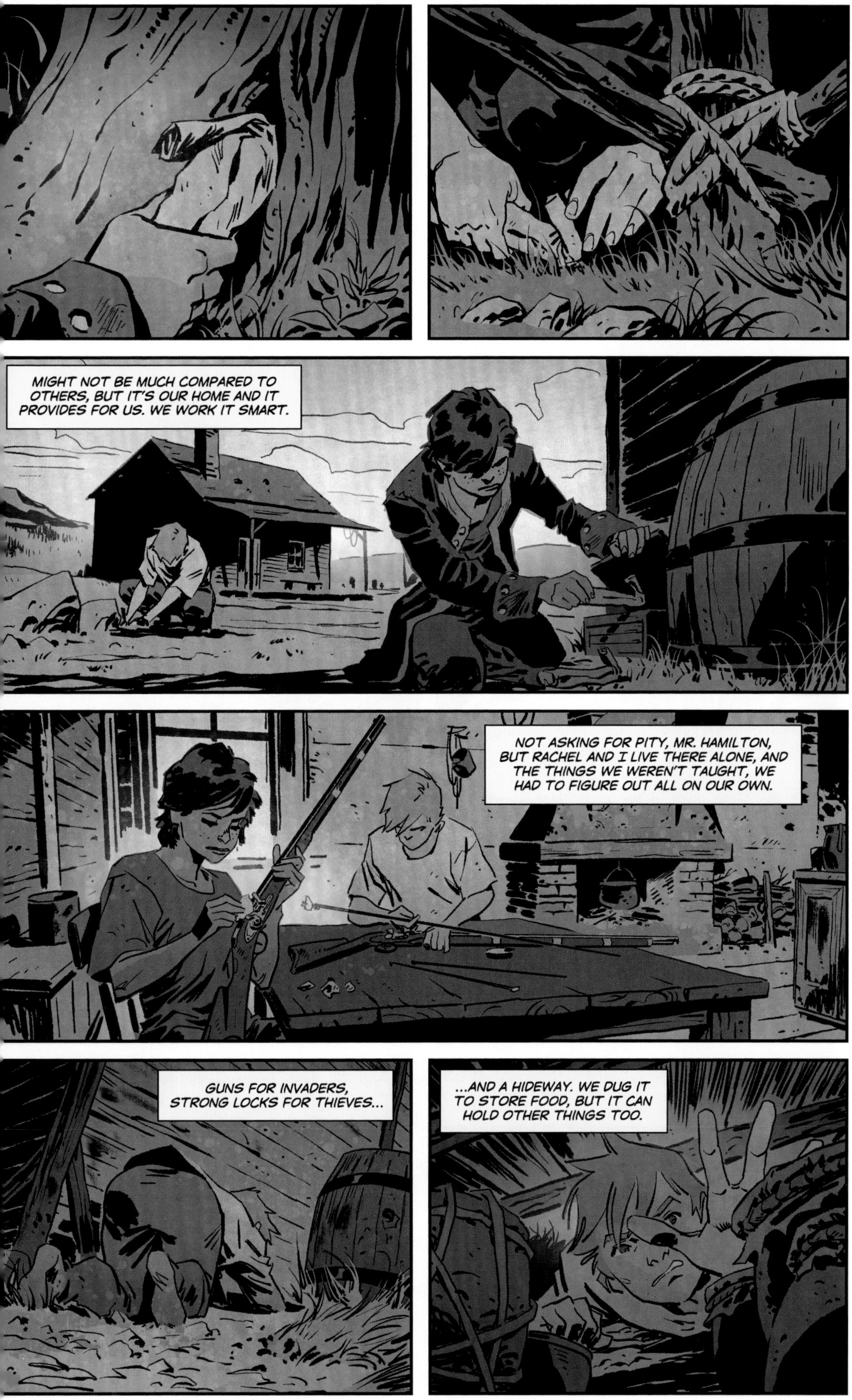
MIGHT NOT BE MUCH COMPARED TO OTHERS, BUT IT'S OUR HOME AND IT PROVIDES FOR US. WE WORK IT SMART.
NOT ASKING FOR PITY, MR. HAMILTON, BUT RACHEL AND I LIVE THERE ALONE, AND THE THINGS WE WEREN'T TAUGHT, WE HAD TO FIGURE OUT ALL ON OUR OWN.
GUNS FOR INVADERS, STRONG LOCKS FOR THIEVES...
...AND A HIDEWAY. WE DUG IT TO STORE FOOD, BUT IT CAN HOLD OTHER THINGS TOO.

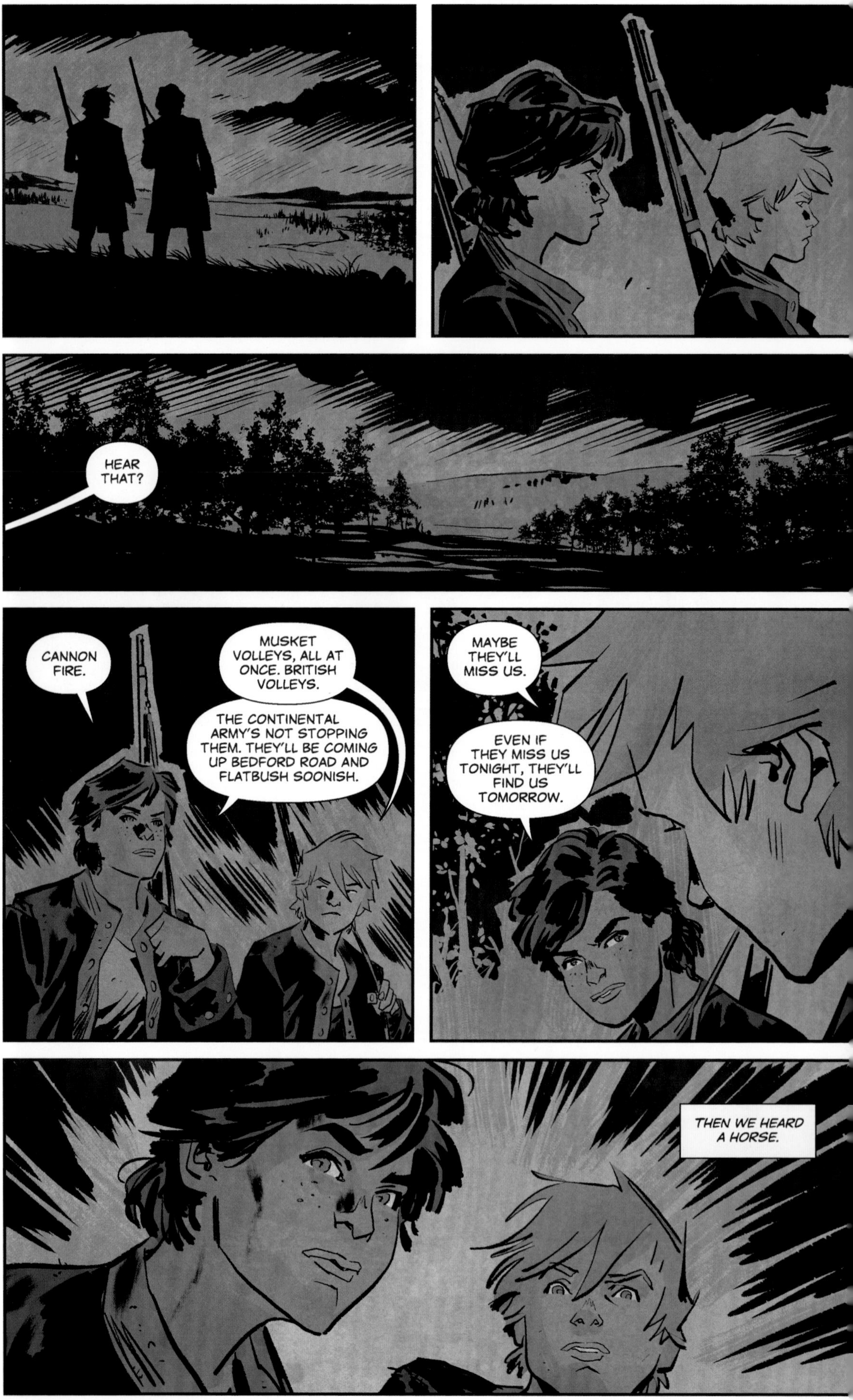
HEAR THAT?
CANNON FIRE.
MUSKET VOLLEYS, ALL AT ONCE. BRITISH VOLLEYS.
THE CONTINENTAL ARMY'S NOT STOPPING THEM. THEY'LL BE COMING UP BEDFORD ROAD AND FLATBUSH SOONISH.
MAYBE THEY'LL MISS US.
EVEN IF THEY MISS US TONIGHT, THEY'LL FIND US TOMORROW.
THEN WE HEARD A HORSE.

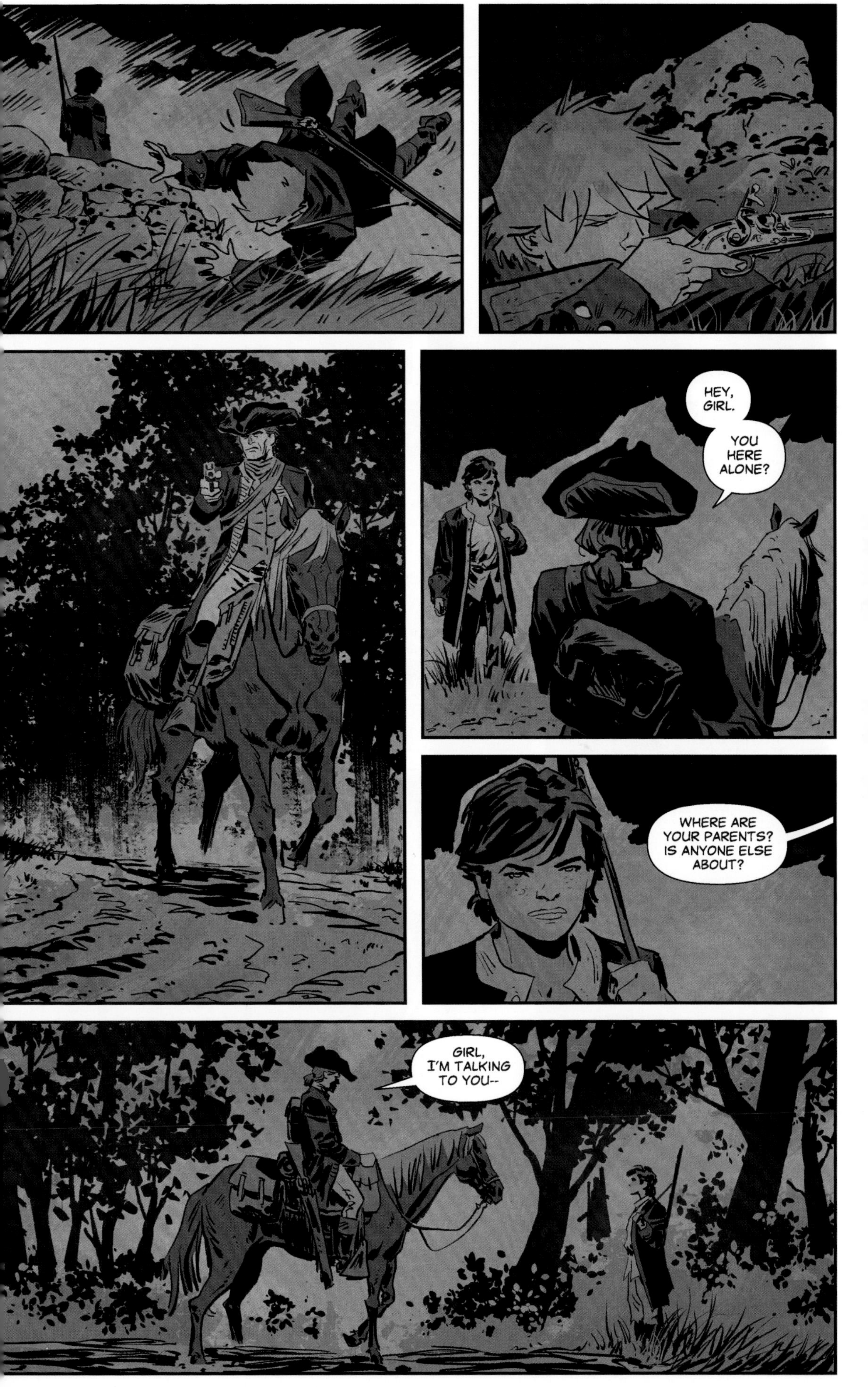
HEY, GIRL.
YOU HERE ALONE?
WHERE ARE YOUR PARENTS? IS ANYONE ELSE ABOUT?
GIRL, I'M TALKING TO YOU--

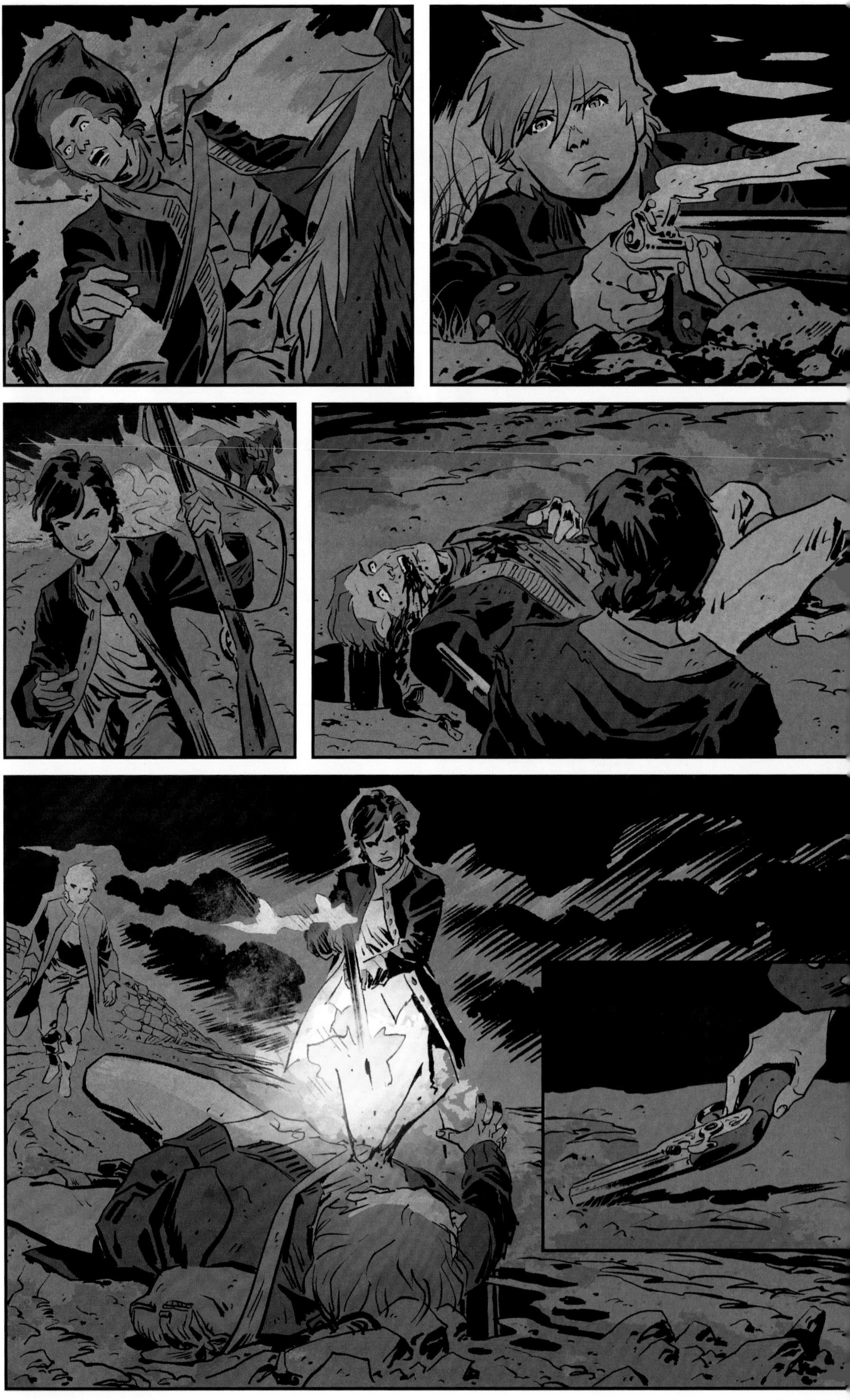

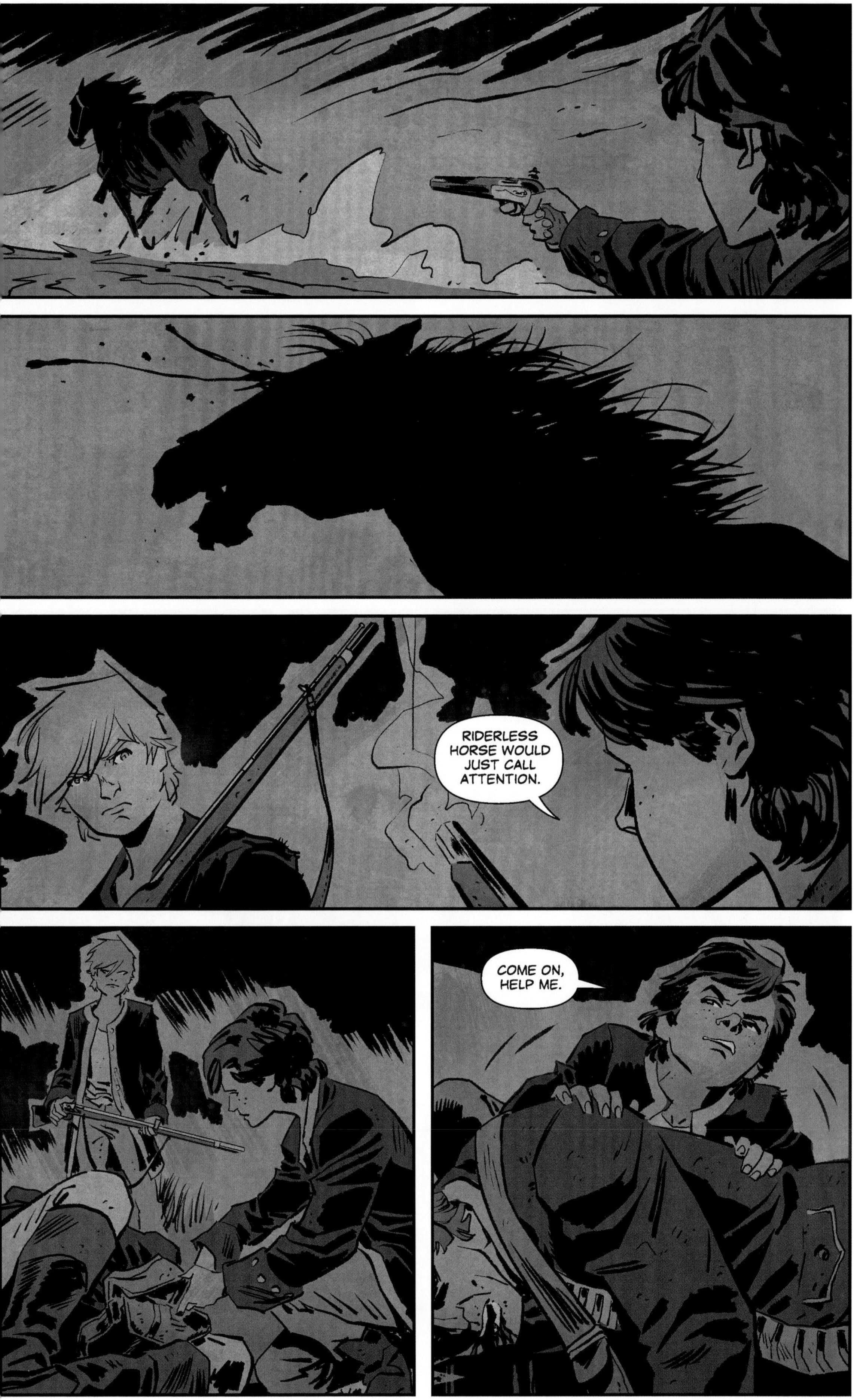
RIDERLESS HORSE WOULD JUST CALL ATTENTION.
COME ON, HELP ME.

RACHEL, CAN YOU READ THIS?

WHAT IS IT?

LETTER. SOMETHING ABOUT A SHIPWRECK.

HELLO THE HOUSE!

I GOT IT.

YOU TWO ALL RIGHT, THEN?

BATTLE MISSED US.

MISSED US AT SPEED. YOU HEARD THE NEWS? WASHINGTON'S HIGHTAILING IT ACROSS THE WATER TO NEW YORK!

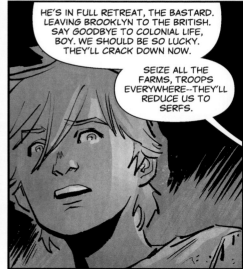

HE'S IN FULL RETREAT, THE BASTARD. LEAVING BROOKLYN TO THE BRITISH. SAY GOODBYE TO COLONIAL LIFE, BOY. WE SHOULD BE SO LUCKY. THEY'LL CRACK DOWN NOW.

SEIZE ALL THE FARMS, TROOPS EVERYWHERE--THEY'LL REDUCE US TO SERFS.

CHARLIE, COME BACK HERE.

YOU CAN RETREAT WITH THE ARMY IF YOU LIKE...

...CROSS OVER TO THE CITY, REGISTER YOUR PROPERTY WITH THE ARMY, AND WITH LUCK RECLAIM IT ONCE THIS IS ALL OVER.

BETTER THAT THAN OCCUPATION!

CHARLIE, THERE'S A BOAT SUNK IN THE RIVER, A SECRET BRITISH BOAT--FULL OF GOLD! TO PAY WAGES, TO BUY SUPPLIES, TO FUND THE WAR...

...SUMMAT WENT WRONG, AND SHE SUNK WITH ALL HANDS. AND I KNOW EXACTLY WHERE!

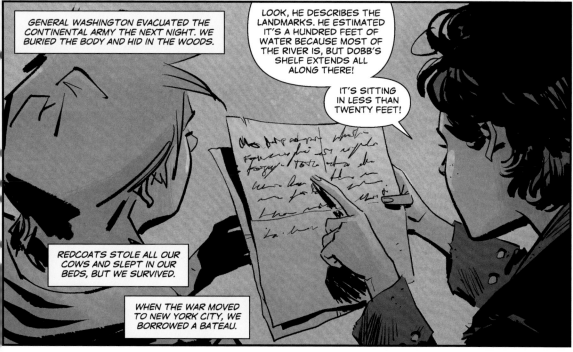

GENERAL WASHINGTON EVACUATED THE CONTINENTAL ARMY THE NEXT NIGHT. WE BURIED THE BODY AND HID IN THE WOODS.

LOOK, HE DESCRIBES THE LANDMARKS. HE ESTIMATED IT'S A HUNDRED FEET OF WATER BECAUSE MOST OF THE RIVER IS, BUT DOBB'S SHELF EXTENDS ALL ALONG THERE!

IT'S SITTING IN LESS THAN TWENTY FEET!

REDCOATS STOLE ALL OUR COWS AND SLEPT IN OUR BEDS, BUT WE SURVIVED.

WHEN THE WAR MOVED TO NEW YORK CITY, WE BORROWED A BATEAU.

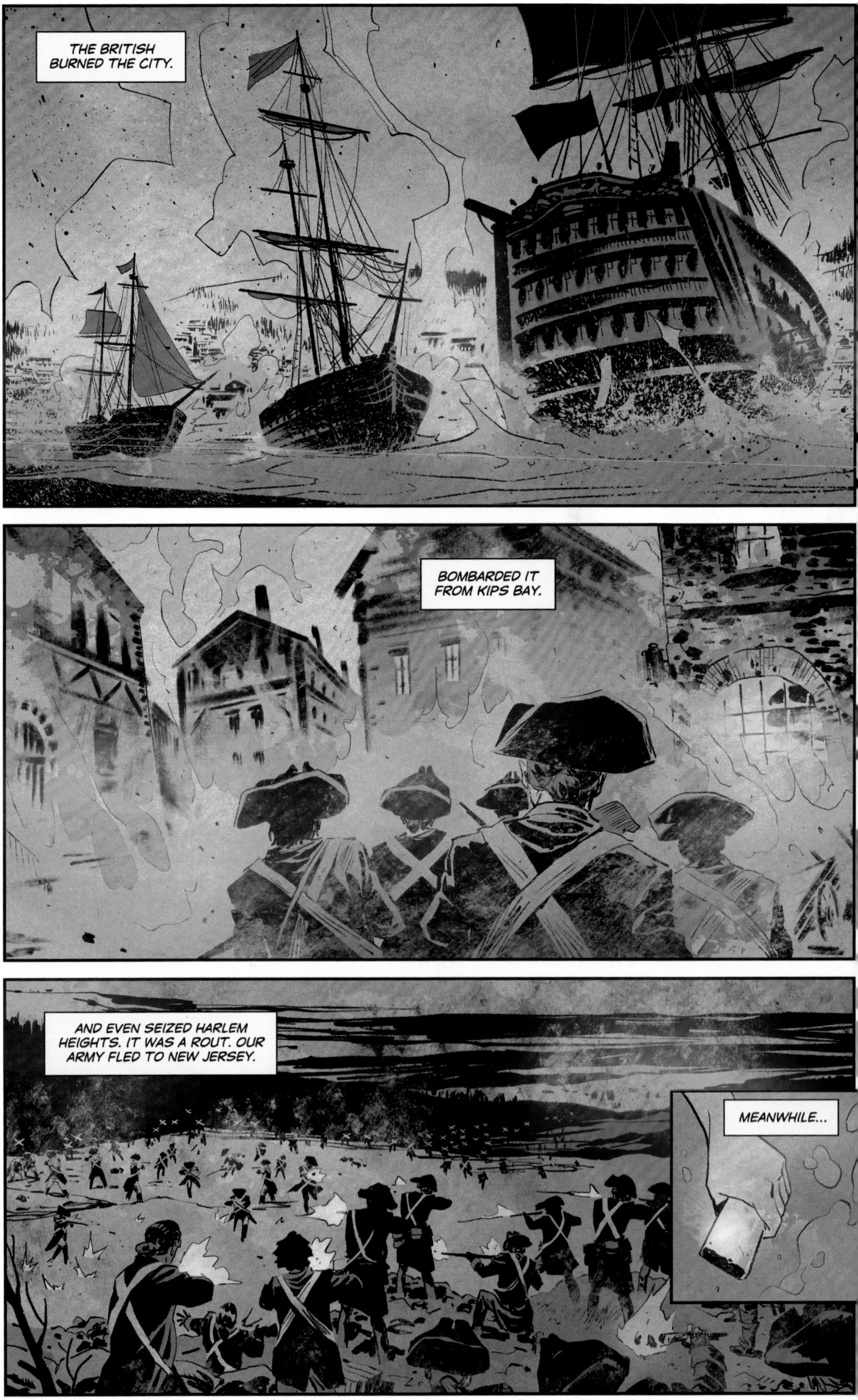
THE BRITISH BURNED THE CITY.
BOMBARDED IT FROM KIPS BAY.
AND EVEN SEIZED HARLEM HEIGHTS. IT WAS A ROUT. OUR ARMY FLED TO NEW JERSEY.
MEANWHILE...

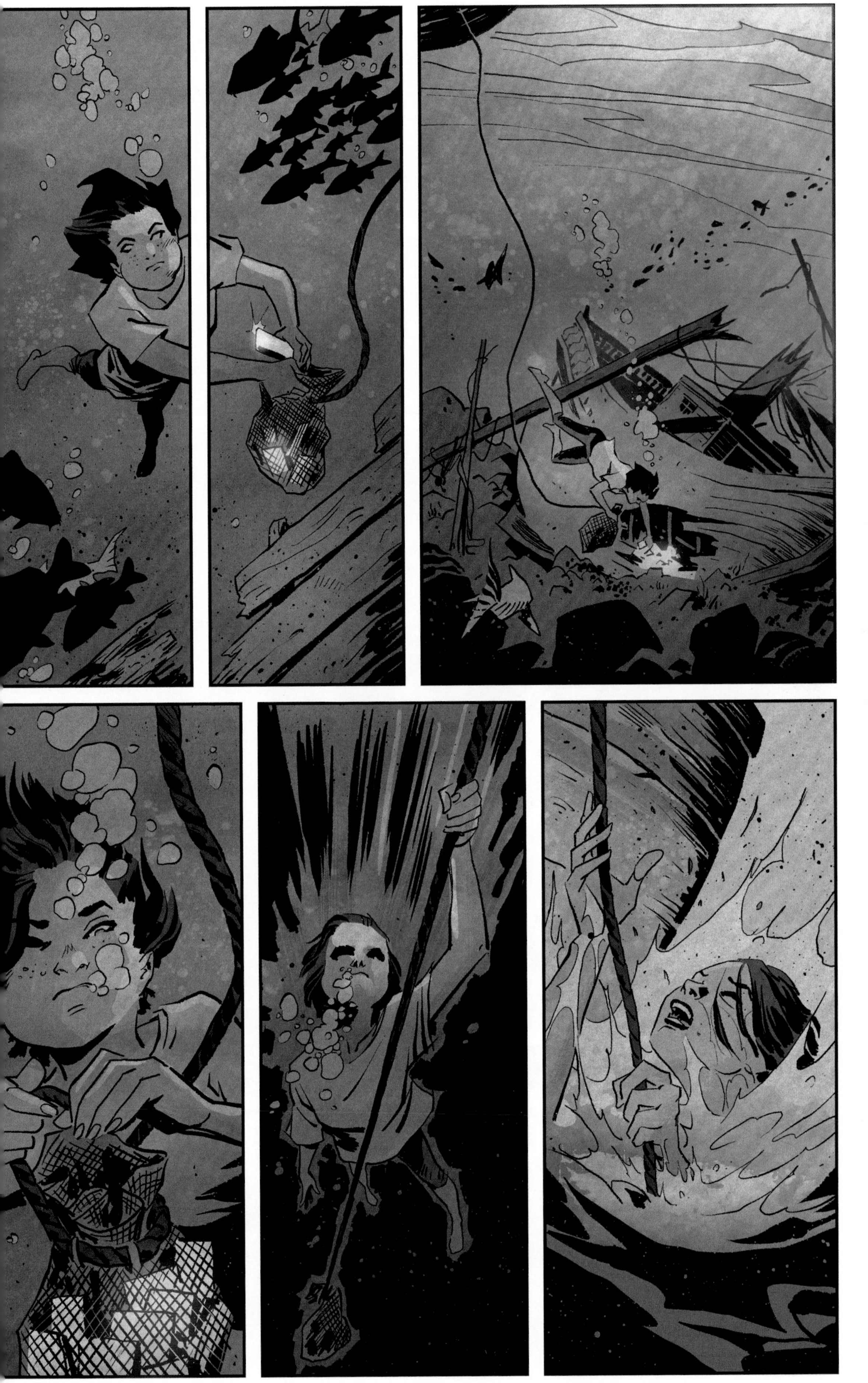

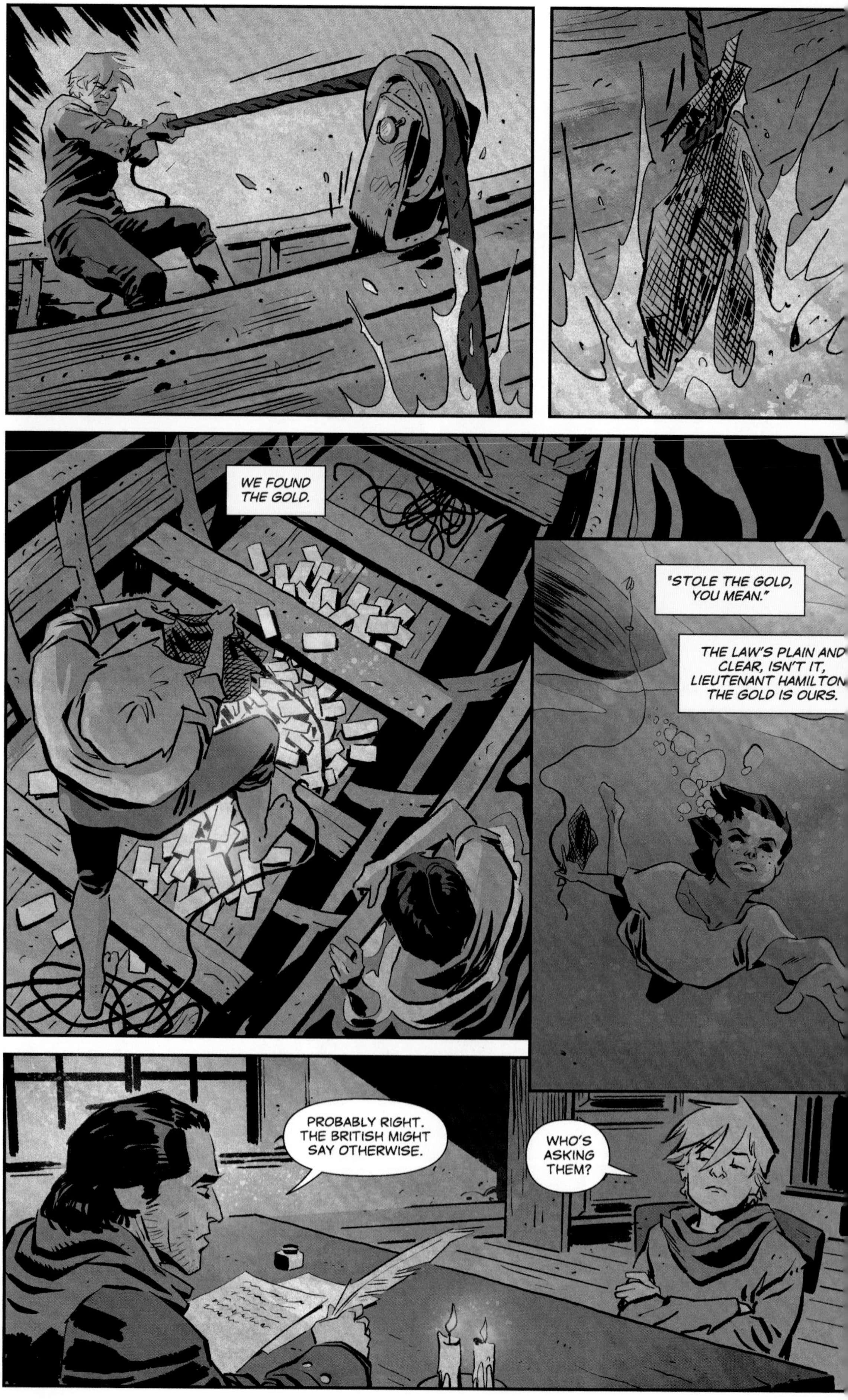
WE FOUND THE GOLD.
"STOLE THE GOLD, YOU MEAN."
THE LAW'S PLAIN AND CLEAR, ISN'T IT, LIEUTENANT HAMILTON THE GOLD IS OURS.
PROBABLY RIGHT. THE BRITISH MIGHT SAY OTHERWISE.
WHO'S ASKING THEM?

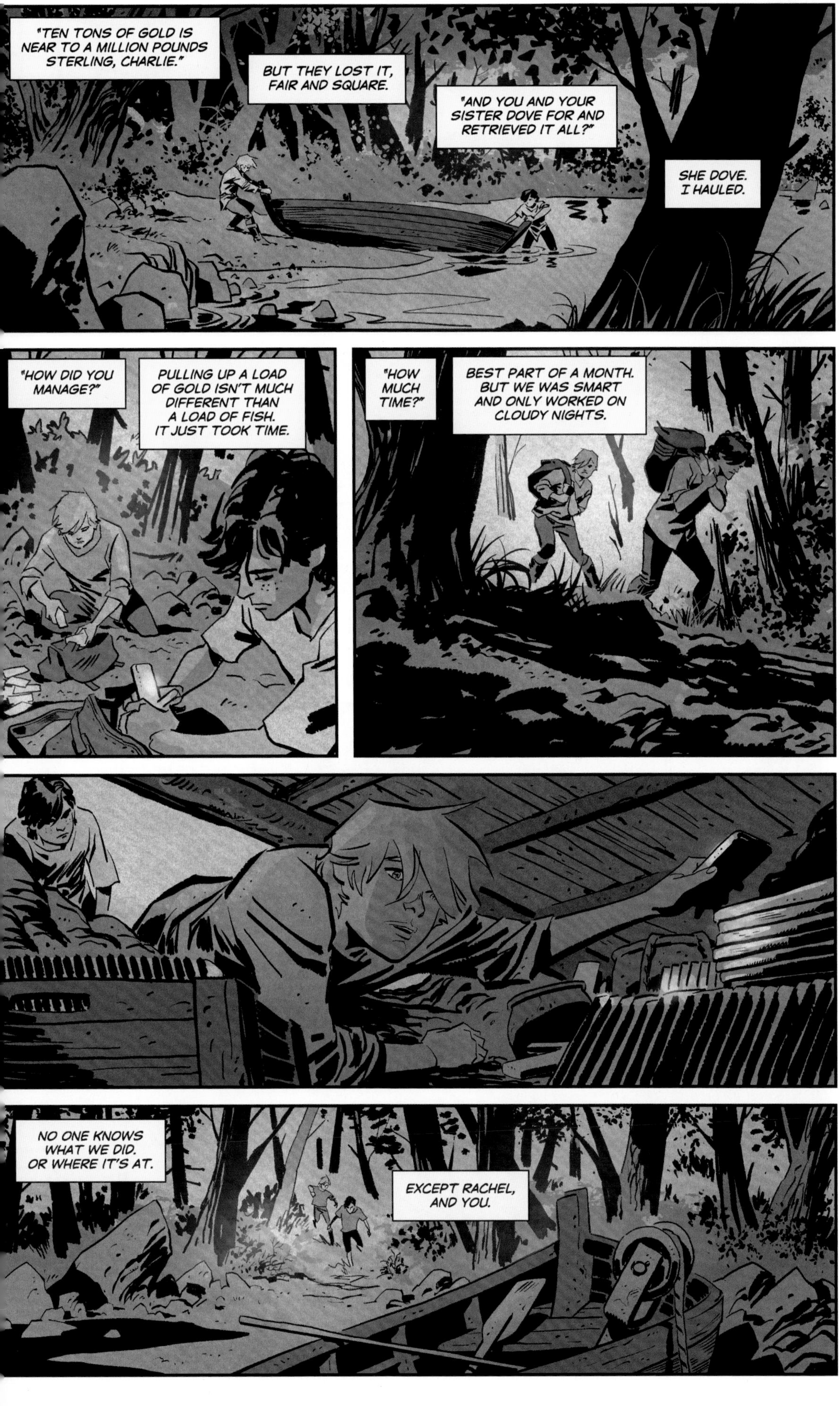
"TEN TONS OF GOLD IS NEAR TO A MILLION POUNDS STERLING, CHARLIE."
BUT THEY LOST IT, FAIR AND SQUARE.
"AND YOU AND YOUR SISTER DOVE FOR AND RETRIEVED IT ALL?"
SHE DOVE. I HAULED.
"HOW DID YOU MANAGE?"
PULLING UP A LOAD OF GOLD ISN'T MUCH DIFFERENT THAN A LOAD OF FISH. IT JUST TOOK TIME.
"HOW MUCH TIME?"
BEST PART OF A MONTH. BUT WE WAS SMART AND ONLY WORKED ON CLOUDY NIGHTS.
NO ONE KNOWS WHAT WE DID. OR WHERE IT'S AT.
EXCEPT RACHEL, AND YOU.

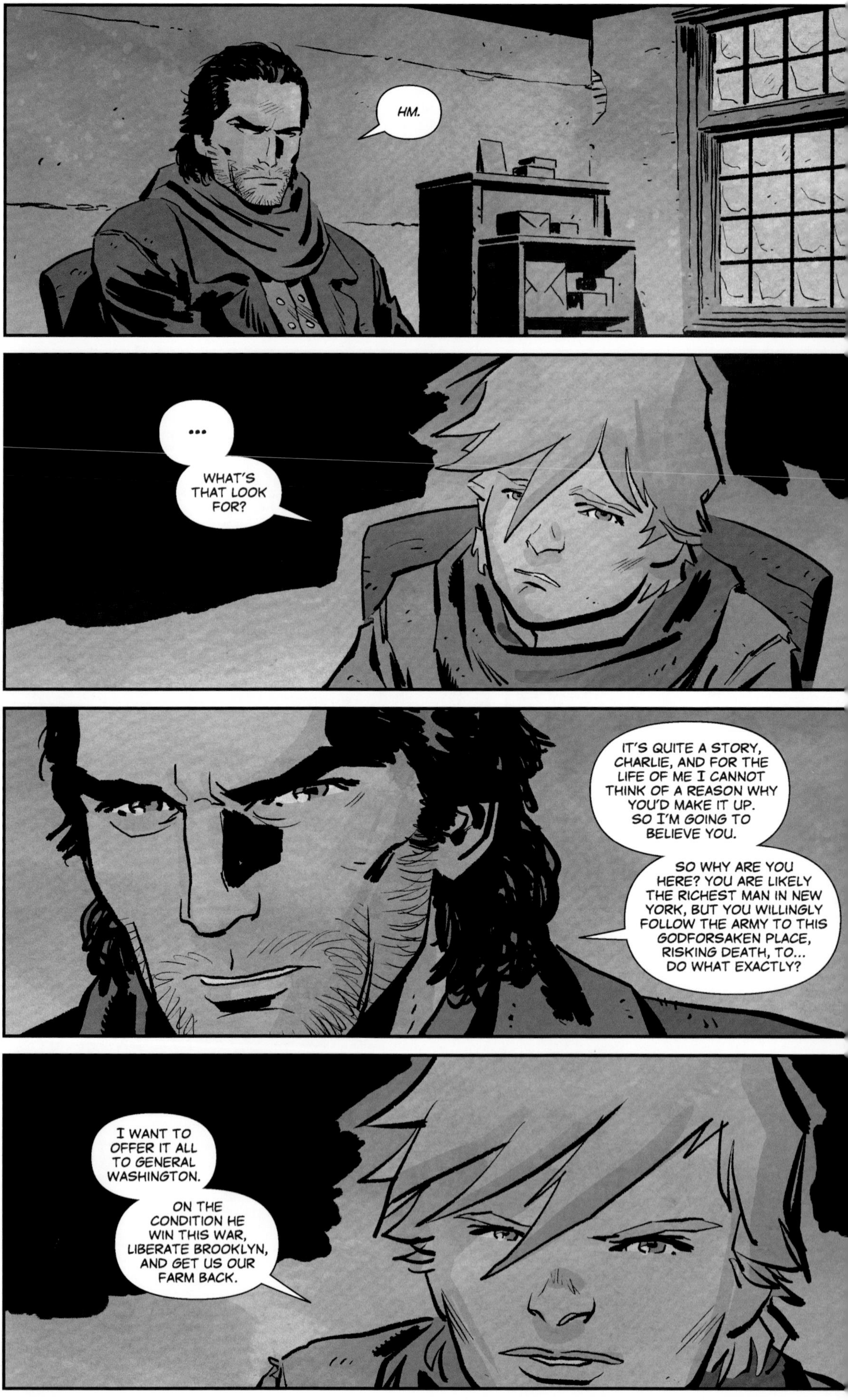
HM.
...
WHAT'S THAT LOOK FOR?
IT'S QUITE A STORY, CHARLIE, AND FOR THE LIFE OF ME I CANNOT THINK OF A REASON WHY YOU'D MAKE IT UP. SO I'M GOING TO BELIEVE YOU.
SO WHY ARE YOU HERE? YOU ARE LIKELY THE RICHEST MAN IN NEW YORK, BUT YOU WILLINGLY FOLLOW THE ARMY TO THIS GODFORSAKEN PLACE, RISKING DEATH, TO... DO WHAT EXACTLY?
I WANT TO OFFER IT ALL TO GENERAL WASHINGTON.
ON THE CONDITION HE WIN THIS WAR, LIBERATE BROOKLYN, AND GET US OUR FARM BACK.

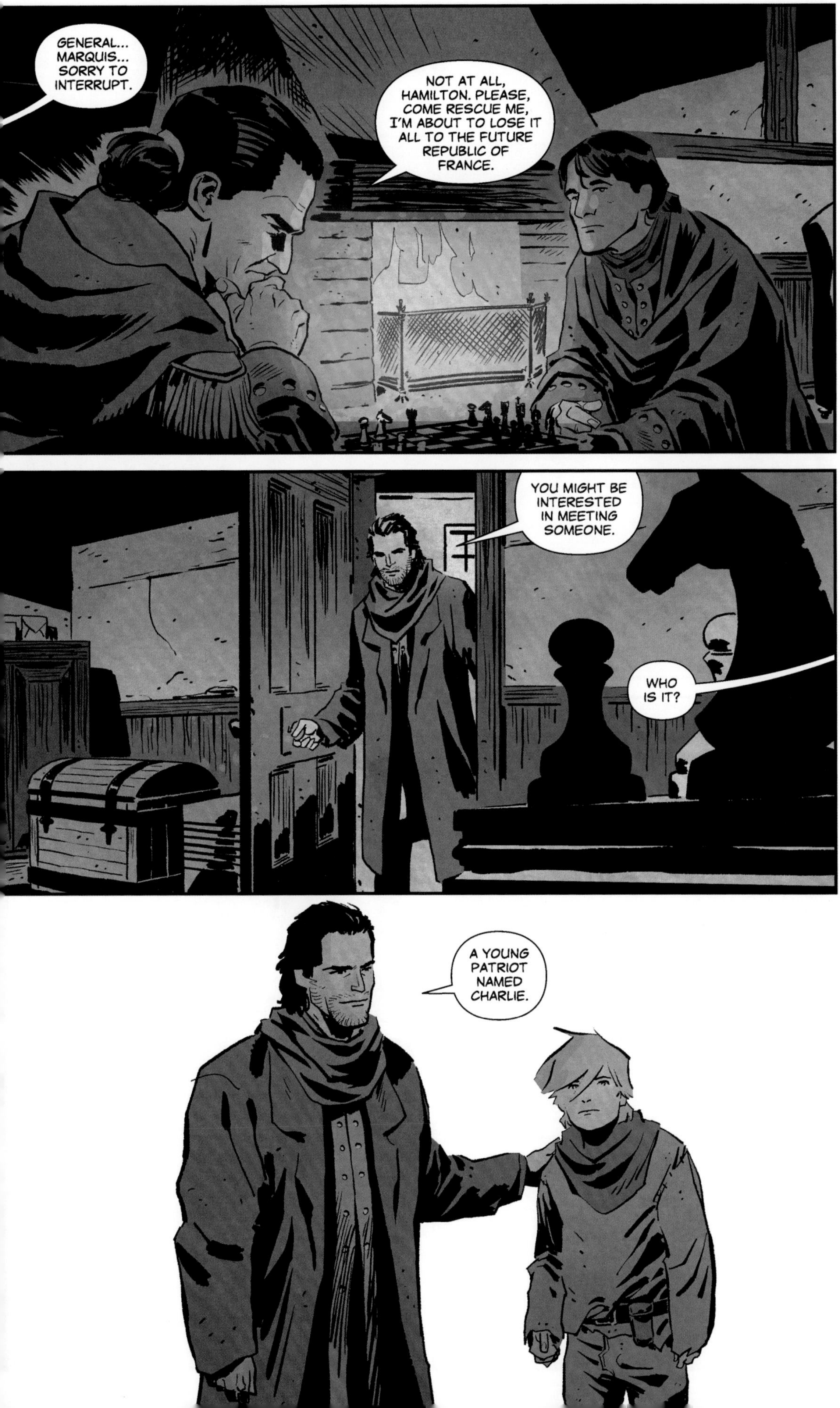
GENERAL... MARQUIS... SORRY TO INTERRUPT.
NOT AT ALL, HAMILTON. PLEASE, COME RESCUE ME, I'M ABOUT TO LOSE IT ALL TO THE FUTURE REPUBLIC OF FRANCE.
YOU MIGHT BE INTERESTED IN MEETING SOMEONE.
WHO IS IT?
A YOUNG PATRIOT NAMED CHARLIE.

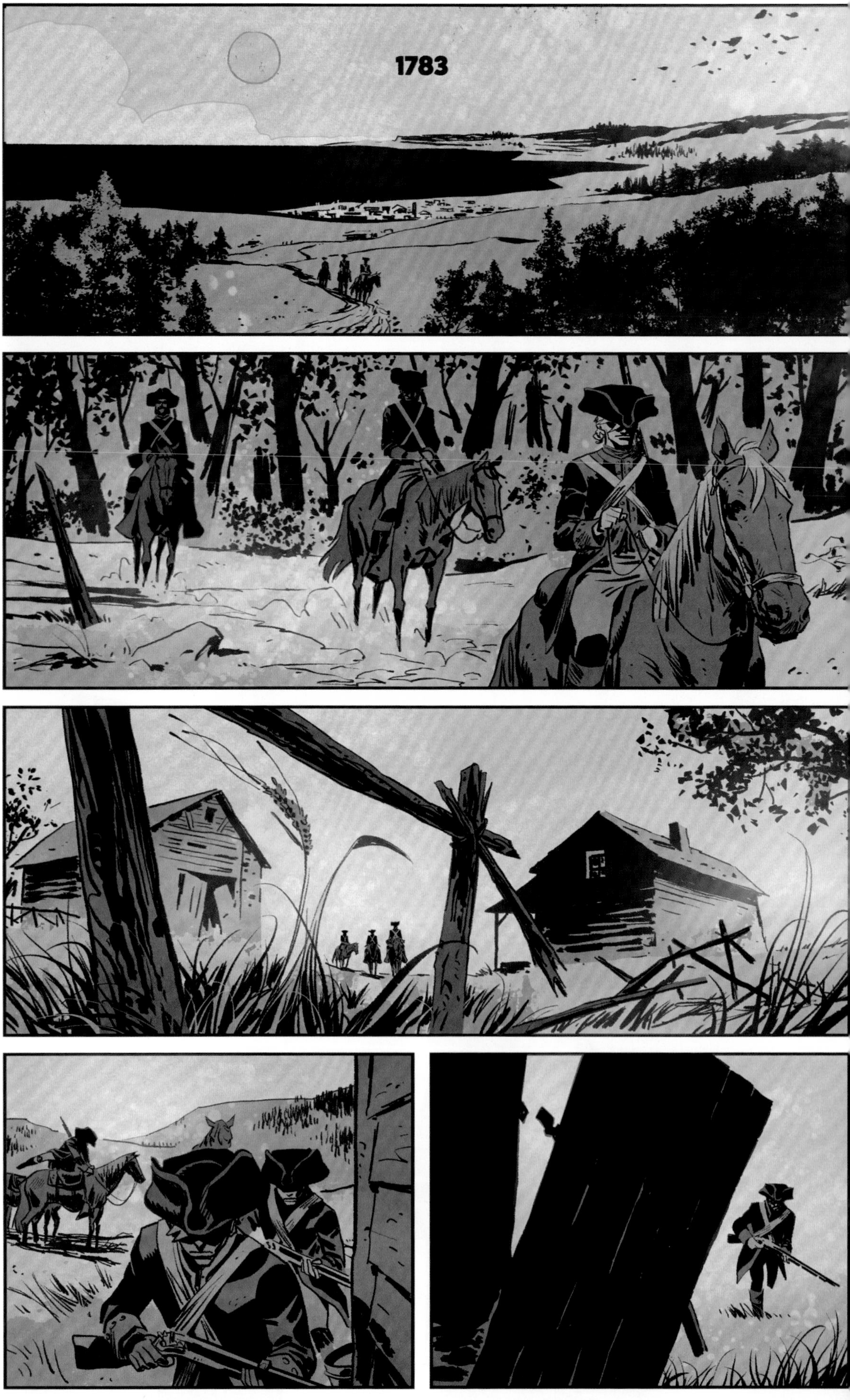
1783

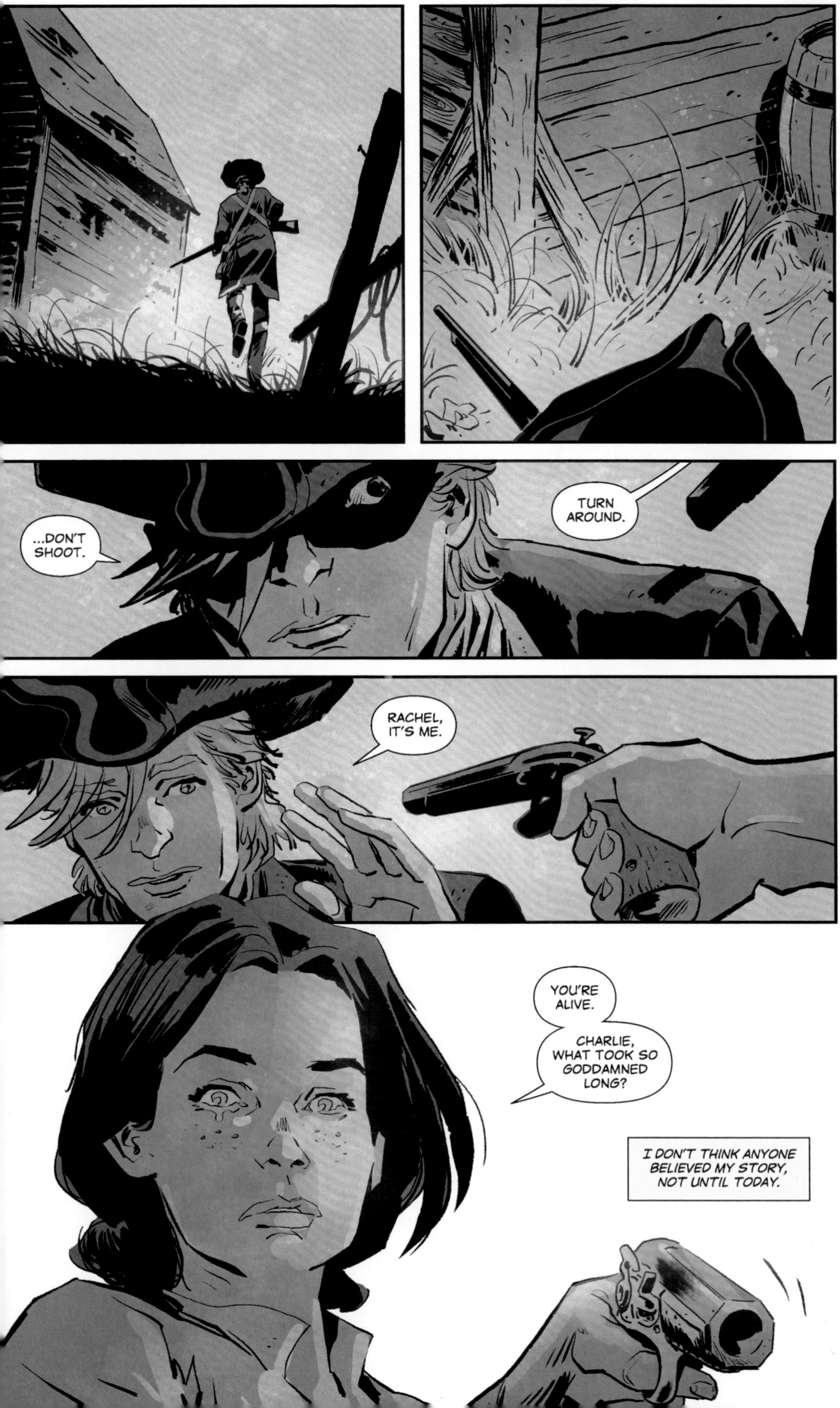
TURN AROUND.
...DON'T SHOOT.
RACHEL, IT'S ME.
YOU'RE ALIVE.
CHARLIE, WHAT TOOK SO GODDAMNED LONG?
I DON'T THINK ANYONE BELIEVED MY STORY, NOT UNTIL TODAY.

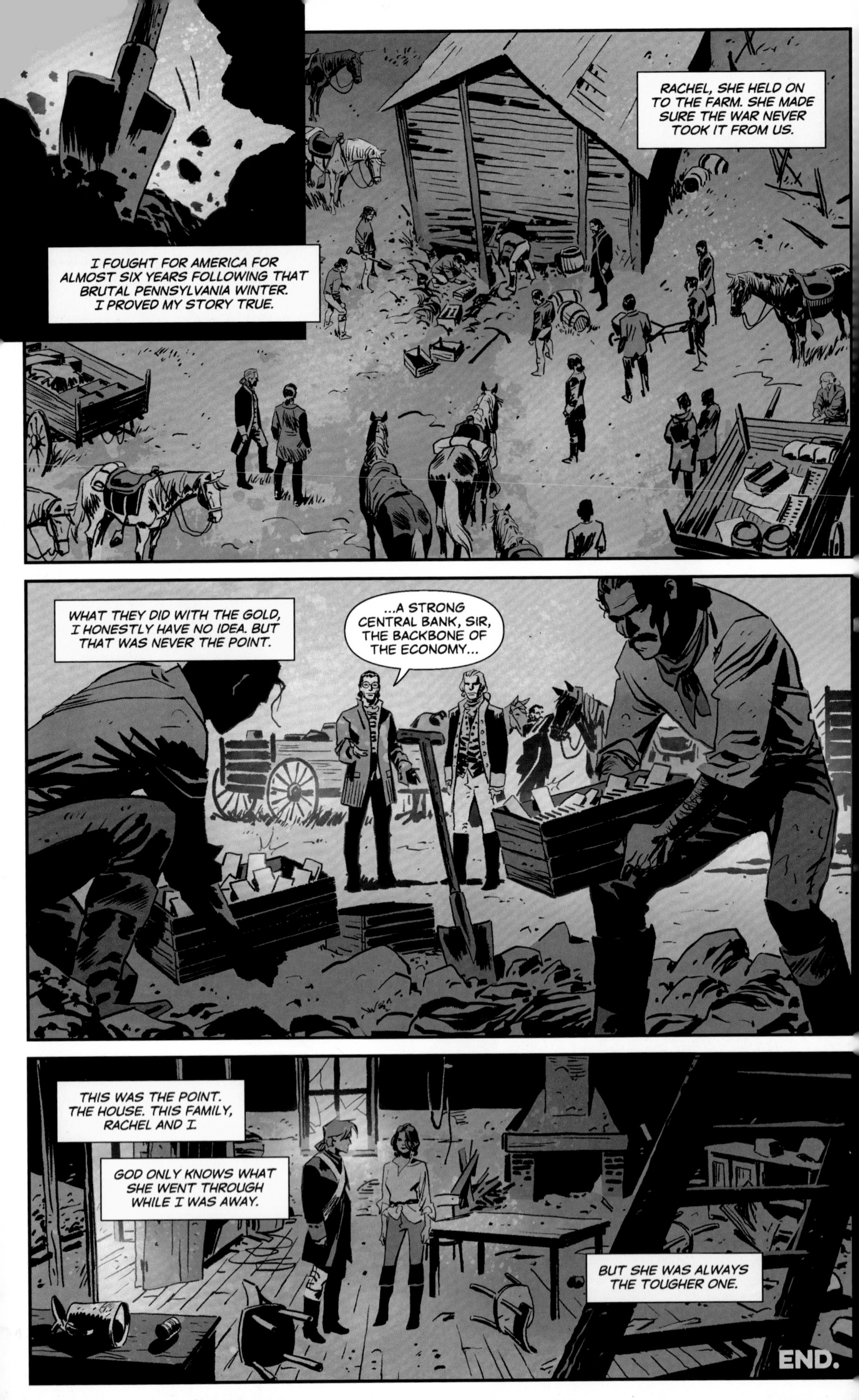
I FOUGHT FOR AMERICA FOR ALMOST SIX YEARS FOLLOWING THAT BRUTAL PENNSYLVANIA WINTER. I PROVED MY STORY TRUE.
RACHEL, SHE HELD ON TO THE FARM. SHE MADE SURE THE WAR NEVER TOOK IT FROM US.
WHAT THEY DID WITH THE GOLD, I HONESTLY HAVE NO IDEA. BUT THAT WAS NEVER THE POINT.
...A STRONG CENTRAL BANK, SIR, THE BACKBONE OF THE ECONOMY...
THIS WAS THE POINT. THE HOUSE. THIS FAMILY, RACHEL AND I.
GOD ONLY KNOWS WHAT SHE WENT THROUGH WHILE I WAS AWAY.
BUT SHE WAS ALWAYS THE TOUGHER ONE.
END.

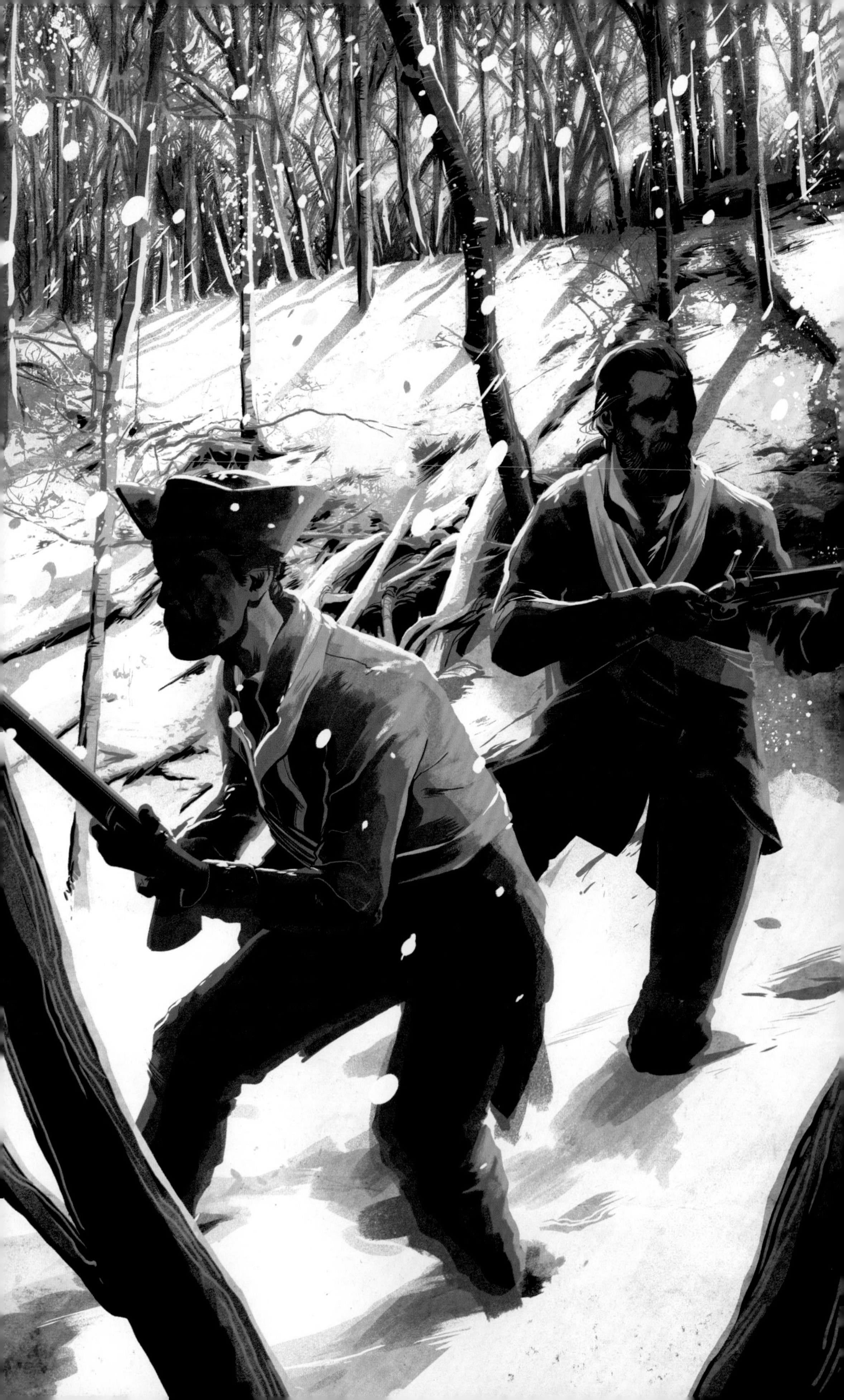

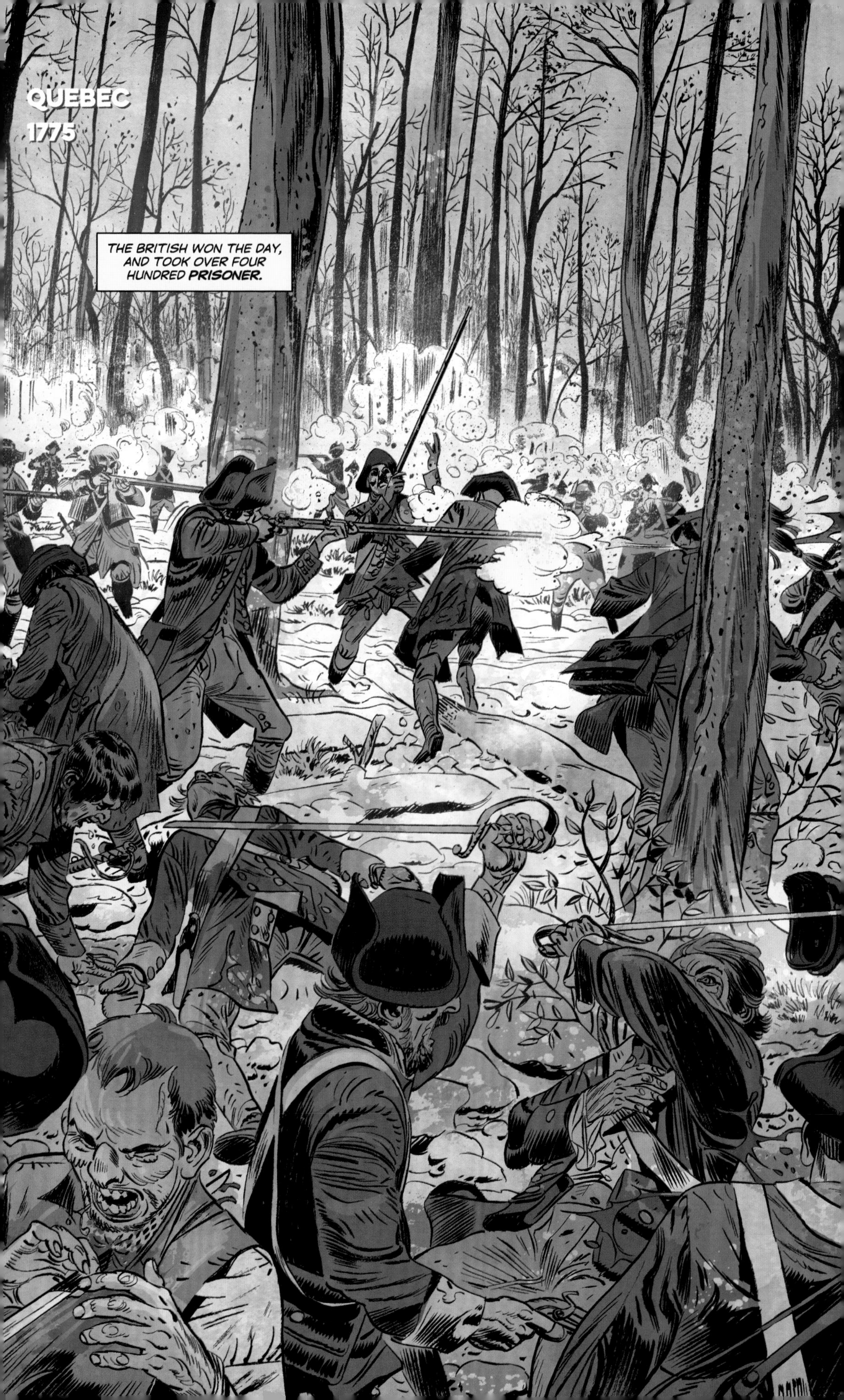
QUEBEC
1775
THE BRITISH WON THE DAY, AND TOOK OVER FOUR HUNDRED PRISONER.

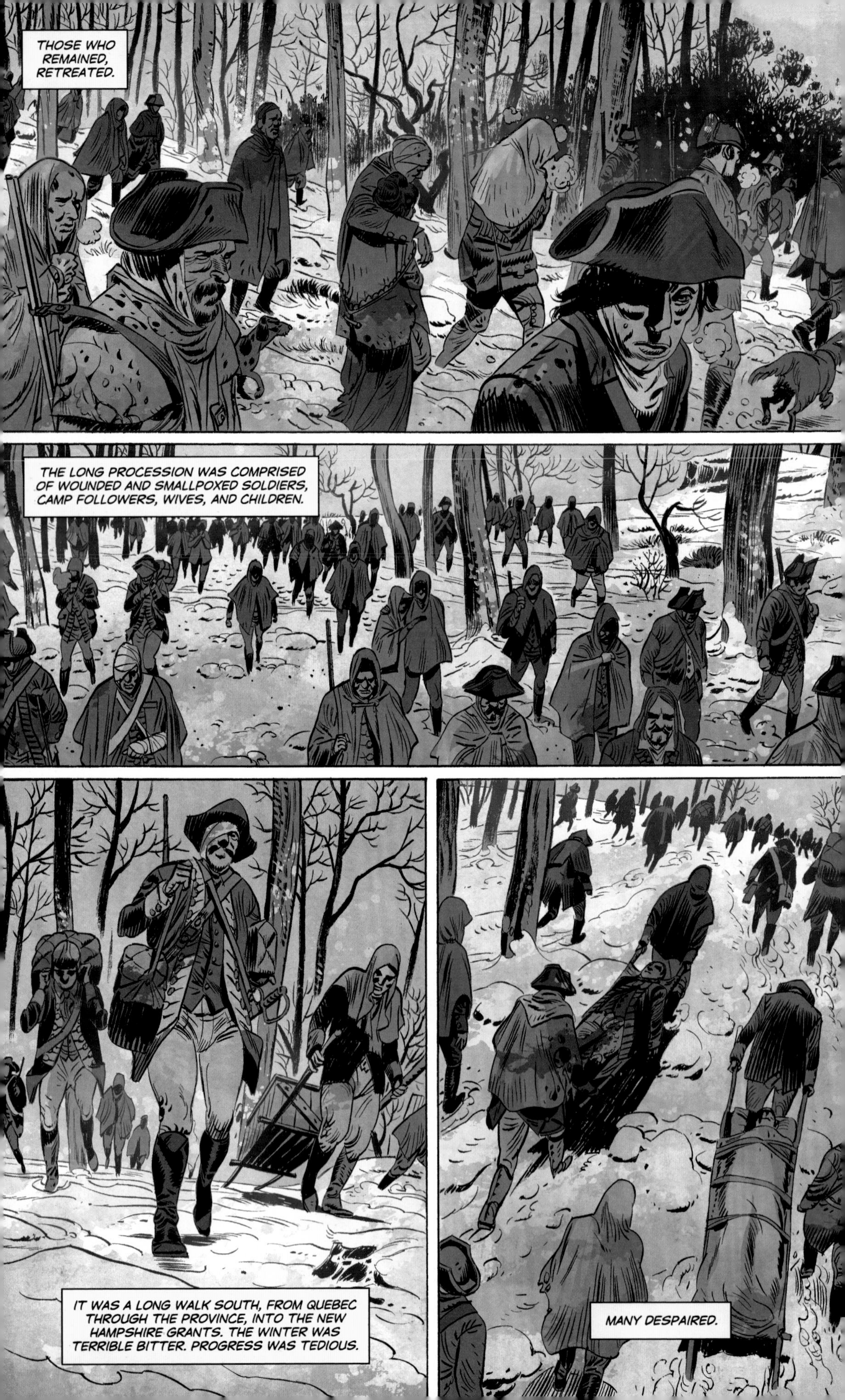
THOSE WHO REMAINED, RETREATED.
THE LONG PROCESSION WAS COMPRISED OF WOUNDED AND SMALLPOXED SOLDIERS, CAMP FOLLOWERS, WIVES, AND CHILDREN.
IT WAS A LONG WALK SOUTH, FROM QUEBEC THROUGH THE PROVINCE, INTO THE NEW HAMPSHIRE GRANTS. THE WINTER WAS TERRIBLE BITTER. PROGRESS WAS TEDIOUS.
MANY DESPAIRED.

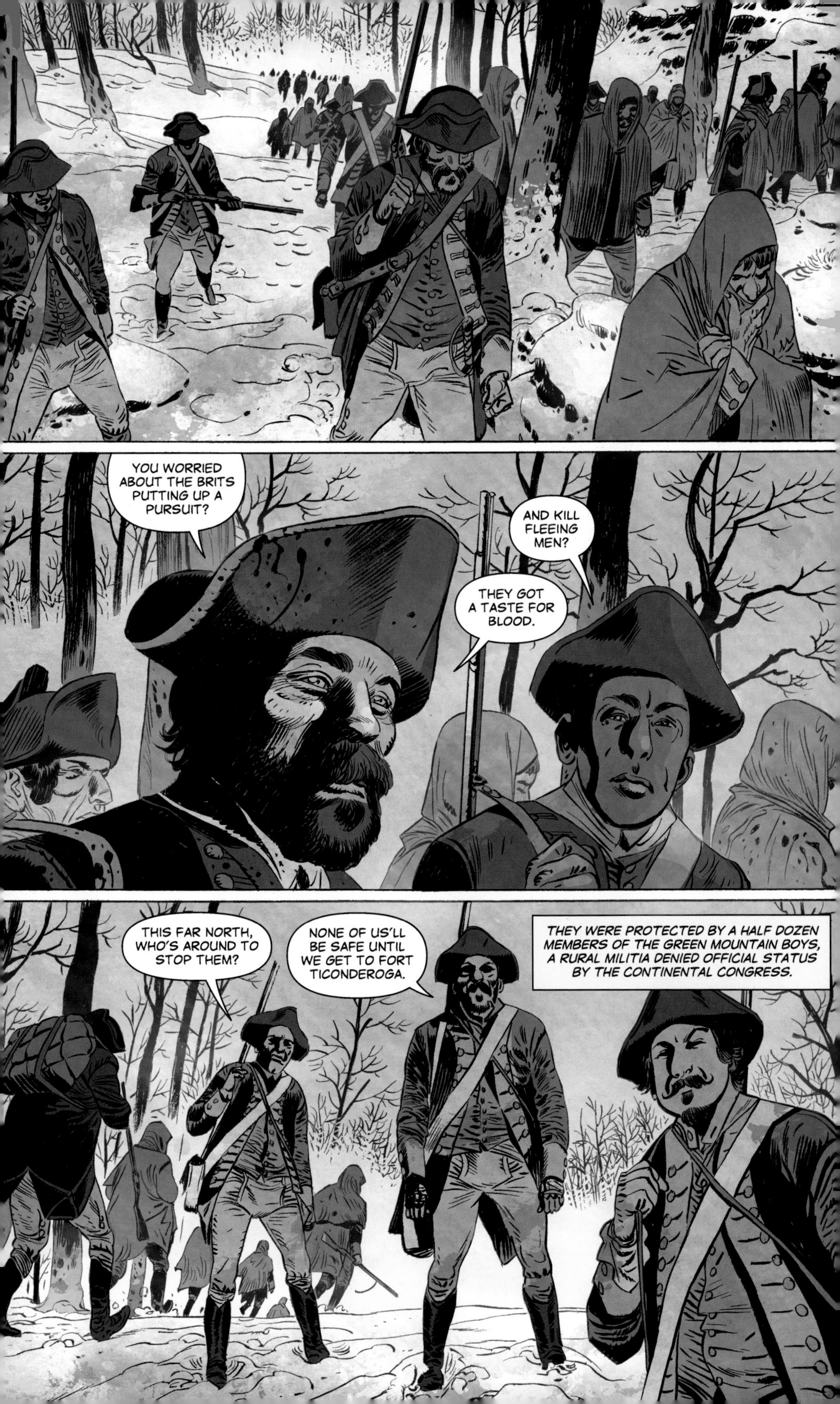
YOU WORRIED ABOUT THE BRITS PUTTING UP A PURSUIT?
AND KILL FLEEING MEN?
THEY GOT A TASTE FOR BLOOD.
THIS FAR NORTH, WHO'S AROUND TO STOP THEM?
NONE OF US'LL BE SAFE UNTIL WE GET TO FORT TICONDEROGA.
THEY WERE PROTECTED BY A HALF DOZEN MEMBERS OF THE GREEN MOUNTAIN BOYS, A RURAL MILITIA DENIED OFFICIAL STATUS BY THE CONTINENTAL CONGRESS.

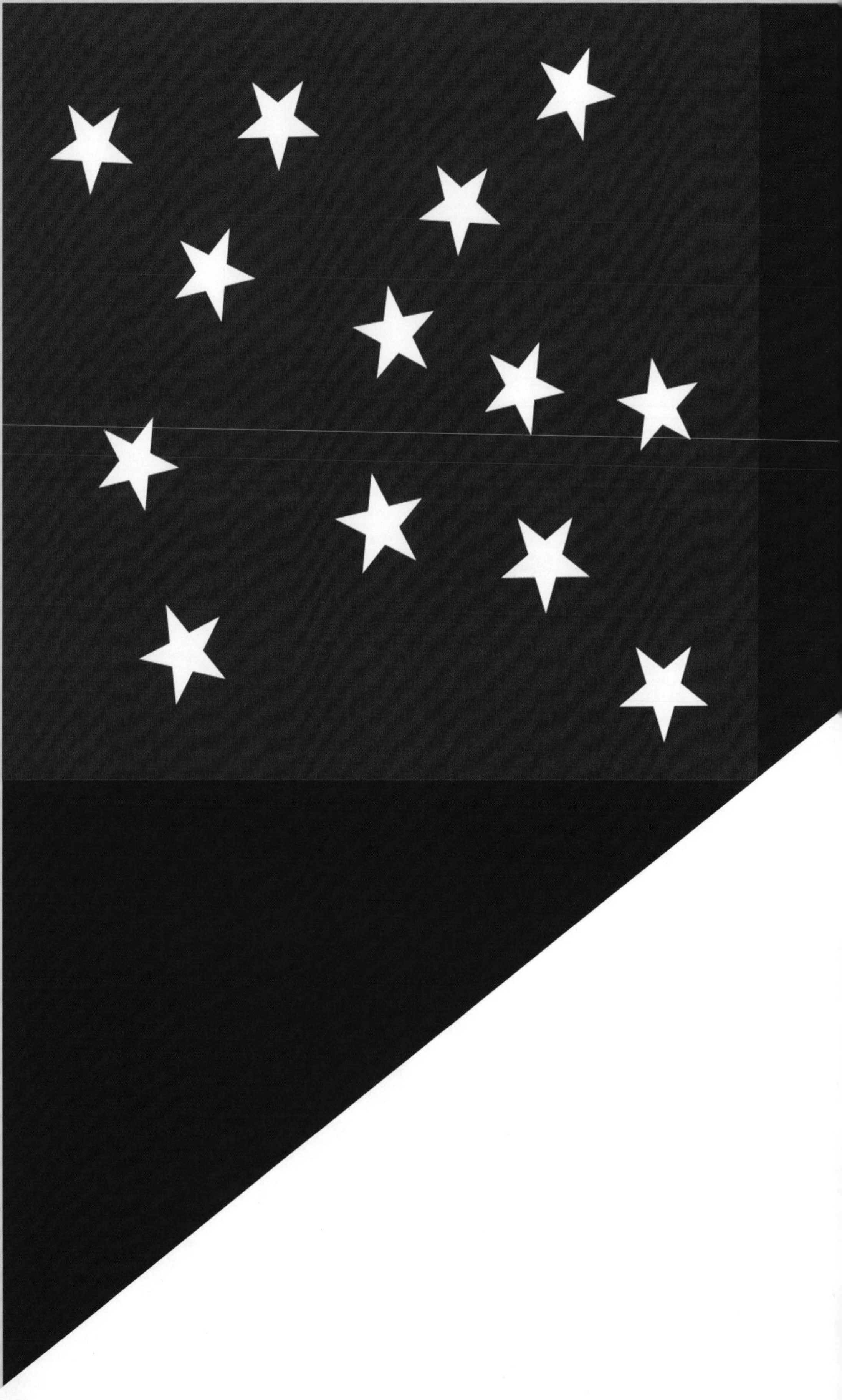

REBELS

"THE GREEN MOUNTAIN BOYS"

IN WHICH A FEW PROTECT MANY.

BRIAN WOOD · JOAN URGELL · LAUREN AFFE · MATT TAYLOR

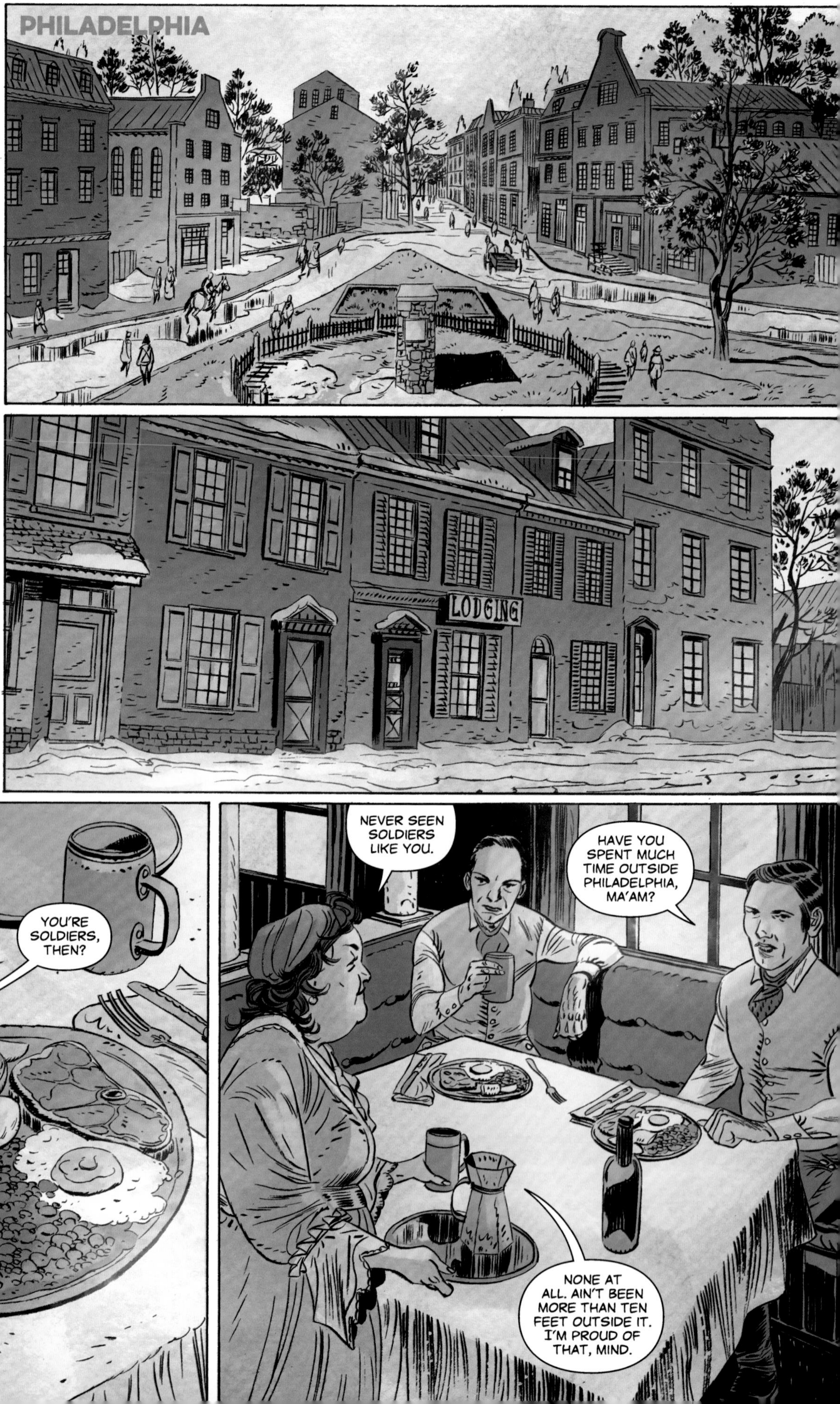
PHILADELPHIA
LODGING
YOU'RE SOLDIERS, THEN?
NEVER SEEN SOLDIERS LIKE YOU.
HAVE YOU SPENT MUCH TIME OUTSIDE PHILADELPHIA, MA'AM?
NONE AT ALL. AIN'T BEEN MORE THAN TEN FEET OUTSIDE IT. I'M PROUD OF THAT, MIND.

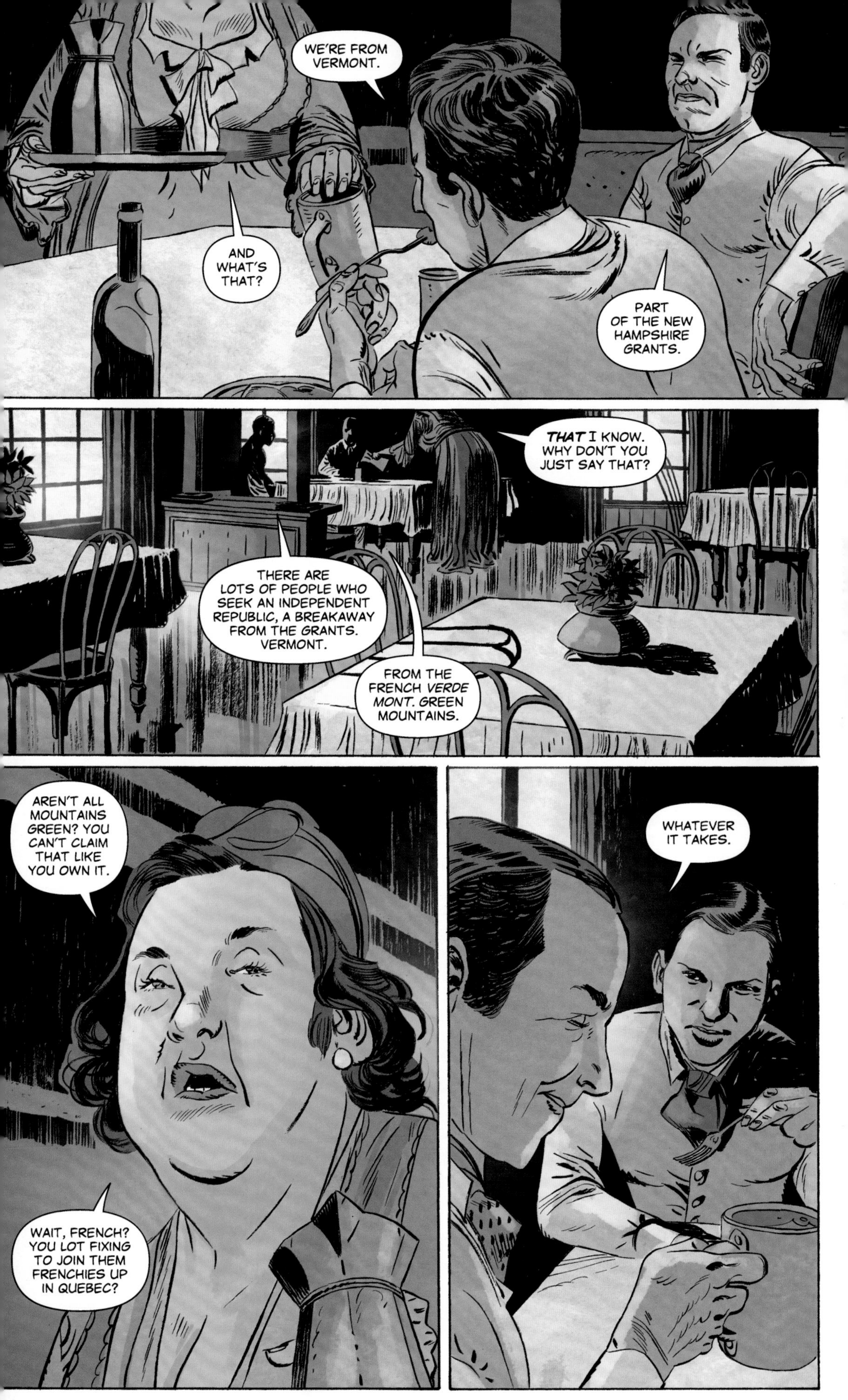
WE'RE FROM VERMONT.
AND WHAT'S THAT?
PART OF THE NEW HAMPSHIRE GRANTS.
THAT I KNOW. WHY DON'T YOU JUST SAY THAT?
THERE ARE LOTS OF PEOPLE WHO SEEK AN INDEPENDENT REPUBLIC, A BREAKAWAY FROM THE GRANTS. VERMONT.
FROM THE FRENCH *VERDE MONT*. GREEN MOUNTAINS.
AREN'T ALL MOUNTAINS GREEN? YOU CAN'T CLAIM THAT LIKE YOU OWN IT.
WAIT, FRENCH? YOU LOT FIXING TO JOIN THEM FRENCHIES UP IN QUEBEC?
WHATEVER IT TAKES.

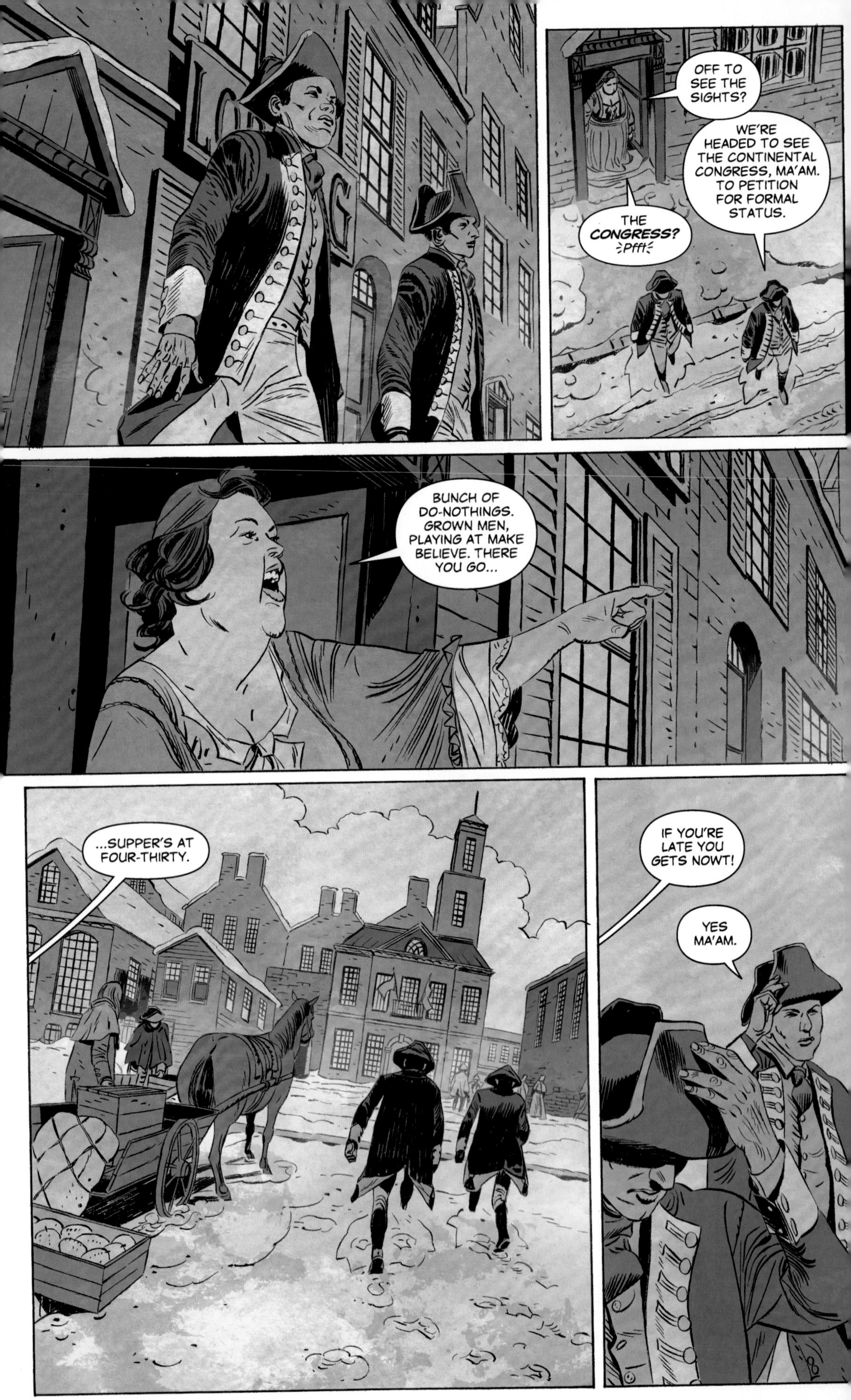

OFF TO SEE THE SIGHTS?
WE'RE HEADED TO SEE THE CONTINENTAL CONGRESS, MA'AM. TO PETITION FOR FORMAL STATUS.
THE *CONGRESS?* Pfft
BUNCH OF DO-NOTHINGS. GROWN MEN, PLAYING AT MAKE BELIEVE. THERE YOU GO...
...SUPPER'S AT FOUR-THIRTY.
IF YOU'RE LATE YOU GETS NOWT!
YES MA'AM.

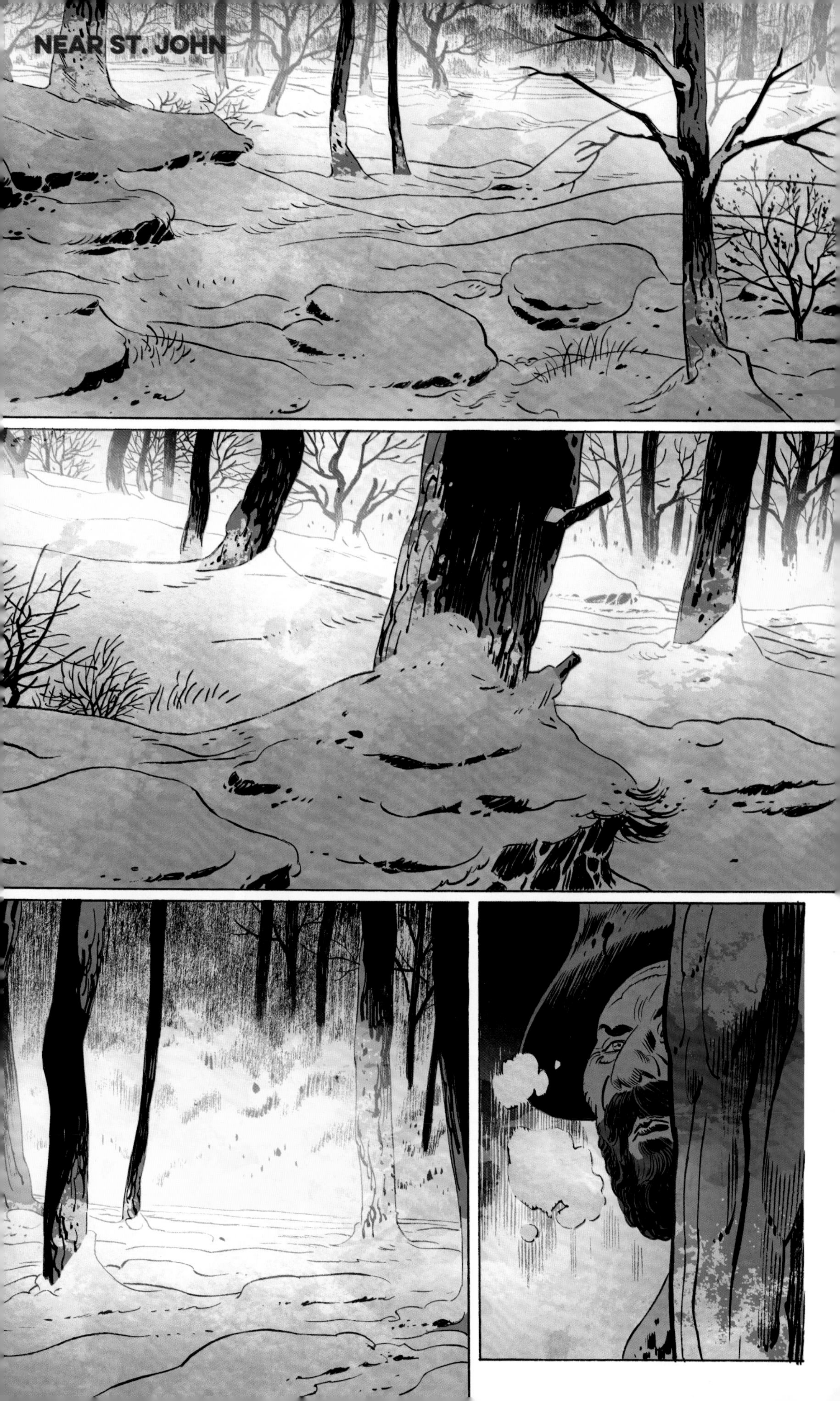
NEAR ST. JOHN

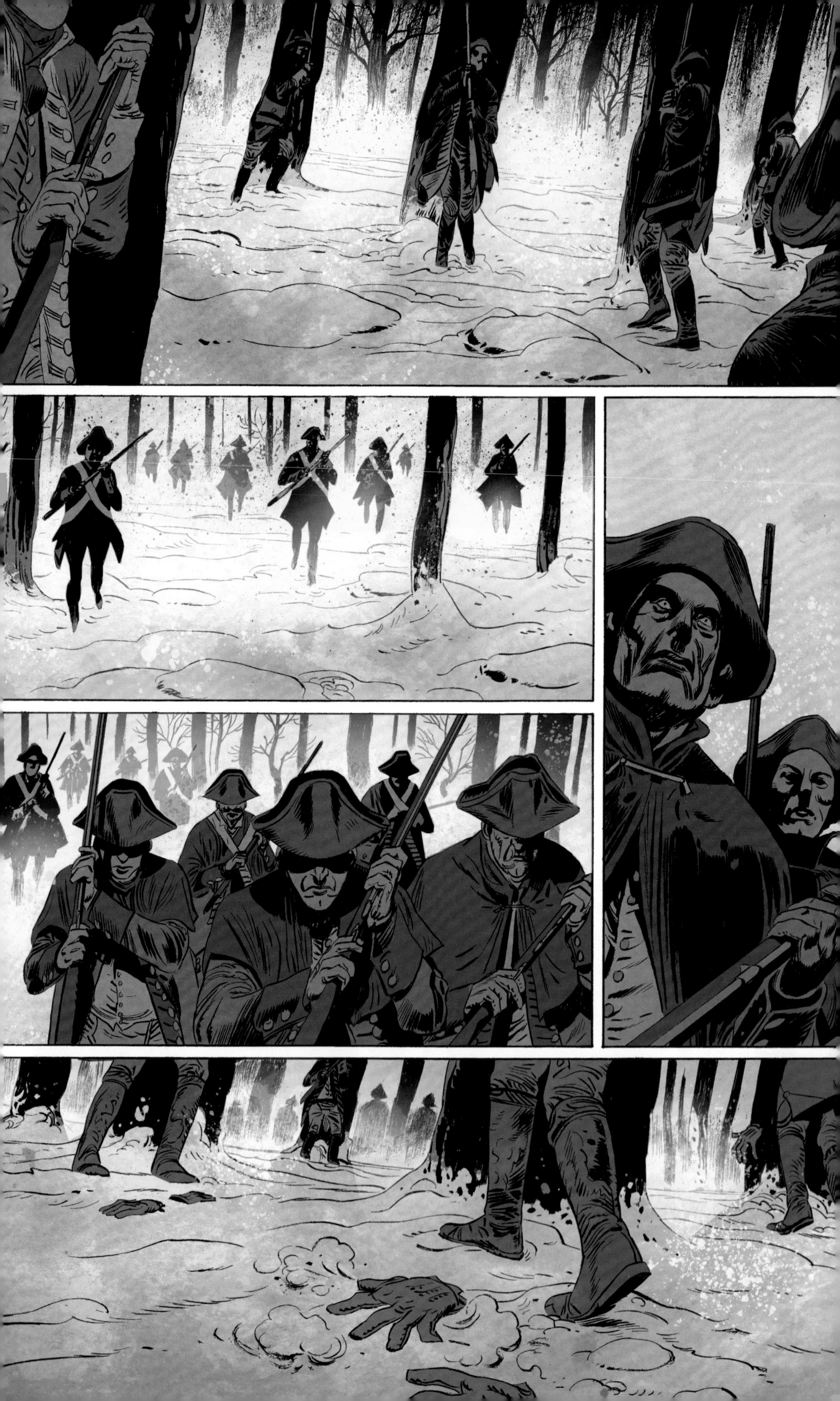

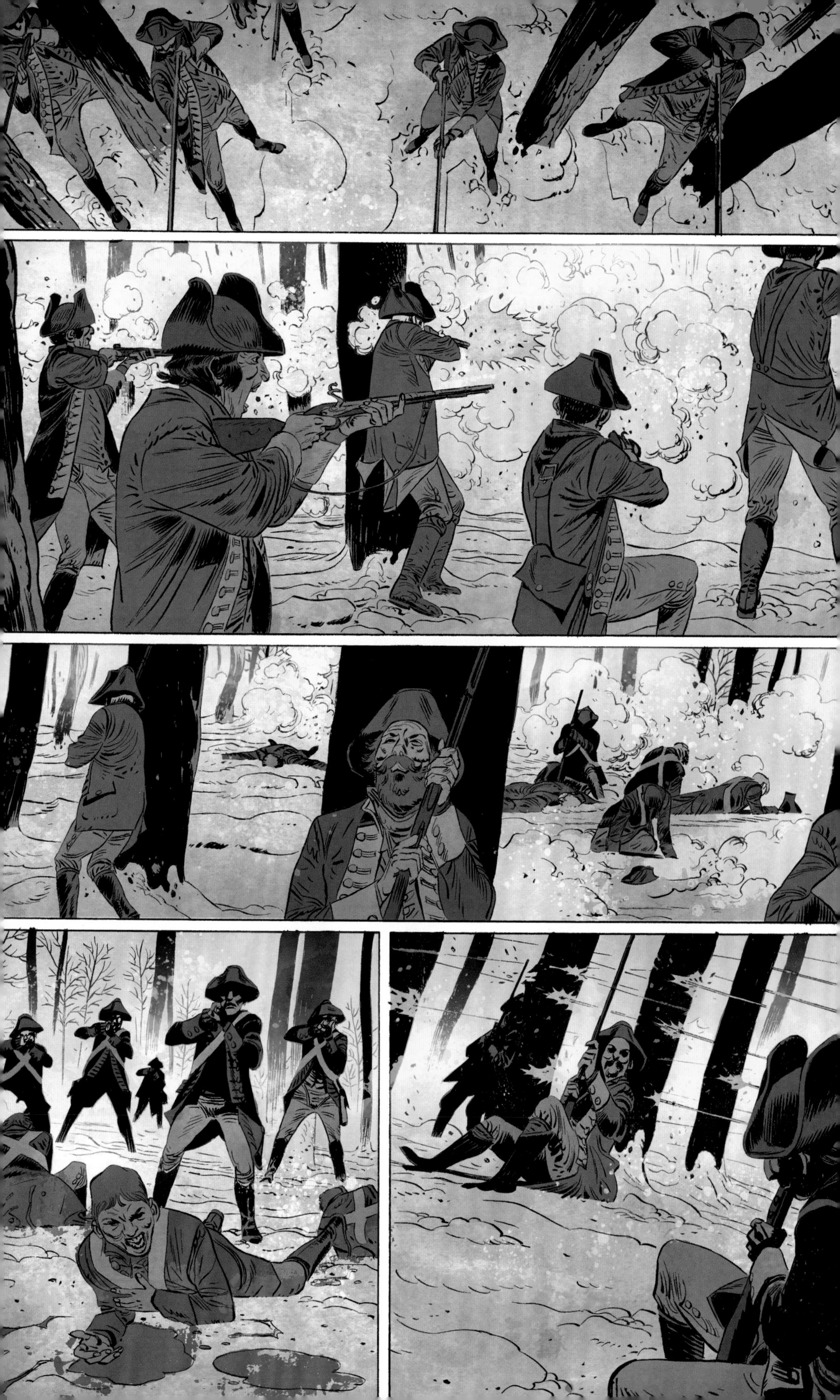

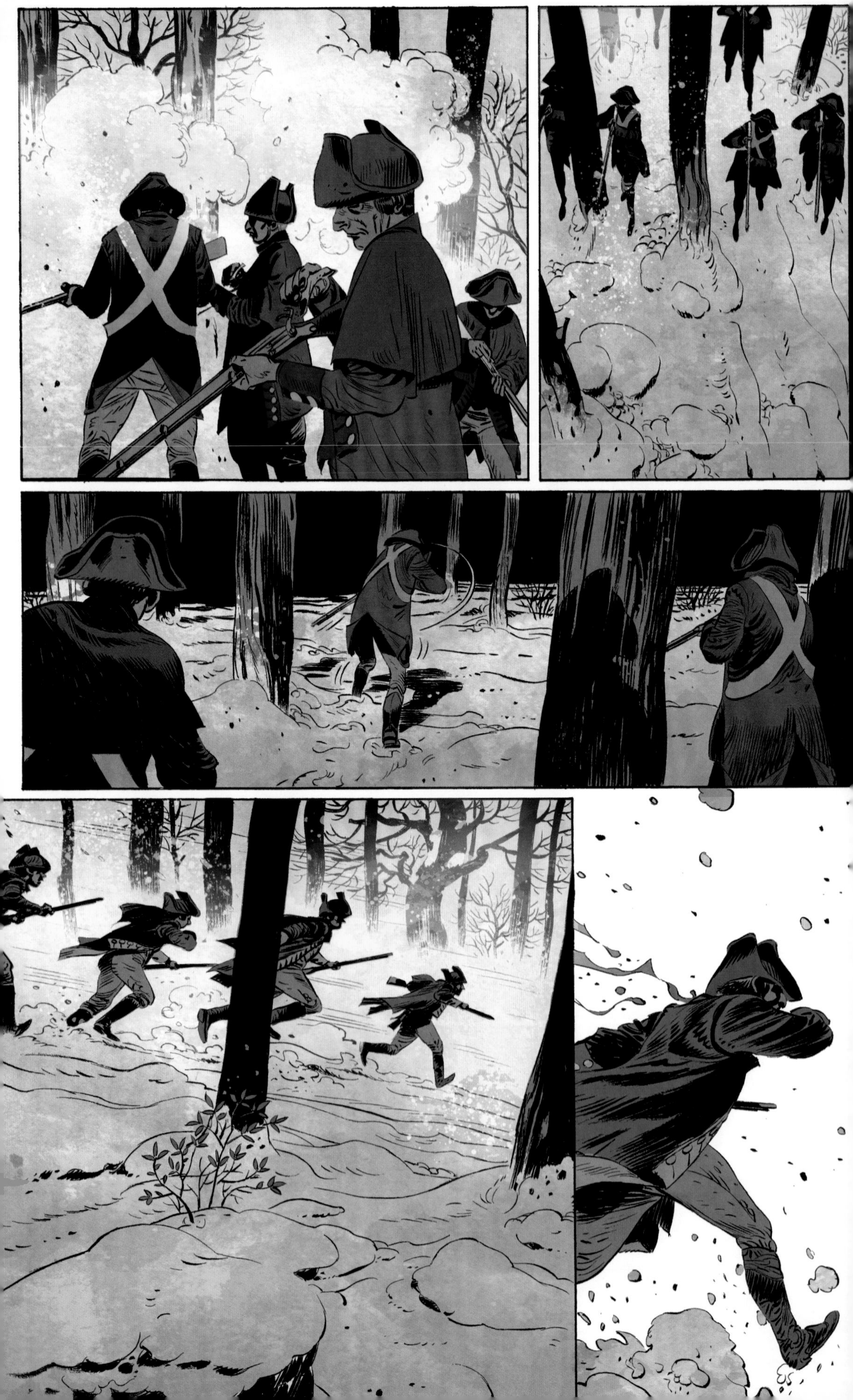

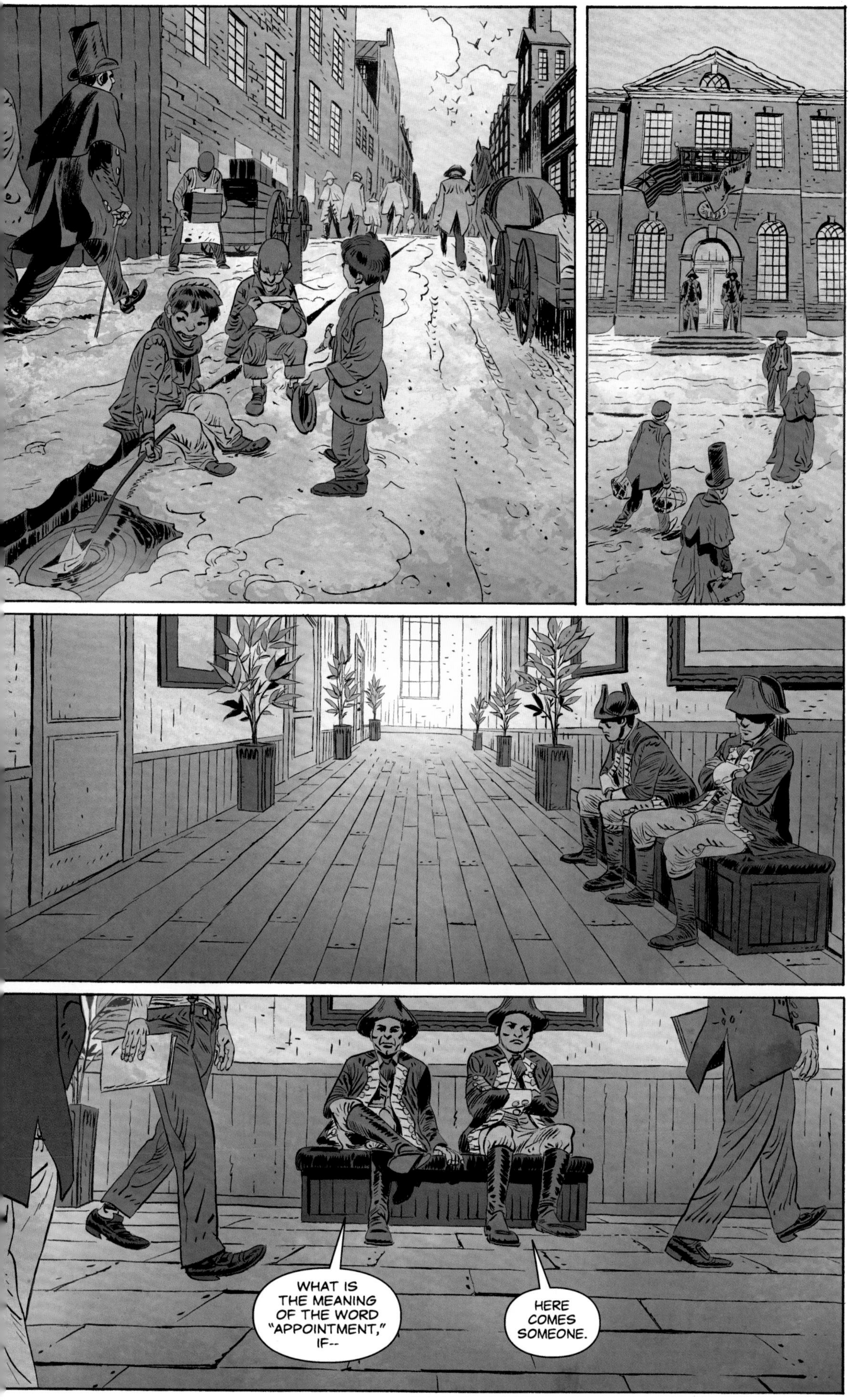
WHAT IS THE MEANING OF THE WORD "APPOINTMENT," IF--
HERE COMES SOMEONE.

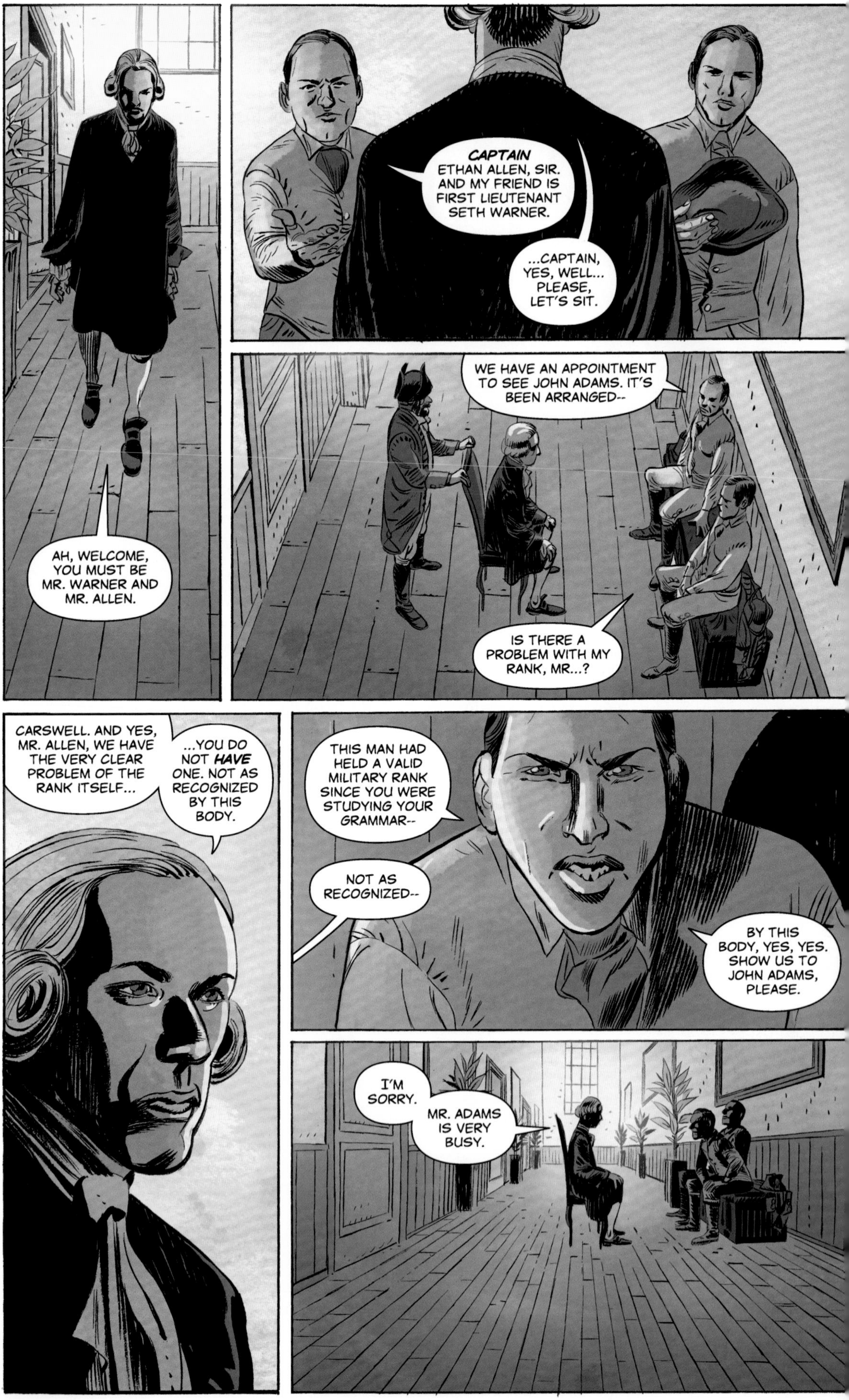
AH, WELCOME, YOU MUST BE MR. WARNER AND MR. ALLEN.
CAPTAIN ETHAN ALLEN, SIR. AND MY FRIEND IS FIRST LIEUTENANT SETH WARNER.
...CAPTAIN, YES, WELL... PLEASE, LET'S SIT.
WE HAVE AN APPOINTMENT TO SEE JOHN ADAMS. IT'S BEEN ARRANGED--
IS THERE A PROBLEM WITH MY RANK, MR...?
CARSWELL. AND YES, MR. ALLEN, WE HAVE THE VERY CLEAR PROBLEM OF THE RANK ITSELF...
...YOU DO NOT HAVE ONE. NOT AS RECOGNIZED BY THIS BODY.
THIS MAN HAD HELD A VALID MILITARY RANK SINCE YOU WERE STUDYING YOUR GRAMMAR--
NOT AS RECOGNIZED--
BY THIS BODY, YES, YES. SHOW US TO JOHN ADAMS, PLEASE.
I'M SORRY.
MR. ADAMS IS VERY BUSY.

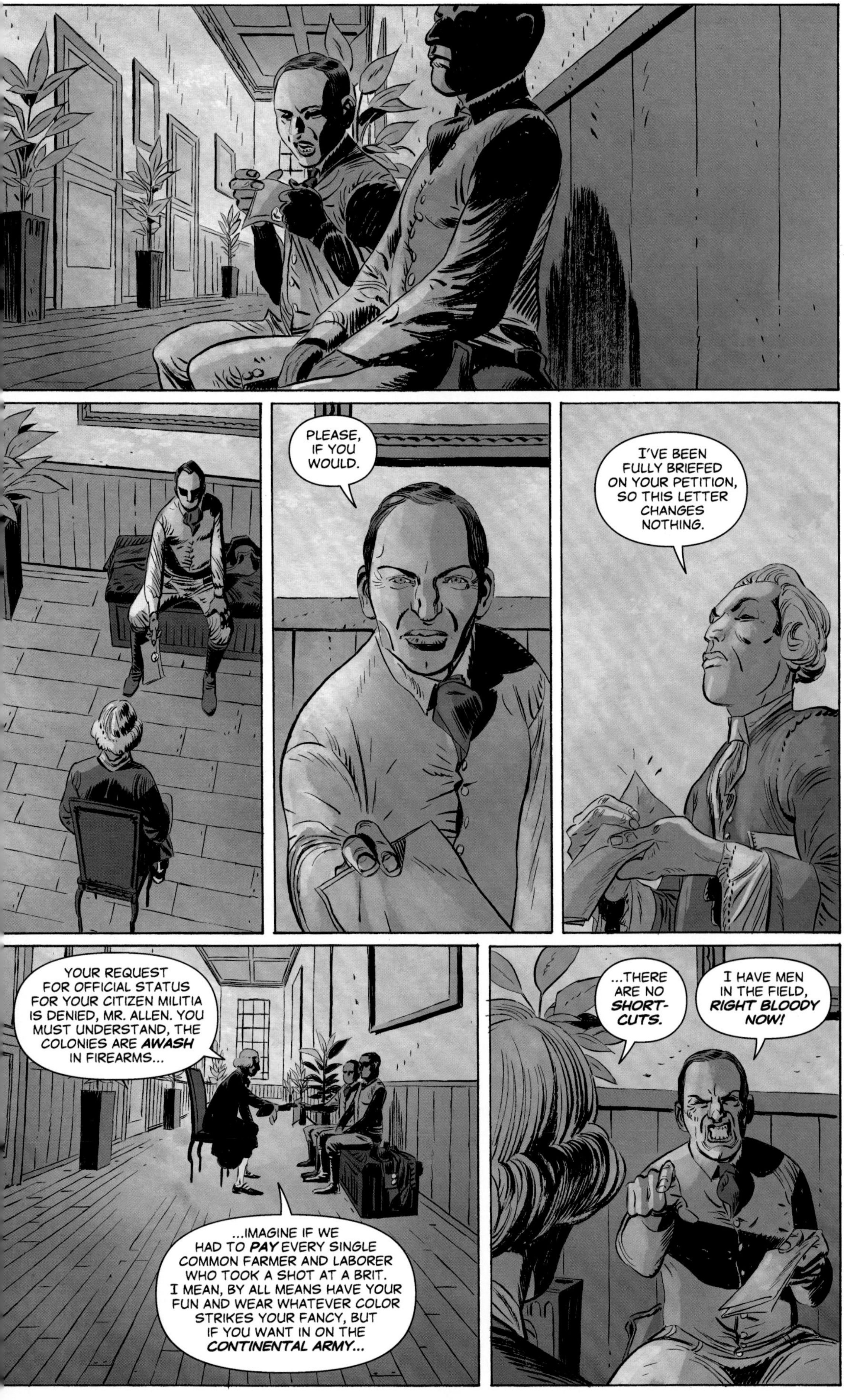
PLEASE, IF YOU WOULD.
I'VE BEEN FULLY BRIEFED ON YOUR PETITION, SO THIS LETTER CHANGES NOTHING.
YOUR REQUEST FOR OFFICIAL STATUS FOR YOUR CITIZEN MILITIA IS DENIED, MR. ALLEN. YOU MUST UNDERSTAND, THE COLONIES ARE AWASH IN FIREARMS...
...IMAGINE IF WE HAD TO PAY EVERY SINGLE COMMON FARMER AND LABORER WHO TOOK A SHOT AT A BRIT. I MEAN, BY ALL MEANS HAVE YOUR FUN AND WEAR WHATEVER COLOR STRIKES YOUR FANCY, BUT IF YOU WANT IN ON THE CONTINENTAL ARMY...
...THERE ARE NO SHORT-CUTS.
I HAVE MEN IN THE FIELD, RIGHT BLOODY NOW!

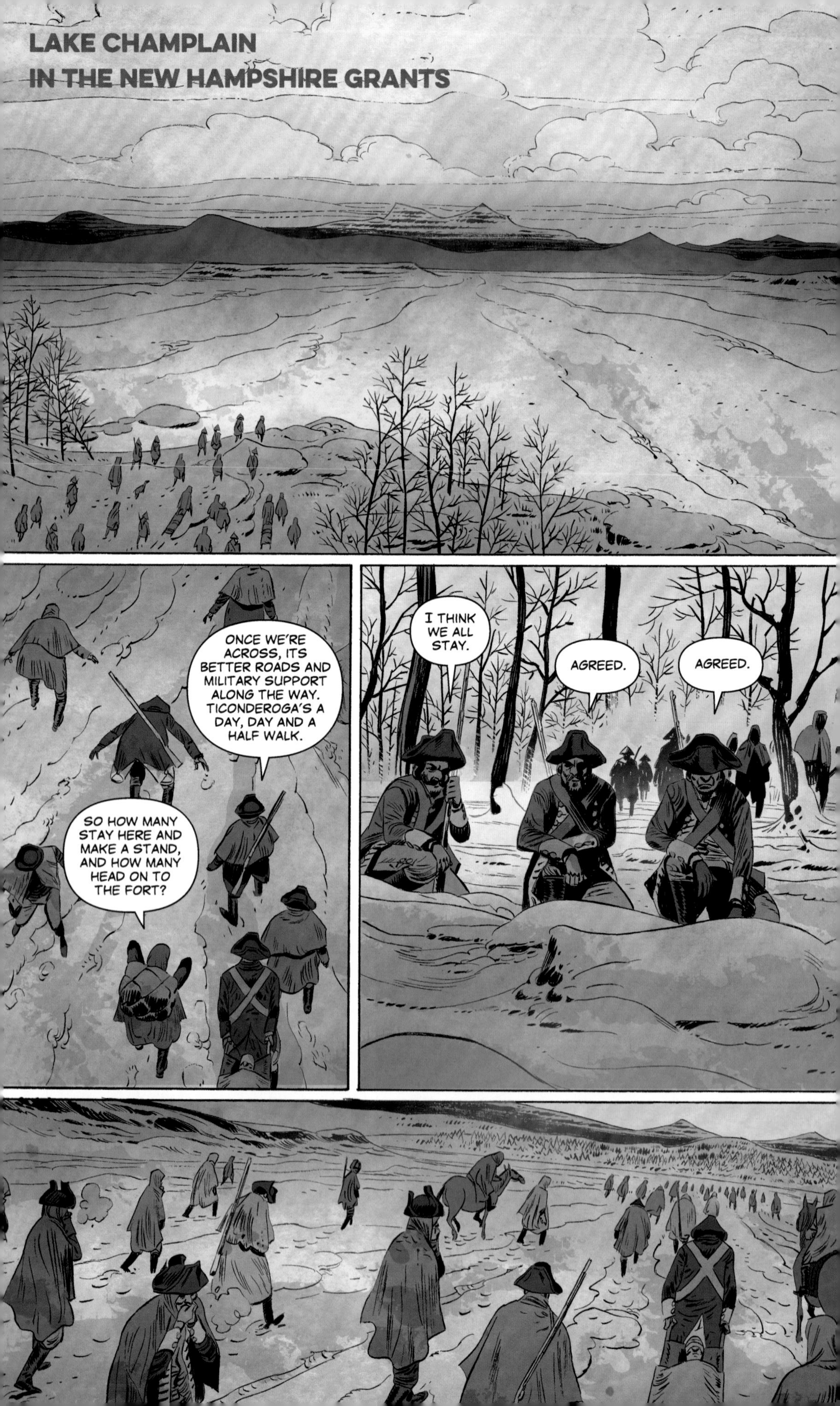
LAKE CHAMPLAIN
IN THE NEW HAMPSHIRE GRANTS
SO HOW MANY STAY HERE AND MAKE A STAND, AND HOW MANY HEAD ON TO THE FORT?
ONCE WE'RE ACROSS, ITS BETTER ROADS AND MILITARY SUPPORT ALONG THE WAY. TICONDEROGA'S A DAY, DAY AND A HALF WALK.
I THINK WE ALL STAY.
AGREED.
AGREED.

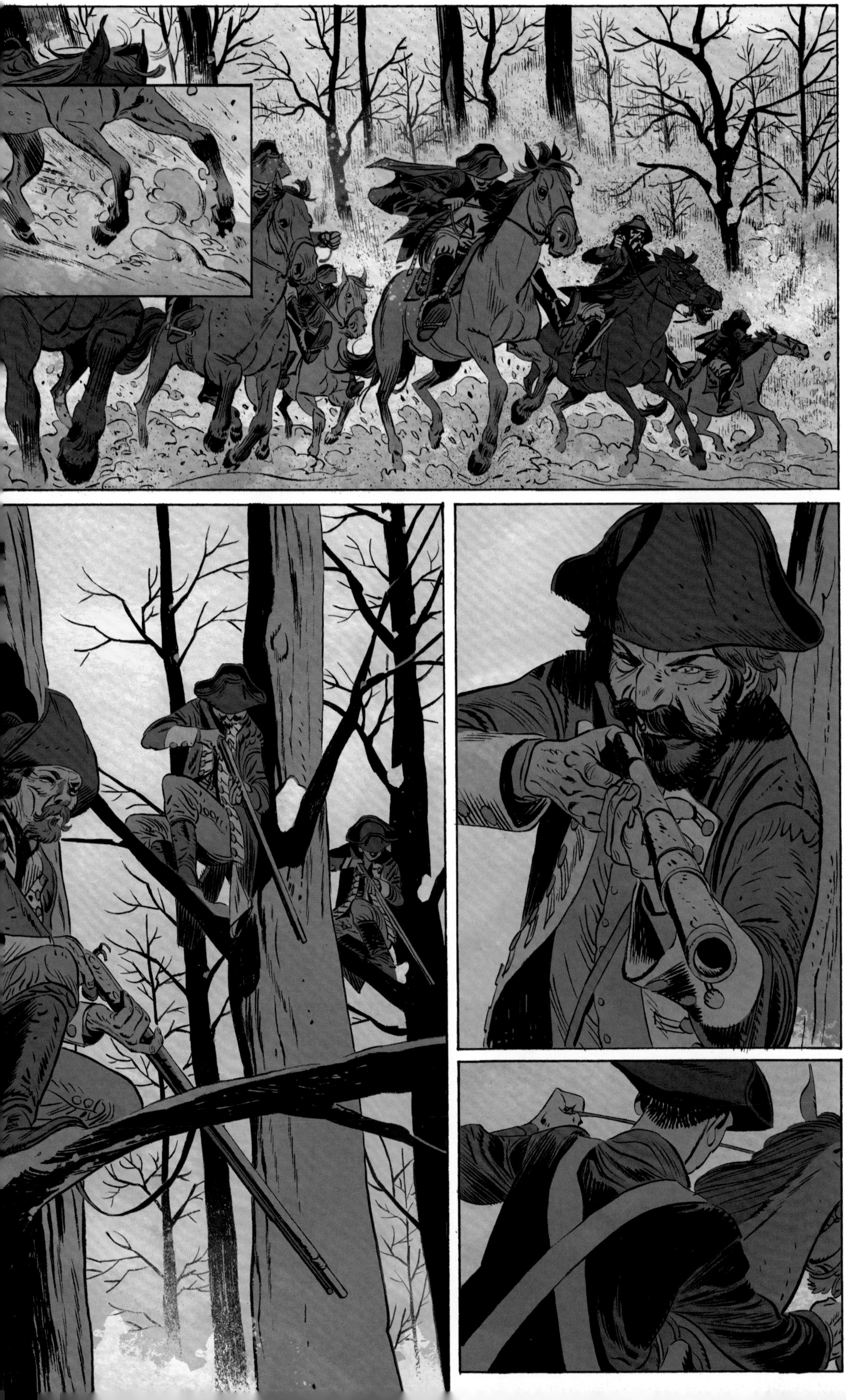

I'M TOLD WE HAVE AN APPOINTMENT.

WE DO, SIR. I CORRESPONDED WITH YOU SOME MONTHS BACK, AND ARRIVED AT AN AGREEMENT ON THIS DATE AND THIS TIME--

YES, YES, FINE, FINE--

--YOU'RE ETHAN ALLEN.

I AM. THIS IS LIEUTENANT WARNER.

CITIZEN MILITIA FROM THE GRANTS.

SIR, THE CITIZEN MILITIA IS--

--IMPORTANT, YES, I KNOW. I'M A MASSACHUSETTS FARMER, AND I NEED ONLY THINK OF LEXINGTON AND CONCORD TO SEE THE WISDOM IN KEEPING FOLK LIKE YOU CLOSE.

HOWEVER--

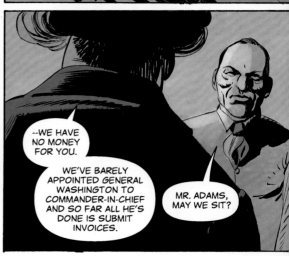

--WE HAVE NO MONEY FOR YOU.

WE'VE BARELY APPOINTED GENERAL WASHINGTON TO COMMANDER-IN-CHIEF AND SO FAR ALL HE'S DONE IS SUBMIT INVOICES.

MR. ADAMS, MAY WE SIT?

I, AND MY LIEUTENANT, REPRESENT THE TERRITORY THAT SPANS THE GRANTS FROM THE CONNECTICUT RIVER TO LAKE CHAMPLAIN, FROM QUEBEC SOUTH TO BENNINGTON, ON THE BORDER OF YOUR MASSACHUSETTS.

YOU MAY BE CONJURING A MENTAL IMAGE OF DENSE FORESTS, GRANITE PEAKS, BUT LITTLE ELSE--

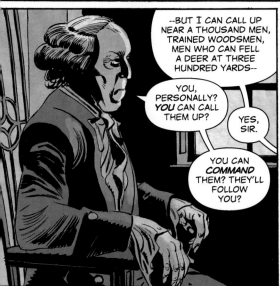

--BUT I CAN CALL UP NEAR A THOUSAND MEN, TRAINED WOODSMEN, MEN WHO CAN FELL A DEER AT THREE HUNDRED YARDS--

YOU, PERSONALLY? YOU CAN CALL THEM UP?

YES, SIR.

YOU CAN COMMAND THEM? THEY'LL FOLLOW YOU?

TO HELL.

AND BACK AGAIN FOR ANOTHER ROUND, IF NEED BE.

I SEE.

WOODSMEN. WHO TOOK TICONDEROGA WITHOUT A SHOT FIRED? WHO OCCUPIED WESTMINSTER?

DON'T LOOK SURPRISED. MY FELLOWS IN THE CONGRESS MAY SCOFF AT THE NORTHERN COLONIES, BUT NOT I.

WE NEED MONEY, MR. ADAMS. AND WE NEED RECOGNITION. FOR OUR SAKE, BUT ALSO FOR YOURS.

WE ARE NOT JUST A MILITIA... WE'RE A DE FACTO GOVERNMENT--

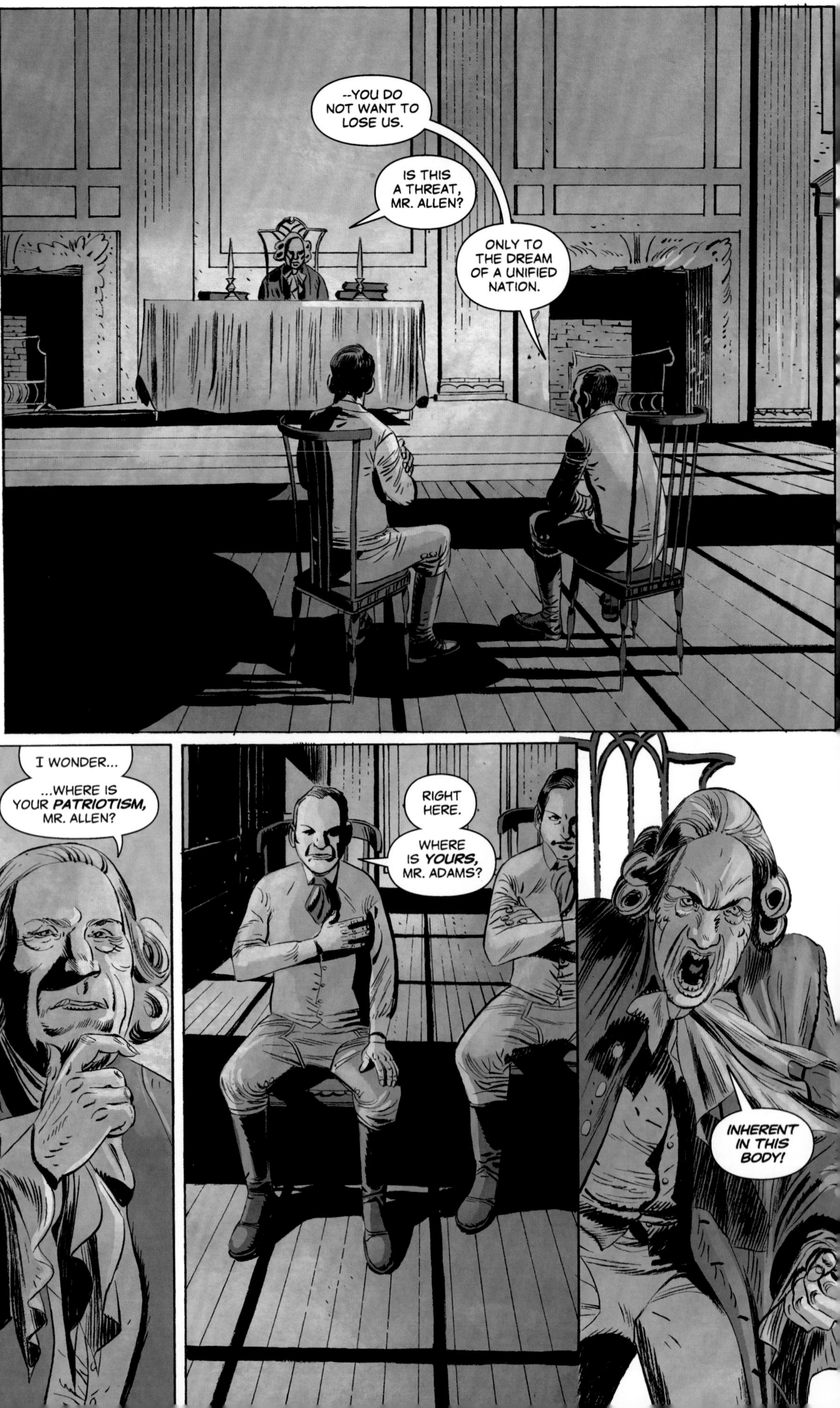
--YOU DO NOT WANT TO LOSE US.
IS THIS A THREAT, MR. ALLEN?
ONLY TO THE DREAM OF A UNIFIED NATION.
I WONDER...
...WHERE IS YOUR *PATRIOTISM,* MR. ALLEN?
RIGHT HERE.
WHERE IS *YOURS,* MR. ADAMS?
INHERENT IN THIS BODY!

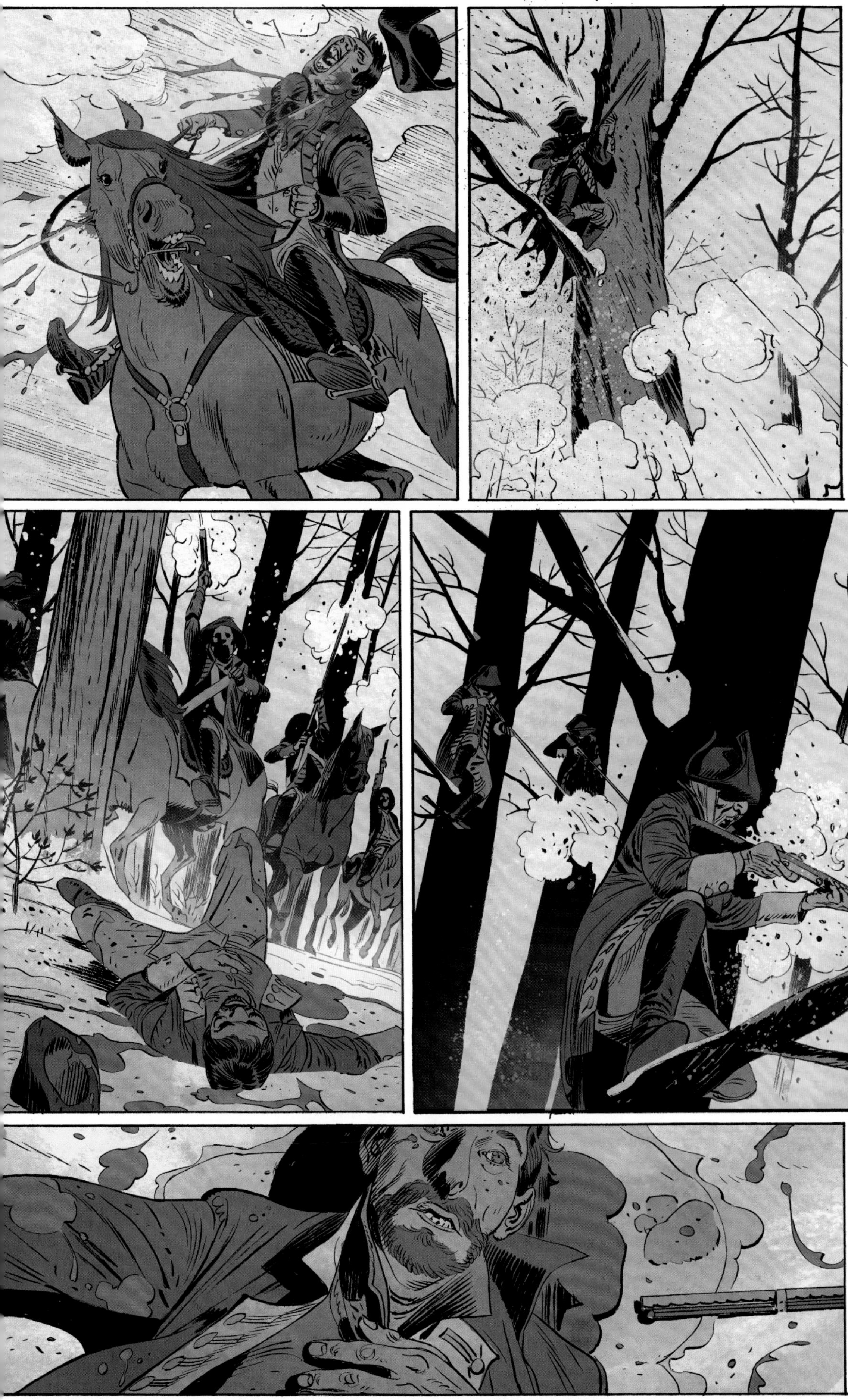

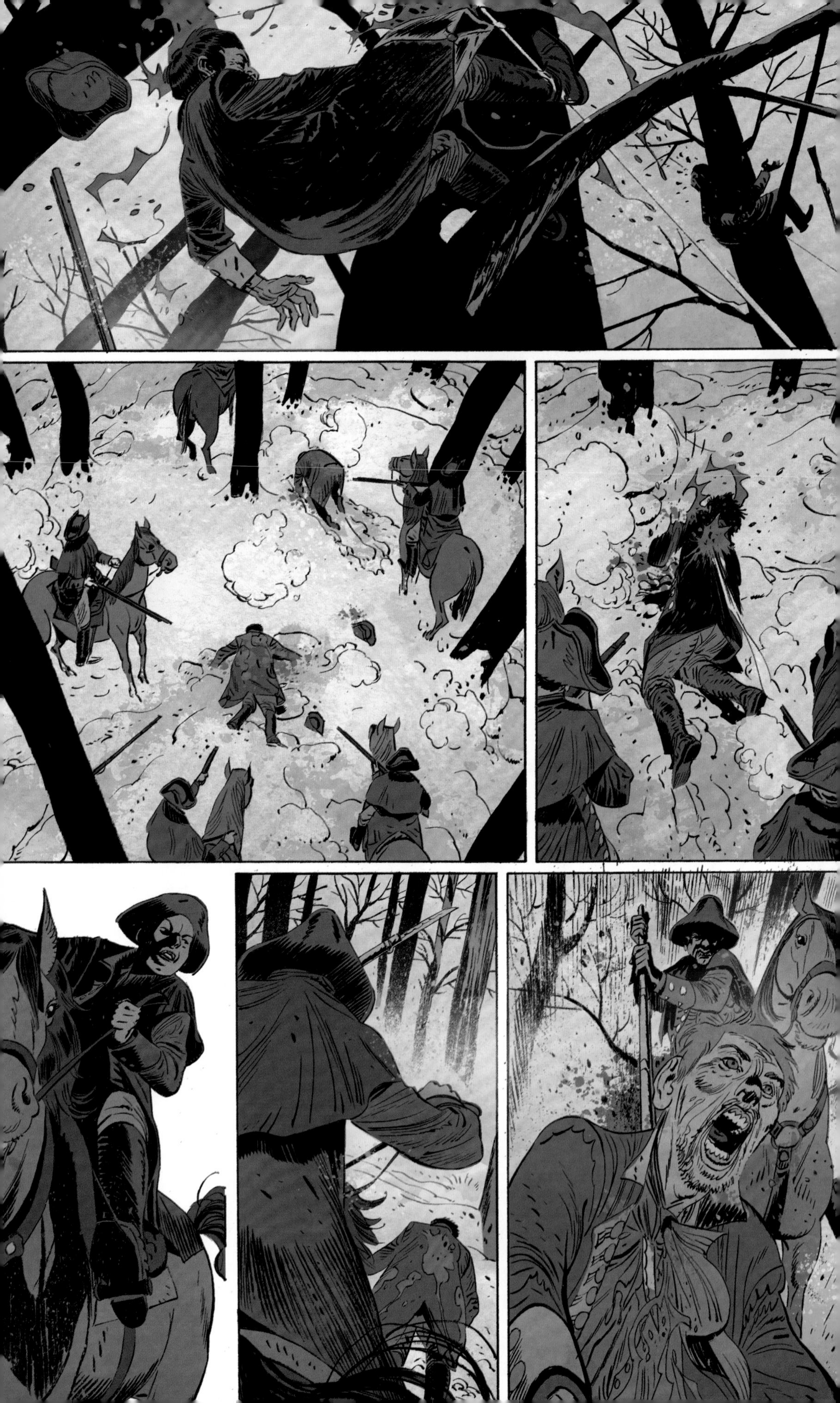

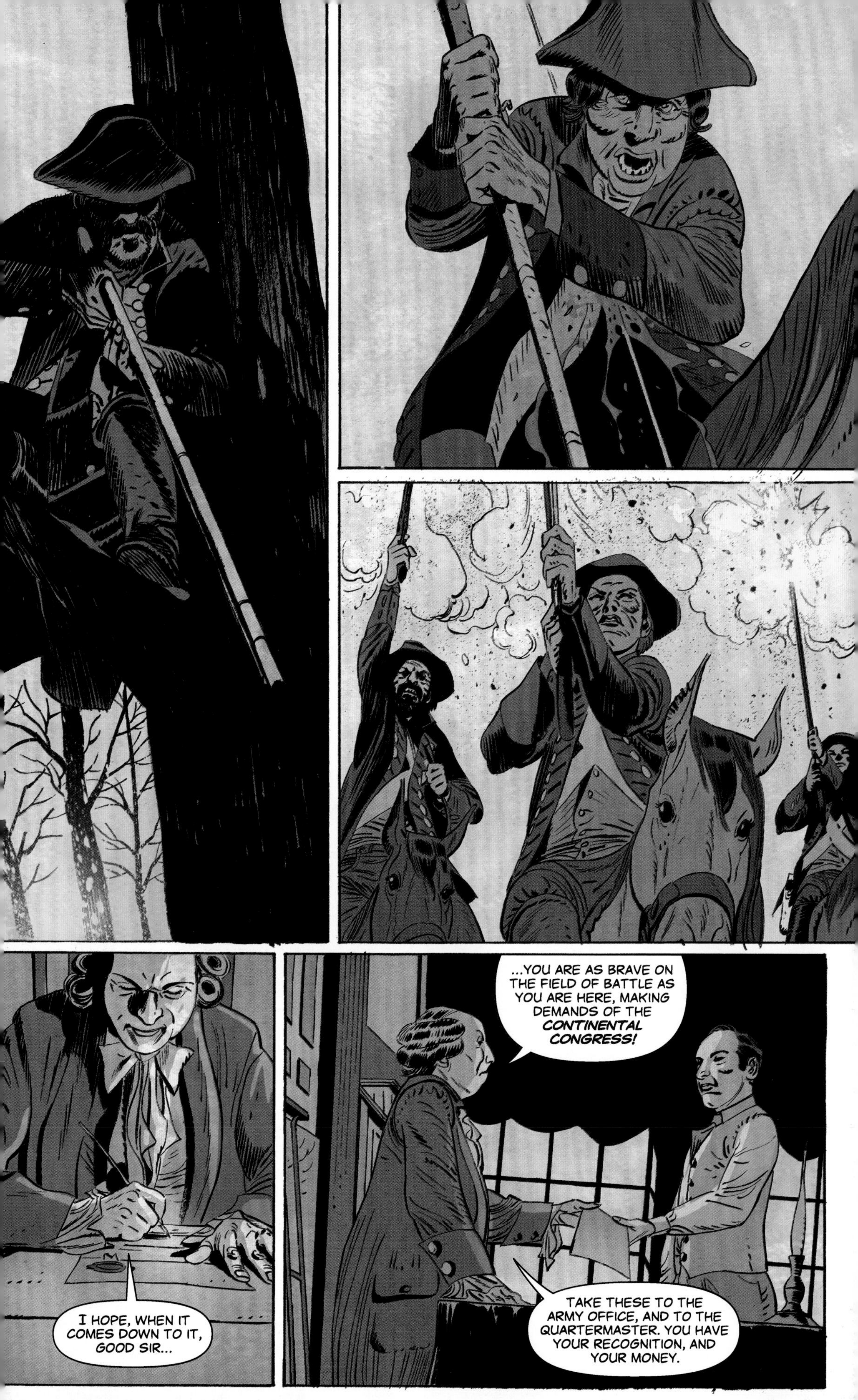

I HOPE, WHEN IT COMES DOWN TO IT, GOOD SIR...
...YOU ARE AS BRAVE ON THE FIELD OF BATTLE AS YOU ARE HERE, MAKING DEMANDS OF THE *CONTINENTAL CONGRESS!*
TAKE THESE TO THE ARMY OFFICE, AND TO THE QUARTERMASTER. YOU HAVE YOUR RECOGNITION, AND YOUR MONEY.

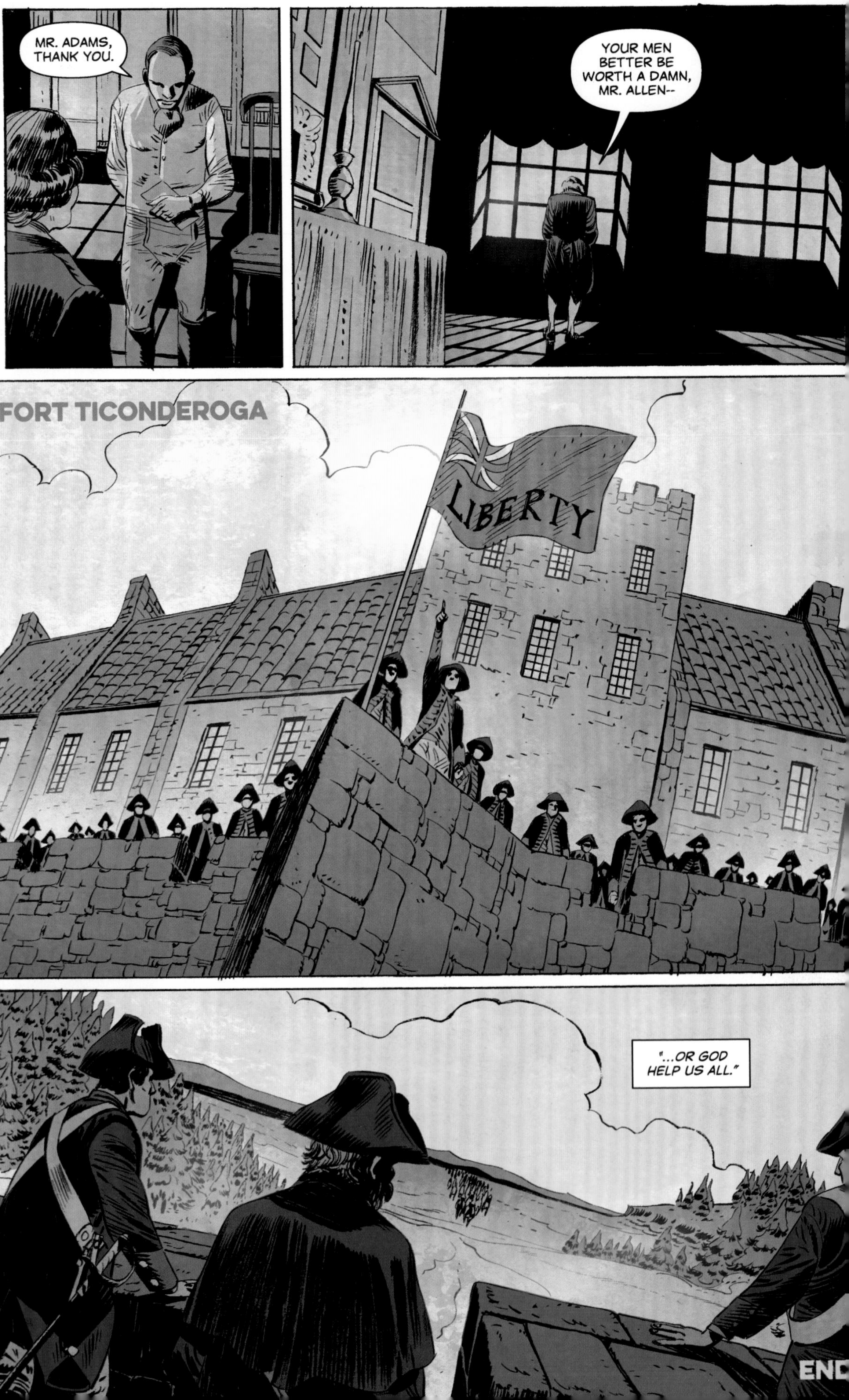
MR. ADAMS, THANK YOU.
YOUR MEN BETTER BE WORTH A DAMN, MR. ALLEN--
FORT TICONDEROGA
LIBERTY
"...OR GOD HELP US ALL."
END